ENVIRONMENTAL PSYCHOLOGY

ENVIRONMENTAL PSYCHOLOGY

Francis T. McAndrew
Knox College

Brooks/Cole Publishing Company
Pacific Grove, California

Brooks/Cole Publishing Company
A Division of Wadsworth, Inc.

Printed in the United States of America

10   9   8   7   6   5   4   3   2   1

Library of Congress Cataloging-in-Publication Data
McAndrew, Francis T., [date]
    Environmental psychology / Francis T. McAndrew.
        p.   cm.
    Includes bibliographical references and index.
    ISBN 0-534-19308-0
    1. Environmental psychology.   I. Title.
  BF353.M39   1992   92-7718
    155.9 — dc20   CIP

Project Editor: *Marianne Taflinger*
Editorial Associate: *Heather L. Graeve*
Production Editors: *Kay Mikel and Kirk Bomont*
Permissions Editor: *Karen Wooten*
Interior Design: *Roy R. Neuhaus*
Cover Design: *Michael Rogondino*
Cover Photo: *Dennis Brack/Black Star*
Art Coordinator: *Susan Haberkorn*
Interior Illustration: *Roger Knox*
Photo Coordinator: *Larry Molmud*
Typesetting: *Graphic World Inc.*
Printing and Binding: *Arcata Graphics/Fairfield*
(Credits continue on page 405.)

To Maryjo, with love

Preface

Teaching a course in environmental psychology is challenging in many ways. Students in the class often range from sophomores to graduate level, and their backgrounds can be quite diverse — architecture, business, and various other disciplines. This diversity reflects the interdisciplinary nature of environmental psychology and its appeal to a broader audience than is often found for other psychology courses. As environmental issues become more pressing and as general interest in the environment continues to grow, this audience will become even larger and more diverse. Keeping this in mind, I have written the book to be as adaptable as it can be. An informal, conversational style and the inclusion of nontraditional topics such as wayfinding in the blind, seasonal affective disorders, Antarctic and outer space environments, and the environmental psychology of zoos should make the book interesting and accessible to students with minimal backgrounds in psychology. At the same time, everything in the text is firmly anchored in the latest empirical work on environment and behavior and is sufficiently rigorous that upper-level psychology students and graduate students will find it a useful survey of the field and a gateway to more in-depth work with primary sources.

I have tried to keep the discussion closely tied to the available data. Each chapter describes for the student what environmental psychologists currently know before dealing with more abstract theoretical issues and controversies. I believe that most undergraduates quickly become bored and confused when confronted with theory building before they have a sense of the empirical information at hand. Consequently, theories are discussed at relevant points in the individual chapters rather than in a separate "theory" chapter, and they follow rather than precede the discussion of empirical findings in most cases. Each chapter includes one or more "boxed inserts," many of which are experiential exercises that will help the student relate the reading to everyday life. There is also a glossary of technical terms at the end of each chapter rather than one large glossary at the back of the book; my own students tell me that this arrangement greatly facilitates studying.

Above all else, I have tried to convey my own sense of excitement about environmental psychology and to help the student discover how much fun it can be. If the book accomplishes nothing more, I will consider it successful.

As much as possible, the chapters are self-contained units that can be read in any order. The ordering of the chapters, however, has not been completely random. Chapter 1 is an introduction to the field, presenting a brief sketch of its history and an introductory-level explanation of the research methods that will be encountered most frequently throughout the book. Chapters 2 and 3 deal with the transfer of sensory information from the environment to the individual; chapter 2 discusses how environmental information is stored and used, and chapter 3 emphasizes the emotional impact that environments have on human beings. Chapter 4 describes the stress that people experience when the input from the environment becomes extreme, intense, or unusual.

Chapters 5, 6, and 7 focus on human spatial behaviors, privacy, territoriality, and crowding. These chapters describe the ways in which the individual relies on the physical environment to structure and regulate relationships with other people.

Chapters 8, 9, and 10 examine the built environment and explore the importance of architecture in human life. The emphasis in these chapters is on the environments in which people live, work, and learn.

Chapters 11 and 12 look at humans in the context of the natural environment, with chapter 11 emphasizing the influence of the natural environment on people and chapter 12 emphasizing the impact of people on the environment.

To keep the book as flexible as possible, I have avoided any rigid, overarching theme that locks the instructor into any particular viewpoint or sequence of topics. However, every textbook that is the work of a single author presents material from *some* theoretical perspective through which the individual chapters are united into a single body of knowledge. To the extent that this is true in this book, you will find that the most common denominator among the topics discussed throughout the text is an evolutionary perspective. I have tried not to make this orientation omnipresent or oppressive. In chapters where it is particularly salient, it will be an important part of the discussion; in other chapters, it may hardly be mentioned but can still be found lurking just beneath the surface. In either case, it is helpful for the reader to be familiar with the author's biases and predilections.

My presentation of the research in environmental psychology is based on the assumption that human beings, as well as other animals, have evolved over a long period of time in response to pressures from the physical and social environment. Environmental preferences, behavior tendencies, and the way in which we process information have been shaped by natural selection to ensure survival and successful reproduction. Granted, we are a long way from understanding the genetic basis of such complex human phenomena, and I am *not* proposing that human feelings and behavior are wired to unfold in an inescapable, predetermined fashion. Nevertheless, I do propose that we approach the physical environment with evolutionary baggage that predisposes us to choose one response or type of environment over another, even though the situation we now face may be quite different from the conditions that shaped these predispositions so long ago. This being the case, I believe that much can be learned from animal research, since our animal cousins have presumably been shaped in their environment by the same processes. Consequently, there may be a somewhat heavier dose of animal research in this text than is found in other environmental psychology books; I also pay more attention to the relationship between humans and the natural environments that guided the development of our species.

Acknowledgments

In any work of this magnitude, a great many people deserve credit. I will try to avoid repeating the phrase "thank you" ad nauseam, but I owe a debt of gratitude to so many that I feel compelled to make public my sincere appreciation for what they have done. First of all, for patience and support of all conceivable varieties, I would like to thank my wife, Mary, and my children, Tim and Maura; it was they who kept me going. I also want to acknowledge the unwavering support of my parents and my parents-in-law. I want to thank Paul Cherulnik for introducing me to environmental psychology and my colleagues at Knox College (especially Gary Francois, Heather Hoffmann, and John Strassburger) for helping me to sustain my interest in it. Paul Harris and Jackie Snodgrass were teaching while I was writing, and Peter Bailley produced much of the fine photography that appears in the book. In one way or another, the trouble taken by many kind people greatly facilitated the completion of this project. I would especially like to recognize the efforts made on my behalf by Paul Gump (Professor Emeritus, University of Kansas), James A. Russell (University of British Columbia), and Kimberly Evard (Lincoln Park Zoo, Chicago). I want to thank everyone at Brooks/Cole. Phil Curson got me started (the easy part), and Marianne Taflinger got me finished (the hard part!). Kay Mikel's and Kirk Bomont's magnificent eye for detail helped make the final manuscript fit for public consumption, and much helpful advice in the acquisition of photographs and rights and permissions was provided by Larry Molmud, Carline Haja, and Karen Wootten. Last, but not least, I wish to thank the reviewers who spent so much time evaluating the eternal earlier drafts of this book. They are Jack Aiello of Rutgers University, Robert Bechtel of the University of Arizona, Kathy Hoyt of Boise State University, Richard Ryckman of the University of Maine, and Edward Sadalla of Arizona State University. Much of what is found between these covers is rightfully theirs.

Frank McAndrew

Contents

C H A P T E R **8** **Work Environments**   **163**

C H A P T E R **9** **Learning Environments**   **185**

C H A P T E R   **12** **Environmental Problems and
Behavioral Solutions**   **265**

ENVIRONMENTAL PSYCHOLOGY

Introduction
and Methods
of Research

WHAT IS ENVIRONMENTAL PSYCHOLOGY?

Have you ever wondered why you seem to be in a better mood on sunny days than on rainy days? Have you noticed that you always seem to get lost in some cities but very quickly learn your way around other cities that are even larger? Perhaps you have struggled with the arrangement of furniture and decorations to create just the right "atmosphere" for a party. If you have ever wrestled with problems like these, then you have pondered some of the same questions that interest environmental psychologists

Environmental psychology is a field that is difficult to define specifically in just a few words. In fact, some psychologists have even proposed that it is impossible to define it and have said that environmental psychology is simply whatever environmental psychologists do (Proshansky, Ittelson, & Rivlin, 1970). For our purposes, however, a description provided by Proshansky (1990) is more useful: **environmental psychology** *is the discipline that is concerned with the interactions and relationships between people and their environments.* While the emphasis in this book will be on the physical environment, Proshansky rightly points out that every physical environment is also a social environment and that it is sometimes impossible to separate these two aspects of environments. Consequently, the complexity of the concept *environment* will be a recurring theme throughout the chapters of this text. Above all else, environmental psychology has been identified by its content (the built, natural, and social environments) and by its emphasis on the reactions of individuals (as opposed to large groups or societies) to the environment.

Traditionally, the emphasis in environmental psychology has been on how human behavior, feelings, and a sense of well-being are affected by the physical environment. The earliest studies focused on how human-made environments such as buildings and cities affected behavior, especially when these built environments resulted in crowding or what Milgram (1970) referred to as **sensory overload.** (Sensory overload is what happens when a person is presented with more sensory information than he or she can effectively deal with.) In recent years, the topics that environmental psychologists study have broadened considerably, with an increased emphasis on how humans are affected by natural environments, more research on the effects that humans have on their physical environment, and the reactions of people to human-made and natural environmental hazards.

A Brief History of the Field

It is misleading to talk about the beginning of environmental psychology as if there were an opening ceremony followed by the *very first* research done in this field. Geographers, architects, and social scientists in many disciplines have long been interested in the relationship between environment and behavior, and many of today's environmental psychologists can trace the roots of their research questions to the work done by the early figures in psychology. For example, psychologists interested in environmental perception have been strongly influenced by the early Gestalt theories of perception developed in Germany by Max Wertheimer (1880–1943), Wolfgang Köhler (1887–1967), and Kurt Koffka (1886–1941). The Gestalt psychologists believed that humans have an innate tendency to organize their perceptual world as simply as possible. In support of this idea, they emphasized the strong human need to determine what in the perceptual field constitutes a clear "figure" that stands out against the background. People discern figure from ground in a variety of different ways since individuals group objects on the basis of similarity or geographic proximity (see Figures 1-1 and 1-2) and perceive configurations of objects that are symmetrical, continuous, and in contrast to the rest of the perceptual field as figures rather than as background.

F I G U R E   1·1 The gestalt principle of proximity. Most people perceive the above configuration as two groups of six dots rather than as four columns of three dots or three rows of four dots.

Later theories of perception, notably Egon Brunswik's lens model (1956), came even closer to the kind of perceptual framework used by environmental psychologists today. Brunswik's model proposes that humans take a very active role in structuring their perceptions of the environment and says that we rely heavily on past experiences with our environment in an attempt to make sense of the sensory information that we are receiving at any given time. According to Brunswik, the raw sensory cues that we receive from the world are often flawed and misleading, sensory information must be used in combination with past experience to come to a useful estimate about the real state of the

F I G U R E   1·2 The gestalt principle of similarity. Most people perceive the above field as triangles and stars instead of dividing it on the basis of top versus bottom, left versus right, or organizing the perception in some other way.

environment. This general approach to perception, with its reliance on humans as active processors of information, was a precursor to many of the current theories that deal more specifically with how we process environmental information.

It is, however, to social psychology as much as to any other area that environmental psychologists trace their disciplinary origins. **Kurt Lewin** (1890–1947), an early disciple of **Gestalt psychology,** is best remembered for bringing the Gestalt perspective to the study of social psychology. According to Lewin (1943), a person's feelings and behavior are a function of tensions between the things in the world that a person is aware of at any one time. Lewin referred to these influences as **psychological facts.** These psychological facts collectively make up what Lewin called the individual's **life space.**

Psychological facts can exert positive, attractive forces on a person or negative forces that push the individual in another direction; some psychological facts are neutral. The interaction of these positive and negative forces push or pull the person through the life space, guiding behavior toward a resolution of tension among conflicting forces. For example, a person graduating from college must make choices among jobs, graduate schools, and places to live. Each of these options (psychological facts) presents that person with an array of forces that produce tension. The nature of the job or graduate school, the distance from one's family, recreational and social opportunities, and other factors interact to produce movement toward some parts of the life space and away from others.

Lewin's approach to thinking about human behavior has been influential in understanding phenomena as diverse as motivation and group dynamics, and it was the precursor of some of the most influential theories in social psychology, including cognitive dissonance theory (Festinger, 1957), which led to ground-breaking research on attitude change, and attribution theory (Heider, 1958), which is the foundation of our current understanding of social perception. Lewin believed that the individual's internal representation of the environment is the crucial factor in determining movement through the life space. In other words, the individual's beliefs about the environment as they are represented mentally influence that person's behavior more than the environment as it actually exists. However, this internal representation ultimately can be traced to the person's perception of the physical environment and, as we shall see in Chapter 2, that perception bears a strong resemblance to the environment as it actually is. Thus, for Lewin, the actual physical environment is one of many powerful psychological facts in the life space. He saw an intimate link between human behavior and the physical environment. This orientation, coupled with a strong interest in research that could be applied directly to the solution of problems in the "real world," resulted in a theoretical perspective that would be comfortable to modern environmental psychologists.

P H O T O 1·1 Kurt Lewin

Two of Lewin's students, Roger Barker and Herbert Wright, founded the first research enterprise that had as its sole purpose the study of how human behavior is affected by real-world environments. **The Midwest Psychological Field Station** was founded in the small town of Oskaloosa, Kansas, in 1947 and memorialized forever as the anonymous town of "Midwest." It was in operation for 25 years and provided a wealth of information about the lives of real people in real situations. Thorough descriptions of the field station can be found in Barker (1990), Wicker (1979), and Gump (1990). At the beginning of the project, it was unclear to the large team of researchers exactly how one could study the everyday behavior of an entire community. They contacted a number of community leaders, explained the goals of the study (to learn about children and their day-to-day living), and described the methodologies they would be using. They began living in the town and making notes each night about the behaviors observed during the day, with an emphasis on the behavior of the 100 or so children. Barker, Wright, and their assistants immersed themselves in the life of the community, joining community organizations and activities. Barker lived there in retirement until his death in 1990 at the age of 87; one of his colleagues, Paul Gump, still lives there. The children and spouses of the researchers were invaluable sources of information about community life (Gump, 1990; Schoggen, 1990). As time passed, more systemic, quantifiable observational techniques were developed. The researchers were pro-

P H O T O   1·2   Herbert Wright and Roger Barker (standing) in 1975

gressively impressed by the data because the clear influence that places and settings have on behavior was obvious. As Gump (1990) noted, "Two children in the same place behaved more similarly than one child in two places" (p. 437).

A new field called **ecological psychology** evolved from Barker and Wright's work in Kansas. The term *ecological* implies a biological perspective (Kaminski, 1989), and for Barker and his colleagues this was certainly appropriate in that the emphasis was on naturally occurring behavior in natural settings. Ecological psychology was a precursor of environmental psychology. It emphasized the role of the physical setting in the generation of human behavior, and it sparked intense interest in the impact of the physical environment on the people who use it.

It was during the final years of the Midwest Psychological Field Station, in the late 1960s and early 1970s, that environmental psychology emerged as a field with an identity of its own. It was during this time that the first graduate programs in environmental psychology were developed, the first journals and professional organizations devoted to environmental psychology were formed, and many psychologists became comfortable identifying themselves primarily as environmental psychologists. Proshansky (1987) has observed that many factors made this time period ripe for the growth of environmental interests in psychology. There were pressing social issues such as civil rights, the environment, and the women's movement, and activists turned to social psychology for answers to the problems confronting society. Unfortunately, these inquiries generally ended in disappointment as there was very little that was useful to these movements in existing social psychological research and

PHOTO 1-3 A scene from Oskaloosa, Kansas, site of the Midwest Psychological Field Station

theory. A heavy reliance on rigorous, often artificial laboratory research left social psychologists unprepared to deal with the bewildering array of complex problems that suddenly presented themselves. The intense pressure for social change demanded a loosening of the traditionally rigid approach to experimentation. The new field of environmental psychology was more eclectic, less rigidly bound to theory, and more interdisciplinary. This seemed to be an apt response to the situation, and as a result the first environmental psychologists tended to be social psychologists with applied interests and a flexible approach to solving problems.

The social psychological heritage is still strong in environmental psychology today, since many environmental psychologists have been trained in social psychology programs. However, this "marriage" has created some tensions. Social psychology has traditionally relied heavily on experimentation growing out of a theory building and hypothesis testing approach to science. In fact, Proshansky (1976), who is himself a social psychologist by training, believes that social psychology has little to offer to environmental psychology, and that environmental psychologists would be better off divorcing themselves from it entirely. On the other hand, Altman (1976a, 1976b) spoke for many in the field when he argued that the theories and experimental methods of social psychology would ultimately prove to be one of environmental psychology's greatest assets. The social psychological influence on environmental psychology is undeniably strong, but it appears to be diminishing as the number of environment/behavior researchers trained in other disciplines (developmental psychology, art, architecture, sociology) continues to grow.

P H O T O   1·4   An observer taking notes in a behavior setting at the Midwest Psychological Field Station

While theory is certainly important in environmental psychology, there are as yet no theories broad enough to be applicable to all environmental issues and much of the research is explicitly pragmatic and atheoretical in nature. Indeed, it is the lack of widely accepted general theories that many perceive as the main weakness of environmental psychology. The field has not yet been unified as to what questions should be asked or even *how* questions ought to be answered, and given the priority placed on solving specific and immediate environment/ behavior problems, it is still relatively rare for most researchers to make any attempt to generalize or construct theory from their data (Ittelson, 1989). Also, the sheer vastness encompassed by the term *environment* has made theory building in environmental psychology difficult. The different-sized environments that must be considered (for example, a living room versus an entire city) and the variety of techniques correspondingly employed defy easy theoretical unification (Kaminski, 1989).

Differences among environmental psychologists may be more the rule than the exception at this point in time (see box on p. 9).

In spite of the diverse backgrounds of the people now engaged in research on the relationship between the physical environment and human behavior, the field is robust and communication channels among the disciplines are wide open. Social scientists involved in environmental research belong to multidisciplinary organizations such as the Environmental Design Research Association (EDRA) and publish their work in interdisciplinary journals such as *Environment and Behavior* and the *Journal of Environmental Psychology*. Much of the excitement and interest in the field can be traced to the fact that today environmental psychology is more than just a means of satisfying intellectual curiosity; it is a discipline driven by environmental problems in the everyday world. Environmental psychologists are involved with problems as diverse as overcrowded prisons, the destruction of natural scenery, the design of low-income housing, and energy conservation. Environmental psychologists work in applied settings with forest rangers, architects, and government agencies of all kinds to create a better match between people and their physical environments.

Increasingly, attempts are being made to bring environmental psychology to the problems faced by planners in developing countries. Before such efforts can bear fruit, the researchers involved must have a thorough knowledge of the cultural, economic, and political factors operating in the countries in question. Consequently, working partnerships are being forged between environmental psychologists in the United States and their colleagues in developing countries. Recent examples

---

Environmental Psychology Around the World

While the emergence of environmental psychology has been primarily a North American phenomenon, research on environmental topics is now going on around the world, with each culture bringing a unique perspective to the field. In the 1987 *Handbook of Environmental Psychology,* many authors have assembled a profile of "what's new" cross-culturally in the study of the environment and human behavior. The researchers in these countries share the same techniques and interests as their Canadian and American colleagues, but their research is flavored by the needs of their home countries and the social context in which the research is conducted. Thus, we find Japanese environmental psychologists interested in the perception of natural disasters such as earthquakes and floods. In a country where the right to be buried in a public cemetery is often determined by lottery, it is not surprising that psychologists are also busy studying problems such as crowding and pollution, which are related to overpopulation. In Sweden, on the other hand, a sparse population and a cold climate have prompted concern for energy conservation and the study of landscapes. In Germany, there is a strong tradition of research on architecture and community planning stemming from postwar reconstruction. The problems accompanying growing urbanization and the depletion of natural resources are at the forefront of environmental research in many Latin American countries. In some countries, the field is being enriched by a tension between competing perspectives on the physical environment that forces an examination of the basic assumptions researchers make as they approach problems. In Australia, tremendous differences between white and aboriginal views of the environment have produced this kind of tension. In sum, the continuing mix of cross-cultural research promises to make the environmental psychology of the future a richer and more diverse enterprise.

include a cooperative arrangement between the environmental psychology program at the University of Arizona and the University of Lima in Peru, and a similar arrangement between the School of Architecture and Urban Planning at the University of Wisconsin–Milwaukee and the Gadjah Mada University of Indonesia (Hardie, 1989).

Many of the problems faced in these countries involve planning housing, towns, and cities to meet the needs of a rapidly growing and, for the most part, poor population. Unfortunately, many of the mistakes made in developed countries are being repeated in the developing countries. As Hardie (1989) has observed, the problem is that the housing crisis is often perceived in strictly technical terms, with little consideration given to the values, behavior, and preferences of the people who must live in whatever new housing is constructed. Houses must reflect social values and the cultural and religious beliefs of the inhabitants if they are to truly feel like "home," and this important fact is often overlooked by planners. (See Chapter 10 for more on this topic.) Housing projects that have been disappointing for exactly this reason have been constructed in many places around the world; good descriptions of such projects in Gourna, Egypt, and Mexicali, Mexico, can be found in articles by Fathy (1973) and Alexander, Davis, Martinez, and Corner (1985).

Environmental psychology may also have many benefits for the casual student of psychology. Throughout this text, you will gain valuable insights into some of the forces that influence your feelings and behavior every day of your life. You will learn how the design of the buildings and cities you live and work in affects you and how much your relationships with other people are controlled by the physical environment. I hope you will come away with practical information that can be put to good use in personal problem solving; at the very least, you should become a more interested and sophisticated observer of human behavior as it relates to the physical environment.

RESEARCH METHODS IN ENVIRONMENTAL PSYCHOLOGY

Now that you have a general idea of what environmental psychology is all about, I want to consider the ways in which environmental psychologists collect information about the world. Since so many of the people who do research on the relationship between human behavior and the physical environment are psychologists by training, they use the same approaches to research that have proven useful in other areas of psychology. However, in addition to these generalized techniques of psychological research, environmental psychologists also have developed unique methods that lend themselves well to the kinds of questions environmental psychologists ask.

Experimental Methods

Experimentation has been at the heart of scientific psychology through-out the 20th century. In an experiment, the researcher actively changes something to create the conditions that he or she is interested in investigating. **Experimental methods** are a very active, interventional style of doing research. The experimenter manipulates one or more **independent variables** to see if they have an effect on a **dependent variable.** Martin (1985) points out that it is easy to remember the difference between the two if you remember that the independent variable is manipulated by the experimenter and is independent of the subject's behavior, while the dependent variable depends on the independent variable and what the subject does. The dependent variable is always what is measured in the experiment. It is possible to manipulate several independent variables in an experiment, and this is usually done to see if they interact with each other in some way. For now, I will discuss an example in which there is just one independent variable.

Suppose that a researcher is interested in the effects that crowding has on blood pressure. The researcher might design an experiment wherein her subjects will experience different conditions of crowding (the independent variable). In one condition, a single subject will sit alone in a 4-meter by 4-meter room for two hours while working on a series of problem-solving tasks. In a second condition, 6 people will spend two hours in the same room working on the same tasks, and in the third condition 12 people will work on the tasks in the same room for two hours. It is absolutely essential that the only systematic difference among the three groups be the number of people in the room. If something else is different between the groups (for example, the length of time spent in the room or the nature of the problem-solving tasks), it will be impossible to tell whether any effects observed are due to changes in the independent variable or to something else. When this occurs, an experiment is said to be **confounded** because something other than the independent variable is different between the groups. For this reason, the experimenter also wants to be sure that the subjects in these groups are as similar to each other as is possible.

The experiment would be clearly confounded if one of the groups had only male subjects while another had only female subjects, or if subjects were allowed to choose the condition they preferred to be in. The most common way to deal with this problem is through a procedure called **random assignment.** In random assignment, each subject has an equally likely chance of being assigned to any of the experimental groups, and where the subject ends up is a matter of chance. This procedure assumes that important individual differences (for example, differences in intelligence) will be randomly distributed across all groups so that the more intelligent (or less intelligent) subjects do not end up in one group in larger numbers than in another group. Random assignment also allows the experimenter to assess the probability that differences will occur by chance between groups. No matter how well controlled an experiment is, there is always the possibility that differences between groups will occur by chance alone. The statistical techniques that the experimenter uses to analyze the data provide an estimate of the probability that the results of the experiment are due to the manipulation of the independent variable and not to chance. Thus, if our experimenter has used random assignment and very carefully followed procedures, an analysis of the data collected on the subjects' blood pressure (the dependent variable) will show whether subjects in the crowded room had a different level of blood pressure overall than did the subjects in the less crowded rooms.

There are many advantages to using experimental methods in research. First of all, an experiment usually allows for greater control of variables than most other research techniques do, and it can be designed to test very specific hypotheses. Perhaps more important, a valid experiment permits the researcher to draw a conclusion about the nature of the cause–effect relationship between the independent and dependent variables.

On the other hand, experiments can also have drawbacks. Limitations are often placed on the independent variable; this may preclude the use of experimental methods for some problems. These limitations may be ethical or more practical in nature. For example, a researcher interested in how people respond to natural disasters such as tornadoes, or how people are affected by their home being burglarized is unlikely to use a well-controlled experiment to test the hypothesis. Even when it is possible to manipulate the independent variable of interest, experiments in environmental psychology are sometimes so costly and inefficient that the researcher is forced to use other techniques.

Whenever experimental methods are used, great care must be taken to ensure that the experiment is valid. An experimenter must be concerned about two kinds of validity: internal validity and external validity. **Internal validity** reflects the degree to which an experiment is free from confounding. If an experiment has been confounded by poor control of extraneous variables (outside variables that the experimenter is not interested in), the experiment lacks internal validity and few meaningful conclusions can be drawn from it. **External validity** refers to the extent to which the results of the experiment can be generalized from that experiment to other situations in the real world. As an example, consider an experiment in which the researcher evaluates the effects of heat on aggressive behavior. College students are placed in rooms that range from comfortable temperatures to very hot temperatures and are asked to administer electric shocks to other college students. If the experiment is carefully controlled and free from confounding, it will be internally valid. External validity, on the other hand, will only exist to the extent that the results of this experiment predict the relationship between heat and very different aggressive behaviors in real situations on city streets or in people's homes. Environmental psychologists, with their emphasis on solving real environmental problems, may be even more concerned with external validity than are their colleagues in other areas of psychology, although among psychologists there is some difference of opinion as to the importance of external validity in the field of psychology as a whole.

Data collected in experiments are not always gathered to predict behavior in the real world (McAndrew, 1984). Psychologists may be interested purely in what *can* happen to behavior under very specific (not necessarily "natural") conditions. External validity is not an issue in these situations. Mook (1983) describes the opposition to this point of view by suggesting that psychologists have come to think of any kind of validity as a "warm, fuzzy, good thing" while any kind of invalidity must be a "cold, creepy, bad thing." After all, who would want to admit that their research is in any way invalid? Mook has also pointed out that if generalizations can be made successfully from a research setting to a real-life setting—even when the two settings are not at all similar—it may be even more impressive because external validity was not the explicit, primary goal of the experiment.

Quasi-Experimental Designs

Perhaps the most common type of data collected by environmental psychologists comes from studies known as **postoccupancy evaluations (POEs)** (Marcus, 1990; Wener, 1989). A POE is the evaluation of a built environment from a social and behavioral perspective in an effort to see how well it meets the needs of the people who must live or work there. POEs provide feedback about the effect that the physical setting has on behavior, and they can provide valuable insights for the design of future environments as well as for the improvement of existing ones. Unfortunately, the highly complex real-world situations in which POEs must be carried out rarely meet the conditions necessary for carefully controlled experiments; researchers must rely on other techniques to collect data. These techniques are known as **quasi-experimental designs.**

Quasi-experimental designs are used in studies that have some components of experiments but lack one or more important features needed for a valid experiment. For example, random assignment may not have been used or it may not have been possible to manipulate the independent variable as cleanly as the researcher would have liked. These designs are not as useful in establishing causal relationships and are not as rigorous as true experiments, but they are quite useful in natural settings where changing conditions and lack of control preclude pure experimentation. Since this is often the case in environmental psychology, quasi-experimental designs are more widely used here than in many other areas of psychology. There are many different kinds of quasi-experimental designs, and in-depth discussions of these can be found in

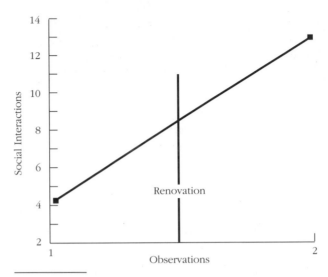

F I G U R E   1·3   Data from a simple time series study

Cherulnik (1983), Campbell and Stanley (1966), or Cook and Campbell (1979). For now, I will focus on one that is used frequently by environmental psychologists—the **time series design.** Time series designs have been used to study a wide variety of environment–behavior problems. Examples include the impact of the renovation of the activity room of a nursing home on its residents (Bakos, Bozic, Chapin, & Neuman, 1980), the effect of a change in office design on the satisfaction of workers (Picasso & White, cited by Wener, 1989), the effect of modifications in an urban plaza on pedestrian traffic (Project for Public Spaces, 1978), and the effects of air pollution on the psychological state and mental functioning of residents of polluted and nonpolluted areas (Bullinger, 1989).

In a time series design, the behavior of a single group of subjects is measured both before and after an experimental treatment or an intervention of some sort. For example, suppose that a researcher were interested in whether the social interaction among residents of a ward in a psychiatric hospital would increase after a renovation of the lounge area. The number of interactions observed during a one-hour observation period before renovation would be compared to the number observed during a similar period after renovation. A graph of how the hypothetical results from such a study might be presented is shown in Figure 1-3.

A problem with this technique is that the fluctuation in the rate of interaction in this ward is not known, so it is impossible to know how well the data reflect the general level of interaction before and after the renovation occurred. This can be partially compensated for by using an interrupted **time series design,** recording data during several observation periods before and after the renovation. Using an interrupted time series design, a clearer picture is formed of the fluctuation in the rate of

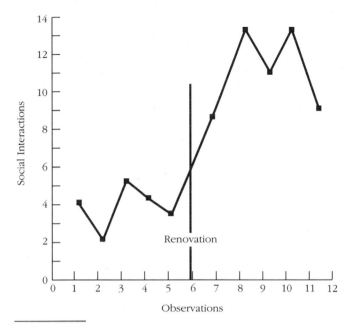

FIGURE 1·4 Data from an interrupted time series study

interaction, and the graph of the results is a better indication of the power of the renovation in affecting social interaction (see Figure 1-4). While this is better, there are still some problems with interpreting the data. For example, since there is no control group, it is possible that some other event may be causing the change. In my example, it may be simply that the residents get to know each other better as time goes on, and this leads to more interaction.

One way to attack this problem is to use a multiple time series design. This design attempts to rule out alternate interpretations by including a control group. If several observation periods before and after renovation are used, and the pattern of results is compared to a similar group of patients in another hospital ward that was not renovated, it can be said with more confidence that any changes observed were due to renovation, provided the patients in the other ward did not show similar changes in interaction across time. A graphic presentation of these hypothetical data can be found in Figure 1-5.

Correlational Methods

Correlational research is an alternative to experiments and quasi-experiments. In correlational studies, the researcher measures two or more variables as they exist in the world. It is a nonexperimental, noninterventional approach to research in which variables are not manipulated and subjects are not assigned to treatment groups. The goal of the

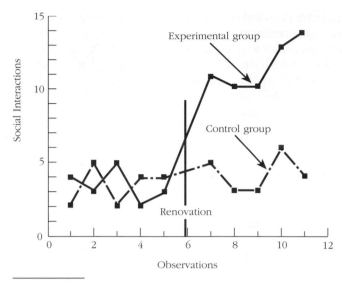

FIGURE 1·5 Data from a multiple time series study

research is to see whether any systematic relationship exists between the variables being measured.

I want to return now to the crowding experiment discussed earlier. Is there a relationship between crowding and blood pressure? Our first experimenter attempted to answer this question with a laboratory experiment, but it is also possible to answer it with a correlational study. In this case, the researcher would identify a target group of subjects to participate in the study and record two pieces of information from each subject: blood pressure and the density of the subject's living conditions. (In this case we will define this as the number of people per room in the subject's house or apartment.) After all the data have been collected, they will be examined to see if a consistent relationship between the variables exists. If there is a strong tendency for high blood pressure readings to be paired with high-density living conditions, the relationship between the two is described as *positive* because when the score for one variable is high the other one also tends to be. On the other hand, if high blood pressure readings tend to be paired with low-density living conditions, the relationship is *negative* because a high score on one variable usually indicates that there will be a low score on the other variable. The researcher assesses this relationship by computing a statistic called a **correlation coefficient.** The correlation coefficient can range from a value of −1.0 to +1.0. The closer the number comes to a −1.0 or +1.0, the stronger and more consistent the relationship is between the variables; the closer the number is to zero, the weaker the relationship is between the two variables. The positive or negative sign in front of the coefficient says nothing about the *strength* of the relationship between the two

variables, but it does indicate whether the relationship is positive or negative. A strong correlation, regardless of whether it is positive or negative,
allows the researcher to make fairly accurate predictions about the value of
one of the variables if the value of the other variable is known.

Correlational studies are useful in many of the situations where
experiments are difficult to perform. They are usually quicker and less
expensive than experiments, and they allow researchers to study things
such as reactions to natural disasters that they cannot study experimentally. As is true for any research technique, correlational designs have
limitations. They provide little control over extraneous variables, and this
often leaves the cause–effect relationship between the variables ambiguous. Even when it provides a researcher with good predictive power, a
correlational study makes it more difficult for the researcher to unequiv-
ocally state that one variable is responsible for changes in the other.

In the example of crowding being related to blood pressure, a strong
positive correlation would make it tempting to say that high-density living
leads to high blood pressure, but this would be completely unjustified.
Statistically, it would be just as legitimate to say that people with high
blood pressure seek out crowded situations. It is also possible that some
third, unmeasured variable (an inability to pay one's bills or afford a
larger house) is responsible for the link between the variables measured.
In spite of these shortcomings, correlational methods are often used by
environmental psychologists because they are frequently the best technique for tackling the applied problems encountered in the field.

Research Settings

One commonly thinks of experiments as something that occurs in a
laboratory and correlational research as a study done in a field setting.
While this is often the case, there is no necessary connection between the
setting of a study and the research technique used. It is possible to do a
perfectly valid experiment in a field setting, and correlational data can be
collected in a laboratory. Thus, a researcher's decisions about the relative
merits of conducting laboratory or field research are made independent
of the technique he or she wishes to use.

Laboratory research   Laboratory studies have the advantage of offering the researcher greater control over the situation than is usually
possible in a field setting — random assignment of subjects, precise control
of the independent variable — and the researcher can be sure of what is
happening to each subject throughout the study. A laboratory setting also
lets the researcher measure the dependent variable in the most sensitive
way. For example, if the emotional response of the subject is the dependent variable, the experimenter may be able to record the subject's
physiological reactions to the situation with a physiograph. The major
disadvantage of the laboratory study is that subjects are aware that they

are in an experiment. This can create **reactive effects** in subjects, and they may change their behavior in ways that will affect the outcome of the study. Subjects in psychological experiments usually try to guess the purpose and hypotheses of the experiment and occasionally will adjust their behavior to "help" the experimenter find what he or she is looking for or even intentionally try to interfere with the results. Even more common is a tendency for subjects to act in ways that will reflect well on themselves; after all, no one wants to appear foolish or incompetent in a psychological experiment.

The cues available to the subject that may reveal the hypotheses of the study are called **demand characteristics** (Orne, 1962), and unless they are carefully controlled, the validity of the study is in doubt. Aside from demand characteristics, there are other problems with laboratory research. The kinds of manipulation that realistically can be done in a laboratory are limited, and there is the question of how well laboratory results can generalize to the real world. Nevertheless, laboratory research has proven to be a valuable tool in environmental psychology.

Field research   Field studies of real people in real situations can compensate for many of the problems faced by laboratory studies. Since subjects usually do not know they are being studied, suspicion is minimized and the researcher will get more "real" results. Additionally, field studies make it possible to study many different types of people (not just college students) and also make it possible to study more powerful variables that cannot be manipulated effectively in the laboratory. On the other hand, field studies do not provide the kind of control found in the laboratory. It may not be possible to randomly assign subjects to conditions or to control extraneous variables. In addition it is usually more difficult to get "pure" measures of the dependent variable. For example, if the emotional response of individuals is the dependent variable, the researcher may have to infer an emotional state from other behaviors (such as facial expressions or posture) rather than measuring it directly as might be possible in the laboratory. Also, field studies are often awkward and more costly than laboratory research since they require transporting researchers and equipment to different locations, a greater number of researchers, and the cooperation of people who are not specifically a part of the research team.

Both laboratory and field studies can be productive sources of information, but the researcher must carefully consider their relative advantages for the problem at hand.

Other Sources of Data in Environmental Psychology

Zeisel (1981) and Webb and his colleagues (Webb, Campbell, Schwartz, & Sechvest, 1966; Webb et al., 1981) have provided a comprehensive description of many of the more specific research techniques used by environmental psychologists. I will provide a brief explanation of some of the most important of these.

Self-report measures   Surveys that use questionnaires or focused interviews are common tools in environmental psychology. In self-report measures such as surveys or interviews, people respond in writing or verbally to questions posed by the researcher. Great care must be taken when constructing survey questions, and the researcher must weigh the relative merits of written questionnaires versus face-to-face or telephone interviews. Interviews have a higher return rate and greater accuracy, but they are also usually more expensive and difficult to do anonymously. The researcher must also pay close attention to the wording of questions and format issues, such as whether open-ended or closed questions are more appropriate. Open-ended questions allow the subject to respond any way he or she wishes with no restrictions placed on length of response or the type of information given. Closed questions are highly structured and employ a forced-choice design that requires the subject to select an answer from a multiple-choice list or to express agreement or disagreement with a statement along a numerical scale. Occasionally, closed, structured questionnaires require that subjects merely answer "yes" or "no," or "agree" or "disagree." Closed questions are easier to score and analyze. But open-ended questionnaires can yield more useful insights into what subjects are actually thinking, and they may leave the respondent more satisfied with his or her responses (Cozby, 1989).

A common use of self-report measures in environmental psychology is in the evaluation of the quality of an environment by the people who use it. An instrument called a **Perceived Environmental Quality Index (PEQI)** is used to quantitatively measure an individual's subjective evaluation of his or her environment. PEQIs are self-report measures that are usually in the form of a questionnaire, and they are used to measure the perceived quality of both human-made and natural environments. Assessing environmental quality with a PEQI can be an important part of judging the effectiveness of environmental protection programs, estimating the environmental impact of building or development projects, and communicating information about environmental quality to those in a position to set environmental policies (Craik, 1983).

A problem with interviews, questionnaires, and other self-report measures is that the implications of the responses are usually obvious to the person being questioned; therefore, they may be motivated to conceal or distort information. For example, in a study of the owners of self-built homes in South Africa, Hart and Hardie (1987) found that female-headed households averaged only half of the income of male-headed households; yet they were able to afford houses that were about the same size. This prompted speculation about the resourcefulness of female-headed households until a follow-up study revealed that many of the women made extra money through independent businesses, such as making clothes or beer, or selling meat and vegetables. Because these activities were illegal, they were hidden from the interviewer in the original study.

Clearly, most self-report measures are reactive, and this may cause problems if the subjects of the study are motivated to conceal or distort information. In these situations, other techniques that are *nonreactive* (subjects are not aware that they are in a study) may be necessary. Nonreactive measures will be considered next.

Archival research   Archival research is the use of data produced for other than scholarly purposes to test hypotheses or to look for relationships between variables (Webb et al., 1966). Archival sources are usually written documents. They may be ongoing societal records such as census data, actuarial records (for example, births, deaths, marriages), directories, newspapers, or the results of past surveys. Archival data may also come from private sources such as diaries, letters, or corporate sales records. Archival research has been employed successfully by environmental psychologists to study problems ranging from the relationship between crowding and health problems (Fleming, Baum, & Weiss, 1987; Paulus, McCain, & Cox, 1978) to the relationship between temperature and violent behavior in cities (Anderson, 1987; Anderson & Anderson, 1984).

While archival data are useful for many purposes, it must be recognized that these data may not be representative. Not all information is equally likely to be preserved (a phenomenon known as **selective deposit**) and of that deposited, not all will be preserved across time (**selective survival**) (Webb et al., 1966). Environmental psychologists exploiting archival sources must be aware of these limitations and attempt to determine how they might affect any conclusions that are drawn. To give yourself a direct experience drawing conclusions from archival data, try it (see box, Interpreting Archival Data).

Unobtrusive observation   In **unobtrusive** (or nonreactive) **observation,** data are generated by observing the actual behavior of people in a specific setting, often without their awareness. The observer may use a variety of techniques for recording data, including checklists, maps, and even videotape. In all cases, great care must be taken to completely describe the setting, behaviors, and people in enough detail to permit analysis of the important factors in the study. This technique involves the observer more with the setting and the people using it than most other research techniques, which leads to a better understanding of the connections between events that occur in that setting. This research also provides a more honest record of what people actually do than interviews or questionnaires do. Still, the observer must be on guard against subjectivity and personal feelings interfering with the objective recording of data. In situations where a visible observer might disrupt the behavior of interest or produce reactivity in those being observed, care must be taken that the observer not be too obvious. In these situations, it may be necessary to hide the observer in a crowd or remove him or her from the scene altogether (for example, via a hidden video camera).

Observing physical traces When **observing physical traces,** the environmental psychologist systematically examines an environment for remnants or reflections of the activities of the people who use that setting. What the researcher looks for depends entirely on what he or she is interested in, but the research is usually being done to make an environment better suited to what people actually do while they are in it. For example, at the college where I teach, the well-worn trampled pathways across the grassy areas of the campus were used as a guide for the location of new sidewalks. Carefully observing how people rearrange the furniture and other props in their environment, the kinds of litter they leave behind, and the nature of the **accretion** (the deposit of material in a setting) and **erosion** (the selective wear of some portion of an environmental setting) that occur in the environment can tell you what people do, and do not do, in an environment and how well that environment is accomplishing what it was designed for. It is often possible to determine when places are most likely to be used and whether the environment is being used in unanticipated ways. By observing how people rearrange their settings, environmental psychologists learn how to construct more satisfying and efficient environments.

TRY IT!

Interpreting Archival Data

An exercise developed by Bernstein (1991) shows how a common archival record, an individual's checkbook register, can provide information about a person's day-to-day whereabouts, his or her spending priorities and habits, important life events and problems, and some of the significant people in his or her life. Ask several students in the class to volunteer to have their checkbook registers examined. The class should be divided into small groups, each of which examines a different register. Ideally, the owner of the register should remain anonymous. Give each group about 15 minutes to come to some agreement and then ask them to report their conclusions about the owner of the register. This exercise is especially useful if the owners of the checkbook registers are willing to be identified so that they can confirm or deny the conclusions drawn by the group.

P H O T O S   1-5A and B Physical traces are forms of "fossilized behavior" that provide insights about how environments are used by people.

Webb and his colleagues (1966) have provided numerous examples of how physical traces can be used in research. They note that wear and tear and rate of repair can be an indication of the extent of library book use, just as the wear of carpeting and floor tiles around museum exhibits can serve as an index of their popularity. Webb and his colleagues also report that the popularity of radio stations has been estimated by observing the dial settings in parked cars and cars brought into a car dealership for repair.

Sir Arthur Conan Doyle's famous fictional detective, Sherlock Holmes, was a master at using physical traces to learn things about the people and places that figured prominently in his adventures. In *The Adventure of the Speckled Band,* Holmes has to solve a series of mysterious murders, and the observation of physical traces plays a significant role in helping him track down a murderer who killed his victims with a well-trained, poisonous snake. When first approached about the case, Holmes deduced that his female visitor had traveled by train because she held a ticket stub in her hand; he also deduced that she had ridden on the left side of a dogcart because of the pattern of fresh mud spattered on her jacket. Important clues to the mystery were provided by examining the seats of chairs to see whether they had been used for standing on as well as sitting, attending to the arrangement of furniture and other items in the murder room, and detecting the odors left by cigar smoke.

The Aventure of the Speckled Band is a colorful example of how physical traces can be thought of as "fossilized behavior." They can provide a researcher with rich impressions and give tremendous insights into the successes and failures of a setting and the characteristics of its users. From traces, investigators can generate questions about what caused the trace, what the person who created it intended, and the sequence of events that led up to it. Observing physical traces also circumvents the problem of demand characteristics, as it does not affect the behavior being observed; and, because physical traces are so durable, they are easy and inexpensive to observe and record.

CHAPTER SUMMARY

Environmental psychology is concerned with the relationship between human behavior and the physical environment. It came into its own as a field in the 1960s but was strongly influenced by earlier developments in psychology. Social psychology, in particular, has played a role in shaping the growth of environmental psychology, with the early influence of Kurt Lewin and his students being especially strong. Today, environmental psychologists study a bewildering array of topics, but all are firmly grounded in empirical research. More than that of many other kinds of psychologists, the research of environmental psychologists involves the resolution of human problems in real environments.

Environmental psychology relies on many of the same techniques used in other areas of psychology. Experimental methods entail the manipulation of one or more independent variables to see if they have an effect on the dependent variable. Quasi-experimental designs have many of the same features of experiments but are used when pure manipulation or random assignment is not possible. Correlational methods are a nonexperimental approach to research, which permits the study of problems that cannot be studied experimentally. While they have many advantages, correlational studies do not allow a researcher to say anything about the cause–effect relationship between the variables studied. All these techniques can be used in both laboratory and field settings. In addition to the standard research methodologies, environmental psychologists employ other techniques that are suited to their special needs. Some of the most popular of these are unobtrusive observation, self-report measures, the observation of physical traces, and the use of archival sources.

GLOSSARY

Accretion   Deposit of material in an environmental setting made by the people who use that setting.

Confounding   Occurs when something other than the independent variable varies between experimental groups.

Correlation Coefficient   A statistic that is calculated in correlational research, which indicates the strength and direction of a correlation.

Correlational Research   A noninterventional style of research in which two or more variables are measured as they already exist, with the goal of the research being to see if any systematic relationship exists between the variables.

Demand Characteristics   The cues available to subjects in laboratory experiments that may reveal the hypotheses of an experiment.

Dependent Variable   In an experiment, this is the variable that is measured.

Ecological Psychology   A precursor of modern environmental psychology that grew out of the work at the Midwest Psychological Field Station.

Environmental Psychology   The discipline concerned with the interactions and relationships between people and their environments.

Erosion   The selective wear of some portion of an environment.

Experimental Methods   An interventional style of research in which one or more independent variables are manipulated to see if they have an effect on a dependent variable.

External Validity   The extent to which the results of an experiment can be generalized to other settings.

Gestalt Psychology   A school of psychology developed in Germany in the early 1900s that was influential in later psychological theories, especially theories of perception.

Independent Variable   In an experiment, this is the variable that is manipulated.

Internal Validity   The extent to which an experiment is free from confounding.

Kurt Lewin (1890–1947)   The person who brought the Gestalt perspective to the study of social psychology. His theories of behavior and the work of his students were important in the development of environmental psychology.

Life Space   In Lewin's theory, this refers collectively to all the psychological facts currently being experienced by an individual.

The Midwest Psychological Field Station   Founded in 1947 in Oskaloosa, Kansas, it was the first research enterprise devoted entirely to the study of human behavior in a real-world environment.

Observing Physical Traces   A research technique in which an environment is examined for remnants or reflections of the activities of the people who used that setting.

Perceived Environmental Quality Index (PEQI)   A quantitative measure of subjective evaluations of an environment.

Postoccupancy Evaluation (POE)   The evaluation of a built environment from a social and behavioral perspective.

Psychological Facts   In Lewin's theory, the influences in an individual's life that he or she is aware of at any given time.

Quasi-Experimental Designs   Research designs that have some components of experiments but lack one or more of the features needed in a good experiment.

Random Assignment   A technique used in experimentation to prevent confounding. In random assignment, each subject has an equally likely chance of being assigned to any experimental condition.

Reactive Effects   Changes in behavior that occur when people are aware that they are being studied.

Selective Deposit   Refers to the fact that not all types of information are equally likely to be recorded in archival sources.

Selective Survival   Refers to the fact that, after being recorded, not all archival information is equally likely to be preserved over long periods of time.

Sensory Overload   What occurs when a person is presented with more sensory information than he or she can process.

Time Series Design   One of the most commonly used quasi-experimental designs: the behavior of a group of subjects is examined before and after an experimental treatment or intervention. Three different forms that this technique may take are the simple time series, interrupted time series, and multiple time series designs.

Unobtrusive Observation   Observing the behavior of people in a specific setting, usually without their knowledge.

Environmental Cognition

2

Have you ever studied a road map of a city that you have never been to, driven there, and then found exactly what you were looking for with little trouble? Perhaps you have had the experience of returning to a place that you have not visited in many years and were surprised when you recognized the landmarks, streets, and other places that you thought were long forgotten.

Our ability to process, store, and retrieve spatial and geographical information is quite impressive. Of course, there are sound evolutionary reasons why our spatial abilities should be so sharply developed. Human organisms survive only if they interact appropriately with the environment. We have to learn the value of different objects encountered in the environment and their location. These objects (for example, predators, mates, food, shelter, hazards) are scattered in space, and it is important that we possess the cognitive and physical skills required to move through this space to approach or avoid these objects. According to Lee (1978), we "plan" our immediate future by evoking and examining long sequences of images of the environment that we construct from past experiences. These plans not only help us move through the environment, but they strongly influence the affective experiences we have in the places we visit and the kind of information we can recall after we have left them (Ward, Snodgrass, Chew, & Russell, 1988).

In short, the ability to successfully anticipate what will happen next has been crucial for survival throughout our evolutionary history, and it depends completely on our ability to accurately store information about the physical environment. This spatial memory allows us to live in a world of expanded space in which we are aware of places and things beyond the immediate grasp of our senses. Passini, Proulx, and Rainville (1990) point out that finding one's way around in the environment is a highly complex activity that involves planning, decision making, and information processing, all of which rely on an ability to understand space and to manipulate it mentally. This ability is usually referred to as **spatio-cognitive ability.** In this chapter, I will examine the ways in which human beings come to know and understand the physical space in the world around them.

ENVIRONMENTAL PERCEPTION

Perception is the process that is at the core of any environmental behavior since it is the source of all information about the environment. Environments stimulate all the senses, providing the individual with far more information than he or she can process efficiently. Therefore, perception is not the same thing as sensation, but rather is the result of a filtering process performed by the individual. In commenting on this phenomenon, Ittelson (1976) noted that in reality the individual is part of the system that he or she is perceiving. It is sometimes difficult to separate the person from the environment in the perceptual process, since the two are always interacting and perceptions depend on what the person is doing in the environment. Perception is also a trade-off between speed and accuracy. However, both speed and accuracy are desirable goals in the perceptual process, and our system of mental representation helps soften this necessary trade-off by quickly recognizing things that are "probable" in spite of changes in perspective or sketchy sensory information (Kaplan, 1978a). For example, if you are driving along a highway and pass a farm, any large dark figure moving in the distance is likely to be quickly recognized as a cow, a horse, or a pig, since these are the stimuli that would be "probable" in that environment. In these situations, the speed of recognition usually will not interfere with accuracy. This process is called **top-down processing** (sometimes called conceptually-driven processing) by cognitive psychologists who study pattern recognition (Glass and Holyoak, 1986). In top-down processing, the recognition process is driven by expectations of what objects are to be found in a particular environment. The search for a stimulus in memory that matches the pattern of sensory input is effectively narrowed when only a small set of items must be considered. In effect, top-down processing causes us to seek specific perceptions in the farm environment (for example, a horse or a cow) before we receive any sensory information at all! While top-down processing usually speeds up the perceptual process, it may slow it down when we encounter an "improbable" stimulus. An octopus in a barnyard would more likely be misidentified or take substantially longer to recognize than a cow would.

That our perceptual expectations are based on experience is supported by research demonstrating that many visual illusions are culture-specific. That is, people are only fooled by illusions that involve shapes and architectural features that are familiar to them from their everyday experience (Allport & Pettigrew, 1957; Altman & Chemers, 1980).

A complementary kind of processing is active in situations where there are no "probable stimuli" expected by the perceiver. This type of processing is called **bottom-up processing** (or data-driven processing). In bottom-up processing, the perceptual process is driven entirely by the nature of the sensory input unguided by any preconceptions or expectations. In those rare situations in which there are no "probable stimuli" whatsoever, recognition would necessarily take longer. Most of the time, however, perception is the result of some combination of bottom-up and top-down processing occurring simultaneously.

Theories of Environmental Perception

Brunswik's probabilistic model   In the study of perception, psychologists have usually focused on the study of object perception and ignored a most obvious and important perceptual problem: the perception of the environment as a whole and its importance to individual functioning (Gärling & Golledge, 1989; Ittelson, 1976). Egon Brunswik's **lens model** (Brunswik, 1956) was mentioned in Chapter 1; it is a good example of a psychological model of perception that addresses the perception of the environment as a whole. Brunswik's theory says that sensory information never accurately reflects the real world and that it is ambiguous by its very nature. Individuals must use this faulty information to make probabilistic judgments about the true nature of the environment. In the lens model, human perceptual processes act very much like the lens in an eye or a camera (see Figure 2-1).

Just as a lens captures a scattered array of light and focuses it on a

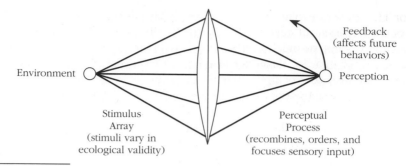

F I G U R E   2·1   Brunswik's lens model (Source: Holahan, 1982)

single point on the retina (or on the film), in Brunswik's lens model the perceptual process receives a scattered array of environmental stimuli (left side of Figure 2-1) which it filters and recombines into an ordered, unified perception (right side of Figure 2-1). With experience, individuals learn which stimuli are the most accurate reflections of the real environment, and these are given greater weight in the organization of future perceptions. From Brunswik's perspective, the world is "inferred" from more or less reliable cues rather than observed (Gärling & Golledge, 1989). Brunswik's model clearly portrays the individual as an active processor of information, constructing perceptions from the interaction of current sensations and past experiences.

Gibson's ecological model   An alternative to Brunswik's model is **Gibson's ecological theory of perception** (Gibson, 1957a, 1958, 1960, 1966, 1979). While most environmental psychologists feel that Brunswik's probabilistic model has been more influential than Gibson's ecological model in theories of environmental perception (Craik, 1983; Holahan, 1982; Saegert & Winkel, 1990), Gibson's model has drawn new interest with the growth of an evolutionary perspective that emphasizes the adaptation and functioning of organisms in their environment.

Gibson's approach to perception was called ecological because it stressed environmental facts that were most relevant to species' biological adaptation such as successful locomotion, prevention of injury and death, and the location of vital resources and sex partners (Lombardo, 1987). Gibson disagreed with Brunswik's position because he did not see how there could be survival in a "world of probable objects" (Gibson, 1957b). Gibson's approach to perception was much less phenomenological than Brunswik's. It posits that sensory information does in fact provide an accurate record of the world as it really is. For Gibson, the senses are an evolved adaptation to the environment, and crucial parts of the environment such as gravity, diurnal cycles, and earth–sky contrasts have been invariant throughout evolutionary history. The invariance of the environment creates stability and provides a framework for life. Hence, evolutionary success required development of sensory systems that accurately reflected the environment. For Gibson, the question is not so much "How do things look?" as it is "What is there to see?" (Lombardo, 1987). From the ecological perspective, perception becomes a process of the environment revealing itself to the perceiver; the nervous system does not construct perceptions as much as it extracts them.

Gibson's theory diminishes the role of learning in perception and proposes that many, if not most, perceptual responses are innate. This position is consistent with research showing innate depth perception in animals that can walk shortly after birth (Gibson & Walk, 1960; Walk & Gibson, 1961). It is also consistent with the finding that single cells in the visual cortex of animals fire only in response to specific kinds of visual stimuli (Ewert, 1974, 1980; Hubel & Wiesel, 1962; Perrett & Rolls, 1983). While Gibson believed that sensory information from the world was essentially correct, he also believed that other perceptual activities, such as exploration, adjusting the intensity of sensory inputs, and selective attention, had to occur for this information to become an effective stimulus for the individual. These activities were especially important so that an individual might take advantage of the useful functions of objects in the environment (for example, the provision of food, safety, comfort, or recreation), functions that Gibson (1966) referred to as **affordances.** For example, a lake might offer affordances such as "fishable," "swimmable," or "float-on-able" but not affordances such as "sleepable" or "walkable." The affordances of objects in the environment can be discovered only through exploration and the efficient allocation of attention.

COGNITIVE MAPS AND WAYFINDING IN THE ENVIRONMENT

The importance of environmental cognition to the functioning of any organism cannot be overestimated, since it forms the basis of an organism's ability to navigate through the world. A diverse array of mechanisms has evolved in many species of animals, resulting in some impressive feats of **wayfinding** (navigating) through the environment. Some green sea turtles swim from Brazil to Ascension Island (a small island in the South Atlantic) to lay eggs, unfailingly locating the five-mile speck of land after crossing 1500 miles of ocean (Carr, 1965). Many species of fish such as shad (Leggett, 1973) and salmon (Hasler & Larsen, 1955) accomplish similar feats using cues such as odor and water temperature as guides through the sea. Migratory birds make use of a variety of cues in their travels, including the position of the sun and, at least in European robins and in homing pigeons, an ability to sense magnetic fields (Ganzhorn, 1990; Keeton, 1974; Petterson, Sandberg, &

Alerstam, 1991). Emlen (1975) described a series of experiments demonstrating how some nocturnal migratory birds use the position of stellar constellations for navigational purposes. Emlen studied the North American Indigo Bunting. Like all migratory birds, the Indigo Bunting shows increased activity levels during the spring and fall migration periods, even when held in captivity. Buntings normally spend the summer months in eastern North America and winter in the Bahamas and Central America. Emlen tested his birds by placing them in a circular cage constructed of a piece of white blotting paper rolled and stapled to form a funnel (see Figure 2-2). The top of the cage was covered with a screen or clear plastic and the floor of the cage was an ink pad. A bird inside the cage would only be able to see objects that were overhead. A bird hopping onto the funneled paper would slide back, leaving ink marks showing where it had hopped. The accumulation of inky footprints provided a record of the amount and direction of the bird's activity. Birds were tested outdoors on clear nights and indoors in a planetarium. The birds in Emlen's study always hopped toward the northern or southern constellations, depending upon the season. Further experimentation in the planetarium revealed that the birds oriented themselves in relation to several star groups near the North Star, flying toward them in the spring and directly away from them in the fall.

Like birds, it is believed that humans rely primarily on visual information to understand the structure of their environment. Although much is still unknown about human environmental cognition, one thing is clear: Memory for pictures and other visual information is different from memory for other kinds of information. In fact, research indicates that our capacity to retain pictorial information is very impressive. Nickerson (1965) presented a sequence of 200 photographs for five seconds each to subjects in an experiment on visual memory. These 200 photographs were followed by 400 photographs—half were duplicates of the originals and half were new ones. The subjects' overall average accuracy in distinguishing the pictures they had seen before from the ones that were new was about 95 percent. Other studies have shown recognition accuracy close to 95 percent when as many as 2560 pictures were used (Standing, Conezio, & Haber, 1970), and Nickerson (1968) found long-term recognition for his 200 photographs at around 63 percent an entire year after his subjects first saw the pictures for a mere five seconds! The superiority of pictorial memory over memory for verbal material has been established in many other studies as well (Lutz & Sheirer, 1974; Nelson, Reed, & Walling, 1976; Shepard, 1967).

The clear superiority of visual memory over verbal memory is difficult to account for without assuming that visual information is coded in a different fashion from nonvisual information. A belief in the existence of visual imagery was common among the founders of modern psychology (Galton, 1883; James, 1890; Titchener, 1910), but by the 1960s the notion

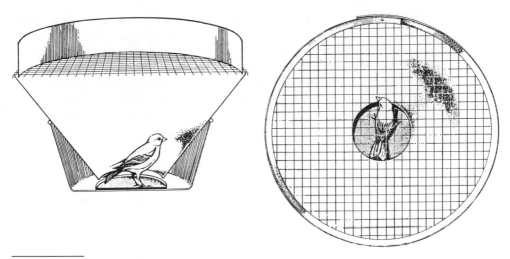

F I G U R E   2-2 Circular test cage for determining the directional preference of an indigo bunting is shown in cross section and in a top view. Funnel portion of the cage is made of white blotting paper. The bunting stands on an ink pad, and each time it hops onto the sloping funnel wall it leaves black footprints. The bird's view is limited to a 140-degree overhead sector of sky when it hops up. (Source: Emlen, 1975)

of visual memory had fallen into disrepute (Wingfield & Byrnes, 1981) and some psychologists continue to argue against any form of visually-based memory codes (Anderson, 1978; Pylyshyn, 1973, 1978, 1984). Nevertheless, most researchers now seem to believe that visual memory codes are the best available explanation for the results of many studies done since the early 1960s, and the concept is enjoying a revival in the field of psychology. Presumably, visual memory codes are instrumental in constructing mental representations of the physical environment.

Mental representations of environments are called **cognitive maps.** The term was introduced by the influential learning theorist E. C. Tolman (Tolman, 1948; Tolman, Ritchie, & Kalish, 1946) to explain how rats learned the location of rewards in a maze when the pathways available to the rat are changed. A cognitive map provides the organism with a useful model of the environment. A model must be an abstraction, leaving out some information if it is to be useful. Consequently, through abstraction and errors of attention, perception, and recall, cognitive maps can be quite different from reality. Cognitive maps may be detailed or very sketchy; they may be of areas as large as the earth or as small as a backyard. In all cases, the cognitive map represents the world as the individual believes it to be (Matlin, 1989) (see Figure 2-3). The kind of information salient to the individual may depend upon whether that person must actually travel through an environment (Sherman, Croxton,

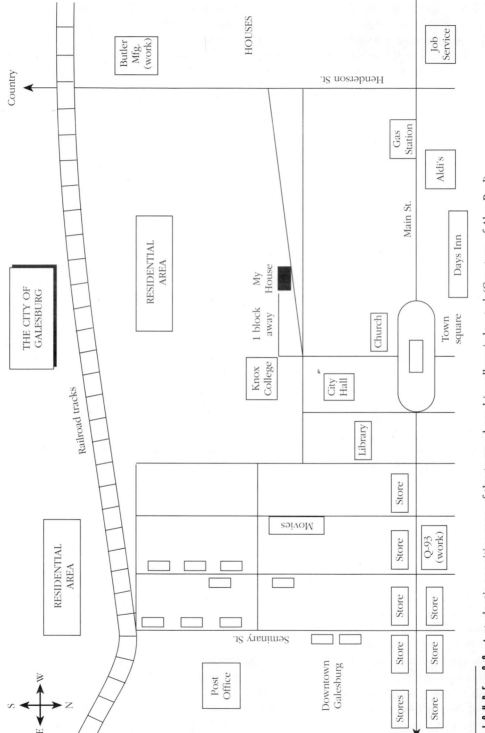

F I G U R E   2·3   A student's cognitive map of the town where his college is located (Courtesy of Alex Paul)

& Smith, 1979), as making sense of the environment is especially important in these situations. Settings that enhance the formation of good
mental maps are strongly preferred (Evans, 1980; Kaplan, 1975, 1978b).

Two different kinds of spatial knowledge can be distinguished: route
knowledge and survey knowledge (Shemyakin, 1962; Thorndyke &
Hayes-Roth, 1982). *Route knowledge* (also known as wayfinding) refers
to a series of actions a person takes in the environment, and it depends
on direct navigational experience. *Survey knowledge,* on the other
hand, is more maplike, conveys global relations between locations, and
can be acquired by studying a map. There is evidence that extensive
navigational experience can produce more flexible spatial knowledge
than map learning because maps alone make it difficult to change one's
perspective and orientation to the environment (Evans & Pezdek, 1980;
Gale, Golledge, Pellegrino, & Doherty, 1990).

The Nature of Cognitive Maps

Most researchers agree that our cognitive maps of larger environments
include a combination of spatial information from maps, direct personal
experience, and a variety of other sources (Evans & Pezdek, 1980; Spoehr
& Lehmkuhle, 1982). Our maps contain both spatial and verbal/
propositional information (for example, "the house I live in") and features as diverse as elevation and the names that we give to places on
maps (Gärling, Böök, & Lindberg, 1985; Gärling, Böök, Lindberg, & Arce,
1990, Russell & Ward, 1982).

Geographical locations are usually described in terms of distance and
direction, but Altman and Chemers (1980) noted that it is common for
people in the Northeastern United States and in urban areas of California to
refer to distance in terms of travel time. Downs and Stea's (1973) finding
that people often mix distance, direction, and estimates of travel time when
giving directions to others, supports the idea that the concept of travel
time is an important ingredient in the cognitive maps of some people.

Studies show that people have fairly accurate cognitive maps of
familiar surroundings (Appleyard, 1970; Evans, 1980; Evans, Marrero, &
Butler, 1981; Foley & Cohen, 1984; Gärling, Lindberg, Carreiras, & Böök,
1986; Holahan, 1978; Holahan & Dobrowolny, 1978; Kaplan, 1976;
Moore, 1974). When asked to give estimates of distances between places,
the time it takes to come up with an estimate increases with the real
distance, which shows a strong relationship between actual physical
distance and distance on cognitive maps (Baum & Jonides, 1977).

When drawing pictures of their cognitive maps, people expand the
size and detail of places that are most familiar to them and place them in
the center of the map. For example, students all over the world tend to
draw their own country in the center when constructing a map of the
world (Saarinen, 1973), indicating that the most familiar territory is used
as an anchor for the overall map (see Figure 2-4).

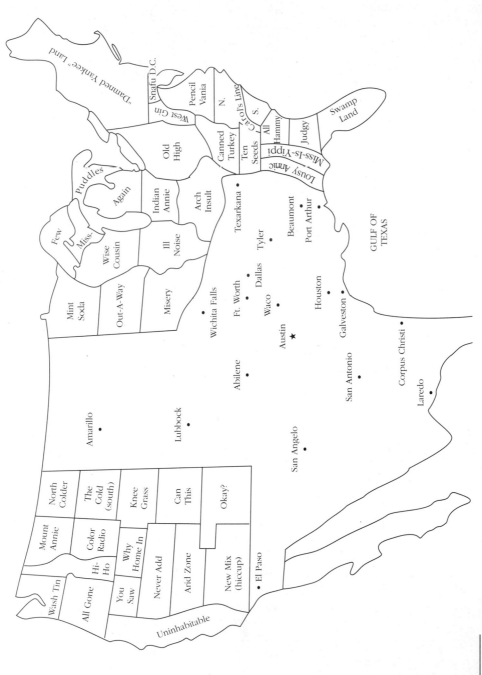

FIGURE 2-4 A Texan's view of the United States. On our cognitive maps we tend to exaggerate the size of areas that are highly familiar to us.

Cognitive Maps of Cities

Most studies of cognitive mapping have been concerned with the cognition of cities (Appleyard, 1969, 1970, 1973; Lynch, 1960; Milgram, 1977). By far the most influential work in this area has been done by an urban planner named Kevin Lynch (1960, 1965, 1977). His book *The Image of the City* (1960) introduced a way of thinking about cities that remains the cornerstone of professional thinking about the spatial organization of urban areas. According to Lynch, one of the most important characteristics of a city is its **legibility.** Legibility refers to the ease with which the features of the city can be recognized, organized into a pattern, and recalled. Humans often prefer environments that are easily "read" and quickly understood, probably because of the strong survival value of these environments throughout evolutionary history (Kaplan, 1987). In this respect, cities are no different from any other environment.

Lynch's research revealed that people use five key dimensions when constructing a mental image of a city. **Paths** are routes or channels along which people move—streets, rivers, and subway lines are common examples. The more the street pattern of a city is dominated by right-angled intersections, the more easily people know and remember directions, and they more quickly learn the location of specific places (Montello, 1991). **Edges** are linear elements that need not be paths; they serve as dividing lines between different parts of the environment. Shorelines, walls, hedges, or legal boundaries are typical examples of edges. Note that things that sometimes serve as paths (such as rivers and railroad tracks) may also function as edges in some cognitive maps. **Districts** are medium to large sections of a city that a person can be "inside of" such as Chinatown, the "red light" district, the Loop (Chicago), or Beacon Hill (Boston). **Nodes** are strategic points in the city that serve as transfer points for travelling to and from places. Major intersections, public squares, and subway or bus stations all serve as nodes. **Landmarks** are physical objects, such as buildings, statues, or fountains, whose primary characteristics are their uniqueness, prominence, and importance. Landmarks are the things you describe when giving directions by saying "You can't miss it!" (See Photo 2-1.)

As you can see from the list in the box Landmarks as Symbols, some landmarks become so well known that they literally become graphic symbols of the cities in which they are located.

Sadalla, Burroughs, and Staplin (1980) believe that landmarks have a cognitive status different from that of other points in space. Landmarks serve as the anchorpoints in our spatial representations of the environment. Our cognitive maps are often oriented around them rather than to compass directions, and people usually learn the location of landmarks long before they have a good grasp of the network paths in a city (Cohen & Cohen, 1985; Evans, Marrero, & Butler, 1981; Evans & Pezdek, 1980; Gärling, Böök, Lindberg, & Nilsson, 1981; Golledge, 1978, 1987; Schouela, Steinberg, Leveton, & Wapner, 1980). Most of the distance estimates we make are estimates of distances between landmarks (or between our current location and a landmark). Sadalla, Burroughs, and Staplin (1980) found that people tend to underestimate the distance from a vantage point to a landmark but, curiously, do not underestimate the distance if they are asked to give it from the other direction—that is, from the landmark to that point. They also found that distance estimates between landmarks are given more quickly than distance estimates not involving landmarks. Smith (1984) found that the accuracy of judging distances between landmarks increased as the "pleasingness" of the landmarks increased.

Many studies (e.g., Aragones & Arredondo, 1985) have confirmed the importance of Lynch's first dimensions of orientation to the urban environment for understanding the cognitive mapping of cities.

Distortions and Errors in Cognitive Maps

Cognitive maps have been studied in a number of different ways. Some researchers have asked people to sketch maps of their cities or neigh-

TRY IT!

Landmarks as Symbols

Downs and Stea (1977) compiled a list of famous landmarks that are so well known that they have literally become visual symbols of the cities in which they are located. To illustrate how effectively these symbols have been identified with their home cities, match the landmark in the left-hand column below with the appropriate city in the right-hand column.

Liberty Bell	Copenhagen
Statue of Liberty	Seattle
Golden Gate Bridge	St. Louis
Little Mermaid Statue	Chicago
Eiffel Tower	Rome
Parthenon	Sydney
Space Needle	New York
Gateway Arch	Philadelphia
U.S. Capitol Building	Paris
Big Ben	Washington, D.C.
Harbor Bridge	London
The Coliseum	San Francisco
Sears Tower	Athens

borhoods (Lynch, 1960); others have asked subjects to recognize photographs of landmarks or other locations from an environment (Lynch, 1960; Milgram & Jodelet, 1976). Each of these techniques has shortcomings, since they can be affected by the individual's drawing ability, experience with maps, or familiarity with other testing procedures (Beck & Wood, 1976; Blaut & Stea, 1974; Dart & Pradham, 1967). Nevertheless, these methods have been consistent in identifying the kinds of mistakes that we are likely to make in our cognitive maps.

As shown in Figures 2-3 and 2-4, we usually exaggerate the size of familiar locations in relation to other areas (Saarinen, 1973). This has implications for the kinds of mistakes we are likely to make in both familiar and unfamiliar territory. Downs and Stea (1973) have categorized errors in cognitive maps as errors of incompleteness, distortion, or augmentation. **Incompleteness** occurs when something in the environment is missing or represented incompletely on a cognitive map. **Distortion** occurs when the geometry, direction, and distances in the environment are represented incorrectly. **Augmentation** is adding things to the environment that aren't really there. One often cited example of augmentation occurred in a study

TRY IT!

Downs and Stea have also shown how cleverly visual images can be incorporated in the names of places in a way that conveys something of the nature of the place. Some examples of Downs and Stea's "word images" are presented in the accompanying figure.

P H O T O   2·1 Landmarks are distinguished by their uniqueness and by how they stand out from the background.

by Appleyard (1970) wherein a European engineer temporarily living in Guyana included a nonexistent railroad on his cognitive map between a steel mill and a port because his experience led him to expect one.

Russell and Ward (1982) report that people have more trouble making East–West judgments than judgments about North and South, although both can be troublesome when the person is not familiar with the area. The estimate of actual distances between places also poses a problem in cognitive mapping. A number of studies have indicated that the amount of information that has been stored about a path between two points may be a crucial factor. According to Sadalla, Staplin, and Burroughs (1979), when people travel a pathway they attend to, encode, and store information about that route. The more information they can retrieve that is relevant to that route, the longer the route is judged to be. Giving prompts or cues that facilitated retrieval of the information increased the distance estimates for individuals in their study. Consistent with this hypothesis, the more turns or intersections that there are on a path, the longer it appears to be. This is especially true if the path and intersections are labeled with familiar names (Sadalla & Magel, 1980; Sadalla & Staplin, 1980). Similarly, estimates of distances between cities increase when there are many cities in between but decrease when there are very few or if they are connected by a straight road rather than an indirect one (Thorndyke, 1981). An interesting distortion of distance occurs when shoppers prefer to use stores in the downtown direction from where they live, even when stores in the out-of-town direction are closer. This curious phenomenon has come to be known as "Brennan's Law" (Lee, 1962; Smith & Sargent, 1948). Brennan was a town planner in Wolverhampton, England, who observed that housewives he interviewed in a planning survey preferred to use shops in the "downtown" direction from their homes, even when there were shops in the other direction that were closer. In this case, direction was apparently more important than proximity in determining where to shop. Lee (1978) determined that this effect probably occurs because people overestimate the distance of outward journeys from a town center and underestimate inbound distances. Lee also thinks that perhaps journeys toward the town center are more complex and interesting (that is, there is a greater variety of things to see), making the trip in that direction seem shorter than it really is.

Errors that occur in cognitive mapping are as likely to be errors of geometry as they are to be errors of distance or location. People have a strong tendency to regularize the angles of paths in their cognitive maps

TRY IT!

How Good Are Your Cognitive Maps?

Stevens and Coupe (1978) and Tversky (1981) explain that many errors in cognitive maps are made because of our tendency to store information in a way that fits our preconceptions of how things "ought to be." Consequently, we tend to remember things as being more lined up and more directly horizontal and vertical to each other than they really are. They have also proposed that we tend to think in terms of "geographical superordinates," meaning that our memory for large places (like countries and continents) may distort our idea of where cities and other smaller places are. They developed a series of tricky geography questions to highlight how easily these mistakes are made. Answer each of the following apparently simple questions. After you have given your answers, consult a map to see if you are correct.

1. Which city is further north: Rome or Philadelphia?
2. Which city is further east: Los Angeles or Reno, Nevada?
3. Which end of the Panama Canal is further west: the Atlantic end or the Pacific end?
4. If you were to travel due south from Detroit, what is the first foreign country you would enter upon leaving the United States?
5. If you were to travel due south from Chicago, what is the first continent you would encounter after leaving North America?
6. Which city is further north: Seattle or Montreal?

so that they come closer to being 90-degree angles than they really are; consequently, settings with 90-degree angles are least disorienting and the most accurately remembered (Moar & Bower, 1983; Sadalla & Montello, 1989). To test the accuracy of your own cognitive maps, try it (see box, How Good Are Your Cognitive Maps?).

A study by Herman, Miller, and Shiraki (1987) demonstrated that the emotions associated with locations can also affect estimates of distance. In their study, first-year college students underestimated the distance to campus locations associated with positive feelings to a much greater extent than they did to locations associated with negative feelings. This was not true for upperclass students, suggesting that the emotions associated with locations may have a greater impact when the environments are unfamiliar.

The legibility of buildings (that is, how easy it is to find your way around in them), especially in large buildings such as hospitals, airports, and government office buildings, is also important in the day-to-day lives of people. The floor plan has a greater influence on the legibility of a building than any other design factor and, not surprisingly, simple and predictable floor plans are the easiest to learn and remember (O'Neill, 1986; Peponis, Zimring, & Choi, 1990; Weisman, 1981).

It had been assumed that cognitive maps of buildings develop more or less automatically following experience with the environment in question, but a study by Moeser (1988) suggests that this may not always be the case. Moeser's study focused on a very confusing, nonlegible five-story hospital building. She compared the cognitive maps of naive subjects who memorized the floor plans of the building to the cognitive maps of student nurses who had worked in the hospital for two years. Although the nurses could find their way around in the building, they failed to form effective "survey type" cognitive maps of the building — even after two years. The naive subjects performed significantly better on several objective measures of cognitive mapping than the nurses did. This study showed that mental representations of survey maps may not automatically develop in complex environments and that they may not be necessary for successfully finding one's way through the environment.

The Development of Cognitive Mapping Abilities

The ability to use cognitive maps to find one's way through the environment changes dramatically from infancy to adulthood, and the problem of understanding the development of environmental cognition across a life span is more complicated than was once thought. Most theoretical approaches to the development of environmental cognition have been influenced by the work of the late Swiss psychologist Jean Piaget (Piaget, 1954; Piaget & Inhelder, 1967; Piaget, Inhelder, & Szeminska, 1960). According to Piaget's model, children pass through a series of predictable developmental stages in their comprehension of spatial relations. These

T A B L E   2·1   Piaget's Developmental Stages and Environmental Cognition

Developmental stage	Spatial ability
Sensorimotor Period (birth to age 2)	Completely egocentric; defines space and the location of objects only in relation to own body
Period of Intuitive or Preoperational Thought (age 2 to age 7)	Still egocentric, but begins to build crude symbolic representations of immediate environment
Concrete Operations Period (age 7 to age 12)	Can conceive of objects and places as existing apart from the self; becomes more sophisticated at using landmarks to locate objects and places
Formal Operations Period (age 12 to adult)	Can use symbols and abstractions to represent space; can form larger and more unified cognitive maps

stages (summarized in Table 2-1) result from a combination of learning and maturation and are thought to represent an unfolding of the child's genetic potential.

In Piaget's first stage, the **sensorimotor period** (from birth until about 2 years of age), the child defines space and the location of objects entirely in relation to his or her own body; for the child, the spatial world is completely egocentric. It is not until the second year that the child is able to generate and hold images of absent objects and relate them to each other.

The second stage is called the **period of intuitive or preoperational thought,** and it lasts from about age 2 until about age 7 or 8. During this period, the child is still very egocentric and finds it difficult to build complex mental images of places divorced from him or herself. Preoperational children can, however, build crude symbolic representations of the environment immediately surrounding them.

The **concrete operations period** follows roughly between the ages of 7 and 12. Here, children begin to break away from their egocentrism and conceptualize places and objects as existing apart from themselves. They also become increasingly sophisticated at using landmarks as reference points for locating objects and places.

The final stage of Piaget's model, the **formal operations period,** begins with adolescence. The individual now becomes comfortable using symbols and abstractions such as compass directions, and he or she begins to form larger, more unified cognitive maps than were possible in earlier stages.

Piaget's theory is still the basic foundation upon which our understanding of cognitive development is built, although several other theorists have extended Piaget's ideas into more specific models of the development of spatial abilities. For example, Siegel and White (1975) developed a model that is more concerned with actual spatial behavior than Piaget's and is, therefore, more of a theory of wayfinding than a theory of cognitive mapping. According to Siegel and White, the child can at first use landmarks only to mark the beginning and end of a journey and to gauge progress. Learning routes between places develops gradually as the landmarks along a route become more familiar. In Siegel and White's model, spatial knowledge is ultimately derived from locomotion through the environment. It is only in the final stage, after routes and landmarks are well known, that mental representations of clusters or configurations of routes, in the sense of true cognitive maps, can develop.

A similar developmental model was developed by Hart and Moore (1973) and Moore (1979). They propose three frames of reference that the child passes through in understanding the spatial world: egocentric, fixed, and coordinated. Like Piaget, they believe that children must begin with fragmented, "egocentric" impressions of their environment before they can develop disconnected mental maps oriented around specific "fixed" places in the environment. These piecemeal maps are in turn a prerequisite to the "coordinated," survey-type cognitive maps that integrate large portions of the environment.

Although these models differ in some respects, they agree on several important ideas:

1. Children pass through a series of predictable developmental stages in understanding their spatial environment.
2. In all cases, a sensorimotor, "wayfinding" skill develops before more abstract cognitive mapping abilities do.
3. Landmarks are the first dimension of the environment to be learned, followed by paths, clusters, or networks of paths, and finally, an overall mental configuration of the environment.

These models are consistent with Heft and Wohlwill's (1987) belief that children first learn about the environment in very functional ways. In the terminology of Gibson's ecological model, Heft and Wohlwill propose that children learn the *affordances* of the environment. They quickly become aware of scary places, places that sell candy, and shortcuts to friends' houses. These affordances take on the importance of landmarks and become the focal points of the organization of cognitive maps.

For the most part, empirical research supports the notion that children pass through a sequence of stages in understanding their environment (Hazen, Lockman, & Pick, 1978; Herman & Siegel, 1978; Siegel, Kirasic, & Kail, 1978). Research on infants suggests that they do in fact progress from an egocentric understanding of space to one that is less self-centered. However, this progress does not seem to be as rigidly fixed as Piaget's theory suggests, and development can be speeded up by opportunities to explore, especially in highly differentiated environments (Acredolo, 1978, 1982; Acredolo & Evans, 1980; Bremner, 1978; Bremner & Bryant, 1977; Hart, 1979, 1981; Heft & Wohlwill, 1987; Presson & Somerville, 1985; Reiser, 1979).

Research with older children leads to similar conclusions. Young children can only read maps that are oriented correctly and have clear, unambiguous landmarks (Blades & Spencer, 1987), and they are more accurate at estimating distances from egocentric reference points like their homes than they are at estimating other distances (Biel, 1982). Not surprisingly, younger children are poorer at estimating *all* distances than older children are (Anooshian & Wilson, 1977; Kosslyn, Pick, & Fariello, 1974). While it is apparent that landmark-based wayfinding precedes a configurational, survey-type understanding of the environment, it also appears that young children are capable of better configurational representation than the theories we have discussed would predict (Acredolo, Pick, & Olson, 1975; Cousins, Siegel, & Maxwell, 1983; Herman & Siegel, 1978; Liben, Moore, & Golbeck, 1982).

Many researchers feel that part of the problem with understanding how children structure environmental information is that inappropriate methods have been used to assess the representational skills of children, especially very young ones. Children don't have the degree of drawing, reading, and test-taking skills available in adult subjects, yet their poor performance on experimental tasks has often been interpreted as a lack of cognitive spatial ability. This may not be a valid interpretation. Consequently, the true spatial ability of children has probably been underestimated (Heft & Wohlwill, 1987; Matthews, 1985).

The current opinion in the field is that the theories on developmental stages are probably correct in identifying the stages children pass through in understanding the environment but that they probably overestimate the time it takes most children to pass through these stages and underestimate the extent to which young children can work with abstract representations of the environment.

Wayfinding in the Environment

Cognitive maps are mental representations of the environment; wayfinding is the process by which people actually navigate through their environment. Passini (1984) has described wayfinding as a sequence of problem-solving tasks requiring the use of stored information about the environment. In wayfinding, an individual must decide on routes, methods of transportation, and a variety of other things necessary for successful completion of the trip. The study of wayfinding is in its infancy, and the methods currently being used to study it range from computer modeling (Leiser & Zilbershatz, 1989) to having people find their way through life-sized mazes (Passini, Proulx, & Rainville, 1990). Even so, it is already clear that humans are very flexible in the strategies they employ in learning routes. Most people prefer to use landmarks in wayfinding whenever possible. These landmarks are especially effective if they are at key locations such as intersections and other decision points along the route (Heft, 1979).

Anything that facilitates the formation of clear cognitive maps will also facilitate wayfinding (O'Neill, 1991a; Rovine & Weisman, 1989). Gärling, Böök, and Lindberg (1986) described several specific characteristics of environments that affect wayfinding. **Differentiation** is the degree to which parts of the environment look the same or are distinctive. For example, a highly differentiated university campus would be one with varied terrain and a wide variety of buildings, ranging from older and ivy-covered to ultramodern glass and metal structures. A highly differentiated environment is easier to navigate through than one in which everything looks very much the same. The **degree of visual access** refers to the extent to which different parts of the setting can be seen from other vantage points. A high degree of visual access also facilitates wayfinding. The **complexity of spatial layout** reflects the amount and difficulty of the information that must be processed to move around in the environment. Research by O'Neill (1991b) has confirmed that complex floor plans increase the difficulty of wayfinding in buildings. He also found that graphic or textual signs placed at key intersections within complex buildings improved wayfinding for most people.

Research on wayfinding promises to have real applications in making environments more hospitable to the people who use them. It should enable tours of settings or simulated tours via slide shows to be more effective, which will make new environments more familiar and less intimidating by giving people the security of a preliminary cognitive map before they must deal with a new environment. Environmental previews have already been used to help kindergarteners adapt to school (Cohen, Evans, Stokols, & Krantz, 1986), to help senior citizen volunteers adapt to an unfamiliar nursing home (Hunt, 1984), and to aid elderly adults find their way around a shopping mall (Kirasic & Mathes, 1990). Three-dimensional maps are also being developed for recreational purposes to prepare bicyclers and hikers for the terrain that they must cross on outings (Hiss, 1990).

Individual Differences in Cognitive Mapping and Wayfinding

As with any other ability, the skills of cognitive mapping and wayfinding vary tremendously from person to person. Not surprisingly, good general spatial abilities as measured by psychological tests seem to be related to a number of wayfinding and mapping activities. There is a correlation between spatial ability and measures of environmental knowledge, such as the ability to locate landmarks and remember routes between points (Pearson & Ialongo, 1986), and with the ability to produce efficient route directions for others (Vanetti & Allen, 1988). Kozlowski and Bryant

(1977) found that people who believed that they had a good sense of direction did in fact remember geographical and directional information more accurately. Kozlowski and Bryant also found that these people were more accurate in pointing out directions of large cities from where they stood and remembering the way through a system of underground tunnels after they had been led through them. Thorndyke and Stasz (1980) studied the differences between people who were good at learning environmental information by studying maps and those who were not. They found that successful learners were more likely than poor learners to split the map into subparts and to systematically study the parts. Successful learners were also more apt to think in spatial, maplike terms rather than in words, and they spent less time rehearsing material they already knew and more time encoding new material.

A variety of demographic variables have been related to wayfinding and cognitive mapping. Adults make better maps than children (Cohen, 1985; Olson & Bialystok, 1983), and people from higher educational and socioeconomic classes make more extensive and accurate maps, probably because of greater opportunities for travel (Appleyard, 1970, 1976; Goodchild, 1974; Karan, Bladen, & Singh, 1980; Orleans, 1973).

Most studies have found no sex differences in overall cognitive mapping ability (Evans, 1980; Evans, Brennan, Skorpanich, & Held, 1984), but there are indications that males and females take different approaches to understanding their environment. For example, females emphasize districts and landmarks in their cognitive maps and males emphasize routes. Males seem to begin their maps by organizing roads and paths; females begin by grouping landmarks, establishing distances, and then filling in the roads and paths. Men are also more likely to give distance estimates or compass directions when giving directions to others (McGuiness & Sparks, 1979; Pearce, 1977). Antes, McBride, and Collins (1988) had the opportunity to compare the cognitive maps of residents for Fargo, North Dakota, before and after the construction of a new overpass over a railroad switching yard that had previously bisected much of the city. They found that the presence of the overpass improved the female residents' estimates of distances between selected points in the city, but that it had no effect on the males' estimates. Antes and his colleagues concluded that females make judgments based on inferences from travel paths and that males relied more on mental representations of the city. There is consistent evidence of superior cognitive mapping ability in male children, but this is apparently due more to extensive exploration of the environment by boys rather than to actual mapping ability (Moore & Young, 1978; Munroe & Munroe, 1971; Webley & Whalley, 1987).

Cognitive Mapping and Wayfinding in the Blind

A literature review by Jones (1975) notes that echo cues, touch, and even muscular feedback from eye movements provide important cues in the location of objects in space and in distance estimation. Nevertheless, blind and visually impaired people appear to be at a clear disadvantage when it comes to understanding the environment and finding their way through it. Downs and Stea (1977) found that congenitally blind people form cognitive maps, but they concluded that the information was stored more as a sequence of actions than as visual images.

Since spatial cognition is so often associated with vision and visual imagery, understanding the degree to which blind people possess spatio-cognitive abilities would help to pin down the importance of these skills in wayfinding and cognitive mapping. Studies indicate poor cognitive mapping in blind people (Casey, 1978), and some researchers feel that this is because they do not possess adequate spatio-cognitive abilities (Hatwell, 1966). On the other hand, many studies show that blind people possess spatial representational abilities comparable to those of sighted people (Byrnes & Salter, 1983; Fletcher, 1980, 1981a, 1981b; Hollyfield & Foulke, 1983; Jones, 1975; Kerr, 1983; Leonard & Newman, 1967; Passini & Proulx, 1988). For example, Passini and Proulx (1988) compared blind and sighted subjects' ability to find their way through a large complex building after two guided tours. Although the blind group made more errors, they demonstrated a good spatial understanding of the setting, and their performance was close to that of the sighted group. Passini and Proulx found that the blind subjects tended to prepare more for the journey in advance and that they used cues such as handrails and tactile features of the building that were ignored by the sighted subjects who relied almost entirely on visual cues. Similarly, Leonard and Newman (1967) found that blind boys could follow routes in unfamiliar territory from memory of a tactile map. The boys could also solve detour problems, showing a clear grasp of the spatial relations among locations.

In a more recent study, Passini, Proulx, and Rainville (1990) compared congenitally totally blind subjects, subjects blinded after age 3, and visually impaired subjects with sighted subjects who were blindfolded and a control group of sighted subjects who were not blindfolded. The wayfinding task was to perform a series of activities in a life-sized, labyrinth-like maze constructed in a laboratory. Subjects had to learn new routes through the maze, retrace their steps through the maze, combine previously learned routes in new combinations, estimate and point out directions, and transfer information from a finger-maze model to the larger maze. Passini and his colleagues found that the performance of the blind subjects was comparable to the other groups on most tasks. They concluded that the visually impaired in general and the congenitally blind in particular are able to perform all of the spatio-cognitive operations necessary for wayfinding. In spite of visual handicaps, spatio-cognitive abilities in blind persons appear to be normal. This indicates that congenitally blind people may readily and effectively substitute the tactile sense for the visual sense.

CHAPTER SUMMARY

The ability to understand space and to manipulate it mentally is called spatio-cognitive ability. It is this ability that enables us to comprehend our spatial environment and to navigate through it successfully.

Environmental perception is the initial source of information about the environment. Perception is a process based on a combination of sensory information and expectations based on experience. Although there are many theories of object perception, only a few theories have focused on the perception of the environment as a unified whole. Brunswik's lens model and the ecological theory of perception proposed by J. J. Gibson have had the greatest impact on environmental psychology.

Environmental cognition refers primarily to the formation of mental representations of our environment (cognitive mapping) and finding our way through it (wayfinding). Although there is still disagreement, many researchers believe that we depend on the use of visual memory codes for these tasks.

Generally speaking, the more familiar we are with an environment, the more detailed and accurate our cognitive maps of that environment will be. Most studies of cognitive mapping have been concerned with the cognition of cities. This research confirms that five dimensions of cities identified by Lynch (1960) are especially important for understanding the organization of cities. These dimensions are landmarks, paths, edges, districts, and nodes. Through abstraction and errors of attention, perception, and recall, cognitive maps may be quite different from reality. The most common errors in cognitive maps are errors of imcompleteness, distortion, and augmentation.

A number of demographic variables, including age, sex, and general spatial abilities, are related to cognitive mapping and wayfinding abilities. Environmental cognition develops throughout childhood in a series of stages. The very young child begins with a fragmented, egocentric view of the spatial environment and over time is able to construct more generalized, abstract representations of the spatial environment.

GLOSSARY

Affordances   From Gibson's ecological theory of perception. The useful functions provided to an individual by objects in the environment.

Augmentation   An error of cognitive mapping in which things are included in a map when they do not actually exist in the environment being mapped.

Bottom-Up Processing   Also known as data-driven processing; a perceptual process that depends entirely on the analysis of sensory information.

Brennan's Law of Shopping Behavior   Preference to shop in stores located in a "downtown" direction from one's home, even when stores may be closer in the other direction.

Cognitive Map   An individual's mental representation of his or her environment.

Complexity of Spatial Layout   The amount and difficulty of the information that must be processed in an environment.

Concrete Operations Period   Piaget's developmental stage (ages 7 to 12) in which children begin to break away from egocentrism and conceptualize places as existing apart from themselves.

Degree of Visual Access   The extent to which different parts of a setting can be seen from other vantage points.

Differentiation   The degree to which different parts of an environment look the same or are distinctive.

Distortion   An error in cognitive mapping in which distances, direction, and geometry are represented incorrectly.

District   A section of a city that a person can be "inside of."

Edge   Linear elements in cognitive maps that divide an environment into different parts.

Formal Operations Period   Piaget's developmental stage (begins with adolescence) in which individuals can use symbols and abstractions to form unified cognitive maps.

Gibson's Ecological Theory of Perception   A theory of environmental perception that emphasizes the adaptation of organisms to their environment. Gibson's theory proposes that sensory information accurately represents the real environment.

Incompleteness   An error in cognitive mapping in which objects in the environment are omitted from a cognitive map or incompletely represented.

Landmark   A physical object in the environment whose chief characteristic is its uniqueness and prominence.

Legibility   The ease with which an environment can be recognized, organized into a pattern, and recalled.

Lens Model   Egon Brunswik's model of environmental perception that proposes that human perceptual processes act like a lens in uniting a disparate array of environmental stimuli into a unitary, cohesive perception.

Node   Strategic point in a city that serves as a transfer point for travelling from one place to another.

Path   Route by which people move through an environment.

Period of Intuitive or Preoperational Thought   Piaget's developmental stage (ages 2 to 7) in which the child begins to form crude symbolic representations of the environment, although he or she is still highly egocentric.

Sensorimotor Period   Piaget's developmental stage (birth to age 2) in which the child's understanding of space is completely egocentric.

Spatio-Cognitive Ability   The ability to understand space and to manipulate it mentally.

Top-Down Processing   Also known as conceptually-driven processing, it is a perceptual process driven by our cognitive expectations about what "ought" to be perceived in a setting.

Wayfinding   The process by which people navigate through their environment. Also known as route knowledge.

Semantic differential

3 Factor Theory of Emotion
Pleasure, Arousal, Dominance

Environmental load intensity
novelty
complexity
Climate & elevation
Temperature
Light
Color
Noise
ERF & Sensation seeking
Arousal levels, Adaptation levels

The A
Envir

The **ambient environment** refers to nonvisual aspects such as sound, temperature, odor, and illumination. These factors are stable daily features of the environment that we may not consciously perceive. Although it often goes unnoticed, the ambient environment has a profound impact on everything we do. Our moods, work performance, and even our physical well-being are affected by the sensory input we constantly receive from the ambient environment. In this chapter, I will examine the responses of human beings to the ambient environment, beginning with a discussion of the relationship between the ambient environment and our feelings.

EMOTIONAL IMPACT OF THE AMBIENT ENVIRONMENT

Take a moment to relax. Read the descriptions of the following two situations. Try to capture the mood of each one, and if you can, imagine that you are actually there. Be aware of how you might feel during each of these experiences described by Mehrabian and Russell (1974a):

> Situation A: You are water skiing behind a speedboat on a mountain lake. As you go by, you watch the sun glinting on the water and look at the thickly wooded shore of the lake as it quickly passes. There are only a few other boats out, and they are down near the other shore of the lake. The water is smooth and glassy, and the air is fairly warm with a slight breeze.
> Situation B: You are at the funeral of a distant relative. It takes place at the funeral home, and everyone is dressed in dark colors. The minister's voice drones on in the service. The casket up front is the only decoration in the otherwise plain room. [pp. 207; 213–214]

As you imagined each of these situations, you probably found that they evoked strikingly different emotional reactions, just as they did in a large number of other people who were exposed to these and other hypothetical situations in research done by Mehrabian and Russell (1974a). To a great extent, the emotions people experience in situations like these are a product of the ambient environment. In fact, Russell and Snodgrass (1987) have argued that the emotional, affective quality of an environment is the most important part of the person's relationship to that environment because the affective quality of the environment is the primary factor in determining the moods and memories associated with a place, which may even affect the individual's health and well-being.

Emotions consist of behaviors, physiological changes, and subjective experiences. For over 100 years a debate has raged within psychology over which of these components truly reflects "real" emotion. Although emotion is a complex construct, which is difficult to define precisely, most current theories of emotion include heightened levels of physiological arousal (also called **activation level**) as an important part of the experience of emotion. Berlyne (1960a) describes arousal or activation as a continuum. That is, a person is not either aroused or unaroused but experiences some level of arousal that ranges from drowsiness or sleep at one extreme to a state of frenzied excitement at the other extreme. The activation level reflects the extent to which a person is hyped-up by adrenalin in the blood, an increased heart rate, and cognitive activity. However, most environmental psychologists think of arousal as a unidimensional factor that varies only quantitatively along an arousal continuum. In other words, they believe that there is only one kind of generalized autonomic arousal, and that differences among different activation states are simply differences involving how much arousal, not differences in the kind of arousal a person experiences. This position is consistent with much of the environmental research and is the perspective I will take in this book. It should be noted, however, that some researchers (Eysenck, 1982; Lacey, 1967) disagree with this view and feel that qualitatively different activation states must be distinguished to accurately describe the effects of arousal. Specifically, they believe that arousal initiated actively by the person, as when paying attention to a demanding task, is different in nature from that produced more passively through exposure to stimulant drugs, intense noise, or other external agents.

Emotional arousal can be measured in many ways, from questionnaires to physiological measures such as brain wave activity and changes in the electrical conductance of the skin caused by sweat (galvanic skin response, or GSR). All these measures have been used with some success, but disagreement continues over the exact role of arousal in the experience of emotion.

Russell and Snodgrass (1987) tried to sort out the confusion by working informally with some definitions of common terms that are useful for this chapter. According to Russell and Snodgrass, a **mood** represents the core feelings of a person's subjective emotional state at any particular moment. Moods fluctuate with events in the evironment and also with the arousal changes that accompany diurnal cycles and other biological rhythms, such as the menstrual cycle (Backstrom et al., 1983; Boyle, 1985; Lacoste & Wirz-Justice, 1989; Sanders, Warner, Backstrom, & Bancroft, 1983; Thayer, 1987, 1989; Thayer, Takahashi, & Pauli, 1988). Moods are ultimately traceable to neurochemical activity at the synaptic level: norepinephrine, dopamine, and serotonin are three of the primary neurotransmitters believed to play an important role in determining mood. The evidence for this is preliminary, however, and much of the discussion about the neurochemical basis of mood is still speculative (Thayer, 1989).

Russell and Snodgrass (1987) refer to very extreme moods brought on by specific places, objects, and events as **emotional episodes.** A person's stable, long-term tendency to respond consistently to emotionally arousing situations is known as **emotional disposition.** Finally, an **affective appraisal** consists of attributing an affective quality (for example, disgusting, pleasant, boring) to a thing or place. In other words, an affective appraisal refers to the capacity of an object or environment to alter moods. In all cases, however, a mood refers to something within a person; an affective appraisal resides in a thing or place in the physical world.

Reactions to environments can be described according to our tendencies to approach or avoid those environments (Mehrabian, 1976b). When we are already in an environment, these same terms may be used to describe whether we explore or withdraw from the environment and whether we affiliate with or withdraw from the other people we encounter there. Our affective appraisals of places guide much of this approach/avoidance behavior. These appraisals are sometimes based on nothing more than memory, the authority of others, or estimates based on bits and pieces of information. Ultimately, our affective appraisals will affect our moods, which can influence much of what we do. For example, researchers know that environments can influence our moods even after we have left them, and mood has been shown to affect memory and performance on cognitive and creative tasks (Bower, 1981; Laird, Wagener, Halal, & Szegda, 1982; Snyder & White, 1982; Teasdale & Taylor, 1981). Gifford (1980) has shown that the direction of the influence between affective appraisals and moods can go both ways. He reports that people in a pleasant prior mood rated settings as more pleasant than people who were in a less pleasant prior mood, demonstrating that anything that affects mood can also affect reactions to environments.

The Three-Factor Theory of Emotion

Moods are subjective experiences and, therefore, must be measured through self-report. A number of questionnaires have been developed to measure moods. Some of the measures that have been widely used in research include the Mood Adjective Checklist (MACL) developed by Nowlis (1965), the Profile of Mood States (POMS) (McNair, Lorr, & Droppleman, 1971), Curran and Cattell's (1976) Eight State Questionnaire (8SQ), and the Multiple Affect Adjective Checklist (MAACL) (Zuckerman & Lubin, 1985). Many measures of mood employ some form of the **semantic differential** developed by Osgood, Suci, and Tannenbaum (1957). The semantic differential consists of pairs of **bipolar adjectives,** or adjectives that are opposites of each other. For example, good–bad or pleasant–unpleasant are typical pairs of bipolar adjectives. The adjectives in each pair anchor the ends of a scale (usually between five and nine points in length). The individual is presented with an abstract concept such as water, churches, hunters, or a specific thing or place (for example, your present mood, this classroom), and he or she then rates the concept, thing, or place on a series of bipolar scales. The subject places a mark along the scale. The distance of the mark from each adjective reflects the person's feelings about the object in question. The different points along the scale are then converted to numbers that can be subjected to quantitative analysis. Figure 3-1 presents an example of a seven-point semantic differential scale that might be used to evaluate your classroom.

Moods have often been measured using a semantic differential. One such influential approach is the **three-factor theory of emotion** proposed by environmental psychologists Albert Mehrabian and James A. Russell (Mehrabian & Russell, 1974a; Russell & Mehrabian, 1974, 1977; Mehrabian, 1976b, 1980). People react emotionally to environments in many different ways. According to Mehrabian and Russell's theory, three dimensions seem to be particularly useful in predicting behavior in environments: pleasure/displeasure, arousal/nonarousal, and dominance/submissiveness. Mehrabian and Russell (1974a) have developed a semantic differential measure of emotional state that contains 18 pairs of bipolar adjectives to assess feelings along these three dimensions.

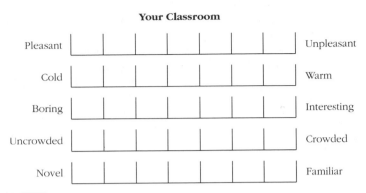

Your Classroom

Pleasant | | | | | | | | Unpleasant

Cold | | | | | | | | Warm

Boring | | | | | | | | Interesting

Uncrowded | | | | | | | | Crowded

Novel | | | | | | | | Familiar

F I G U R E   3·1   A semantic differential scale for evaluating a classroom

The arousal/nonarousal dimension can be thought of as a combination of activity (excited versus calm) and alertness (wide awake versus sleepy). Arousal scores on this dimension will be high when both activity and alertness are high, moderate when one is high and the other is low, and low when both feelings of activity and feelings of alertness are low. The dominance/submissiveness dimension reflects the extent to which a person feels in control, free, and unrestricted in a situation as opposed to feeling confined, intimidated, or controlled by others. The pleasure/displeasure dimension is quite straightforward: it reflects the degree to which a person feels happy, satisfied, and contented as opposed to feeling unhappy, dissatisfied, and discontented.

Each of these dimensions is independent of the others. Thus, feelings along one dimension may change completely while the others remain the same. Different combinations of arousal, pleasure, and dominance result in different emotional experiences. For example, feelings of low pleasure, low arousal, and high dominance might result in boredom; feelings of low pleasure, high arousal, and low dominance might reflect anxiety. These dimensions can be used to describe affective appraisals of places as well as emotional states. Figure 3-2 shows how subjects ordered descriptions of places along the dimensions of pleasure (horizontal axis) and arousal (vertical axis) in a study conducted by Russell and Lanius (1984).

The three-factor theory has been useful not only in predicting the reactions of people to large-scale environments but also in predicting preferences for more specific objects and people (Amato & McInnes, 1983; Hines & Mehrabian, in Mehrabian, 1980). For example, several studies of children's preferences for video games show that stronger feelings of arousal, pleasure, and dominance lead to an increased preference for the games. Unfortunately, most games have been shown to increase feelings of arousal and *displeasure,* which leads to feelings of

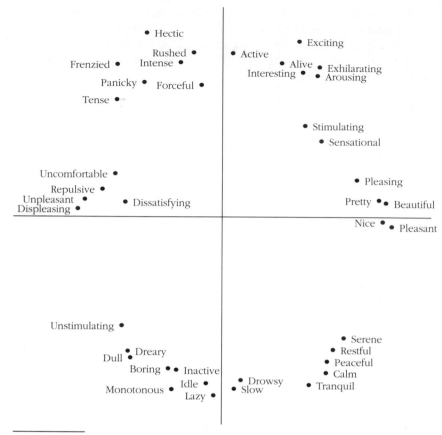

FIGURE 3-2 Ordering affective appraisals along the arousal and pleasure dimensions (Source: Russell & Lanius, 1984)

aggression, anger, and hostility during play, and often to increased aggressive behavior after play (Greenfield, 1984; Mehrabian & Wixen, 1986; Silvern, Williamson, & Countermine, 1983).

The Concept of Environmental Load

Any environment will cause some sensory stimulation, whether it is visual, auditory, or tactile. This sensory information may be intense and varied or mild and repetitive. Sensory stimulation from the ambient environment leads to generalized arousal of the autonomic nervous system; as a result, where persons fall along the arousal dimension (described in the previous section) will depend to some extent on the amount of sensory information they are receiving. Mehrabian (1976b) has proposed that environments can be described in terms of the rate of information they deliver to an individual—a concept he refers to as **environmental load.** Thus, a "highly loaded" environment is one that delivers a great deal of sensory information, and a "low load" environment is one with a less stimulating information rate. All other things being equal, high-load environments are more arousing than low-load environments, and they induce higher activation levels in individuals in that environment.

According to Mehrabian, three aspects of the information in an environment contribute to environmental load: intensity, novelty, and complexity. Intensity refers to the absolute magnitude of the sensory stimulation. Music played at 85 decibels is much more intense than music being played at 60 decibels, and results in a more highly loaded, arousing environment. Novelty is a function of how familiar the individual is with the information he or she is receiving. Anything that is strange or different requires more attention and "cognitive work" than something that is very familiar. This cognitive arousal results in higher arousal levels. Your arousal levels would be higher if you were confronted by a calculus problem than if you were asked to do simple third-grade arithmetic. By the same token, your arousal levels are higher when you examine a painting or photograph that you have never seen than when you are looking at a picture you have seen a hundred times before. Complexity operates in much the same way. The more different kinds of information an environment contains, the more cognitive effort it demands of us when we try to comprehend it. An empty classroom with paintings hanging on the wall is a more complex environment than an identical room with bare walls. If the classroom contains paintings and is crowded with chairs and tables, it becomes even more complex; adding audiovisual equipment to the room further increases the complexity. The more complex an environment is, the more arousing it is. Perceptually interesting, complex environments encourage exploration and stimulate attention and are highly preferred by pedestrians in both rural and city environments (Rapoport, 1990).

There may be sound evolutionary reasons why intensity, novelty, and complexity increase environmental load and demand our attention to such stimuli. From an evolutionary point of view, our present system of adaptation to the environment is a result of natual selection over time. Our psychological reactions to external stimuli are adaptations to recurring stimuli encountered throughout our evolutionary history (Tooby & Cosmides, 1990). Intense or novel stimuli in an organism's environment are potential threats or resources that must be comprehended quickly if a creature is to have any chance for long-term survival. To a great extent, this is still true for human beings. From the standpoint of survival, there is little difference between a charging predator and a speeding truck. Along these same lines, a complex stimulus is one that might offer great rewards to an organism with the curiosity and patience to exploit it. It is plausible, then, that individuals with strong activation responses to intense, novel, and complex stimuli survived longer and reproduced more successfully than did those who lacked this response pattern.

SPECIFIC FEATURES OF THE AMBIENT ENVIRONMENT

Much of what passes for common knowledge about the effects of the environment on humans has little basis in fact. For example, there is no evidence to support the widely held belief that a full moon causes bizarre or unusual behavior (Campbell & Beets, 1978; Rotton & Kelly, 1985). This section will review the empirical evidence regarding the effects of the ambient environment on human beings.

Climate and Elevation

The climate, elevation, and terrain of the places in which you live and work dictate everything from the clothing you wear to the kinds of driving problems you encounter. The skills you develop and the experiences that shape your life are determined to a great extent by your environment. After all, not many hockey players come from Florida; few rodeo riders hail from New York City; and surfing is uncommon in Nebraska. Given the obvious importance of climate, terrain, and elevation in daily life, it is surprising that so little is actually known about their effects.

In a review of the research on how people adapt to high elevations, Frisancho (1979) explains the many ways in which altitude affects human beings. Living at extremely high elevations, where barometric pressure is lower and oxygen is thinner, produces many short-term effects. For example, enlargement of the heart may occur; red blood cells increase in number; hemoglobin concentration increases, while plasma volume decreases; also, light sensitivity in the retina decreases. At high altitudes people often experience an increased desire for sugar. There is an increase in adrenal activity and a decrease of thyroid activity. Testosterone and sperm production decrease in men, and women may experience more uncomfortable menstrual periods than usual. However, after about six months at high altitudes, most people become acclimated and the severity of these symptoms is greatly reduced. There are some long-term effects as well. Natives of high elevations have larger lung capacity and chest size and different patterns of blood pressure than natives of lower elevations. They also are more likely to exhibit lower birth weight and slower growth and sexual maturation. Additionally, some areas of the heart may be enlarged (Frisancho, 1979).

Climate is just as important as elevation. Indeed, some have argued that climate is *the* most important factor in shaping a culture's values and "personality" (Tetsuro, 1961). For quite some time, scholars have proposed that a cool or moderate climate was required for the development of technology and civilization as we know it, since these climates present problems that must be mastered for human survival (Huntington, 1915, 1945; Markham, 1947). Although there is little in the way of hard data to support such an extreme position, climate has been shown to have predictable effects on human behavior. Sommers and Moos (1976) report that residents of regions that are regularly subjected to warm, dry winds attribute depression, nervousness, pain, irritation, and even traffic accidents to these winds. Research in Switzerland and Israel implies that this link may in fact be real (Moos, 1964; Rim, 1975). Similarly, changes in barometric pressure have been associated with changes in the suicide rate (Digon & Block, 1966; Sanborn, Casey, & Niswander, 1970) and disruptive school behavior (Auliciens, 1972; Russell & Bernal, 1977).

There is evidence that even atmospheric electricity influences the behavior and feelings of human beings. The number of **ions** found in the air at a particular location determine atmospheric electricity. Ions are positively or negatively charged particles that are formed when air molecules are split by lightning, wind, and other atmospheric events. For a long time, psychologists believed that electricity in the air might be related to changes in human social behavior; archival data confirm that suicides, accidents, and crime become more frequent as the atmosphere becomes more highly charged (Muecher & Ungeheuer, 1961; Sulman et al., 1974; Baron & Byrne, 1987).

Recently, research spearheaded by psychologist Robert A. Baron has used equipment that can generate atmospheric electricity artificially to study the behavioral effects of ionization in the laboratory. These studies found that high levels of positive ions influenced mood and arousal level (Charry & Hawkinshire, 1981) and that negative ions influenced a wide range of behaviors, possibly because they increase arousal that then enhances the behaviors or feelings that are dominant at that moment (Baron, 1987b). In effect, increasing the concentration of negative ions intensifies whatever is happening, regardless of whether it is pleasant or unpleasant. Thus, Baron and his colleagues have found that negative ionization intensifies mood states (Baron, Russell, & Arms, 1985), affects memory (Baron, 1987a), and increases the aggressive behavior of individuals who are predisposed to behave aggressively (Baron, Russell, & Arms, 1985). In one of his most recent studies, Baron (1987b) had female undergraduates interact with another person whom they were predisposed either to like or dislike. He found that these feelings became even more pronounced in the presence of high levels of negatively charged ions.

Temperature

Extreme heat or cold changes arousal levels and produces discomfort; cold temperatures reduce manual dexterity and tactile sensitivity and increase reaction time. Not surprisingly, both hot and cold temperatures can disrupt performance on a variety of tasks such as typing or driving an automobile (Bell, 1981, 1982; Bell & Greene, 1982; Buck & McAlpine, 1981; Fox, 1967; Provins, 1958; Wyon, 1974). The relationship beween temperature and task performance is extremely complex, and the details are still a bit murky. This complexity is due in part to the influence that other factors such as humidity, air movement, adaptation level, and the type of task have on the relationship.

Extremes of temperature also have been shown to affect health (Bell & Greene, 1982; Folk, 1974) and social behaviors such as aggression and attraction to other people (Baron, 1978; Bell & Baron, 1977; Cunningham, 1979). Most of this research has been concerned with **ambient temperature,** which refers to the air temperature in the immediately surrounding environment. **Effective temperature** refers to an individual's perception of the ambient temperature and is strongly influenced by the humidity of the air. In general, high humidity makes temperatures seem hotter than they actually are. Humidity is negatively correlated with vigor and other positive moods (Howarth & Hoffman, 1984; Sanders & Brizzolara, 1982). Because heat from air conditioners, motor vehicle engines, and industrial sources makes cities up to 10 to 20 degrees (F) hotter than the surrounding countryside (Fisher, Bell, & Baum, 1984), and because the health and social problems thought to be associated with high temperatures appear most frequently in cities, most of the field research has focused on the effects of high temperatures on city dwellers. Heat waves in North American cities correspond with increased death rates (Buechley, Van Bruggen, & Truppi, 1972; Oechali & Buechley, 1970; Schuman, 1972), and the effects of prolonged heat stress can range from exhaustion, headaches, irritability, and lethargy to delirium, heart attacks, and coma. Rotton, Shats, and Standers (1990) found that pedestrians even walk faster in hot or cold temperatures than they do in moderate temperatures!

Social behaviors of many kinds are affected by temperature. Anderson (1987) used archival sources from cities across the United States to gather data on the rates of murder, rape, assault, robbery, burglary, and motor vehicle theft. He confirmed that violent crime increases with temperature but that nonviolent crime does not. Subjects exposed to very warm conditions in the laboratory are less likely to help others even after the experiment is over (Page, 1978), and field studies also indicate that extreme temperatures in winter and summer make people less willing to help others (Cunningham, 1979). High temperatures lead to a reduced attraction toward other people we encounter, especially when the heat is accompanied by crowding (Griffit, 1970; Griffit & Veitch, 1971).

Perhaps the most complicated relationship is that between heat and aggression. During the 1960s, the civil disturbances and riots that occurred during the summer in many United States cities gave rise to the expression "long, hot summer." This expression reflected the common belief that hot weather made people behave aggressively and that the amount of violence that occurred was highly dependent upon the temperature. Testing this belief was the impetus behind an extensive program of laboratory research designed to pin down the relationship between temperature and aggression. Most of these studies placed subjects in an artificial situation where they could behave aggressively toward someone else. Often, they employed a **sham-shock procedure** in which the subjects believed they were administering an electric shock to another person (Buss, 1961). The number and intensity of intended shocks was the dependent variable, while temperature, degree of anger, and other factors were manipulated as independent variables. In a review of this laboratory research, Baron and Byrne (1987) conclude that it strongly supports an "inverted U-shaped" relationship in which aggression increases with temperature to a certain point, then decreases when the temperature goes even higher (Baron & Bell, 1975, 1976; Bell & Baron, 1976, 1981; Palamarek & Rule, 1979).

The conclusion of the laboratory research, however, is at odds with the results of recent field studies that overwhelmingly support a linear relationship in which increasing temperature is *always* accompanied by increases in the incidence of violent behaviors such as murders, rapes, and assaults (Anderson, 1987, 1989; Anderson & Anderson, 1984; De Fronzo, 1984; Cotton, 1986; Kenrick & MacFarlane, 1986; Harries & Stadler, 1988). In these studies, hotter regions of the world and hotter years, seasons, months, and days all are linked with more aggressive behaviors (Anderson, 1989). One study even suggested that baseball pitchers pitch more aggressively in hot weather. There is a significant, positive relationship between temperature and the number of batters hit by pitches in major league baseball games (Reifman, Larrick, & Fein, 1991). In spite of these field results, Bell and Fusco (1989) believe that the curvilinear model is correct and that many important factors such as the time of day were not controlled in these field studies, which obscured the nature of the temperature–agression relationship. At this point, the only conclusion that can be drawn is that there definitely is a relationship between heat and aggression. It is too early to describe exactly what the nature of that relationship is.

This discussion has focused on the effects of hot temperatures because little research has been done on the effects of extremely cold temperatures, and almost all of that has focused on task performance. Although a few studies suggest that cold temperatures increase aggression (Bell & Baron, 1977) and decrease helping behavior (Bennett, Rafferty, Canivez, & Smith, 1983; Cunningham, 1979), there is too little research available to draw even preliminary conclusions about the effects of cold temperatures on social behavior.

Light

Throughout history, people have believed that sunlight can help decrease feelings of lethargy and depression. In fact, recent research has confirmed that sunlight as well as bright artificial lighting does have antidepressant effects on people suffering from depressive disorders (Kripke, Gillin, Mullaney, Risch, & Janowsky, 1987; Kripke, Risch, & Janowsky, 1983; Rosenthal & Blehar, 1989; Wehr, 1989). Regular exposure to light seems to be especially important for people suffering from **seasonal affective disorder (SAD),** which is a form of depression common in the fall and winter when the hours of daylight decrease. Rosenthal and his colleagues (1984) refer to people who suffer from SAD as "light hungry." Light-hungry people tend to gain weight, sleep a lot, withdraw socially, and generally exhibit low energy levels during the winter, although they may occasionally experience bouts of depression in the summer as well (Rosenthal et al., 1984; Wehr et al., 1989). Not surprisingly, people who are light hungry express a stronger preference for brightly lit rooms than do people who do not suffer from SAD (Heerwagen, 1990). **Phototherapy** (treatments with bright lights during the winter months) has been shown to be an effective remedy for SAD (Heerwagen, 1990; Hellekson, Kline, & Rosenthal, 1986; James, Wehr, Sack, Parry, & Rosenthal, 1985; Rosenthal et al., 1985; Rosenthal, Sack, Skwerer, Jacobsen, & Wehr, 1989; Kasper, et al., 1989). The brightness of the light and the duration of exposure are the most important factors. The neurotransmitter serotonin has also proven effective in treating SAD (Jacobsen, Murphy, & Rosenthal, 1989).

The level of illumination preferred also depends to a great extent on the situation. Presumably you would want more light for operating a table saw than you would for a romantic encounter. Research has confirmed that this is indeed the case (Biner, Butler, Fischer, & Westergren, 1989; Butler & Biner, 1987). Generally there is a strong preference for natural over artificial lighting; evidence shows that full-spectrum daylight lamps that radiate light more like natural sunlight may facilitate the school performance of elementary school children and that cool-white fluorescent lamps may increase the activity levels of children (Colman, Frankel, Ritvo, & Freeman, 1976; Mayron, Ott, Nations, & Mayron, 1974; Munson & Ferguson, reported in Gifford, 1987; Painter, 1976–1977). Some researchers are skeptical of these effects, however, and believe that any differences in task performance under full-spectrum as opposed to fluorescent lighting are too small to have practical implications (Boray, Gifford, & Rosenblood, 1989). In a recent attempt to resolve this controversy, Veitch, Gifford, and Hine (1991) manipulated subjects' beliefs about full-spectrum lighting: They told one group that it improved performance and decreased fatigue; told another group that there was no evidence to support claims that lighting affects humans in any way; and provided a third group with only neutral information about full-spectrum lighting. Their results indicated that subjects' self-reports of arousal changes and improved performance on reading tasks during the course of the experiment were probably due to demand characteristics (see Chapter 1) rather than to any real effects of full-spectrum lighting.

Brighter lighting increases arousal levels in human beings (Mehrabian, 1976b). Given our evolutionary history as a species that is active during daylight, it is logical that activation levels would increase in response to stimuli that increase our chances of survival. In keeping with this, researchers find that other diurnal animals, such as monkeys, respond to light with increased arousal and that nocturnal animals, such as cats and rats, show decreased activity levels in response to light (Alexander & Isaac, 1965; Isaac & DeVito, 1958; Isaac & Kendall, 1967; Isaac & Reed, 1961).

Even though brightly lit rooms are more arousing than dimly lit rooms, darkness tends to release social inhibitions. People are more likely to engage in intimate, aggressive, or impulsive behavior under cover of darkness (Gergen, Gergen, & Baron, 1973; Zimbardo, 1969). An interesting example of the disinhibition that can occur in the dark is provided in the box that follows.

Deviance in the Dark

Gergen, Gergen, and Barton (1973) conducted an interesting demonstration of how darkness leads to disinhibition of social behaviors. Subjects (mostly college students) volunteered for the experiment entitled Environmental Psychology. Each person was escorted alone to a completely darkened chamber. They removed their shoes, emptied their pockets, and were left in the pitch-black room with the other subjects in that session. In each group there were four males and four females. They were told that they would be left in the chamber for no more than an hour, that they would be escorted from the chamber alone, and that they would never meet the other participants. Control groups had the same experience in the same chamber with one important difference: in the control groups, the lights were left on. The question was, would the subjects in the totally dark room with people they would never meet feel freer to "let down their guard" and be less encumbered by the rules that regulate interactions between strangers?

The difference between the behaviors of the people in the lighted and darkened rooms was marked. People in the lighted room kept a continuous stream of conversation going for the whole session, and they tended to sit in one spot throughout the experiment. On the other hand, people in the dark room talked much less and moved around much more. There was also more touching in the darkened room. All dark room subjects touched one another accidentally, and over 90 percent of them purposely touched someone else. In the lighted room, accidental touches were rare and intentional touching was almost nonexistent. About 50 percent of the subjects in the dark room hugged someone else, and almost 80 percent reported feeling some sexual excitement. Many of the dark-room subjects even engaged in kissing. Interestingly, these intimate behaviors decreased dramatically in dark-room groups where the participants thought that they would meet each other after the session.

Clearly, the deindividuation and anonymity encouraged by the darkness left the participants feeling freer to deviate from the usual societal restraints about interacting with strangers. Perhaps the "dark side" of human nature is not so dark after all!

The level of illumination in a work environment can affect task performance directly, by improving or hindering the worker's ability to see well enough to work efficiently, or indirectly, by creating uncomfortable or distracting conditions (Boyce, 1975). Brighter light increases visual acuity and comfort and makes task performance easier, unless the person is looking directly toward the light and experiences glare (Bennett, 1977; Boyce, 1975; McCormick & Sanders, 1982). The worker's age is an important consideration in establishing the amount of light needed for a task. Because the flexibility of the lens of the eye decreases with age, older people require more light than younger people do for office work (Hughes & McNelis, 1978), for driving an automobile at night (Sivak, Olson, & Pastalan, 1981), and for distinguishing objects from a background (Blackwell & Blackwell, 1971).

Color

There has been a great deal of popular and professional speculation about how vivid colors affect the feelings and performance of individuals (Birren, 1965). Unfortunately, little of this speculation is supported by empirical research. Psychologists do, however, know some things about how people react to color.

Color has three dimensions: brightness, hue, and saturation. **Brightness** refers to the intensity of the light coming from the colored stimulus. **Hue** refers to the color, which is a function of the wavelength of the light reflected from the stimulus. **Saturation** refers to the amount of white light in the color; the less white there is, the more highly saturated the color. In a review of the literature, Mehrabian and Russell (1974a) note that there is generally a positive relationship between brightness and pleasure and between saturation and pleasure. Most studies indicate that people prefer light to dark colors, saturated colors to unsaturated colors, and colors from the "cool" end of the spectrum (green, blue) to "warm" colors such as orange or red (Bennett, 1977; Child & Iwao, 1969; Mehrabian & Russell, 1974a). Our reactions to color can be affected by the context in which the color appears. For example, Malandro, Barker, and Barker (1989) reported women's reactions to colored granules in laundry detergent:

> One detergent manufacturer sprinkled red granules through his white soap powder, and housewives subsequently complained that the detergent was too rough on their hands. He changed the color to yellow, and women said it was easier on the hands but that the clothes were not as clean. Finally, he changed the granules to a blue color, and the women said it was just right. Nothing had changed but the color of the granules (p. 157).

Although variations in room color may affect physiological reactions such as blood pressure and respiration rate (Acking & Küller, 1972), there seems to be little support for the common belief that changing the color of a room changes the perceived room temperature (Green & Bell, 1980).

When asked to ascribe moods to various colors, people readily do so. In a study by Wexner (1954), subjects agreed substantially that certain colors were associated with the following moods:

Blue — secure, comfortable, tender, soothing, serene, calm
Red — exciting, protective, defiant
Orange — distressed, upset
Black — despondent, powerful
Purple — dignified
Yellow — cheerful

These affective associations may have implications for the way people perceive their environment. Lighter colored rooms are seen as bigger and more spacious than darker rooms, but dark colored rooms are perceived as richer and more expensive (Acking & Küller, 1972; Baum & Davis, 1976). Srivastava and Peel (1968) recorded visitors' movements in an art gallery by concealing a system of switches under the carpet. They compared visitor movement when the walls and carpet were light beige and during periods when they were a chocolate brown. They found that people moved around more when the gallery was brown but spent less time in the room than they did when it was beige.

Perhaps the most consistent results are obtained when behavior that might be affected by changes in arousal levels is measured. Colors differ in their ability to arouse, and red in particular appears to be a highly arousing color. Red consistently induces higher levels of arousal in experimental subjects than cooler colors such as green and blue (Gerard, 1958; Mehrabian & Russell, 1974a; Wilson, 1966). Nakshian (1964) showed that subjects engaged in a tracing task had more hand tremor and speedier movement when seated in front of red wall panels than when seated in front of gray panels. Gray also evoked faster tracing than green. Consistent with these findings, Seaton (1968) found that people walk faster in hallways painted in warm colors (red or orange) than in hallways painted in cooler colors, and in a study by Profusek and Rainey (1987) pink rooms reduced anxiety more than red rooms.

One hypothesis growing out of this work is that physical strength can be affected by the color than an individual sees while undergoing testing. Schauss (1979) believes that the color pink causes relaxation and can be used to reduce aggression. Pellegrini and his associates (Pellegrini & Schauss, 1980; Pellegrini, Schauss, & Birk, 1980) found that subjects could exert more strength with their hands and legs while staring at blue than while staring at pink cardboard plates. There were, however, several problems with these studies. The colors used as stimuli (pink and blue) have very strong gender associations and also reflect differences in preference and perceptions of pleasantness (Child, Hansen, & Hornbeck, 1968). O'Connell, Harper, and McAndrew (1985) controlled for these factors and examined the grip strength of 40 male undergraduates as they were exposed to red and green visual stimulation. Their results showed that these students did in fact have stronger grips when exposed to red than they did when exposed to green.

One final, interesting study is that of Goldstein, conducted in 1942. In this experiment subjects estimated the length of time intervals and judged the heaviness of weights while sitting under colored lights. Under red light, the subjects consistently overestimated both the passage of time and the heaviness of the weights. Green or blue lights had the opposite effect, leading subjects to underestimate time and weight. This study indicates that color can affect both mental tasks and physical tasks, such as grip strength.

Noise

Sound is a change in air pressure created by wave-like motions of air molecules that are caused by vibrating objects. Sound waves are described by their frequency and amplitude; these characteristics determine the pitch and intensity of the sound we hear. Intensity is the physical characteristic of sound that corresponds most closely with the psychological experience of loudness, which is measured along a logarithmic scale in **decibels (dB).** An increase of three decibels doubles the intensity of the sound we hear. The bottom of the decibel scale (zero decibels) represents the weakest sound that a person with unimpaired hearing can detect in an extremely quiet environment. At the other end of the scale, 125 to 140 decibels represents the point at which the sound is so intense that it causes pain. A sample of the decibel levels associated with some common sounds is presented in Figure 3-3.

While sound is a physical entity, **noise** is a psychological concept that is defined as unwanted sound; you might say that "noise is in the ear of the beholder." Loud, high frequency, unpredictable, and intermittent sounds are most likely to be perceived as noise, especially if they are interfering with some ongoing activity. It may not be the type of noise per se, but the degree to which it is perceived as abnormal and avoidable that determines how annoying it is to different individuals (Levy-Leboyer & Naturel, 1991). As with other ambient stimuli, there is strong evidence that loud, unpredictable noise is arousing and that individuals differ in their sensitivity to noise (Cohen & Weinstein, 1982; Glass & Singer, 1972; Topf, 1989; Weinstein, 1978).

Prolonged exposure to noise in the home or workplace has been associated with hearing loss (Alexander, 1968; Lebo & Oliphant, 1968) and a variety of health problems, especially high blood pressure and strokes (Cameron, Robertson, & Zaks, 1972; Cohen, Evans, Krantz, Stokols, & Kelly, 1981; Cohen & Weinstein, 1980; Colligan & Murphy, 1982; Dellinger, 1979; Peterson, Augenstein, Tanis, & Augenstein, 1981).

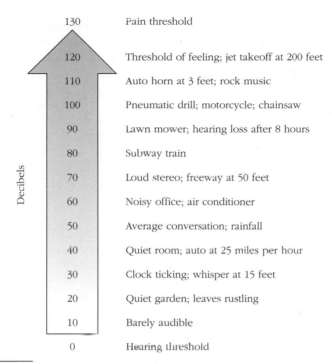

Decibels		
130	Pain threshold
120	Threshold of feeling; jet takeoff at 200 feet
110	Auto horn at 3 feet; rock music
100	Pneumatic drill; motorcycle; chainsaw
90	Lawn mower; hearing loss after 8 hours
80	Subway train
70	Loud stereo; freeway at 50 feet
60	Noisy office; air conditioner
50	Average conversation; rainfall
40	Quiet room; auto at 25 miles per hour
30	Clock ticking; whisper at 15 feet
20	Quiet garden; leaves rustling
10	Barely audible
0	Hearing threshold

F I G U R E   3·3   Decibel levels associated with common sounds

Some researchers have even proposed that high levels of noise are associated with higher admission rates to mental hospitals (Napp, 1977).

The relationship between noise and human learning and task performance is complex, and researchers disagree as to why noise has the impact that it does (Broadbent, 1978; Poulton, 1977, 1978, 1979). Most explanations focus on the arousing and distracting qualities of noise, but other researchers believe that an individual's feelings of control in a situation are just as important (Glass & Singer, 1972; Sherrod, Hage, Halpern, & Moore, 1977). All these explanations agree that intermittent, unpredictable noise is the most aversive and disruptive; Glass, Singer, and Friedman (1969) have shown that this kind of noise has an impact on task performance even after a person is no longer experiencing it.

The effects of noise on learning depends to some extent on the sex, age, and academic ability of the individual (Christie & Glickman, 1980; Zentall, 1983). Similarly, the nature of the task is crucial in determining how it will be affected by noise. Noise that is novel, unusual, or "psychologically meaningful" in some way will interfere with almost any task (Cohen & Weinstein, 1982; Kryter, 1976, 1980), but some tasks can be easily disrupted by almost any noise. Tasks that require focused attention, memorization, simultaneous attention to several different things, or maintaining vigilance are the most easily affected. On the other hand, visual judgment tasks, search tasks, and repetitive manual tasks requiring strength or dexterity seem relatively unaffected by noise (Broadbent, 1958; Cohen & Weinstein, 1982; Glass & Singer, 1972; Kryter, 1970; Poulton, 1970; Smith, 1991; Theologus, Wheaton, & Fleishman, 1974). Under some conditions, noise may actually improve performance, especially if it helps the person pay attention or stay awake (Corcoran, 1962; Poulton, 1976; Warner, 1969). Evans and Cohen (1987) have surmised that although noise reduces overall memory capacity, it may speed up processing the information already in working memory and facilitate performance of some tasks.

Most of the research about the effects of noise on performance discussed so far has been laboratory research, but field studies in everday settings tend to be consistent with the laboratory data. A well-known program of field research on the effects of noise was the Los Angeles Noise Project undertaken by Cohen and his colleagues (Cohen, Evans, Krantz, & Stokols, 1980; Cohen et al., 1981, 1986). These studies examined elementary school children who lived in the flight paths around Los Angeles International Airport. All the children were exposed to very loud aircraft noise in their homes both day and night. The studies found that these children were more likely to suffer from high blood pressure, that they had lower mathematics achievement scores, and that they were less capable and persistent at problem solving than children from similar racial and socioeconomic backgrounds who did not live near the airport. Other studies have confirmed that children who live or attend school near noisy elevated railways or on streets with heavy traffic show similar effects (Bronzaft, 1981; Bronzaft & McCarthy, 1975; Cohen, Glass, & Singer, 1973; Crook & Langdon, 1974). In all cases, there is a negative relationship between school noise and academic achievement. Children in classrooms on the noisy side of school buildings performed more poorly than children on the quiet side of the same building. On a more optimistic note, studies have determined that moving children from noisy to quiet classrooms leads to gradual improvement in performance. While there have been fewer well-controlled studies on the effects of exposure to noise in the workplace, studies indicate that decreasing noise levels in industrial settings may increase productivity (Broadbent & Little, 1960; Hockey & Hamilton, 1970).

Noise also affects social behavior. Appleyard and Lintell (1972) discovered that there are fewer interactions between neighbors in noisy neighborhoods. Other studies have indicated that we are less likely to help strangers in noisy environments than in quiet settings (Mathews & Canon, 1975; Page, 1977). Finally, a number of experiments have linked noise to heightened levels of aggression in laboratory situations (Donnerstein & Wilson, 1976; Geen & O'Neal, 1969; Konecni, 1975).

RESPONSE TO THE AMBIENT ENVIRONMENT: STIMULUS SCREENING AND SENSATION SEEKING

From the preceding discussion, it is clear that the arousing, emotional qualities of the ambient environment are important determinants of human behavior. However, people do not all react to their environment in the same way. Some individuals seem to be involved in a constant quest for excitement and fill their lives with loud parties and white-water rafting. Others prefer to spend their time more quietly; viewing slides of Philadelphia on a Saturday night is the most adventure they can handle at one time. No doubt, you have some friends who can study effectively while listening to loud music in a room filled with people, and other friends who need solitude and silence before they can work. Intuitively, you understand that the emotional disposition of individuals varies and that this affects how people respond to their environment.

Environmental psychologists have tried to use general personality inventories like the Minnesota Multiphasic Personality Inventory (MMPI) (Hathaway & McKinley, 1951) and the California Personality Inventory (CPI) (Gough, 1975) to predict environmentally relevant behaviors such as environmental concern and sense of direction (Borden & Francis, 1978; Bryant, 1982); however, these scales were developed primarily for clinical use and their utility for environmental psychologists is limited. Consequently, a number of personality measures have been developed to assess characteristics more directly of interest to environmental psychologists (Sonnenfeld, 1969; McKechnie, 1974; Kaplan, 1977; Bunting & Cousins, 1983). For the most part, these were "global" measures of many different dispositions relevant to the interaction between people and their environment. One of these scales is the **Environmental Response Inventory (ERI),** developed by McKechnie (1974). The ERI, constructed very carefully over a long period of time, contains a number of different subscales. To gain a better understanding of McKechnie's subscales, try it (see box The Environmental Response Inventory).

Gifford (1980) used the ERI to predict how people might evaluate the interiors of buildings. Scores on the ERI differentiated optometrists who practiced in urban areas from those in suburban or rural areas (Kegel-Flom, 1976). The ERI has also successfully identified differences in orientation toward the natural environment between conservation group members, government officials, and sports enthusiasts (McKechnie, 1977).

Many personality measures have been developed that measure a single trait or disposition. Of special concern to environmental psychologists interested in responses to the ambient environment are those measures that predict how individuals will react to environmental stimulation. Central to many of these traits is the concept of the **orienting response (OR).** Imagine that you are all alone (or so you think) late at night in a big house. What happens when you hear a mysterious, muffled noise somewhere in the house? In all probability, your muscles become tense. You turn your head in the direction of the sound, and your eyes and ears strain as you probe the darkness for more information. Your heart rate increases as you struggle to control your breathing. You have just exhibited an orienting response. Orienting responses have evolved in all organisms as a means of focusing the senses on novel stimuli in the environment. During the OR, sensory thresholds are lowered, brain activity increases, heart and respiration rates change, and blood flow to the limbs is altered as the individual prepares for an appropriate response to the new stimulus (Weiss & Baum, 1989). The OR habituates (decreases in intensity) with repetitions of the stimulus and leads to investigation or approach to the stimulus. An OR is not to be confused with a startle response, which occurs in response to very sudden, intense stimuli and leads to freezing or flight.

TRY IT!

The Environmental Response Inventory (ERI)

George McKechnie's (1974) Environmental Response Inventory (ERI) was the first successful attempt to construct a multidimensional personality measure specifically designed to describe the ways in which the dispositions of individuals affect how they deal with their physical environment. The ERI was developed very carefully over a period of several years until McKechnie finally arrived at a 184-item questionnaire that assesses a person's standing on nine different dimensions. The person's interactions with his or her physical environment will be a function of the pattern of their responses to the nine scales of the ERI. As you can see, there are potentially as many different orientations to the environment as there are combinations of scores on the nine subscales of the ERI. Bunting and Cousins (1983) have even developed an ERI for children, aptly called the Children's Environmental Response Inventory (CERI). Get a feel for your own orientations toward the environment by evaluating your reactions to each of McKechnie's nine dimensions of the ERI described below.

Antiquarianism Measures a person's enjoyment of and interest in historical places and things and in places that convey a sense of great age.

Communality Measures the person's need for human contact and the extent to which he or she is socially involved with friends and neighbors.

The strength of the OR can be measured by the strength of the initial reaction and the speed with which it habituates. The OR's strength varies from person to person, and Maltzman and Raskin (1965) determined that the OR is a stable individual difference (that is, consistent in the individual across different situations). As it happens, this difference in response to environmental stimulation has strong implications for the types of environments people prefer as well as how they deal with the load found in different environments.

Orienting responses are set off by novel, unpredictable stimuli. The strength of an individual's OR reflects the ease with which he or she becomes aroused by environmental stimulation. Clearly, all environmental stimuli are not equally important. Efficient functioning in the environment requires that a person be able to rank sensory inputs in some order of importance, attending to the most relevant ones and screening out the less relevant stimuli. Mehrabian (1977a, 1977b) has developed a person-

TRY IT!

Environmental Adaptation Measures the willingness of the person to change the physical environment for the benefit of human beings and the degree to which he or she perceives technological advances as "good."

Environmental Trust Measures the extent to which the person is comfortable exploring new environments and the extent to which he or she feels comfortable and secure in environments that lack human influence.

Mechanical Orientation Measures the individual's interest in how machinery works and the extent to which he or she enjoys manual work.

Need for Privacy Measures the extent to which a person enjoys isolation and solitude.

Pastoralism Measures the extent to which the individual wishes to preserve nature and stem the development of natural environments.

Stimulus Seeking Very similar to the sensation-seeking trait discussed in this chapter, stimulus seeking reflects the tendency of the individual to explore the environment and seek out and enjoy intense physical stimulation.

Urbanism Measures the extent to which an individual likes cities and high-density living.

ality scale called **stimulus screening** or "arousability" that measures how effectively individuals screen out irrelevant environmental stimulation. Mehrabian refers to people who effectively screen out the less important information from their environment as **screeners**. Screeners tend to be not easily aroused, and they function quite well in situations where there is a lot of distraction and noise in the environment. Your friend who can study in a crowded, music-filled room is probably a screener. **Nonscreeners,** on the other hand, are less able to filter out unwanted stimuli. Their nervous systems are subject to more sensory information than is tolerable. They are more easily aroused than screeners and experience environments as more highly loaded. Nonscreeners tend to show stronger and longer-lasting ORs, and they respond to any increase in the information rate of their environment with accelerated levels of arousal. Your friend who needs a quiet, isolated study place is probably a nonscreener. Mehrabian (1976a) has described a number of situations in which stimulus screening might be an excellent predictor of the problems and preferences that people exhibit in different environments. He believes that nonscreeners will be more strongly attracted to pleasant, arousing situations and be more likely to avoid unpleasant, highly arousing situations than screeners. Thus far, this prediction has received only mixed support (Hines & Mehrabian, 1979; Mehrabian, 1978, 1980; McAndrew & Clark, 1983; McAndrew & Thornton, 1987).

In addition to differences in how arousable they are, individuals also differ on the levels of arousal that they prefer to maintain. Some people prefer relatively high activation levels and seek out situations that will produce them; others desire lower activation levels and are more comfortable in environments sympathetic to that need. Several different measures of preferred activation levels have been developed, and the trait has variously been called stimulus seeking (McKechnie, 1974), sensation seeking (Zuckerman, Kolin, Price, & Zoob, 1964; Zuckerman, 1971, 1974, 1979), and arousal seeking (Mehrabian, 1973). All of these scales measure the same predisposition in slightly different ways. Here, the terms will be used interchangeably, and for ease of discussion the trait usually will be referred to as sensation seeking, since Zuckerman's scale is the best known and most widely used of these measures.

Sensation seeking is a complex trait with a number of different components. For example, Zuckerman's sensation-seeking scale consists of four subscales. These subscales separately assess an individual's interest in physical risk-taking activities, the pursuit of new sensory and mental experiences, the disinhibited pursuit of pleasure, and susceptibility to boredom. While these scales are positively correlated, it is possible to score higher on one dimension than on another.

The reliability and validity of the sensation- and arousal-seeking scales have been well established, and the trait has been related to a bewildering array of different behaviors. High sensation seekers have stronger orienting responses (Neary & Zuckerman, 1976; Zuckerman, Eysenck, &

P H O T O   3·1   High sensation seekers engage the environment in ways that will increase their arousal levels.

Eysenck, 1978) and find high arousal more pleasant than low sensation seekers do (Ridgeway, Hare, Waters, & Russell, 1984; Zuckerman, 1980). High sensation seekers are more likely to smoke and to experiment with drugs, and are more strongly attracted to pleasant settings than are low sensation seekers (Mehrabian, 1978, 1980; Newcomb & McGee, 1991; Segal & Singer, 1976; Zuckerman, Neary, & Brustman, 1970; Zuckerman, Bone, Neary, Mangelsdorff, & Brustman, 1972). Low sensation seekers are more likely to suffer from phobias (Mellstrom, Cicala, & Zuckerman, 1976). High sensation seekers consistently engage in behaviors that result in risk, change, or sensory and social stimulation. They are more likely to be skydivers and rock climbers (Hymbaugh & Garrett, 1974; Levenson, 1990), to ride motorcycles, and to commit traffic violations (Brown, Ruder, Ruder, & Young, 1974). High sensation seekers are more likely to volunteer for unusual experiments or encounter groups (Stanton, 1976; Zuckerman, Schultz, & Hopkins, 1967) and express a greater willingness to take drugs that might produce strange side effects or hallucinations (Carroll, Zuckerman, & Vogel, 1982; Neary, 1975).

Sensation seeking also influences social behavior. High sensation seekers are better at maintaining eye contact with strangers (McAndrew & Warner, 1986), are more likely than low sensation seekers to be attracted to dissimilar others (Mehrabian, 1975; Williams, Ryckman, Gold, & Lenney, 1982), and have had a greater variety of sexual partners and experiences and a stronger interest in seeing erotic films (Brown, Ruder, Ruder, & Young, 1974; Zuckerman et al., 1972; Zuckerman, Neary, & Brustman, 1970; Zuckerman, Tushup, & Finner, 1976). Jacobs and Koeppel (1974) and Zuckerman (1979) report that high sensation seekers are more likely to change locales and entertain the idea of travelling to exotic places, even if the travel is risky. Berkowitz (1967) has even found that high sensation seekers prefer warm colors such as red and orange. Raju (1980) found that this trait is also related to consumer behavior such as switching brands and seeking more information about new products.

Not surprisingly, sensation seeking is related to a person's occupational choice. High sensation seekers are more likely than low sensation seekers to have risky occupations such as firefighting, police work, race car driving, and underwater rescue and salvage diving (Bacon, in Zuckerman, 1979; Kusyszyn, Steinberg, & Elliot, in Zuckerman, 1979). Sensation-seeking scores correlate positively with vocational-preference test scores in scientific occupations and social professions such as psychologist, physician, social worker, and minister; they also correlate positively with an interest in being a musician. Sensation seeking is negatively correlated with vocational interests in business or clerical fields such as banking and accounting; and for women, interest in being a housewife, elementary school teacher, or dietician is usually associated with low sensation-seeking scores (Kish & Donnenwerth, 1969, 1972; Kish & Leahy, 1970). Rape crisis counselors score high on sensation seeking (Best & Kilpatrick, 1977). Interestingly, sensation seeking declines as people get older (Brownfield, 1966; Coursey, Buchsbaum, & Frankel, 1975; Zuckerman, Eysenck, & Eysenck, 1978).

Zuckerman (1979) has noted that a moderate amount of sensation seeking has an obvious adaptive value for organisms with a capacity to acquire and retain information, as it may enhance the organism's chances of discovering new sources of food and other resources. Individual differences in sensation-seeking temperaments and behaviors are found in many different species of animals. This tendency seems to be genetically based (Hall, Rappaport, Hopkins, Griffin, & Silverman, 1970; Lukas & Siegel, 1977; McLearn, 1959; Redmond & Murphy, 1975).

Increasing evidence shows a biological, genetic component for sensation seeking in humans as well (Fulker, Eysenck, & Zuckerman, 1980; Zuckerman, 1979, 1983, 1990; Zuckerman, Buchsbaum, & Murphy, 1980). A genetic basis has been established for similar personality traits such as extraversion/introversion (Eysenck, 1967), and consistent biological differences are found between high and low sensation seekers. Higher levels of gonadal hormones in the blood are associated with high sensation seeking in males and females (Daitzman, Zuckerman, Sammelwitz, & Ganjam, 1978).

Monoamine oxidase (MAO) is an enzyme found in the brain of humans and animals. The level of MAO found in each individual's brain is a stable biological trait. Drugs that inhibit MAO production dramatically increase activity in rodents (Murphy, 1977a, 1977b) and cause euphoria, aggression, and hallucinations in humans. Low MAO levels in humans have been associated with restless and uninhibited behavior and with high probabilities for criminality, drug abuse, and psychopathy (Ellis, 1991). Not surprisingly, high MAO concentrations are negatively correlated with sensation seeking (Ellis, 1991; Schooler, Zahn, Murphy, & Buchsbaum, 1978), and high scores on the sensation-seeking scale have been directly related to delinquent and criminal behavior in adolescence and young adulthood (Newcomb & McGee, 1991). Although there is no firm evidence yet, Zuckerman (1979, 1983) believes that the sensation-seeking trait is at least partly a function of the levels of the neurotransmitters norepinephrine and dopamine in the reward areas located in the limbic system of the brain.

Although there seems to be a biological basis for sensation seeking, experience may influence how strongly the trait is displayed. Several studies have shown that some sensory deprivation increases stimulus-seeking behavior in animals (Butler & Alexander, 1955) and humans (Jones, 1969; Persky, Zuckerman, Basu, & Thorton, 1966); however, monkeys raised under conditions of extreme social and sensory deprivation were unwilling to expose themselves to new situations (Sackett, 1972).

For more details on the many ways human personality relates to the physical environment, the reader should refer to Little's (1987) excellent chapter in the *Handbook of Environmental Psychology*.

CHAPTER SUMMARY

The ambient environment refers to the nonvisual aspects of the physical environment. Ambient factors considered in this chapter included climate, elevation, temperature, light, color, and noise. Each of these environmental factors has been shown to have strong, predictable effects on human behavior and feelings.

To a great extent, the moods and emotions that people experience are a product of the ambient environment. Moods are influenced by physiological arousal and the individual's enduring emotional disposition.

Reactions to environments can be described as approach or avoidance, and the extent to which we engage in one or the other of these tendencies will be a function of the intensity of the pleasure elicited by the environment. Mehrabian and Russell (1974a) have proposed that three dimensions, arousal/nonarousal, pleasure/displeasure, and dominance/submissiveness, predict moods and reactions to environments. Their model is called the three-factor theory of emotion.

Mehrabian (1976b) introduced the concept of environmental load to describe the sensory information rate of different environments. High-load environments are full of information and are highly arousing; low-load environments are not. The intensity, novelty, and complexity of an environment are the chief features contributing to its load.

An individual's personality, especially as it relates to reactions to changes in arousal, strongly affects how he or she will respond to the ambient environment. Sensation seeking and stimulus screening are two examples of personality traits that are very important in this regard.

GLOSSARY

Activation Level   An individual's current, generalized level of autonomic arousal.

Affective Appraisal   The attribution of an emotional quality to a thing or place.

Ambient Environment   The nonvisual aspects of an environment such as noise, temperature, odor, and illumination.

Ambient Temperature   The objective air temperature in an environment.

Bipolar Adjectives   Pairs of adjectives that are opposite in meaning.

Brightness   The intensity of the light coming from a stimulus.

Decibel   The unit by which loudness is measured.

Effective Temperature   An individual's perception of the ambient temperature.

Emotional Disposition   A stable, long-term tendency to respond consistently to emotionally arousing situations.

Emotional Episode   An extreme mood brought on by a specific place, object, or event.

Environmental Load   The sensory information rate of an environment.

Environmental Response Inventory (ERI)   A personality scale developed by McKechnie (1974) to predict environmental behavior.

Hue   The color of a stimulus.

Ion   Positively or negatively charged particle caused by splitting air molecules.

Mood   The core feelings of a person's subjective emotional state at any particular moment.

Noise   The psychological experience of unwanted sound.

Nonscreener   A person who is highly aroused and unable to efficiently screen out unwanted environmental stimuli.

Orienting Response (OR)   Reflexively focusing attention on novel, intense, or complex stimuli.

Phototherapy   An antidepressant treatment consisting of exposure to bright lights during the winter months.

Saturation   The amount of white light in a color.

Screener   A person low in arousability who effectively screens out unwanted environmental stimuli.

Seasonal Affective Disorder (SAD)   A form of depression that occurs during fall and winter months when the number of daylight hours decreases.

Semantic Differential   A type of questionnaire based on bipolar adjectives that is commonly used in self-report measures of emotion.

Sensation Seeking   A personality measure developed by Zuckerman to assess the degree to which individuals seek out and enjoy stimulation.

Sham–Shock Procedure   A laboratory technique for studying aggression in which a person believes that he or she is administering electric shock to another person.

Stimulus Screening   A measure of arousability developed by Mehrabian.

Three-Factor Theory of Emotion   A theory of emotion developed by Mehrabian and Russell that proposes that the dimensions of arousal, dominance, and pleasure best explain emotional reactions to environments and events.

Environmental Stress

4

THE NATURE OF STRESS

Think of some of the Hollywood versions of torture you have seen. In many of these movies, prisoners are interrogated under hot lights or confined in dark, tiny rooms with featureless stone walls. In spite of their theatrical excesses, these films have correctly recognized the physical environment's potential for exerting pressure on human beings. When the environmental load that an individual experiences becomes too high or too low for extended periods of time, environmental stress occurs. Most definitions of environmental **stress** imply that stress occurs when the demands that an environment makes on people do not mesh with their capacity to cope with those demands (Evans & Cohen, 1987; Lazarus, 1966; Lazarus & Launier, 1978). In some cases, environmental stress can be traced to an information overload that exceeds the limited attentional capacities of the individual. This results in mental fatigue that may ultimately have physical consequences (Cohen, 1978, 1980; Cohen &

Spacapan, 1978; Cohen & Williamson, 1991). At other times, the stress reaction seems to be a response to the perceived unpredictability and uncontrollability of the environment, which leaves the person feeling helpless and unable to cope with the situation (Cohen, 1980; Mechanic, 1978; Seligman, 1975; Sherrod, 1974; Stokols, 1972). Consistent with this second interpretation, many studies have shown that individuals who assume some personal responsibility for stressful situations adjust better to those situations than those who blame others or in some way believe that the source of stress is completely out of their control (Baum, Fleming, & Singer, 1983; Tennen, Affleck, Allen, McGrade, & Ratzan, 1985; Timko & Janoff-Bulman, 1985).

Selye (1956) provided one of the earliest general descriptions of the body's reaction to prolonged stress. He described what he called the **general adaptation syndrome (GAS),** which consists of three stages. The first is a period of general alarm and excitement in which the body musters its "fight or flight" resources to deal with whatever is causing the high information load from the environment. This physiological arousal is measurable through the usual channels—heart and respiration rates, blood pressure, muscle tension, and skin conductance. The first stage can persist only for a limited time before a second stage marked by weariness, depression, and possibly illness, sets in. If the stress continues, the person eventually reaches a point of total exhaustion (the third stage). Prolonged stress can lead to illness and physical complaints ranging from high blood pressure to stroke (Cox, Paulus, McCain, & Karlovac, 1982; Sundstrom, 1978; Welch, 1979) and to psychological problems such as substance abuse, depression, and personality disorders (Keane & Wolf, 1990). Cohen and Williamson (1991) also believe that stress is a contributor to infectious diseases such as colds, flu, and bacterial infections. Cohen and Williamson believe that stress can lead directly to these diseases by disrupting the operation of the immune system and that it can indirectly contribute to illness by inducing people to rely on their social networks and interact with others more frequently and intimately. A recent study by Cohen, Tyrrell, and Smith (1991) confirms that people are twice as likely to catch a cold after a period of prolonged stress.

Green (1990) outlines three major aspects of the stress process (see Figure 4-1). First, an event external to the person must occur, such as a flood, a period of imprisonment, or the death of a loved one. Second, the individual must perceive and appraise the event. This is followed (third) by a psychological reaction. Thus, stress results from an interaction between external events, cognitions, and emotional responses. The nature of the stress experienced by any particular person will depend to some extent on whether the stress is chronic or acute. **Chronic stress** lasts longer and is frequently caused by events that last longer than those causing **acute stress** (Baum, O'Keefe, & Davidson, 1990). The problem in defining stressors as chronic or acute, however, is more complicated than it appears. Events can be categorized as acute or chronic in any of the

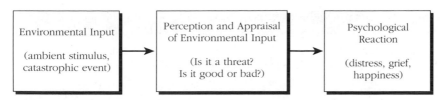

F I G U R E   4·1   The three aspects of the stress process (Source: Green, 1990)

stages in Green's model. For example, an earthquake or a serious automobile accident may be acute in that it lasts only a few seconds, but the
person's psychological reactions to this event can be long-lasting and
recurrent. Thus, the duration of an acute stressor can be effectively
increased if the victim continues to reexperience the event vicariously
(Baum, O'Keefe, & Davidson, 1990). Both acute and chronic stress can
result in extended periods of heightened arousal, endocrine imbalances,
and permanent changes in a number of brain mechanisms (Ver Ellen &
van Kammen, 1990). Acute or chronic stress can cause changes in sex
hormone levels, a loss of lipids from the adrenal cortex, and a decrease in
the number or activity of lymphocytes (Weiss & Baum, 1989).

Some responses to stressful events habituate over time. Studies of
animals show that the novelty of the stressor is a crucial factor in determining the extent to which habituation will occur. These studies show
that many days of exposure to the same stressor usually leads to habituation, but an equal number of days of exposure to a series of different
stressors does not (Kant et al., 1985). Hence, stress is more than simply
a question of biochemical change or psychological exhaustion as Selye's
early model suggests, because the individual's perceptions and appraisals
of the source of the stress must be involved as well (Aldwin & Stokols,
1988; Baum, O'Keefe, & Davidson, 1990). Baum and his colleagues have
observed that repetitive acute stressful situations that involve different
stressors probably pose the most serious risks to individuals.

Usually, environmental stressors fall into one of four categories:
cataclysmic events such as natural disasters or war, stressful life events
such as major illness or family problems (see the box on pages 80–81),
daily hassles such as dealing with crowding or commuting (see the box
on page 82), or overstimulation from factors in the ambient environment
(Baum, Singer, & Baum, 1982; Campbell, 1983; Evans & Cohen, 1987;
Lazarus & Cohen, 1977). Often ambient stressors are perceived to be
beyond the individual's control. They can be tolerated for short periods
of time without obvious harm (Campbell, 1983). Nevertheless, prolonged
exposure to any ambient stressor that is too intense causes heightened
arousal levels that may interfere with task performance and affect moods
and physical well-being. Individuals who perceive that others are available

TRY IT!

Stress and Life Events

Major changes in an individual's lifestyle can be traumatic and may collectively represent a tremendous source of stress. The most widely used measure of the long-term effects of stress resulting from the events in one's life is the **Life Events Scale (LES)** (also known as the Social Readjustment Rating Scale [SRRS]) developed by Holmes and Rahe (1967). Holmes and Rahe ranked life events according to the degree of change they require of the individual; the values assigned to each of the life events are called **Life Change Units (LCUs).** According to Holmes and Rahe, accumulating too many life change units in a short time constitutes a major life crisis, and studies have linked an increase in LES scores with significant medical problems, including respiratory illnesses, heart problems, and even sudden death (Rahe, 1972).

Examine your own current life stress by noting which of the events on the LES you have experienced during the past 12 months (see table). Add up the values assigned to each of these events. Scores from 150 to 199 represent a mild life crisis. Scores from 200 to 299 indicate a more severe life crisis, and scores over 300 indicate a major life crisis. Eighty percent of the participants in a study by Rahe (1972) scoring over 300 suffered serious health problems shortly after a stressful year.

The Life Events Scale

Rank	Life Event	Value
1	Death of Spouse	100
2	Divorce	73
3	Marital Separation	65
4	Jail Term	63
5	Death of Close Family Member	63
6	Personal Injury or Illness	53
7	Marriage	47
8	Fired at Work	47
9	Marital Reconciliation	45
10	Retirement	45

11	Change in Health of Family Member	44
12	Pregnancy	40
13	Sex Difficulties	39
14	Gain of a New Family Member	39
15	Business Readjustment	39
16	Change in Financial State	38
17	Death of a Close Friend	37
18	Change to a Different Line of Work	36
19	Change in Number of Arguments with Spouse	35
20	Mortgage over $10,000	31
21	Foreclosure of Mortgage or Loan	30
22	Change in Responsibilities at Work	29
23	Son or Daughter Leaving Home	29
24	Trouble with In-Laws	29
25	Outstanding Personal Achievement	28
26	Spouse Begins or Stops Work	26
27	Begin or End School	26
28	Change in Living Conditions	25
29	Revision of Personal Habits	24
30	Trouble with Boss	23
31	Change in Work Hours or Conditions	20
32	Change in Residence	20
33	Change in Schools	20
34	Change in Recreation	19
35	Change in Church Activities	19
36	Change in Social Activities	18
37	Change in Sleeping Habits	18
38	Mortgage or Loan less than $10,000	17
39	Change in Number of Family Get-Togethers	15
40	Change in Eating Habits	15
41	Vacation	13
42	Christmas	12
43	Minor Violations of the Law	11

Source: Holmes and Rahe (1967).

to provide assistance and comfort usually adapt better to environmental stress (Cohen & Wills, 1985; Wethington & Kessler, 1986), but environmental stressors that are persistent and long-lasting eventually erode this social support and diminish the extent to which it can spare individuals from severe psychological distress (Lepore, Evans, & Schneider, 1991).

The stressful properties of normal ambient environments were discussed in detail in Chapter 3; stressors such as crowding and air pollution will be considered at some length in later chapters. This chapter focuses on stress resulting from cataclysmic environmental events and from extreme or unusual ambient stimulation.

ENVIRONMENTAL HAZARDS AND NATURAL DISASTERS

On Tuesday, October 17, 1989, at 5:04 P.M. (Pacific daylight time), millions of people were glued to their television awaiting the start of game three of the World Series between the San Francisco Giants and the Oakland Athletics. The game was being held at Candlestick Park in San Francisco. The pregame festivities were well under way when an earthquake measuring 7.1 on the Richter scale rocked northern California. Although there was little damage to the stadium itself, many people died as high-

The Stress of Commuting

Several years ago, media stories about motorists on California freeways shooting at each other out of frustration over slow-moving traffic began to appear with alarming frequency. Could freeway commuting actually have become so stressful that people would resort to violence against strangers? Surveys of Orange County residents during this period of time confirmed that nearly 50 percent of that county's residents considered traffic congestion to be the county's most pressing problem (Baldassare & Katz, cited by Novaco, Stokols, & Milanesi, 1990).

For about the last 15 years, psychologists Raymond Novaco and Daniel Stokols and their colleagues (Novaco, Stokols, Campbell, & Stokols, 1979; Novaco, Stokols, & Milanesi, 1990; Stokols & Novaco, 1981; Stokols, Novaco, Stokols, & Campbell, 1978) have studied the relationship between stress and commuting to and from work. They have paid particular attention to "high-impedance" commut-

ing in which people must travel long distances in heavy traffic on freeways. This type of commute requires frequent braking, slow driving speeds, and long periods of time stuck in traffic jams. Their research has shown that high-impedance commuting does in fact raise blood pressure, create negative feelings, reduce tolerance for frustration, and decrease overall satisfaction with life. Evans and Carrère (1991) found that urban bus drivers exhibit their highest levels of psychophysiological stress during peak traffic conditions. Commuting stress may also decrease job satisfaction and even cause people to change their residence to cope with the hassles of commuting. Perhaps most serious is the finding that high-impedance commuting is related to more frequent illnesses, especially head colds and flu, and that it is associated with significantly more frequent absences from work due to illness.

way overpasses collapsed onto rush-hour traffic. Ultimately, the extent of property damage and injuries reflected a disaster of major proportions. (Incidentally, the World Series was also postponed.) Television anchorman Dan Rather observed that the earthquake served as a reminder that "even in a high-tech age, man is at the mercy of nature" (CBS News, October 20, 1989). This quake occurred less than a year after an even more deadly earthquake in Armenia, and followed Hurricane Hugo's devastation of the South Carolina coast by just a few weeks. These events vividly impressed on North Americans that natural disasters are real and ever-present dangers that are not confined to "far off" places like Armenia or the Philippines. Between 1974 and 1980 there were 37 major catastrophes in the United States; from 1979 to 1980 alone, the American Red Cross reported that more than 688,000 people received emergency aid following some sort of disaster (Ursano & Fullerton, 1990). Worldwide, about 250,000 people are killed by natural events each year (Burton, Kates, & White, 1978).

Natural disasters are traumatic because they are intense, unexpected, and infrequent in individual's lives and cause fear, anxiety, and withdrawal in the victims (Ursano & Fullerton, 1990). Even for those not originally involved in the disaster, subsequent association with the victims can be traumatic. For example, Ursano and his colleagues (1988) report that those who must handle the bodies of people killed in disasters frequently report anxiety, grief, and an inability to sleep or continue work. Often, they develop coping strategies such as not looking at the victims' faces or hands in an attempt to avoid identifying with them.

The natural environment becomes a potential hazard whenever it intersects with human populations, and according to Kates (1976), natural hazards have the greatest impact in rural societies. In urbanized societies, human-made hazards present even more of a threat than natural hazards. Natural events can be **intensive** in nature, which means that they are brief, sudden, intense, and unpredictable. Earthquakes and tornadoes are good examples of intensive natural events. Many other hazards such as drought and pollution are described as **pervasive.** Pervasive events tend to be more widespread and longer-lasting than intensive hazards (Kates, 1976).

Perceptions of Environmental Hazards

While it is unusual to find people who are completely unaware of the risks they face from the natural hazards in their area, research shows that residents of communities rarely grasp the true potential for disaster that they live with, in spite of educational programs that may be in place (Sorensen, 1983; Nasar & Greenberg, 1984; Lehman & Taylor, 1987). Even when people are aware of the magnitude of the threat, this rarely leads to action (Sims & Baumann, 1983), which indicates that simply educating people about threat may not be enough.

Environmental psychologists have become interested in finding out why people ignore the hazards that they face from their environment and why they seem to prefer reacting to disasters after they occur rather than taking active steps to avoid them in the first place. Why do people consistently fail to perceive threat and believe that it will not affect them? Even more puzzling, why do so many people move back into disaster areas after a tragedy occurs? Burton, Kates, and White (1978) found that residents of natural disaster areas construct elaborate belief systems that justify remaining in the area, and studies reveal that people often grossly misperceive the real statistical probability that a future disaster may occur (Saarinen, 1966; Burton, Kates, & White, 1978; Slovic, 1978; Jackson, 1981; Kushnir, 1982). Kates (1962) studied how residents of flood plains comprehend flood hazards. If an individual had experienced flooding firsthand, he or she was more likely to expect future flooding and to take protective measures. On the other hand, many who had experienced a serious flood still did not expect future floods and often expressed a belief that their faith in God or future flood-control programs would protect them.

There are also cases in which people exaggerate the risks associated with environmental hazards. For example, pervasive feelings of dread and revulsion are common responses to the disposal of waste from commercial nuclear reactors, despite expert opinion that nuclear waste can be stored safely in deep underground chambers (Slovic, Layman, & Flynn, 1991). The resultant emotional and political opposition to disposal programs complicates the problem of nuclear waste disposal and tremendously increases its cost. A study by Slovic, Layman, and Flynn (1991) demonstrated the intense feelings aroused by nuclear waste disposal. In a telephone survey, 3,334 people were asked to respond to the term *underground nuclear waste depository* by naming the first six thoughts that came to mind when they heard it. The four most frequent single-word associations to this stimulus were "dangerous," "danger," "death," and "pollution." There were also many responses pertaining to war, weapons, and annihilation and many that the researchers classified as "NIMBY" (not-in-my-backyard).

The tendency to think unclearly about environmental hazard is called **bounded rationality** (Slovic, Kunreuther, & White, 1974), and researchers are attempting to establish the factors that lead people to misperceive risks and to opt for responses to disasters rather than preparation. Fischoff, Svenson, and Slovic (1987) provide a comprehensive description of the decision-making process individuals employ when dealing with environmental hazards. They point out that a major difficulty people face when making these kinds of decisions is that they are trying to make decisions under conditions of uncertainty. Any good model of decision making must take the degree of uncertainty into consideration as well as the level of risk that people find acceptable and the amount of information they have. This problem is complicated further by the fact that people's estimates of the risks posed by environmental hazards can be influenced and changed by the format of the questions asked in studies of the perception of environmental risks (Eiser & Hoepfner, 1991).

Ultimately, the kind of action a person takes (or does not take) comes down to the perceptions and the personality of that individual. Rochford and Blocker (1991) studied victims' responses to a flood that occurred in eastern Oklahoma during the fall of 1986. The flood caused two deaths and $283 million in damages. Those who viewed the flooding as within human control were more likely to feel threatened by future flooding and were more likely to become active in efforts to see that it did not happen again. Conversely, those who viewed the flooding as uncontrollable focused on adjusting emotionally to the recent event and were uninvolved in trying to prevent future floods.

While preliminary research has failed to find that personality is a good predictor of who will prepare for possible future hazards (Schiff, 1977), instruments are being developed to reliably assess perceptions of environmental hazards. One of the most recent and promising of these is the **Environmental Appraisal Inventory** (EAI) developed by Schmidt and Gifford (1989). It is a 72-item, paper-and-pencil measure that independently measures perceptions of threat to the self, perceptions of threat to the environment, and perceptions of how much control the individual feels in response to threat. The EAI is a good example of an objective, general measure of environmental perceptions, but perceptions of environmental hazards have been studied in a number of other ways as well. Brown, Henderson, and Armstrong (1987) analyzed drawings of nuclear power stations made by English schoolchildren in their art classes to learn about the children's perceptions of this potential hazard. They found that the children's images of nuclear power stations changed over time as a function of pictures and stories about nuclear power in the popular media.

Taylor, Stewart, and Downton (1988) studied farmers' perceptions of drought in the Ogallala Aquifer region of the western United States' Great Plains (the famous "dust bowl" of the 1930s) by conducting in-depth personal interviews. Farmers were asked about their farming practices, about droughts they had experienced, and about their expectations concerning the frequency and severity of future droughts. The interviews revealed that classic, severe droughts, recent droughts, and the first drought that the farmer experienced were best recalled. Intermediate or mild droughts tended to be forgotten as time passed. The researchers also found that farmers over age 60 were much less likely to feel that they had found effective ways to deal with drought losses than young farmers were.

The research to date is not encouraging: People seem determined to live in natural hazard areas despite the dangers. Burton (1972) observed that this is not merely a problem of faulty perception. He points out that people remain in hazard areas for economic and many other reasons. For example, people continue to live in flood plains because the soil is fertile

P H O T O   4·1 Natural disasters can be highly stressful events for those who experience them.

and transportation is good. Societal constraints may also make it difficult for people to leave an area where they have lived for so long. On the bright side, evidence suggests that simulations and field exercises do in fact improve preparedness (Foster, 1980), so that with appropriate training it may be possible to minimize the hazards these populations face.

Finally, an important point to remember is that empirical evidence about perceptions of environmental risks and hazards should not be generalized too freely across cultures or even across different ethnic groups within one society. Studies have shown that a subject's ethnic background is a variable often overlooked in risk research. Ethnic groups differ in the levels of exposure or amount of experience they have had with various hazards; they may have values or worldviews relevant to risk or to the environment that make them diverge sharply in their perceptions of the hazards posed by the physical environment (Kleinhesselink & Rosa, 1991; Vaughan & Nordenstam, 1991).

Stress and Environmental Hazards

The problems caused by environmental disasters go far beyond the death toll and the dollar value of property damage. Coping with the long-term stress that results from the disaster is a serious concern among survivors of these events. There is considerable evidence that natural disasters change many areas of a person's life and that these changes are stressful (Janney, Minoru, & Holmes, 1977; Melick, 1978; Murphy, 1984; Hutchins & Norris, 1989). Persons who survive a natural catastrophe find that they must deal with the loss of loved ones, a home, and a job or business all at the same time. This is complicated even further if the person is struggling to recover from physical injury. The emotional trauma people suffer in this situation is often severe.

Rubonis and Bickman (1991) reviewed 52 studies that reported quantitative measures of psychopathology among populations that had experienced a disaster. They concluded that after a disaster occurs, higher levels of psychopathology reliably follow, and as the death rate from the disaster increases, so does the amount of psychopathology. Natural disasters such as volcano eruptions result in more psychopathology than human-caused disasters, perhaps because they are perceived as less controllable. Although the rate of psychopathology depends to some extent upon the nature of the disaster and the characteristics of the victims, a 17 percent increase over normal levels appears to be typical.

Steinglass and Gerrity (1990) did longitudinal studies of individual and family responses to two natural disasters. One was a 1985 tornado in northwestern Pennsylvania that killed 12 people, injured 200, and left 100 families homeless in a community of only 1800 persons. The second disaster was a 1985 flood in a small West Virginia town where more than 400 households were destroyed. In West Virginia, severe economic problems existed for most of the families before the flood, and the fact that very few households were insured exacerbated the disaster. In both communities, stress declined somewhat between 4 and 16 months after the disaster, but stress levels remained quite high 16 months after the event. In both cases, the female residents of the community reported more stress than the males. More than ten years after the 1972 Buffalo Creek flood (also in West Virginia), survivors still exhibited higher levels of anxiety, depression, and hostility than nearby, culturally similar groups that had not experienced the disaster (Green et al., 1990). In a similar study, Adams and Adams (1984) examined the stress reactions of residents living near Mount Saint Helens after its eruption in 1980. There were definite increases in alcohol abuse, family stress, illness, and domestic violence among families who survived that disaster.

Foster (1980) developed a system for estimating the stress that results from different environmental hazards and preliminary research indicates that it may be more important for victims of natural disasters to focus on their emotional reactions and vent their feelings than to block feelings, focus on the problem, and make plans to act (Collins, Baum, & Singer, 1983). However, a study of earthquake victims reveals that people who focus too strongly on their symptoms tend to retain them longer than those who spend less time worrying (Nolen-Hoeksema & Morrow, 1991).

In the United States, the threat from human-made environmental hazards is probably greater than the threat from natural hazards. Although some of these technological hazards are intensive (for example, oil spills, large explosions), human-made hazards are more likely than natural ones to be pervasive (for example, radiation leakage, toxic waste seepage). For example, lead contamination in paint, soil, and air is associated with mental retardation, hyperactivity, and many illnesses, but most people continue to ignore it (Spreen, Tupper, Risser, Tuokko, & Edgell, 1984). In fact, one of the features that distinguishes natural disasters from technological disasters is the ambiguity and uncertainty about the degree of harm that has actually occurred in a technological disaster; this is almost never true in natural disasters (Freudenburg & Jones, 1991).

Probably the most closely studied technological disaster was the malfunction at the Three Mile Island (TMI) nuclear power plant in Pennsylvania in March, 1979. This accident created contaminated water and also radioactive gas, which leaked from the building into the atmosphere for a year after the incident. In December, 1985, a second reactor at the same plant developed a small radioactive leak. While researchers now believe that radiation levels released at Three Mile Island were too low to have harmful physical effects, the stress nearby residents experienced undoubtedly has had profound psychological consequences. Several studies showed that after the accident people felt less control over their lives, were less able to perform well on tasks requiring persistence, and showed multiple symptoms of stress (Davidson, Baum, & Collins, 1982; Schaeffer & Baum, 1984; Baum, Gatchel, & Schaeffer, 1983). These ill effects seem to result partially from the uncertainty of future risk and the continued uncertainty about the long-term effects of the last accident. Bromet (1990) reports that ten years after the TMI accident 60 percent of a sample of mothers who lived near the plant at the time of the accident admitted that they still thought about the accident, and 62 percent worried that it might happen again. Forty-two percent still worried about their own health and 51 percent worried about their children's health. Dew, Bromet, and Schulburg (1987) found that residents' stress levels during the restart of the TMI facility six years after the accident were higher than during the period immediately following the accident. Some studies indicated that younger, better educated individuals were especially stressed following the TMI accident. Researchers concluded that this was related to the coping strategies these individuals employed (Goldhaber, Houts, & Disabella, 1983; Sorensen, Soderstrom, Copenhaver, Carnes, & Bolin, 1987). More specifically, they believed that the younger people's more active, problem-focused coping style (Folkman, Lazarus, Pimley, & Novacek, 1987) might backfire when faced with conditions that could not be changed. Residents in the TMI vicinity who attended a public health and information series on cancer, radiation, and epidemiology six years after the nuclear accident were better educated, less worried, more cynical of experts, more likely to report disturbances in concentration, and more likely to be male than a normative sample of area residents (Prince-Embury, 1991).

More recent studies of TMI victims confirm that coping styles are related to age and levels of stress, but disagree with the conclusion that older residents of the TMI area experienced significantly lower levels of stress than younger residents (Prince-Embury & Rooney, 1988, 1990). There seems to have been no relationship between the severity of stress experienced by an individual and his or her attitudes toward the nuclear power facility prior to the accident (Freudenburg & Jones, 1991). The stress people experienced around Three Mile Island may prove to be relatively mild compared to the stress experienced from the April 1986 Chernobyl nuclear disaster in the former Soviet Union, a tragedy that involved significant loss of life and the release of massive amounts of radiation.

EXTREME AND UNUSUAL ENVIRONMENTS

The study of how human beings react to extreme or unusual environments occupies a unique niche in the overall study of environmental stress. Extreme environments provide combinations of sensory stimuli not found elsewhere and an ambient environment for which people are evolutionarily unprepared. Often, a mixture of isolation, emotional up-heaval, and physical hazard coupled with extreme temperatures and air or water pressure make individuals' responses to these situations especially unpredictable and interesting. Suedfeld (1987) discusses the difficulty of defining "extreme and unusual" environments precisely. Often, these are environments where survival without advanced technology, or at least special equipment, is impossible. Vision, hearing, and the sense of touch are often restricted by bulky clothing or space or diving suits, and normal spatial cues are often missing or dramatically changed. All these factors increase the likelihood of hallucinations or mirages. Nevertheless, to a great extent the novelty of the environment is a function of the individual's experiences. While the Sahara Desert and the polar ice cap would qualify as extreme and unusual for a college professor from Illinois, such would not be the case for lifelong residents of these areas. On the other hand, environments such as outer space or the ocean floor would be alien to anyone.

Occasionally, an event can turn a familiar setting into one that seems extreme and unusual. Generally, these are natural or human-caused catastrophes such as tornadoes, floods, or war. However, any event that significantly alters the nature of the ambient stimuli may have this effect. Unfortunately, it is difficult to do controlled research in extreme or unusual environments, and much of what psychologists know is anecdotal. Weil (1977) reports something called the **eclipse experience** in which persons in the path of a total eclipse of the sun can "experience dramatic alterations of consciousness if they allow themselves to view the event" (p. 38). There is often a sense of derealization, and time perception changes in that experienced time seems much shorter than actual elapsed clock time. "In the unique light of the corona, reality becomes dreamlike and people report unusually intense feelings of detachment. Immediately after the eclipse, euphoria is pronounced among those who have watched it, and many people continue to feel high and energetic for hours" (p. 39). Witnesses often report that they can remember the period of the eclipse only "as if in a dream," and some yearn to repeat the experience so much that they chase eclipses all over the world, year after year.

Many encounters with harsh environments are the product of accidents in which people are unexpectedly and unwillingly thrust into traumatic situations. The sudden shock of entering such an environment is severe. Survivors of shipwrecks and airplane crashes show a high mortality rate in the first few days, even if they are not injured and there is plenty of food and water available (Bombard, 1953; Suedfeld, 1980). Even after the ordeal, survivors may suffer a posttraumatic stress disorder for years. While these unfortunate episodes are informative, they cannot provide the carefully controlled, systematic information necessary for drawing scientific conclusions. More useful for this purpose are studies of people voluntarily living and working in spacecraft, submarines, polar scientific stations, and other unusual environments.

In one recent experiment, an Italian woman named Stefania Follini lived for 130 days alone in a cave in Carlsbad, New Mexico. Her only contact with other humans was through a computer terminal. In the absence of night, day, or clocks, Follini's menstrual cycle stopped and her sleep–wake cycle changed radically. She tended to stay up for 20 to 25 hours at a time and then sleep for about 10 hours. She believed that only about two months had passed when in reality four months had gone by; she was surprised when she was told that the experiment was over. Researchers believe that the level of calcium in her bones and her muscle tone decreased and that her immune system became depressed during her stay in the cave. On a more positive note, her ability to concentrate deeply seemed to improve.

Antarctica

Most of the data available on human reactions to prolonged isolation in extreme environments have been collected from volunteers at research stations in Antarctica, especially during the "wintering-over" period. One such research project is the Polar Psychology Project (PPP), devoted to comparing people who work in Arctic and Antarctic research stations with similar groups in nonisolated environments. The psychologists involved have used tools such as participant observation, diaries, interviews, physiological measures, and psychological testing to study the effects of polar environments on individuals who must work there for prolonged periods of time (Steel & Suedfeld, 1991; Suedfeld, Bernaldez, & Stossel, 1989). Good work adaptation in polar environments demands not only job competence but mental stability and strong social skills

(Suedfeld, 1991b). The extreme temperatures, long periods of darkness, alien landscapes, and severely reduced sensory input during this period provide a perfect laboratory for the study of isolation and confinement (Levesque, 1991). Cornelius (1991) describes the winter-over in an Antarctic field station:

The "winter-over" varies from station to station. The isolation period for Palmer Station on the coast is about 7 months, and the South Pole winter-over is about 9 months. The isolation is almost complete: no mail, no visitors, no leaving, and no fresh supplies. . . . The crewmembers must adjust to many stressors, which include things that people in a normal environment take for granted. For example, absent are windows, privacy, living green things and animals, the sun, thick moist air to breathe, freedom to travel, or freedom to leave a rumor-infested isolated human outpost. The "rumor mill" can be quite potent. Cliques can develop and be quite cruel and stressful to an individual with a different background than the rest of the crew. Cliques can also be quite insensitive to their own kind. Lack of acoustic privacy in the small "private" rooms can also lead to stress. Privacy becomes a cherished commodity. Time away from the group alone is very important for "charging one's batteries." Lack of a partner of the opposite sex can also lead to stress. Married couples who have wintered tend to handle the isolation much better. Constant low light levels can cause stress too. It was observed that much higher light levels inside the dome at South Pole Station during the isolation period seemed to increase the morale of the crew. The higher light levels tend to decrease stress. . . . The plateau (ice sheet) is flat and almost featureless. It extends over most of the continent. . . . The surface altitude at South Pole Station is about 3,150 m. In addition, there is an intense low-pressure system that makes the effective physiological altitude vary between 3,300 m and a high of 4,000 m. Breathing can be quite difficult for the first few days, but most people can acclimatize fully within a month. The humidity is extremely low and causes drying of the eyes, nose, mouth, and skin. This can complicate sunburns caused by the lack of water vapor in the air and the harsh sunlight during the 6-month day [in the summer]. The temperature usually rises to about −25 degrees C on the warmest day of the summer and drops to about −80 degrees C during the winter. . . .

Off-duty activities depend on the individual but include conversation, watching movies and videos, listening to music, short excursions outside, looking out of the only set of windows in the station; finding an excuse for a party (sunset, midwinter, birthdays, holidays); and group projects (for example, one crew built a jacuzzi). . . .

Some customs at South Pole Station appear strange to the uninitiated observer. For example, the custom of the 300 Degree Club may appear foolhardy. During the winter, usually just past midwinter in September, the outside temperature drops below 100 degrees F. At this time, all of the crew proceeds to the sauna which is set to 200 degrees F (a dry heat, but tolerable). They dress in only their tennis shoes. After a heat-soak period of about 10 to 15 minutes, their bodies are sweating profusely. The liberal amount of sweat is quite important. Then the crew madly dashes out of the dome to the pole (about 100 m) and poses for a quick picture and dashes back into the dome. One must be extremely careful not to fall down, because the snow is very cold and would quickly cause burns like dry ice. The whole gloriously mad custom is possible because of the quick freezing of the sweat on the bodies of the candidate club members, just like the orange buds are protected in Florida during cold weather with a mist of water, which, when it freezes, protects them. (Source: Harrison, Clearwater, & McKay, 1991, pp. 10–13)

In spite of the fact that volunteers are carefully screened, wintering-over is almost always a stressful experience for those involved. People with past experience, however, are subject to less stress than those who experience polar conditions for the first time (Taylor, 1991). The extreme altitude, darkness, and cold cause a variety of physical symptoms (Guenter, Joern, Shurley, & Pierce, 1970; Moyer, 1976; Palinkas, 1991b; Rothblum, 1990). Changes in appetite and sleep patterns occur, and people usually gain weight. Changes in one's sense of time occur; and memory, concentration, and the ability to maintain attention suffer. Psychosomatic complaints are not uncommon; and depression, irritability, hostility, and insomnia are frequent complaints during winter-overs (Blair, 1991; Palinkas, 1991b). Antarctic isolation increases hypnotic susceptibility and daydreaming, and may alter consciousness in other ways (A. Barabasz, 1991a, 1991b; M. Barabasz, 1991).

Although the experience is undeniably stressful, individual differences are extremely important in determining reactions to winter-over; for many, it can be a positive experience (Carrère, Evans, & Stokols, 1991; Mocellin, Suedfeld, Bernaldez, & Barbarito, 1991). An analysis of early polar explorers' diaries reveals many references to beauty, serenity, and self-growth experiences (Mocellin & Suedfeld, 1991). Potentially good effects from the experience include decreased dependency, an increased capacity for intimate involvement, and enhanced self-esteem from having successfully met the challenge of winter-over (Oliver, 1991; Palinkas, 1991b). A high need for achievement, an internal locus of control (a belief that one's actions determine one's outcomes), and social compatibility with the other individuals all lead to more successful adaptation to the Antarctic environment (Palinkas, 1991a). Even under the best circumstances, however, returning home after wintering-over poses readjustment problems, and the "re-entry shock" is itself quite stressful (Harris, 1991; Oliver, 1991).

All these problems are compounded because the isolation occurs in a small group. Involvement and familiarity increase among individuals who are often from different cultural backgrounds and who had been strangers at the beginning of the winter-over. The boredom that results from limited sources of entertainment and unchanging group membership is quite stressful. After a while, another person's slightest habit or mannerism becomes grating, annoying, and an inescapable source of torment. The emergence of an accepted leader and the efficient division of labor and responsibility are crucial to the success of these isolated groups. In spite of this, when these groups are together so long, tension grows and

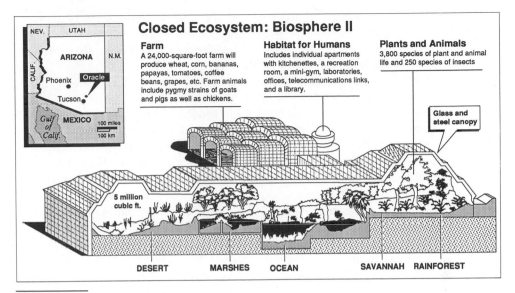

Closed Ecosystem: Biosphere II

Farm
A 24,000-square-foot farm will produce wheat, corn, bananas, papayas, tomatoes, coffee beans, grapes, etc. Farm animals include pygmy strains of goats and pigs as well as chickens.

Habitat for Humans
Includes individual apartments with kitchenettes, a recreation room, a mini-gym, laboratories, offices, telecommunications links, and a library.

Plants and Animals
3,800 species of plant and animal life and 250 species of insects

Glass and steel canopy

5 million cubic ft.

DESERT   MARSHES   OCEAN   SAVANNAH   RAINFOREST

NEV.   UTAH
ARIZONA   N.M.
Phoenix   Oracle
Tucson
Gulf of Calif.   MEXICO   100 miles / 100 km

F I G U R E   4·2   Biosphere II (AP/Wide World Photos)

group deterioration inevitably occurs. This is marked by decreased communication among group members, less regard for each other, and less cooperation (A. Barabasz, 1991a; Foushee, 1982; Gunderson, 1973; Rivolier, Cazes, & McCormick, 1991; Sharma, Vaskaran, & Manhotra, 1976; Taylor, 1991).

An interesting experiment on group isolation under less extreme conditions is currently under way in the Arizona desert. Four men and four women are living inside a two and one-half acre glass and steel dome called **Biosphere II.** The participants entered Biosphere II in September 1991 and will reemerge in September 1993. They share the biosphere with 3,800 varieties of plants, animals, and insects scattered among reproductions of desert, ocean, rain forest, savannah, and marsh habitats. For two years the "Biospherians" will grow their own food, make their own social arrangements, and for the most part be out-of-touch with the outside world. A schematic diagram of Biosphere II is presented in Figure 4-2.

Outer Space

The problems that groups of people in polar regions and underwater environments encounter are similar to the problems that humans will face in outer space, and data from experiments in these environments are becoming increasingly important to the progress of the space program (Ursin et al., 1991). In the future, those who plan and manage missions to outer space will have to accommodate larger, more diverse flight crews who will spend longer periods of time in space than ever before. Evaluations of hypothetical space environments by nonastronauts confirm that larger numbers of people and longer missions will make planning habitats in space a challenging proposition (Harrison, Struthers, & Putz, 1989, 1991). In an effort to prepare for this not-too-distant future, the National Aeronautics and Space Administration (NASA) now employs architects along with systems engineers. Recently the National Space Society (NSS) sponsored a nationwide architectural competition to encourage new designs for habitats in lunar or martian environments. All entries had to describe closed-cycle living environments that would not need constant resupply and that would have an economically self-sustaining reason to exist. The designs also had to deal with the critical problems of radiation, transportation, recreation, and differences in gravity (Bernard, 1991).

Special attention must be paid to the aesthetic qualities of the interiors of space environments. Studies of Soviet cosmonauts (Gurovskiy, Kosmolinsky, & Melnikov, in Clearwater & Coss, 1991) report that gazing out the windows at the earth was the favorite leisure activity and that videotapes depicting natural scenery were very popular. The studies confirm the importance of varied visual stimulation on spaceflights and reaffirm the importance of windows in confined environments (Haines, 1991). Clearwater and Coss (1991) summarized a number of studies that showed that painting spacecraft interiors to provide a natural floor-ceiling relationship (bright colors above, dark colors below) facilitated comfort and reduced motion sickness. Decorative pictures, especially those conveying a strong sense of depth and simulating outside views, enhanced feelings of well-being in space station mock-ups and Antarctic work stations.

Weightlessness is the source of many problems experienced in outer space and is a phenomenon for which human beings are especially unprepared. During weightlessness, fluids move to the upper part of the body, and congestion of inner ear canals is common. Weightlessness and reduced gravity lower cardiovascular activity, degrade reflexes and coordination, and atrophy muscles. All these effects severely hamper work performance (Canby, 1986; Levine, 1991; Money, 1981; Pogue, 1974). A rapid loss of body minerals makes bones fragile. The disruption to the organs that control balance in the inner ear causes severe space sickness called **space adaptation syndrome.** The syndrome, which can last for five days, is marked by a loss of appetite, queasy feeling in the stomach, and unexpected vomiting. Readjusting to earth's gravity also can be difficult, and occasionally results in unconsciousness (Chaikin, 1984; Money, 1981).

Fear that equipment might fail is a constant source of stress in space. Moreover, incessant machinery noise degrades perceptual abilities and contributes to fatigue and irritability (Coleman, in Levine, 1991; Levine, 1991). Alterations of consciousness also occur during spaceflight (Connors, Harrison, & Akins, 1986; Oberg & Oberg, 1986).

Other unsafe environments, particularly underwater habitats, pose similar challenges to designers of the environments of the future. For example, because of rapid pressure changes and different dosages of

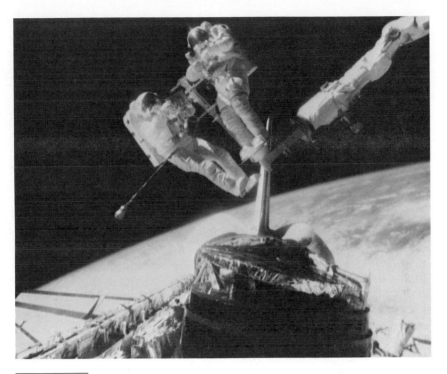

P H O T O   4-2 The ability of humans to work in outer space will become more important as missions to outer space become longer in the future.

oxygen, deep-sea diving can cause hazards that range from simple bruises and vertigo to burst lungs and fatal air embolisms (Bachrach, 1982; Lanphier, 1974).

Obviously, work performance in extreme environments will be affected by excessive stress, but the many successes of groups and individuals in isolated situations indicate that problem solving and good performance are certainly possible. Perhaps an individual's disposition is relevant; thus, people who view the environment as a challenge to be met may cope better and be more likely than others to interpret arousal as excitement rather than fear (Suedfeld, 1987). Other research indicates that more rigidly structured groups react more negatively than less structured groups under stressful environmental conditions, possibly because a rigid structure decreases the group's flexibility and inhibits its ability to cope with changing or unforeseen environmental conditions (Worchel & Shackelford, 1991).

Great care must be taken not to generalize from sensory deprivation studies performed in the laboratory or from research in polar stations or submarines to the problems of crews working in outer space. While there are similarities, space crews are competitively chosen individuals in a unique adventure that will advance their careers and bring great prestige and fame (Suedfeld, 1991a). These strong motivational factors may make spaceflight a qualitatively different experience. According to Suedfeld, studies must focus on the nature of the experience rather than on the nature of the physical environment alone.

Restricted Environmental Stimulation Technique (REST)

Laboratory studies of unusual environments concentrate on the effects of sensory deprivation. Traditionally, two major techniques have been used. In one, subjects lying on a bed were exposed to monotonous stimulation, such as white noise and constant lighting, or to reduced stimulation in silence and darkness. Another early technique involved immersing subjects in a tank of water where they breathed through a tube and had their vision and hearing impaired (Zubek, 1969).

For many years psychologists believed that water immersion was highly stressful, but apparently this was due to poor experimental procedures and popular but misleading anecdotal accounts of the experience (Suedfeld, Ballard, & Murphy, 1983). Now with improved techniques, immersion in water is seen as a generally relaxing, enjoyable, and pleasant experience; indeed, the use of commercial flotation tanks for relaxation is growing throughout North America. Suedfeld, Ballard, and Murphy (1983) describe the type of tank currently used: "Each tank is approximately four feet × eight feet with a ten inch deep solution of epsom salts in 93–94 degree (F) water. The cover of the tank opens easily from both the inside and the outside. With the cover closed, the tank is completely dark" (pp. 151–152). Unlike the earlier immersion method, subjects in these tanks float on their backs with their faces out of the water. This procedure is known as **REST,** short for **restricted environmental stimulation technique.** A "dry" flotation tank has also been developed. It is a similar chamber in which floaters lie on a waterbed mattress instead of floating in a solution. Dry floats are relaxing and pleasant, but so far the "wet" floats receive higher ratings, especially from female floaters (Forgays, Forgays, Pudvah, & Wright, 1991).

Although REST leads to increased arousal in some cases, floaters who receive a non-anxiety arousing orientation to it usually experience deep relaxation, a state that has been verified by physiological measures as well as self-report (Barabasz & Barabasz, 1985; Fine & Turner, 1982; Jacobs, Heilbronner, & Stanley, 1984; Stanley & Francis, 1984; Suedfeld, 1980; Turner & Fine, 1983, 1984). Flotation seems to relax everyone, but Forgays and Belinson (1986) report that the degree of relaxation depends on the gender and personality of the floater; all other things being equal, females find the experience more relaxing than do males. Suedfeld, Ballard, and Murphy (1983) found that floaters score higher on arousal seeking and consciousness of bodily sensation than most people and report a significant reduction in stress following flotation. While it is too early for any practical applications of REST to have surfaced, there are indications that it may facilitate creative thought and learning (Suedfeld, Metcalfe, & Bluck, 1987; Taylor, 1985).

THE SENSED PRESENCE IN EXTREME ENVIRONMENTS

One of the most fascinating aspects of human experience in extreme and unusual environments is the **sensed presence** of another being. People who have spent a long time in strange settings report a perception or feeling that another person is there to help them cope with some kind of hazardous situation. The vividness of the presence ranges from a vague feeling to a clearly perceived, seemingly flesh and blood entity. This entity might be a god, spirit, an ancestor, or someone personally known to the observer. Sensed presences usually appear in environments with little variation in physical and social stimulation; low temperature is also a common ingredient (Critchley, 1955; Suedfeld & Mocellin, 1987).

Possible explanations for a sensed presence include the motion of boats, atmospheric or geomagnetic activity, and altered sensations and states of consciousness induced by changes in brain chemistry that are triggered by stress, lack of oxygen, monotonous stimulation, or a buildup of hormones (Budzynski, 1985; Dubrov, 1978; Jaynes, 1976; Jilek, 1982; Joralemon, 1984; Lindsley, 1961; Lloyd, 1981; Sulman, 1980). Suedfeld (1980) and Suedfeld and Mocellin (1987) base their explanation on shifting attention from external, ambient stimuli to internal information, which most individuals are inexperienced at processing. Any of these factors may contribute to the experience of a sensed presence. At this time, psychologists do not know exactly why it occurs. Undoubtedly, an individual's personality, expectations, and cultural norms play a role.

Some of the most compelling descriptions of sensed presences come from lone sailors who also experience hallucinations and out-of-body experiences. In one famous incident, Joshua Slocum, the first person to circumnavigate the globe single-handedly, saw and spoke with the pilot of Columbus's *Pinta*. He claimed that the pilot steered his boat through heavy weather as Slocum lay ill with food poisoning. Many other startling, vivid examples of such apparitions reported by sailors, mountain climbers, and polar explorers are described by Suedfeld and Mocellin (1987).

The phenomenon of the sensed presence may account for religious experiences people have during times of stress. These episodes often occur after extended periods of meditation and internal reflection and may be facilitated by unusual and intense physical stimulation. Early religious figures such as Moses, Jesus, and Mohammed all reportedly met supernatural beings while wandering in the desert; indeed, fasting, prolonged meditation, and stimulation of the body through pain and fatigue are part and parcel of most religions (MacDermott, 1971; Suedfeld & Mocellin, 1987).

Many societies have included a period of isolation and unusual environmental stimulation as a rite of passage from adolescence to adulthood. The transcendental altering of consciousness is an important part of the experience, and physical hardship or torture are often important ingredients (Suedfeld & Mocellin, 1987). In this ritual, known as a "vision quest" or a "spirit quest," seekers hope to encounter a spirit or being that will provide them with guidance and advice. These spirit quests involve solitude in a harsh environment or intense sensory bombardment (for example, drumming, chanting, sweating, dancing) in a confined area. Both approaches to the quest include starvation, thirst, sleeplessness, and torture as means of further altering arousal levels (Jilek, 1974, 1982).

Many American Indian tribes constructed dwellings that functioned as the equivalent of modern sauna baths but were used for ritual sweat bathing. This is still practiced by some North American Indians, notably the Sioux. Weil (1977) described the ceremony: "Bathers sit unclothed on the ground around a pit filled with red-hot rocks taken from a bonfire; the sweat lodge is sealed from the outside, leaving the participants in darkness and increasing heat. The experience may be accompanied by chanting, praying, burning incense, or smoking. The medicine man in charge of the sweat periodically throws water on the glowing rocks. This creates an "explosive hiss and a wave of intense heat that envelops the body. It is possible to get first- or second-degree burns from this, but, curiously enough, one's mental state seems to be the most important determinant of the fate of one's skin" (pp. 44–45). Practitioners of sweat bathing report that burning occurs only when one loses contact with the "psychic energy" of the group and sees oneself as an isolated individual trying to defend oneself against the heat. In some tribes, the bathers are doused with icy water as they leave the sweat lodge. Sweat bathers report that at the end of the sweat session, they feel euphoric, purged of anxiety and depression, healthy, and full of energy. The "high" lasts for about an hour and gradually gives way to a relaxed feeling and a desire to rest.

Furst (1977) described another ritual, the **Mandan vision-seeking ordeal.** Variations of this ordeal were practiced by several tribes of Plains Indians at the end of the summer bison hunt. From most accounts, this ordeal could produce an intense consciousness-altering experience. Following a period of "hunger, thirst, and four consecutive sleepless nights, the participant had holes pierced by knives through the flesh of the shoulder and breast. Through these holes, he was suspended by skewers and thongs from the center pole of the great medicine lodge" (pp. 70–71); many of the vision-seeker's belongings were suspended from skewers passed through other parts of the body. In some cases, a heavy bison skull was attached to each arm and leg and the individual was spun in circles until he lost consciousness. After recovering, the vision seeker sacrificed the little finger of his left hand to the great spirit. The ordeal ended with a race around an alter with bison skulls and other weights dragging behind the vision seeker until he fell in a dead faint. According to Furst (1977), other cultures practice similar acts of self-mutilation and physical trauma to conjure up spirits or deified ancestors to give counsel or validate priestly or royal succession. While these ceremonies have little practical relevance in today's society, they testify to the long-standing human tradition of altering consciousness by manipulating bodily sensation and environmental load.

CHAPTER SUMMARY

Environmental stress occurs when the demands of the environment exceed an individual's capacity to cope with those demands. Stress has physical as well as psychological effects and can disrupt task performance.

Environmental stressors fall into one of four categories: cataclysmic events, stressful life events, daily hassles, and overstimulation by stressors in the ambient environment. This chapter focused on the stress that accompanies environmental disasters and on the stress experienced under conditions of extreme or unusual ambient stimulation.

The natural environment is the source of a great many hazards. Unfortunately, human beings tend to ignore these risks and try to deal with disasters after they occur, rather than preparing for them in advance. One of the serious aftereffects of environmental disasters is the long-term stress that can result in severe physical and psychological problems for the survivors of these events.

The study of human responses to extreme and unusual environments is in its infancy. This research focuses on the performance of small, isolated groups in underwater and polar environments as well as in outer space. Laboratory studies have employed a sensory deprivation technique called the restricted environmental stimulation technique (REST) to see how people respond to abnormally low levels of sensory information.

A unique subjective experience associated with unusual environments is the sensed presence phenomenon, wherein the observer reports that another person is present when, objectively speaking, this is not actually the case.

GLOSSARY

Acute Stress   Stress that is relatively brief.
Biosphere II   An enclosed ecosystem in Arizona currently being studied.
Bounded Rationality   The tendency to think unclearly about environmental hazards.

Chronic Stress   Stress that is recurrent or long lasting.

Eclipse Experience   The alteration of conscious experience felt by some people as they view a total eclipse of the sun.

Environmental Appraisal Inventory (EAI)   A paper-and-pencil measure of perceptions of environmental threat.

General Adaptation Syndrome (GAS)   Selye's (1956) description of the body's reaction to prolonged stress.

Intensive Environmental Hazard   A natural event that is brief, sudden, and unpredictable (for example, a tornado).

Life Change Units (LCUs)   Stress value assigned to individual events on the Life Events Scale.

Life Events Scale (LES)   A measure of stress resulting from events in one's life. Developed by Holmes and Rahe (1967), it is also known as the Social Readjustment Rating Scale (SRRS).

Mandan Vision-Seeking Ordeal   A traumatic, consciousness-altering ritual practiced by some tribes of North American Plains Indians.

Pervasive Environmental Hazards   Natural events that are widespread and long lasting (for example, drought).

Restricted Environmental Stimulation Technique (REST)   A laboratory sensory deprivation procedure.

Sensed Presence   The perception or feeling that another person or entity is present; the sensed presence occurs most frequently in isolated, harsh environments.

Space Adaptation Syndrome   Space sickness, marked by loss of appetite, a queasy feeling in the stomach, and sudden vomiting.

Stress   The emotional reaction that occurs when the demands of an environment do not mesh with the needs and coping abilities of the individuals in that setting.

Personal Space

5

Whenever you observe a group of people, it quickly becomes apparent that the spatial arrangement of the individuals in the group is not random. Where people position themselves reflects the status and friendship relationships within the group as well as the limitations the physical environment places on the group. Generally, we do not realize the importance of spatial behavior in our lives until something unusual happens to call it to our attention. For example, you may feel uncomfortable when other people sit too close to you in an otherwise empty movie theater, or you may find it unpleasant to deal with "pushy" people who stand too close, or cold, "standoffish" people who position themselves too far away during conversations. You certainly notice whenever a stranger or casual acquaintance touches you; this is often accompanied by a strong positive or negative emotional reaction. In all these cases, your feelings have been affected by the spatial behavior of others. Holahan (1982) noted that the language you and I use to describe our dealings with other people is full of spatial metaphors. We demand that

P H O T O S   5-1A and B Humans are just one of many species of animals exhibiting regular spacing in natural settings.

other people "get out of our face" or "off our back" before they "push us too far." We need "elbow room" so we don't feel "cornered." We need to "have our own space," although we don't want to feel "separated" from the people we are "close to." Extraverted people like to "rub shoulders" while introverts are "distant."

Our use of space is a way to communicate with others and an important determinant of our feelings about the people we encounter. Humans are not the only animals that have spatial needs (see Photos 5-1A and 5-1B), a fact that lion tamers and animal trainers have been aware of for quite some time (Hediger, 1950, 1955). However, it is human spatial behavior that greatly interests environmental psychologists, since human needs are a concern in environmental design.

In 1966, anthropologist Edward Hall published *The Hidden Dimension* and introduced **proxemics,** which he defined as the scientific study of human spatial behavior. In his book, Hall explored the meanings that people attach to the use of space and furnished the first reliable accounts of the spatial norms in many different cultures. According to Hall, interactions between people in the United States usually occur at one of four distances: intimate, personal, social, and public.

Intimate distance ranges from 0 to 18 inches. At this distance, the head and face are the only parts of another person that can be seen clearly; people interacting at this distance often receive additional sensory signals such as body heat and odors. This distance is reserved for highly intimate interactions and usually is not considered proper for adult Americans to use in public.

Personal distance extends from 18 inches to about 4 feet. At this distance, olfactory and fine visual cues begin to fade, and a person is more aware of cues from other parts of his or her partner's body. Touching is usually possible and it is a common distance for casual conversation between friends.

Social distance includes a zone ranging from 4 to 12 feet. The closer distances (4 to 7 feet) tend to be used by people who work

P H O T O S   5·2A, B, C, and D Hall's interaction distances for Americans.
Views of a person using intimate distance (A), personal distance (B), social distance (C), and public distance (D).

together and those conducting informal business. The longer social distances (7 to 12 feet) require raising the voice level and are reserved for more formal business and social interaction.

   Public distance (12 to 25 feet or more) is very formal. At this distance, evasive or defensive action can easily be taken, and it is used with strangers with whom no interaction is desired and as a sign of deference when approaching important public figures.

It should be noted that these distances were based on observations of white, middle-class adults. Hall himself points out that even within American society, other groups such as African Americans, Hispanic Americans, or Asian Americans may have very different standards. Hall's work was vitally important to the growth of cross-cultural research and was the major stimulus for the growing interest in human spatial behavior that occurred in the late 1960s and 1970s.

THE CONCEPT OF PERSONAL SPACE

Closely related to Hall's study of interaction distances is the concept of **personal space.** Personal space has been defined as the area around a person's body into which others may not intrude without arousing discomfort (Hayduk, 1983; Sommer, 1969). It is not a fixed geographical location; it moves with the individual and grows larger or smaller depending on the situation. It has often been described as a "bubble of space" that surrounds a person. Many researchers have tried to burst the bubble analogy because they feel that it leads to incorrect conclusions about the nature of personal space (Hayduk, 1983; Patterson, 1975; Winkelhake, 1975). Objections to the bubble analogy are that it is not a good way to describe the ease with which the size of personal space can change, and that the image of two bubbles bouncing off each other does not resemble what actually happens when people interact with each other. In a review of the literature, Aiello (1987) argues that even the name *personal space* is misleading and that perhaps it is better to talk about the distance between people without resorting to any specific labels. In spite of these criticisms, the term is still widely used and it is difficult to discuss human spatial behavior without using the language common to so many of the researchers in this area. Thus, the term *personal space* will be retained in this chapter.

In most cases the invasion of one's personal space by another person is an unpleasant, stressful experience. You probably have noticed yourself altering your behavior on many occasions to avoid invading the personal space of others and, at the same time, positioning yourself so that an invasion of your own space would be unlikely. Where you choose to stand or sit in public places like elevators, libraries, parks, and snack bars is often dictated by your attempts to maximize the distance between yourself and the other people using these areas. Research confirms that people avoid invading the personal spaces of others whenever possible (Barefoot, Hoople, & McClay, 1972; Reid & Novak, 1975; Sommer & Becker, 1969), and that touching, especially between opposite-sex strangers, is very carefully avoided (Anderson, Anderson, & Lustig, 1987). In the study by Barefoot, Hoople, and McClay (1972), the researchers placed a person at various distances from a water fountain in a busy corridor. Baseline data was gathered on the number of people who usually stopped at this fountain for a drink during the times that were studied. Barefoot and his colleagues found that the number of people stopping to drink at the water fountain dropped markedly in direct proportion to how close the confederate sat to the water fountain. When someone sat very close to it, relatively few people stopped to drink. Interestingly, those who did violate the confederate's space drank for significantly longer times than people who did not have to violate anyone's space to get a drink. Perhaps these people were especially thirsty (or at least tried to appear so!) if they were willing to invade someone's personal space to get a drink. Another interpretation of this research is that spatial invasions that occur in task-oriented situations, such as getting a drink, using a public telephone, or looking for a book on a library shelf, may be distracting and make the activity take longer than it would ordinarily (Ruback, 1987; Ruback, Pape, & Doriot, 1989). Another study (Thalhofer, 1980) found that it gets easier to invade space at a water fountain if the area is already crowded, perhaps because the invaders are paying less attention to others' social cues or possibly because they think the invasion will be less aversive under these circumstances.

Invasions of personal space often cause people to give up their place and go elsewhere (Barash, 1973; Felipe & Sommer, 1966; Sommer, 1969). And the evidence confirms that these spatial invasions increase the arousal levels of the people who are invaded. This evidence is based on studies using physiological measures of arousal such as palmar sweating (Dabbs, 1971) and changes in the electrical resistance of the skin (Aiello, Epstein, & Karlin, 1975; McBride, King, & James, 1965) as well as studies in which the subjects' behaviors, postures, and facial expressions clearly indicated heightened arousal levels (Efran & Cheyne, 1974; Konecni, Libuser, Morton, & Ebbeson, 1975; Smith & Knowles, 1979). For example, Konecni and his colleagues found that pedestrians crossed the street more quickly if their personal space was invaded while they were waiting for the light to change. In fact, some experiments on the relationship between arousal and invasions of personal space became notorious when psychologists began to study this problem by observing the behavior of people in public restrooms (Brandeis, 1972; Middlemist, Knowles, & Matter, 1976; Reid & Novak, 1975). This research was controversial because it raised the issue of the ethical responsibility of investigators who observe people in public without their knowledge or consent. These studies and the ensuing controversy are described in the box on page 106.

While there is widespread agreement that invasions of personal space are arousing, explanations differ for why this occurs. Some researchers feel that arousal is a reflexive, automatic response to spatial intrusion, while others believe that the arousal reflects the surprise we experience when our expectations about the behaviors of others are violated (Burgoon, 1978, 1983; Burgoon & Jones, 1976; Cappella & Greene, 1982; Hale & Burgoon, 1984; Patterson, 1982).

Functions of Personal Space

Given the intensity of our responses to invasions of our personal space, it is likely that the maintenance of a personal space served a number of adaptive functions for human beings throughout the history of our species. I will briefly describe a number of functions that may be important.

Self-protection   One apparent function of our "body-buffer zone" is to protect us from physical or emotional threat (Dosey & Meisels, 1969; Horowitz, Duff, & Stratton, 1964). With a larger personal space, an individual is better prepared to flee from physical danger or soften the impact of emotional threat. According to Evans and Howard (1973), personal space has evolved to control aggression and reduce stress, and much of the available data are consistent with this interpretation. For example, several studies show that people maintain greater interaction distances following insult or when receiving negative feedback about their performance on a task (Karabenick & Meisels, 1972; O'Neal, Brunault, Carifio, Froutuine, & Epstein, 1984). People also use larger interaction distances in potentially threatening situations such as when their sexual attractiveness or social competence is being assessed by others

---

Is Unobtrusive Observation Always Ethical?

Of all the studies of personal space, none have been more controversial than those that have studied people's behavior in public restrooms (Brandeis, 1972; Middlemist, Knowles, & Matter, 1976; Reid & Novak, 1975) The study by Middlemist and his colleagues in particular sparked outrage in some quarters over what many saw as a violation of ethical guidelines psychologists should follow in field research. In the Middlemist study, the subjects were men urinating in a public lavatory. During the course of the study, these men had their personal space invaded by a confederate, were spied on with a periscope that was cleverly concealed in a toilet stall, and had the duration of their urination timed by a confederate with a stopwatch. The experiment successfully demonstrated a relationship between invasions of personal space and physiological arousal, as urination onset and duration change predictably by increases in arousal level.

While the information gained from this study was undoubtedly valuable, many psy-chologists felt that the invasions of privacy were unjustified. They argued that when psychologists stoop to spying on people in such highly personal situations, they refuse to acknowledge the subjects' rights of privacy and treat them in ways that they would never treat people in other relationships.

The response to this positions is that any behaviors that occur in public places are open to public scrutiny, and the psychologist is only taking advantage of valuable information freely available to anyone who cares to observe. Also, to make any progress in understanding behavior in real environments, research must be done in real-life situations. In all field studies, the subjects' identity remains anonymous and the behavior of any particular person will never be made public. Thus, the argument is that the subjects' privacy is protected and no harm is done.

Consider your opinion on this issue: Do you think this kind of research is ethical or not?

(Brady & Walker, 1978; Dosey & Meisels, 1969). Edney, Walker, and Jordan (1976) believe that personal space reassures us of our ability to maintain control of social situations. Strube and Werner (1982, 1984) have confirmed that personal spaces are larger for individuals possessing a higher need for control and for individuals faced with the threat of control by another.

Along these same lines, Karabenick and Meisels (1972) report that people who generally are anxious in social situations or whose self-esteem is low also maintain greater interaction distances. A number of prison studies have found that men with a history of violent behavior (and who presumably frequently feel threatened by others) have much larger personal spaces than other people, especially behind them (Kinzel, 1970; Roger & Schalekamp, 1976). In one of these studies, Dabbs, Fuller, and Carr (1973) found that inmates had larger personal spaces than college students, but that both groups showed larger spaces when "cornered" than when they were in the center of a room.

Adjusting sensory input   People will often behave in ways to maintain an optimal level of stimulation, meaning a level that is neither too high nor too low. Yet another function of personal space may be to help individuals regulate the amount of sensory information that they receive from other people. Nesbitt and Steven (1974) explored this possibility in a study that they conducted at an amusement park in California. They enlisted the help of a young woman with dark hair to serve as the "stimulus person" for the experiment. She stood in lines for various rides and attractions while a photographer unobtrusively took pictures. Half the time she was a high-intensity stimulus person who wore brightly colored, shiny clothing and too much perfume. The rest of the time she wore conservative clothing and no perfume. After examining the photographs, the researchers determined that the other people in line stood further away from the high intensity stimulus person than they did from the low-intensity person. In a second study, they replicated the results with a male stimulus person. Thus, it appears that changing the size of our personal space may be one of many techniques we use when adjusting the amount of sensory stimulation we receive from our environment.

Communication and the regulation of intimacy   One tends to associate the word *intimacy* with positive, good feelings between people, but for psychologists, intimacy merely refers to the amount of involvement between individuals. By this definition, two people who are arguing or fighting are still considered to be intimately involved with each other (see Photos 5-3A and 5-3B). Personal space is one of the most important components of a system of nonverbal behaviors that is used to communicate and regulate the amount of intimacy in an interaction between two people. These behaviors have been called **immediacy behaviors** (Mehrabian, 1967, 1969b) and **involvement behaviors** (Patterson, 1987). In

P H O T O S   5-3A and B   Intimate nonverbal behaviors can be used to express both positive and negative feelings.

addition to interpersonal distance they include such things as smiling, eye contact, body orientation, posture, and touching. Perhaps the most influential theory of how these behaviors work is the **affiliative-conflict theory** proposed by Argyle and Dean (1965). They chose the term *affiliative-conflict* because they believed that every encounter between people involves both approach and avoidance tendencies. For instance, you might be drawn toward your partner to express liking or to get information, but you also might be held back by fear of being rejected or revealing too much about yourself. A comfortable level of intimacy will exist in the interaction when these two conflicting forces are balanced and an equilibrium point is reached. Over time, Argyle and Dean's theory has become known as **equilibrium theory.** Thus, at the beginning of each interaction there is a period of nonverbal instability during which each person tries to establish equilibrium. Once equilibrium is reached, any change on the part of one person will be compensated for by changes in the other person's nonverbal behaviors. For example, if Gary is speaking to Heather and he suddenly changes the intimacy level of the interaction by moving farther away from her, she would try to restore the previous level of comfort by moving after him, increasing the amount of eye contact, or making her body orientation more direct.

A good example of nonverbal behaviors used to regulate intimacy can be seen in people's behavior in crowded elevators (see the box on page 109). As an elevator becomes crowded, people must stand close together, often touching. Ordinarily, this closeness signals increased involvement and high levels of intimacy. However, since these people are strangers who do not desire intimate interaction, they adjust other nonverbal behaviors to compensate for the unwanted closeness. Everyone faces forward and avoids eye contact (usually by looking at the floor numbers displayed above the door). Postures are rigid, and everyone avoids touching as much as possible. If you have any doubt that these behaviors are important, try facing the "wrong way" in an elevator while leaning on the people near you, and watch the discomfort of your fellow passengers. (If you are brave enough to try this, be sure to note the intense discomfort you feel as you violate personal space norms.)

In studies testing the accuracy of Argyle and Dean's model, subjects interact with a stranger in a laboratory setting where one of the stranger's immediacy behaviors changes during a conversation. Argyle and Dean predict that this change will be compensated for by a change in the subject's nonverbal behaviors. Most of these studies support their prediction, with eye contact and interpersonal distance being the most frequently measured behaviors (Aiello & Jones, 1971; Argyle & Ingham, 1972; Baxter & Rozelle, 1975; Carr & Dabbs, 1974; Coutts & Ledden, 1977; Goldberg, Kiesler, & Collins, 1969; Patterson, Mullens, & Romano, 1971). Over time, equilibrium theory has become a generally accepted descriptive model.

While most of the research supports the equilibrium model, some studies have found that individuals reciprocate their partner's increased nonverbal intimacy rather than compensate for it, as Argyle and Dean predicted (Breed, 1972; Jourard & Friedman, 1970; Schneider & Hansvick, 1974). This problem, coupled with new information from subsequent research, has led to modifications of the theory (Aiello, Thompson, & Baum, 1981; Argyle & Cook, 1976) and the growth of completely different perspectives on the workings of nonverbal immediacy behaviors

---

TRY IT

The Ups and Downs of Elevator Behavior

Elevators provide a perfect opportunity to observe individuals' attempts to maximize the distance between themselves and the other people in the elevator. To see this firsthand, go to a building where elevator usage is heavy and spend some time riding and observing. Watch where the riders position themselves as they enter the elevator. Typically, the first four people (one of whom will be you!) will stand in the four corners of the elevator. The fifth person may choose the exact center of the car. After these obvious positions have been chosen, how might you predict where other people will stand? What characteristics of your fellow passengers might make them more or less vulnerable to a spatial invasion? Be sure to note the kinds of behaviors such as smiling and direction of gaze that emerge as the elevator becomes so crowded that interpersonal distances become uncomfortably close.

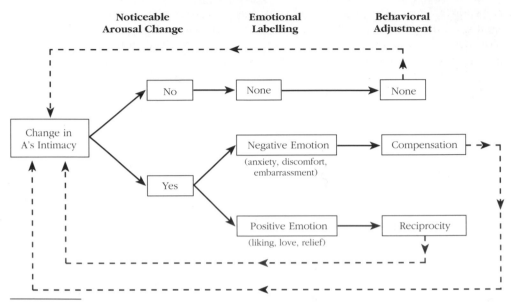

B's Reaction

FIGURE 5-1   Patterson's arousal model of interpersonal intimacy (Source: Patterson, 1976)

(Burgoon & Jones, 1976; Cappella & Greene, 1982; Markus-Kaplan & Kaplan, 1984; Patterson, 1976, 1982).

Patterson (1976) attempted to explain why reciprocation of nonverbal intimacy might sometimes occur. As you have seen, the arousal levels people experience are strongly affected by the nonverbal behaviors of those around them, especially interpersonal distance and gaze behaviors. However, Argyle and Dean's model fails to consider effects that changes in arousal levels might have on nonverbal behaviors. Patterson proposed that arousal change (and the evaluation of that change as positive or negative) experienced by the person in an interaction was the mediating agent in deciding how he or she would respond to the partner's behavior. According to Patterson's model, the intimacy changes reflected in the behaviors of person A in an interaction with person B resulted in arousal changes in B; person B's evaluation of this arousal change as pleasant or unpleasant was critical. If the arousal change was perceived as pleasant, B would recipro-cate the new intimacy level expressed by person A to maintain or enhance the pleasant arousal level. If the arousal change was unpleasant, person B would compensate for A's behavior by altering his or her distance or other behaviors to adjust the intimacy level more satisfactorily. Patterson's model is represented schematically in Figure 5-1.

Patterson's model makes sense intuitively and is in keeping with the general empirical evidence. However, it has not been tested comprehensively. Schaeffer and Patterson (1980) found that direct gaze by a male confederate produced strong negative reactions in male subjects when that confederate was perceived as being incompatible but not when he was seen as compatible. Similarly, a number of studies have demonstrated that increasing nonverbal intimacy increases favorable reactions to others in positive social contexts, but increases unfavorable reactions when the context of the interaction is negative (Ellsworth & Carlsmith, 1968; Ellsworth, Freedman, Perlick, & Hoyt, 1978; Kleinke & Pohlen, 1971; LeCompte & Rosenfeld, 1971; Schiffenbauer & Schiavo, 1976; Storms & Thomas, 1977). A few studies have attempted to relate affective reactions to the nonverbal behaviors of the subjects themselves, but they provide only weak or limited support for Patterson's model (Foot, Chapman, & Smith, 1977; McAndrew, Gold, Lenney, & Ryckman, 1984; Patterson, Jordan, Hogan, & Frerker, 1981).

While all aspects of personal space behavior are not completely understood yet, it is clear that personal space is involved in regulating our intimacy with other people and that it is important in regulating our affective reactions to others while controlling their response to us (Burgoon, 1985; Patterson, 1987).

Measurement of Personal Space

The crucial issue in any research on personal space is the way in which the investigator chooses to measure the personal space of individuals in the study. A wide variety of techniques have been used, but all of them can be lumped into one of three categories: simulation/projective measures, laboratory **stop-distance methods,** and **naturalistic observation.**

Simulation/projection measures   Simulation of social situations and projective techniques were the most popular ways to study personal space, especially during the early years of research. The earliest simulation techniques relied on the use of cloth silhouettes of adults, children, males, females and, occasionally, dogs or other figures that might be important in relationships (Kuethe, 1962a, 1962b, 1964; Little, 1965; Pederson, 1973). Subjects in simulation studies are asked to imagine that these figures represent real people and to place the figures in an appropriate spatial arrangement for the situation the experimenter describes. Presumably, the relative distances they maintain between the cloth figures reflect the distances found in real social situations. Over time, other projective measures that are paper-and-pencil tests were developed. One of the most popular is the **Comfortable Interpersonal Distance Scale (CID)** developed by Duke and Nowicki (1972) (see Figure 5-2). In this scale, respondents imagine that they are standing in the center of a room. They are told that another person is approaching them from one of eight

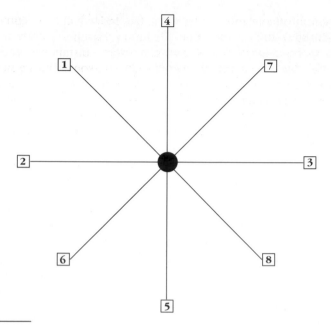

FIGURE 5·2 Duke and Nowicki's comfortable interpersonal distance scale
(Source: Duke & Nowicki, 1972)

directions indicated on a questionnaire. They mark the appropriate line
to indicate the point at which they would begin to feel uncomfortable
with the approacher's distance. This is repeated for each direction until
the subject's personal space is completely mapped out.

The reasons for the popularity of projective measures are apparent:
They are easy to administer and score, they are quick, and they are less
costly than other ways of measuring personal space. Some researchers
maintain that projective personal-space measures do in fact provide consistent, valid estimates of personal space (Knowles, 1980), and these
measures are still used in research (Gifford, 1982; Sanders, Hakky, &
Brizzolara, 1985). However, there is a growing sentiment among researchers that relying on such hypothetical situations is inadequate, and
that the reliabilities of the projective measures currently in use are not
good enough (Aiello, 1987; Hayduk, 1983; Love & Aiello, 1980; Sundstrom & Altman, 1976). Consequently, researchers' reliance on projective
measures to study personal space is declining.

Laboratory stop-distance methods The use of stop-distance measures in the laboratory has overcome some of the problems associated
with projective measures. In this kind of study, the subject is confronted
with an actual person and is asked to indicate the distance at which he or

she feels comfortable interacting with that individual. Sometimes, the subject stands still while the other person approaches, and the subject stops the approaching person when a comfortable distance is reached. In other studies, the subject approaches the other person and stops when the distance is comfortable. This is more realistic than simply manipulating cloth figures but is artificial to the extent that it does not represent a real social interaction. The method also has the same limitations as any laboratory study — the possibility of demand characteristics and uncertainty about how well the results can be generalized to the "real world." In spite of these problems, the technique remains popular and has been used in many studies (for example, Bailey, Hartnett, & Gibson, 1972; Hartnett, Bailey, & Gibson, 1970; Hayduk, 1981; Horowitz, Duff, & Stratton, 1964).

Naturalistic observation   Psychologists agree that the ideal is research conducted in situations that are as natural as possible, since these situations are ultimately what they want to understand. You will recall from Chapter 1, however, that field research is fraught with difficulties. Random assignment usually is not possible. Many ethical and logistical obstacles must be overcome, and measurements may not be as precise as those taken in the laboratory. Nevertheless, there is a strong tradition of field research in personal space studies. Usually the investigator videotapes or photographs people in natural settings and uses floor tiles, sidewalk blocks, or discreet grids made out of tape to measure the distances between the people observed. Field studies of personal space have been done in a wide variety of settings, including nursery schools (Smetana, Bridgeman, & Bridgeman, 1978), amusement parks (Nesbitt & Steven, 1974), beaches (Thomas, 1973), zoos (Baxter, 1970), discussion groups (Henrick, Giesen, & Coy, 1974), and city streets (Dabbs & Stokes, 1975; Heshka & Nelson, 1972; Jones, 1971).

The Shape of Personal Space

Considering the wide variety of techniques available to researchers, it is surprising that so little research has focused on the overall shape of personal space; most studies concentrate on face-to-face interaction distances. The shape of personal space, consistent with the "bubble" analogy, has traditionally been thought of as circular. This assumption has grown out of research that measures personal space only in one plane (usually around the head). It is more appropriate to think of personal space in three-dimensional terms, considering its vertical and horizontal components (Holahan, 1982). Preliminary research within this framework indicates that the size of personal space is different for different parts of the body, which results in an irregular cylindrical shape (Hayduk, 1981). The issue is complicated further by research indicating that variables such as an individual's gender also affects the shape of personal space (Fisher & Byrne, 1975; Harris, Luginbuhl, & Fishbein, 1978).

VARIABLES THAT INFLUENCE PERSONAL SPACE

Many variables have been shown to influence the size and shape of personal space. A brief description of some of the most important of these follows. In keeping with the growing skepticism of studies based on simulations or projective measures, in these summaries I have relied more heavily on research that uses other techniques.

Situational Factors

"Perhaps the best supported general proposition about personal space is that positive affect, friendships, and attraction are associated with close proximity" (Sundstrom & Altman, 1976, p. 50). Ordinarily, people report that they are more comfortable when a friend stands close to them than when a stranger does (Ashton, Shaw, & Worsham, 1980); in mixed-sex pairs, attraction is almost always associated with closer physical distance (Allgeier & Byrne, 1973; Byrne, 1971; Byrne, Ervin, & Lamberth, 1970). Other studies indicate that it is primarily the females in these couples who adjust their personal space to reflect attraction to their partners; the relationship between attraction and interaction distance also holds true in female-female pairs, but not in pairs of males (Edwards, 1972; Heshka & Nelson, 1972). Generally, anything that is associated with greater attraction between people (for example, similarity) is also associated with closer interaction distances. The affective relationship between individuals affects the size of their personal spaces, but the status relationship between them is also important. The higher status person in the relationship almost always owns, controls, and uses more space than the lower status individual (Henley, 1977; Sommer, 1969).

The actual structure of the physical space being used exerts a powerful influence on personal space. Fisher, Bell, and Baum (1984) summarized the effects that architecture has on spatial behavior by observing that human use of space usually reflects a bottom-line concern about safety: when we know that escape (if it should become necessary) is easy, you and I require less space than we would otherwise. Accordingly, we need more space while sitting than while standing (Altman & Vinsel, 1977), more space indoors than outdoors (Cochran, Hale, & Hissam, 1984; Little, 1965; Pempus, Sawaya, & Cooper, 1975), and more space when we are in a corner than when we are in the center of a room (Dabbs, Fuller, & Carr, 1973; Tennis & Dabbs, 1975). When ceilings are lower or rooms are smaller, people require more personal space (Cochran & Urbanczyk, 1982; Daves & Swaffer, 1971; Savinar, 1975; White, 1975). Baum, Reiss, and O'Hara (1974) found that the strategic use of partitions reduced feelings of spatial invasion and maximized the amount of comfortable space available in offices, waiting rooms, and other public places where crowding might be a problem.

Other factors are related to the use of personal space. If a person asks for a favor, it is more likely to be granted when a close interaction distance or touching occurs (Baron, 1978; Willis & Hamm, 1980). It has even been reported that people standing in line for a movie that contains a lot of explicit sex line up twice as densely as people waiting to see a family film (Sommer, 1969).

Age

Although there have been dozens of studies on developmental changes in the use of personal space, the results of these studies have been inconsistent. Thus, it is unclear exactly when children start using consistent spacing between themselves and others, but psychologists agree that children's personal space needs increase steadily with age (Burgess, 1983; Hayduk, 1983). Very young children play closer together and touch more than older children (Burgess, 1981). What *is* clear is that spatial norms very similar to those used by adults emerge about the time of puberty (Aiello & Aiello, 1974; Aiello & Cooper, 1979; Altman, 1975; Evans & Howard, 1973) and that sex differences appear fairly early, with girls using closer distances than boys (Guardo, 1976). Apparently, adults are aware of the instability of children's spatial behavior, since spatial invasions by children under age 10 rarely evoke negative responses (Dean, Willis, & LaRocco, 1976; Fry & Willis, 1971).

Although Heshka and Nelson (1972) indicate that elderly people may use smaller interpersonal distances than younger people do, there has been no other research on possible changes in the use of personal space after a person reaches adulthood.

Sex

A person's gender is a very important factor in determining his or her spatial behavior in most situations. Since sex interacts with so many other personal and situational variables, one must be cautious about making firm predictions about spatial behavior based on sex alone (Aiello, 1987; Hayduk, 1983). Traditionally, the common wisdom (supported by a great deal of empirical evidence) is that females use smaller interaction distances than males at all ages (Aiello & Jones, 1971; Lott & Sommer, 1967; Pellegrini & Empey, 1970; Sussman & Rosenfeld, 1982; Wittig & Skolnick, 1978). Males have a lower tolerance for distances that are too close (Aiello, 1987), and male invaders produce more distress and flight in people of both sexes than do female invaders (Ahmed, 1979; Bleda & Bleda, 1978; Krail & Leventhal, 1976; Murphy-Berman & Berman, 1978; Rüstemli, 1986). Given this information, it is not surprising that everyone approaches women more closely than men (Kassover, 1972; Long, Selby, & Calhoun, 1980).

Much of what is known about sex differences in spatial behavior has been acquired in field studies where a confederate of the experimenter invades the personal space of unsuspecting people in public places. These studies show many differences between male and female responses to spatial invasion. Fisher and Byrne (1975) invaded the space of college students studying at library tables and found that females were most disturbed by spatial invasion from the side, while males found invasions from the front most unsettling. Undoubtedly this is related in some way to the observation that males prefer face-to-face seating while females prefer side-to-side seating arrangements (Sommer, 1959). Fisher and Byrne concluded that males and females have differently shaped personal spaces. However, the issue is more complicated because many other factors operating in these situations affect the responses. For example, when the personal space of college students was invaded on campus benches, males left more quickly when the invader remained silent, and females left more quickly if the invader first asked permission to sit (Sundstrom & Sundstrom, 1977). Similarly, Harris, Luginbuhl, and Fishbein (1978) invaded the personal space of shoppers from behind on escalators in a mall. Regardless of the invader's sex, males were more likely to move and females were more likely to pretend that they did not notice the invasion.

A series of studies investigating reactions to spatial invasions in elevators have also come up with some interesting sex differences. In these studies, subjects enter an elevator that contains people and are put in a position where they are forced to invade someone else's personal space. Most people violate a female's space rather than a male's (Buchanan, Juhnke, & Goldman, 1976). In a series of three experiments, Buchanan, Goldman, and Juhnke (1977) found that females preferred to stand closer to other females who looked at them, but avoided males who gazed at them. Males, on the other hand, always preferred to invade the space of someone who did not look at them. Other studies confirm that when females are forced to invade another's space, they are more likely to choose someone who acts friendly by looking at them or smiling, but males are more likely to choose someone who pretends not to notice them (Hughes & Goldman, 1978; Lockard, McVittie, & Isaac, 1977).

The issue is complicated further by studies that indicate that a female's preferred interaction distance with males might depend on the interval in her menstrual cycle, with interpersonal distance probably being affected by fluctuations in discomfort, tension, and interest in sexual activity (O'Neal, Schultz, & Christenson, 1987; Sanders, 1978). A study by Lombardo (1986) indicated that not only a person's sex, but also his or her sex-role orientation (for example, how strongly that individual identifies with expected masculine or feminine roles) might also be important in regulating spatial behavior.

Racial, Cultural, and Ethnic Background

Hall's (1966) ground-breaking work on cultural differences in spatial behavior distinguishes between "Mediterranean cultures" and "North

European cultures" to describe spatial behavior. He admitted that these were very crude, fuzzy categories and that some cultures, particularly oriental societies, might not fit well into either group. According to Hall, Mediterranean cultures include Arabs, Southern Europeans, and Latin Americans. Individuals from these societies display a tremendous amount of intimacy through their spatial behaviors, using extremely close interaction distances and a great deal of touching and eye contact. North European cultures include North Americans and Northern European countries such as Germany and Great Britain. These societies have a norm of less nonverbal intimacy with others and prefer greater interaction distances and larger personal spaces in general. Hall points out the obvious problems that arise when people from different cultures interact without being aware of the other's spatial needs.

Hall's observations were carefully done and richly described, but they were not quantitative or experimental in the tradition familiar to most environmental psychologists. Follow-up research generally supports Hall's conclusions (Sommer, 1969; Watson & Graves, 1966), but this research is not extensive. Much of it is methodologically suspect and depends on using subjects residing away from their home countries (Aiello, 1987; Aiello & Thompson, 1980). Also, many cross-cultural studies of personal space (Forston & Larson, 1968; Little, 1968; Sander, Hakky, & Brizzolara, 1985) rely entirely on simulation and projective techniques. This is not to say that Hall's descriptions are inaccurate, but only that they have not been explored completely enough. Because so much of this research has been done in the United States, there may be more information available on differences among subcultures in this country than on differences between countries.

Studies frequently demonstrate that interaction distances between people of different racial groups are greater than distances between members of the same subgroups (Booraem, Flowers, Bodner, & Satterfied. 1977; Hendricks & Bootzin, 1976; Rosegrant & McCroskey, 1975; Willis, 1966). Hispanic-Americans appear to interact more closely than Anglo-Americans (Aiello & Jones, 1971; Ford & Graves, 1977; Pagan & Aiello, 1982), and it is clear that black Americans and white Americans have different spatial and nonverbal norms (Aiello & Thompson, 1980; LaFrance & Mayo, 1976). These subcultural differences may have important consequences. Garrett, Baxter, and Rozelle (1981) report a study in which white police officers were trained to use either black (somewhat larger) or white (somewhat smaller) interaction distances in a series of interviews conducted with black citizens. The black citizens strongly preferred the officers displaying "black" spacing behavior and judged them to be more personally, socially, and professionally competent. Scherer (1974) suggests that socioeconomic status can override subcultural distances. In a study of middle- and lower-class children, boys and girls from the same socioeconomic groups used the same distances, regardless of race.

CHAPTER SUMMARY

Proxemics is the scientific study of human spatial behavior. It was pioneered by anthropologist Edward T. Hall who provided the first scheme for describing the interaction distances people use in social interactions. Subsequent research on human spatial behavior has focused on the concept of personal space, which is the area around a person's body into which others may not intrude without arousing discomfort. Invasions of one's personal space by others is a stressful, arousing event that will often cause us to withdraw from an intruder.

Personal space serves many different functions. It serves as a buffer zone that protects us from physical and psychological threat, and it helps us adjust the intensity of the sensory input we receive from other people. It is also the primary mechanism we use to regulate the amount of intimacy we experience in our interactions with others.

Personal space has been measured in several ways. Some studies rely on projective paper-and-pencil measures; some on laboratory measures taken under artificial, controlled conditions; and some rely on the unobtrusive observation of behavior in natural situations. Currently, the trend in the field is moving in the direction of more naturalistic studies and away from using simulation and projective tests.

Many variables influence the size and shape of personal space, including the individual's age, sex, and cultural background, and also a number of interpersonal and architectural features.

GLOSSARY

Affiliative-Conflict Theory (Equilibrium Theory) A theory proposed by Argyle and Dean (1967) that describes how interpersonal distance and other nonverbal behaviors maintain the intimacy level of interactions between individuals.

Comfortable Interpersonal Distance Scale (CID) A popular paper-and-pencil measure of personal space developed by Duke and Nowicki (1972).

Immediacy Behaviors (Involvement Behaviors) Nonverbal behaviors that serve to regulate intimacy between individuals, including interpersonal distance, eye contact, touching, smiling, body orientation, and posture (Mehrabian, 1967, 1969b). Also known as involvement behaviors (Patterson, 1987).

Intimate Distance The distance reserved for highly intimate interactions (0 to 18 inches).

Naturalistic Observation The measurement or observation of behavior in a real-life setting.

Personal Distance The common distance for casual conversations between friends (18 inches to 4 feet).

Personal Space The area around a person's body into which others may not intrude without causing discomfort.

Proxemics The scientific study of human spatial behavior.

Public Distance The distance used by noninteracting strangers and with important public figures (12 to 25 feet and beyond).

Social Distance   The distance used for formal business and social interactions (4 to 12 feet).

Stop-Distance Method   A laboratory technique for measuring personal space.

Territoriality

6

Distortions in some popular treatments of territoriality (Ardrey, 1966) have led many people to think of territorial behavior as something bad that causes conflict and aggression. In fact, exactly the opposite is true. Imagine, if you can, a society with no system of territorial behavior in which every person has equal access to every location. Strangers could wander freely into your bedroom and bathroom, evict you from seats in public places, and drive your car whenever they chose. Fences would not exist, burglary would not be a crime, and locksmiths would become an endangered species. You would have no legal right to inherit your parent's possessions, and there would be no sure way to locate people you wanted to find. In short, such a society would be chaotic, unworkable, and unable to survive.

Unlike personal space, which moves with the person and expands and contracts according to the situation, a territory is a fixed geographical location. Territoriality refers to those behaviors a person uses to exert control over the activities that occur in that space. Researchers have proposed over a dozen definitions of territoriality, all differing in the emphasis they place on observable behaviors such as territorial marking and defense (Becker, 1973; Sommer, 1969) as opposed to more affective or cognitive reactions to space that are less directly observable (Altman, 1975; Brower, 1980; Malmberg, 1980). While all the definitions are useful, a definition similar to one Sack (1983) proposed comes closest to the way the term will be used in this chapter: Territoriality refers to the attempt to influence or control another's actions through enforcing control over a geographic area and the objects in it.

Territoriality and Privacy

The concept of privacy is closely related to the concepts of personal space and territoriality. In fact, these ideas are so intimately linked that it is sometimes impossible to say which is the most inclusive (Taylor & Ferguson, 1980). Like personal space and territoriality, privacy helps us manage our social interactions to maintain order and avoid conflict with others. Insufficient opportunities for privacy have been linked to antisocial behavior and aggression in a variety of settings, including prisons (Glaser, 1964) and naval ships (Heffron, 1972).

Privacy is commonly thought of as being away from other people, but Altman's (1975) definition captures more precisely the spirit of the term as it is used by environmental psychologists: **Privacy** is the selective control of access to the self or to one's group. Therefore, privacy is not just shutting others out. It is a boundary control process through which individuals control who they interact with, and how and when these interactions occur. Maintaining some degree of control over interactions with others is crucial to most people's psychological well-being. Different mechanisms are used toward this end. In North America, the physical environment is manipulated with doors, windows, separate rooms, and other architectural props being the primary means of regulating privacy. Miller and Schlitt (1985) offer an excellent summary of the relationship between privacy and the physical environment. (The problem of privacy is central to many of the design concerns discussed in subsequent chapters on built environments.) Nonverbal communication and the observance of social customs (for example, not calling your psychology professor after midnight) are important supplements to environmental regulators of privacy. People are more likely to pursue privacy aggressively and ask unwanted others to leave them alone when such cues in the physical or social environment clearly support the legitimacy of their claim to privacy (Haggard & Werner, 1990).

Westin (1967) describes four different states of privacy that individuals must regulate at one time or another. **Solitude** refers to the commonplace notion of privacy—the opportunity to separate oneself from others and be free from observation. However, other forms of privacy are also quite important. **Intimacy** is the freedom to be alone with others such as friends, spouses, or lovers without interference from unwanted others. **Anonymity** describes the freedom to be in public but still be free from identification or surveillance by others. Anonymity is the kind of privacy that public figures such as movie stars, politicians, and professional athletes find increasingly difficult to achieve. A fourth type of privacy, **reserve,** occurs when the individual's need to limit communication about himself or herself is protected by the cooperation of those around them.

According to Westin (1967), privacy serves a number of functions. It is necessary for intimate communication with other people, and it allows us to maintain a sense of control, autonomy, and self-identity in our lives. It also allows for an emotional release that might be inappropriate under nonprivate circumstances. Lewis (1961) provides a touching and extremely insightful portrait of what life can be like with too little privacy in *The Children of Sanchez.* The book describes the lives of low-income Mexican families who live with as many as nine or ten family members in a single room, where simple functions such as getting dressed or using the toilet become a struggle against a daily routine dictated by the needs of others.

Many things affect our perceptions of the amount of privacy we have. Personal characteristics such as age, sex, and cultural background undoubtedly play a part, as do our privacy experiences while growing up and our expectations about the privacy to which we are entitled (Marshall, 1972; Smith, 1982; Walden, Nelson, & Smith, 1981). Privacy is difficult to measure empirically. Several questionnaire measures of privacy have been developed (Westin, 1967; Marshall, 1972; Pedersen, 1982), but these have not become sophisticated enough to be very useful in applied settings.

Societies vary tremendously in the degree of privacy they allow and in their assumptions about the amount of privacy individuals need. Hall (1966) explores these differences in his description of North European and Mediterranean cultures. According to Hall, Germany represents one extreme of the privacy continuum. In Germany, visual and auditory privacy is extremely important, and office doors are rarely left open as they are in the United States. It is considered rude to look into rooms or to move furniture even slightly. In Mediterranean cultures, on the other hand, there is little visual or auditory privacy in public, and eye and body contact with strangers is frequent. In fact, there is not even an Arabic word for privacy!

Even though privacy norms differ from place to place, all societies have developed social conventions that permit individuals to control access to themselves in some way. This is true even in societies that appear to allow very little opportunity for individual privacy, such as Gypsies (Yoors, 1967) and the Pygmies of Zaire (Turnbull, 1961). One

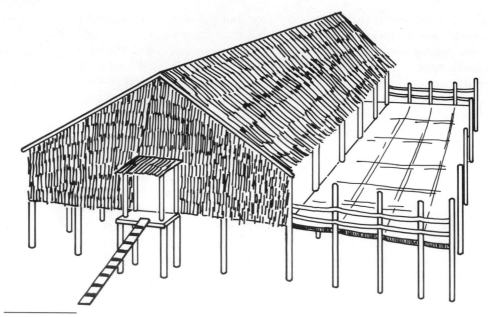

F I G U R E   6·1   An Iban longhouse (Source: Patterson & Chiswick, 1981)

such society is the Iban people of Indonesia and Malaysia studied by Patterson and Chiswick (1981). The Iban live in elevated communal structures called longhouses (see Figure 6-1), structures that range from about 20 yards long that are occupied by as few as three families, to 300-yard-long buildings that accommodate more than 40 families. A typical family consists of parents, four or five children, and a grandparent or two. The longhouse has a thatched roof and a large open porch that runs the entire length of the building. Each family occupies a single rectangular room (approximately 20 feet by 15 feet) that serves as a kitchen, bed-room, and living area. Each room opens onto a common gallery area that is semipublic, as is the open porch. These living arrangements result in high density, no auditory privacy (thin partitions between rooms readily transmit noise), and little visual privacy since many activities occur in the public gallery and porch areas.

The high level of social contact in the longhouse permits little privacy in the Western sense of the word, but the Iban have adopted norms that help to compensate for this. Whenever possible, relatives occupy adjoin-ing rooms. There is a rigid division of labor according to traditional sex roles (the men farm and fish; the women cook, keep house, and look after children), and there is great freedom to disassociate one's self from family or to dissolve friendships without negative sanctions. It is considered impolite to ask personal questions of strangers, and criticizing or disciplining other people's children is forbidden. At night, public areas become semiprivate and individuals do not wander freely throughout the longhouse as they do in the daytime. The headman of the longhouse mediates disputes and has the power to impose fines for the violation of norms. Each Iban family is a self-contained unit that is economically independent of its neighbors. Within the family, norms about changing clothing and sex-segregated sleeping arrangements for unmarried people over the age of 12 afford some degree of privacy.

Privacy and the integrity of personal space are crucial to the lives of individuals, and territoriality is the primary mechanism that ensures that these are protected. It is hard to overstate the importance of territorial behavior in the day-to-day organization of our lives. In fact, territoriality serves a vital function in the organization of social behavior throughout the animal kingdom, and much has been learned about territoriality by studying animal behavior.

TERRITORIAL BEHAVIOR IN ANIMALS

Origins of Animal Territoriality

Some animals such as impalas, ants, and redwing blackbirds are so intensely territorial that their entire social organization revolves around territories. Other animals (for example, mice) are more flexible in their territorial needs and are able to adopt other ways of organizing their social world when conditions preclude the efficient defense of territories. While there is agreement that territorial behavior is widespread throughout the animal kingdom, scientists still disagree about how much of this behavior can be thought of as biologically based instinct.

The first scientists to study animal territoriality seriously were ethologists who took an explicitly evolutionary approach to their work (Lorenz, 1966; Wilson, 1975; Wynne-Edwards, 1962). These researchers invariably describe territorial behavior as being shaped by evolutionary forces, appearing in its current form as a function of the selection pressures faced by the species throughout its evolutionary history. Thus, animals inherit a predisposition to behave territorially because individual animals who did so in the past survived and reproduced more successfully than animals who did not. This position is much more controversial for environmental psychologists because they still cannot agree on the origins of territoriality. Taylor (1988) is comfortable with the evolutionary perspective on the development of territoriality in humans as well as animals, while Brown (1987) argues that animal territorial behaviors are extremely flexible and based on learning and that the notion of a "territorial instinct" is too simpleminded to be acceptable.

The position taken here will be similar to that taken by sociobiologists such as Wilson (1975) and Barash (1982): Territoriality is a system of social behaviors that evolved because it has been adaptive. Individual members of territorial species may vary in the strength of their genetic predisposition to behave in a territorial fashion, but all members of the species share a biological basis for these behaviors.

Functions of Animal Territoriality

While maintaining and defending a territory costs an animal time and energy, there are very clear advantages to a well-defined system of territories for individuals and for the species as a whole. For example, by clearly marking the boundaries of their territories and signalling their presence to other members of their species, animals minimize the number of encounters that might result in fighting. Howler monkeys and songbirds continually advertise their location with vocalizations that carry over great distances, giving themselves ample opportunity to avoid confrontation. Wolves and many other carnivores urinate and defecate at key locations on the perimeter of their territories, and bears stretch to their full length to scrape the bark off trees, conveying information about the size of the territory holder as well as the boundaries of the territory.

When confrontations do occur, territorial systems provide other safeguards against the serious injuries that can result from fighting. Perhaps the most important of these is a phenomenon known as the **prior-residence effect.** This occurs when animals in their home territory display dominance over intruders in that territory. If you have ever observed a small dog chase a much larger one from its yard, you have witnessed this phenomenon. Whether the animal is a robin or a dog, there is a definite advantage inherent in being on one's own turf. A chicken is more likely to peck a strange bird in its home cage than in the stranger's cage (Rajecki, Nerenz, Freedenburg, & McCarthy, 1979), and a fish in a familiar aquarium invariably assumes dominance over other fish that are introduced later (Figler & Evensen, 1979). When two members of a species of territorial fish are introduced simultaneously into an aquarium, each will take over some portion of the tank as its own territory. Apparently there is an easily recognized territorial boundary between the two areas (easily recognized by the fish at least) because when a fish strays into its partner's space it is immediately attacked and chased across the boundary. However, during the chase, the attacker often goes too far, suddenly finding itself in the other fish's territory. At this point, the fishes change directions; the formerly fleeing fish becomes the attacker, and the chase goes back and forth until the two fish finally settle face-to-face on either side of the boundary line, "glowering" at each other, each secure and dominant in its own territory. Thus, territoriality does not increase aggressiveness, but actually decreases conflict by keeping animals from running into each other unexpectedly and also by giving such a clear advantage to the animal in its home territory that serious fighting seldom occurs. Recent research lends support to the notion that the prior-residence effect may also occur in humans. For a description of this research, see the box below.

The only time that territorial behavior seems to be associated with increased aggression is in those animal species that have a lek system of territoriality in which aggressive encounters between males for possession of territories is a prelude to mating (Davies, 1982; Gould, 1982). A **lek** is the location where the males gather to compete for territories. While many animals exhibit this form of territorial behavior, antelopes of

---

The Prior-Residence Effect in Human Beings

There is long-standing evidence that animals in their home territories have an advantage in confrontations with other animals, but only recently have psychologists confirmed that this may also be true for humans.

Research consistently shows a relationship between the length of time people have occupied a space and the degree to which they feel ownership and control of it, which leads to greater feelings of security and dominance. Subjects in experiments on the prior residence effect are often undergraduate students engaged in a task or conversation in their own or someone else's room. In their own rooms subjects almost always feel more relaxed, are more successful on tasks, and dominate the conversation more than those visiting the room (Conroy & Sundstrom, 1977; Martindale, 1971). Taylor and Lanni (1981) discovered that residents who were normally low in dominance even tended to dominate discussions among three people if they occurred in their own rooms. Harris and McAndrew (1986) found that people could resist signing offensive petitions better when approached in their own rooms than when they were approached somewhere else. Finally, Taylor (1988) has noted that even in the story

of Peter Pan, the only place where Wendy was able to resist Peter's suggestions was in her own room.

Many studies show that home teams have a distinct advantage over the visitors in competition. This is especially true for indoor team sports like basketball (Greer, 1983; Schwartz & Barsky, 1977; Silva & Andrew, 1987). A recent study of the results of over 2,000 high school wrestling matches indicates that this also happens in individual sports (McAndrew, 1992). While the strength of this home advantage depends to some extent on factors such as the length of time the visiting team has been travelling (Courneya & Carron, 1991), the effect is clearly due to the fact that one of the teams is playing in a familiar setting. Athletes have more intense feelings of control and dominance when playing in front of a supportive crowd. However, when the pressure to win becomes extreme, as it does in a championship game, playing in front of one's own fans actually may hurt performance. Teams play more poorly at home during the championships than during the regular season (Baumeister & Steinhilber, 1984; Heaton & Sigall, 1989).

P H O T O S   8-1A, B, and C   The Uganda kob on the lek

the African plains, such as the Uganda kob, provide the best example of how this system operates. Just before the females begin their estrous cycle, the males leave the bachelor herds they live in the rest of the year and gather at traditional communal display grounds (the lek). The males then begin highly ritualized fighting as they attempt to stake out and defend territories, which are usually small bare areas of ground seldom more than several meters in diameter. The fighting that occurs for these territories involves much horn locking, pushing, and noise but rarely results in serious injury to either of the combatants. The winners stand victoriously in their territories, while the losers either leave the lek or move on to challenge other animals. The females visit the leks to mate, and they gravitate toward the males who hold the central territories on the lek. Thus, only males who have a territory will have any contact with females, and the males with the most desirable central territories will have the greatest number of opportunities to mate. This system ensures that the healthiest, strongest males will mate most often, and the highly ritualized rules of fighting ensure that few injuries or deaths occur. This system also helps to preserve the young, inexperienced animals for future mating (Alcock, 1984).

Aside from its role in decreasing aggression and regulating mating, territoriality provides other benefits for animals. It may spread animals out so food supplies and other resources do not become overloaded; it helps localize waste disposal; and it reduces the rate of spread of disease.

HUMAN TERRITORIAL BEHAVIOR

While many political scientists might disagree, Taylor (1988) asserts that human territorial behavior can only be discussed meaningfully in relation to individuals and small groups, and not on a larger scale such as nations. This is especially true if it is discussed within an evolutionary framework, which presupposes that human territoriality as it exists today has been shaped by biological and cultural evolution over millions of years. This approach does not demand that we think of human territorial behavior as being completely fixed, inflexible, and biologically determined, but only that we have an innate tendency to exhibit territorial behavior in some form because it has proven beneficial in the past. A more detailed discussion of the evolutionary origins of human territoriality can be found in Malmberg (1980) and King (1976a, 1976b).

Different cultures vary widely in the types of privacy/territory problems they face, and therefore the specific forms that territoriality takes in humans living in different societies may be quite dissimilar. Nevertheless, all societies have some way of recognizing boundaries, punishing transgressors, and negotiating territorial rights. This has been true throughout human history.

The ancient Greeks and Romans were extremely sensitive to the boundaries separating private properties. In fact, the Romans had a deity named Terminus who was the god of land boundaries. **Termini stones** had his likeness carved on them and were used to separate fields and define ownership boundaries. Those who tampered with these stones were punished harshly according to religious as well as civil laws. For example, farmers in ancient Rome who plowed under a Terminus stone were burned alive along with their plow animals (Stilgoe, 1976). In Western cultures, annual ceremonies were often held to serve as reminders of the location of town and private property lines. These ceremonies eventually gave way to fences, surveys, and land filings. Some of our current holidays, especially Halloween, are thought to be remnants of these early pagan and medieval boundary customs. In fact, some think the jack-o'-lantern is "the ghost of a long-ago remover of landmarks forever doomed to haunt boundary lines" (Stilgoe, 1976, p. 14).

Today, many of our most popular spectator sports reflect this strong human territorial orientation. Football, soccer, basketball, and hockey all require the successful defense of a primary territory (the goal) against invasions by the opponents. The language used to describe the action in these sports (for example, possession, stealing, control, offsides, neutral zone, and, in football, "territory") makes the sports–territory metaphor explicit. Even in baseball, teams battle for control of the basepaths, with the most important area of the diamond referred to as "home."

Given this brief background on the early roots of human territorial behavior, let us examine the way that it operates today.

P H O T O   6·2 The jack-o'-lantern represents the ghost of those who tampered with territorial markers, forever doomed to haunt boundary lines.

The Functions of Human Territories

One of the major functions of territorial behavior for humans is the preservation and regulation of privacy. Having a place where the individual can regulate privacy and exert control over other activities seems to be an essential part of healthy, normal functioning for most people. The inability to maintain such a place can result in stress and other problems (Lyman & Scott, 1967). In most societies, being "homeless" is one of the greatest misfortunes a person can experience, and it immediately places that person at the bottom of society's status hierarchy. The ability to recognize certain objects and places as "belonging" to one's self is an important stage in the social development of every child (Furby, 1978), and there is evidence that one's attachment to territories intensifies with age (Rowles, 1980). Research consistently shows that people develop a sense of "ownership" over certain places where their activities regularly occur, and that these feelings of territoriality increase with the amount of time the person spends in that place. Sommer (1969) reported that when a person seated at a snack-bar table for 5 minutes was approached by a stranger and asked to move, he or she always did so, often with an apology. However, when people were approached after being seated for 25 minutes, they invariably refused to move. Similarly, Edney (1972) conducted a study to see if there were any differences between people who displayed aggressively **territorial markers** at their homes and those who did not. These aggressive markers might include signs (for example, No Trespassing, Beware of Dog), fences, or other warnings. He found that people who displayed aggressively defensive territorial markers had lived in their homes longer than homeowners who did not display such aggressive territorial behavior, that they planned on living there longer in the future, and that they even answered the doorbell significantly faster!

Given the importance of territories for exerting control in our lives, it is not surprising that psychologists have found that people quickly move to personalize and preserve space for themselves in a variety of settings. Several studies on people dining in restaurants showed that diners touch objects more when there is a need to establish territorial ownership, and that these touches serve no other apparent purpose (Taylor & Brooks, 1980; Truscott, Parmelee, & Werner, 1977). Specifically, these studies found that a person was more likely to touch a plate in a territorial fashion when it was being claimed from another person, when the plate was full rather than empty, and when the diner was a stranger to the restaurant and did not already feel a sense of control in that setting. In a series of similar studies, Werner, Brown, and Damron (1981) found that this same kind of touching behavior is used to claim machines in a video-game arcade, and that the touches are especially lengthy and obvious after an intrusion or the threat of an intrusion by another person.

Territories also allow people to manage and communicate their sense of personal identity. The **personalization of territories** is probably even more important when that territory is going to be a long-standing part of a person's life. When a person moves into a new office, house, or apartment, among the first things unpacked and displayed are highly personal possessions or decorations associated with the permanent places in that person's life. There is evidence that this personalization of territories may sometimes predict other aspects of a person's behavior. Hansen and Altman (1976) conducted a study that showed that the amount and the kinds of room decorations used were actually related to the likelihood that a university student would stay in school! They visited newly enrolled first-year students at the University of Utah during the second week of the autumn quarter and photographed the walls above students' beds. The volume of decorated space was measured, and seven categories of personalization were examined. These categories reflected decorations related to personal relationships; political, religious, or philosophical values; areas of personal interest; reference items; entertainment; or abstract/artistic decorations. The researchers found that students who left school by the end of the year were less likely to decorate their walls than students who stayed in school; those who left covered less space with the decorations they did use and were much more likely to use decorations that reflected a strong connection with their personal lives away from the university. Pictures of boyfriends or girlfriends back home, family pictures, or

P H O T O   6·3 The decorations used in dormitory rooms often reflect the interests of the student as well as how strongly committed that person is to the college environment.

clippings from hometown newspapers are items that fell into this category. A follow-up study at the same university failed to find that the amount of decorated space was related to staying in school, but it did confirm that dropouts showed less diversity and commitment to the university setting with their decorations than "stayins" did (Vinsel, Brown, Altman, & Foss, 1980).

Werner, Altman, Oxley, and Haggard (1985) proposed that decorating the outside of one's home might be a way to increase contact with neighbors and deepen attachment to the neighborhood. Brown and Werner (1985) confirmed that Halloween decorations on a home do indeed predict the number of social contacts homeowners have in the neighborhood and how strongly attached to the neighborhood they feel. These decorations not only increase neighborhood cohesiveness but also may serve as cues to elicit visits from neighbors. In a similar study Werner, Peterson-Lewis, and Brown (1989) found that college students could make accurate judgments about the sociability of homeowners based partly on the nature of the Christmas decorations displayed on their homes.

Greenbaum and Greenbaum (1981) determined that homeowners personalize their residences with markers more than renters do. Brown (1987) noted that the very act of personalizing one's territory may increase feelings of attachment to that territory, and the personalization

P H O T O S   8-4A, B, and C   The style and decoration of a house reflect the lifestyle and personality of its owner. What differences might you expect to find among the owners of each of these homes?

also may foster impressions of one's self in others that may or may not be accurate. A series of studies by Cherulnik and his colleagues clearly demonstrate that people are judged by the places in which they live and work, which makes the personalization of home and work territories a valuable strategy for making good impressions on other people. Cherulnik and Souders (1984) asked college students to make judgments about the traits and occupations of the residents of 24 different neighborhoods depicted in slides of street scenes. Not only did these students agree about the probable occupations of each neighborhood's residents, but they also often agreed on the personality traits of the residents. For example, residents of lower-status neighborhoods were often described as gullible, irresponsible, and lazy. In another study, people photographed in upper-middle-class residential neighborhoods were judged to have more desirable traits and more prestigious occupations than the same people shown in a lower middle-class setting (Cherulnik & Bayless, 1986). Other studies confirm that subjects make similar judgments about people based on individual houses as well as neighborhoods (Nasar, 1989; Sadalla, Vershure, & Burroughs, 1987); the standards that are used to judge the status of homeowners appear to be quite consistent over time as subjects accurately judged the socioeconomic status of the original owners of houses built in Boston 100 years ago (Cherulnik & Wilderman, 1986).

As with animals, territoriality also plays a crucial role in the organization of human social systems. Without coherent ownership, occupancy, and control over various spaces, human interaction would be chaotic. Territories are used to support and clarify social roles, to regulate interactions, and to minimize conflict. Clear, unambiguous territories have been found to decrease aggressive behavior in groups of retarded boys (O'Neill & Paluck, 1973), juvenile delinquents (Sundstrom & Altman, 1974), and street gangs (Ley & Cybriwsky, 1974). Research on pairs of sailors living in small, isolated rooms found that the pairs who established clear territories during the first day or two of the study performed better while working, showed less stress, and were able to endure isolation longer. Less territorial pairs were disorganized and could not tolerate isolation as long (Altman & Haythorn, 1967; Altman, Taylor, & Wheeler, 1971).

Types of Human Territories

Altman (1975) provides a very useful way to distinguish among different types of human territories. Territories differ according to how important they are in the lives of their owners; some territories are much more central than others. Centrality refers to the amount of security and control that an individual experiences in a territory. Altman proposes that most human territories fall into one of three categories: primary, secondary, and public territories.

Primary territories   Places in which the owners feel they have complete control over access and use most of the time are **primary territories**. They include homes, offices, or bedrooms that are central to the lives of their users. Primary territories are owned and used exclusively by one individual or group and are clearly recognized as primary by other people. The law recognizes primary territories as such, and usually it is considered justifiable to use force in defending them.

Primary territories such as homes are often complex combinations of "mini-territories" controlled by different individuals. Sebba and Churchman (1983) interviewed 185 adults and children in a middle-class neigh-

---

TRY IT!

How Territorial Is Your Family?

Most of the day-to-day behaviors that maintain smooth territorial functioning in a home go unnoticed by family members. Think about the norms that have developed in your own family and compile a list of behaviors that might be considered "territorial." Here is a series of questions to help you think territorially; however, these are only a beginning. You will probably be surprised at the length of the list you can generate.

1. Do the members of your family lock the bathroom door?
2. Do people sit in the same chairs at the table for every meal?
3. Do family members knock before entering each other's rooms?
4. Does your family close bedroom doors at night when they are sleeping?
5. Are there any special rooms at home (for example, a den, an office, a workshop) that are used only by one individual?
6. Is there a chair that "belongs" to one individual in the living room or TV room?
7. Does anyone in your family have his or her own telephone or television?

borhood in Haifa, Israel. These interviews revealed that individuals within each family fully agreed to territorial classifications inside the home. Some areas such as living rooms, hallways, and bathrooms were public areas that were not controlled by any one family member. Bedrooms and studies, on the other hand, were individual areas that were considered to belong to one person (or more if the bedroom was shared); usually the "owners" of these areas felt very strongly that these places represented them and were places where "nobody disturbs you." Interestingly, everyone used kitchens but usually the family classified them as belonging to the mother since she was responsible for all that took place there. Other studies confirm that the territorial division of the home reflects the activity patterns of family members, and these patterns are affected by other factors such as the employment status of the mother (Ahrentzen, Levine, & Michelson, 1989). To help you think about territoriality in your own family, try it (see box How Territorial Is Your Family?).

Secondary territories   Less psychologically central to the lives of their users, less exclusive, and less under the occupants' control than primary territories, **secondary territories** have a blend of public availability

TRY IT!

8. Do people freely use each other's possessions (for example, bicycles, stereos, clothing) or must you ask permission first?
9. Does your family share hairbrushes or combs?
10. Is it acceptable in your family to eat food from someone else's plate or to drink from their glass?
11. When there is a dispute over which television program to watch, how is it resolved?
12. Does the same person do the outdoor and indoor cooking?
13. If you have a garden, does everyone in the family have equal responsibility in caring for it?
14. Are visitors to your home entertained in a different area from that usually used by the family?
15. Do the adults in the family have equal control over what decorations are used in the home?
16. When the family travels together by automobile, does the same person always drive?

and private control and serve as a bridge betweenprimary and public territories. Examples of secondary territories include a neighborhood bar, the street in front of a person's home, or seating areas in a cafeteria or lounge. Because they are usually more difficult for outsiders to identify, the potential for misunderstanding and conflict over the use of secondary territories is great. For several years, my family and I lived in an apartment in a college dormitory where we served as dormitory directors. This building was our home, and in the summer we were the only people living there. Just inside the front door of the building between two staircases was a space large enough to store two bicycles. We quickly adopted this space as a secondary territory and regularly kept our bicycles there. When the students returned in the fall, however, they took the space as soon as we moved our bikes for even a brief time. Since we had enjoyed exclusive daily use of the space for so long, we had developed a sense of ownership over the space and felt violated and angry whenever someone else took it away. Knowing, however, that from the students' point of view this was a public area that we had no more right to than anyone else, we usually kept our discontent to ourselves. Disagreements over secondary territories are especially likely to occur when these areas are not under frequent surveillance, when they are difficult to personalize, and when they do not appear to be owned. These areas lack what Newman (1972) called **defensible space,** and we will see in later chapters that the lack of defensible space can result in very serious problems for the residents of some neighborhoods and buildings.

Public territories   Places that are available to anyone on a temporary, short-term basis — provided they do not violate the rules associated with their use — are **public territories**. Common sites for public territories include telephone booths, tennis courts, space on public beaches, or seats in libraries, parks, or shopping malls. Individuals use these territories for brief periods of time to achieve some short-term goal. They are not central to their users' lives, and they are not associated with the same feelings of ownership and control that are typical of primary and secondary territories. If a public territory is used repeatedly by the same person, eventually it may function more as a secondary than as a public territory (Cotterell, 1991). On university campuses, students often choose the same seats in a library or the same shower stalls in a dormitory, and if they find someone else using them and are forced to go elsewhere, students experience a bit of discomfort. In classrooms, students tend to sit in the same seats day after day even when they are not assigned by the instructor; if students are unable to use the same seat, they usually will sit as near to it as possible. Even so, most of the times we use public spaces, they fit the description of a public territory better than any other type.

The research evidence to date indicates that Altman's distinctions between these three types of territories is valid, since people do in fact exhibit greater control in primary territories than in secondary and public

P H O T O   8·5 Territorial marking is an effective way of reserving space in public places.

territories. Subjects in studies report that they experience greater feelings of control in more central territories (Edney, 1975; Taylor & Stough, 1978), and while in their own home territories they exhibit more dominance behaviors than visitors in their territory do (Conroy & Sundstrom, 1977; Taylor & Lanni, 1981). In a study by Harris and McAndrew (1986), college students were asked to sign a petition. Half were asked to sign an inoffensive petition about which most students held no firm opinion (increasing the number of hours per week that leaf burning would be permitted in the city where the college was located). The other half were asked to sign a petition requesting an increase in the number of required courses at the college. (Needless to say, this petition was quite unpopular.) Students were better able to resist signing the unpleasant petition if approached in their dormitory rooms than if they were approached in the library or while walking on campus. For the neutral petition, no differences in the rate at which students signed were found between locations since, in this case, students did not need to resist or attempt to exert control over the situation.

Territorial Marking and Defense

An important part of human territorial behavior is territory marking. Brown (1987) points out that primary territories are often marked in ways that reflect the values and personal characteristics of their owners, while secondary and public territories are more often marked in a

P H O T O   6·6   Graffiti is frequently used as a territorial marker by gangs.

straightforward, conscious, claiming of space. Becker (1973) investigated the way people use markers to reserve territories in public places. People use almost anything available, so that suitcases and coats might be used in a bus station, while books are used in a library. In all locations, territorial markers that are clearly personal possessions are more effective than objects that might be mistaken for litter or public property. Psychologists who studied territorial behavior on beaches found that blankets, radios, and other beach gear are the markers of choice in that setting (Edney & Jordan-Edney, 1974; Jason, Reichler, & Rucker, 1981).

Territorial markers create an effective warning system that allows people to avoid confrontations with others over public space. These markers are almost always respected by other individuals. Sommer and Becker (1969) found that the effectiveness of territorial markers varies with population pressure; that is, when the demand for a space is high, personal markers such as clothing are even more effective than less personal markers. A study of a territorial marker's effectiveness at reserving tables in a tavern indicated that under conditions of high demand, male territorial markers (coats clearly belonging to males) may be more effective than female markers (Shaffer & Sadowski, 1975).

While it is clear that people often mark their public territories, they usually will not defend these territories when they are invaded. Sommer and Becker (1969) found that neighbors would not defend a marked public territory if it was invaded during its owner's absence; Becker and Mayo (1971) discovered that even the territory's owners failed to defend their seats in a college cafeteria when they were taken by an intruder.

McAndrew, Ryckman, Horr, and Solomon (1978) found that territory holders failed to reassert their claims even when the intruder was not physically present. In this study, subjects returned to their seats in a library to find their markers pushed aside and replaced by someone else's belongings. Not a single person ever sat back down in his or her seat. These results are surprising, especially since everyone questioned in a preliminary survey said that they would definitely reclaim their space under these circumstances.

Only a few studies have found any significant defense of public territories by either occupants or neighbors. In one such study conducted at a racetrack (Aronson, 1976), 63 percent of the people sitting next to a seat that was invaded during its owner's absence confronted the invader and defended the territorial rights of the original occupant. You should note, however, that the majority of these "good neighbors" were friends or relatives of the territory holder. Another study indicated that the territory's value to the holder is an important determinant of whether it will be defended. Taylor and Brooks (1980) found that only 50 percent of those who left a marker on a library table asked intruders to move following an invasion, but 100 percent of those discovering an intruder in a previously marked library carrel did so.

Residential Burglary: When Primary Territories Are Invaded

For obvious reasons, most of the experimental studies of territorial invasion have examined public territories. However, a recent series of field studies is beginning to add important data on what happens when an individual's home is burglarized—a clear violation of a primary territory. Brown and Altman (1983) examined the territorial displays of 306 burglarized houses and compared them to nonburglarized houses. They found that certain kinds of territorial displays were much more likely to exist in nonburglarized homes than in homes that had been robbed. These included actual and symbolic boundaries such as fences, walls, alarm systems, and territorial borders. A visible owner's name and address on the property was effective as was other important evidence of the homeowner's presence, such as parked cars, toys in the yard, or yard sprinklers operating. Nonburglarized houses were more visible from neighboring houses, especially those that were immediately nearby. In contrast, burglarized houses were more likely to resemble public territories, show no traces of people's presence, and were visually more secluded. Based on this information, the sketches in Figures 6-2A and 6-2B illustrate the prototypical burglarized and nonburglarized homes.

MacDonald and Gifford (1989) asked 43 convicted male burglars to evaluate photographs of 50 single-family dwellings as potential targets for a burglary. The burglars confirmed that houses easily surveilled were the least vulnerable targets, and that visibility from a road was especially

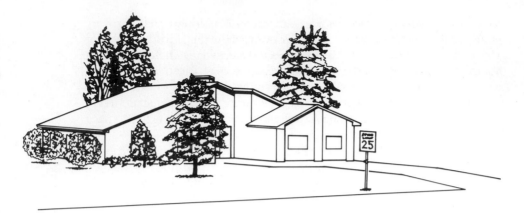

FIGURE   6-2A   Prototypical burglarized home (Source: Brown, 1979)

important. On the other hand, the burglars did not feel that homeowners' territorial behavior decreased vulnerability, and the use of symbolic barriers actually seemed to encourage these men to consider the house as a target for a robbery. MacDonald and Gifford surmised that the burglars often assume that occupants who take care of their house's exterior probably possess goods that make the house a profitable target.

A few studies have focused on the homeowners' reactions to a burglary. The emotional impact goes far beyond the amount of monetary loss the homeowner experiences. Most burglary victims express deep feelings of shock, victimization, disorder, and defilement. Many compare it to rape, highlighting the central importance of primary territories in their lives (Korosec-Serfaty & Bolitt, 1986). These effects linger after the burglary and can result in permanent fears of entering or being in the home alone (Waller & Okihiro, 1978). Brown and Harris (1989) found that these negative reactions become even more extreme when property damage and ransacking accompany the burglary, or when goods high in sentimental as well as monetary value are taken. Ransacking and the loss of very personal objects underscore the victim's loss of territorial control, making the experience even more unsettling.

CHAPTER SUMMARY

Territoriality refers to influencing or controlling another's actions through enforcing control over a geographic area. Territorial behavior is widespread throughout the animal kingdom, and in many species it is the basis of mating and of social organization in general.

Privacy is closely related to the concepts of personal space and territoriality. It is the selective control of access to the self or to one's group. Privacy is the process through which individuals control who they interact with and when and how these interactions will take place. Westin

F I G U R E   6-2B   Prototypical nonburglarized home (Source: Brown, 1979)

(1967) described four different states of privacy: solitude, intimacy, anonymity, and reserve. Each of these aspects of privacy is important in its own right; too little privacy can seriously impair a person's sense of well-being and his or her ability to function effectively. Although different societies have different privacy needs and norms, all have developed social conventions that permit individuals to control access to themselves in some way.

Territoriality serves to reduce conflict and contributes to the smooth regulation of social interaction. Humans personalize their territories to increase feelings of ownership and advertise this ownership to others.

Altman (1975) provides a scheme for distinguishing among different types of territories. Primary territories are places in which the owners feel they have complete control most of the time, as in their own home. Secondary territories are less central in the lives of their users and less under their control but are still important. They have a blend of public availability and private control. Public territories are available to anyone for temporary, short-term use. Research clearly supports the idea that people experience greater feelings of security and control in more central, primary territories. The invasion of a primary territory, as in a home burglary, is an extremely unsettling, highly emotional experience. The invasion of public territory seems much less aversive, since most people do not even defend their public territories when they are invaded.

GLOSSARY

Anonymity   A form of privacy in which the individual can appear in public and be free from identification or surveillance by others.

Defensible Space   An area that readily lends itself to territorial control.

Intimacy   A form of privacy in which an individual is free to be alone with friends, spouses, or lovers without interference from unwanted others.

Lek   A communal display area used by many species of animals. Males compete for small territories on the lek, which are necessary for attracting females and mating.

Personalization of Territory   Decorating a territory to increase feelings of ownership and advertise this ownership to others.

Primary Territories   Places that are central to the lives of their owners and in which the owner has complete control over access and use most of the time.

Prior-Residence Effect   The advantage enjoyed by the owner of a territory over visitors or intruders in that territory.

Privacy   Selective control of access to the self or to one's group.

Public Territories   Public areas that are available to anyone on a temporary, short-term basis.

Reserve   The form of privacy in which the individual's need to limit communication about himself or herself is protected by the cooperation of others.

Secondary Territories   Less psychologically central than primary territories and less exclusive, these have a blend of public availability and private control.

Solitude   The opportunity to separate one's self from others and be free from observation.

Termini Stones   Stones with the carved likeness of the god Terminus used by the ancient Romans to separate fields and define territorial boundaries.

Territorial Defense   The active attempt to reassert territorial control following an invasion.

Territorial Markers   Items used to indicate that a space is controlled by an individual or group.

Crowding

7

In the last two chapters I examined human spatial behavior and how territoriality, privacy, and personal space all meet important human needs and facilitate smooth interactions among the members of social groups. In this chapter, I will discuss what happens when these safeguards break down and crowding occurs.

I will begin by defining two terms that are often used interchangeably but actually refer to two different things: density and crowding (Saegert, 1973; Stokols, 1972). **Density** is an objective measure of the number of people per unit space, and it can be specified precisely. When discussing density, one must carefully describe what measures of density are being used. For example, density might be discussed meaningfully as the number of persons per nation, per square mile, or per room. It might be described in more architectural terms as in the number of rooms per housing unit or the number of housing units within each structure or acre. Many researchers have distinguished between these different measures of density by referring to "inside" and "outside" density (Galle,

Gove, & McPherson, 1972; Jacobs, 1961; Zlutnick & Altman, 1972). The measure that seems most strongly related to interpersonal relations and the one showing the strongest effects on behavior is density defined by the number of persons per room (Galle, Gove, & McPherson, 1972).

There are two basic forms of density that can be manipulated experimentally: social density and spatial density (Baum & Valins, 1977; Paulus, 1980). **Social density** is changed by having different numbers of people occupy the same physical space, while **spatial density** changes when the same number of people occupy physical spaces of different sizes. The distinction between the two types of density is important, as one increases the number of people one must deal with and the other does not. Also, they have been shown to have different effects on feelings and behavior depending upon the situation in which the density changes occur (Baum & Koman, 1976; Baum & Valins, 1979; McGrew, 1970; Paulus, 1980, 1988; Stokols, 1976).

While density refers to an objective physical state, **crowding** is a subjective, psychological state that results in negative feelings. Crowding occurs when an individual perceives that there are too many people in a given space. Of course, many things affect the perception of crowding, including the personalities and relationships of the people involved and situational factors such as heat, noise, odor, and the tasks to be performed in that environment. Nevertheless, density is probably the most influential factor in determining the extent to which people will feel crowded.

Crowding has been defined as a negative, unpleasant state, and the folklore on human crowding has almost always been consistent with this definition. There are many famous incidents of human crowding. One of the most notorious occurred in "the black hole of Calcutta" in 1756 (Ashcraft & Scheflen, 1976). Fort William, a British settlement in Calcutta, was captured by forces led by Siraj-ud-daula. One hundred forty-six prisoners were forced into the fort's 18-by-14.10-foot guardroom where they were held overnight. In the morning, only 23 were alive. Many less celebrated and less extreme tales of crowding also point to the negative consequences of high density on humans. For example, Ashcraft and Scheflen (1976) report a firsthand account of crowding on an American troop transport train during World War II:

> The trip should have taken no more than two hours. . . . Unfortunately that particular trip took sixteen hours. For some unexplained bureaucratic reason the train was held up at one siding after another. No food was provided, as it was meant to be a short trip. By the end of the third hour, water supplies had also been exhausted.
>
> Gradually joking ceased and tempers flared. Arguments became more frequent and the normal GI complaining took a more seriously bitter tone. The almost continual tactile contact often became unbearable, and what had been joked about a few hours previously occasionally erupted into a fist fight. Some soldiers were resourceful. . . . Others withdrew into themselves

and one fellow went berserk, attempting to jump from the train while it was moving. Obviously, some adapted to the prolonged crowding and others did not [p. 90].

In spite of these colorful examples and the common wisdom, it is increasingly accepted that although high density often has negative consequences for human beings, this is not always the case (Choi, Mirjafari, & Weaver, 1976; Ditton, Fedler, & Graefe, 1983; Freedman, 1975; Westover, 1989).

THE EFFECTS OF HIGH DENSITY ON ANIMALS

There is little question that prolonged periods of high-density living can result in strong negative consequences for many species of animals, and it appears that the number of animals in the group is more important than the amount of space available for each animal (Baum & Paulus, 1987; Freedman, 1979). Thus in animals, changing social density triggers more powerful effects than changing spatial density. These effects are physiological, behavioral, and affective in nature, as animals in groups are consistently less emotional, more active, and have larger adrenal glands than animals who are alone (Freedman, 1975). These effects occur for a number of different reasons: The animals face increased competition for vital resources such as space and food; the increased density leads to a greater interference with goal-directed activity; and there is more frequent and intimate exposure to various stimuli that might trigger disruptive behavior.

Physiological Consequences of High Density

High-density living has a severe impact on the health of animals. Research on the physiological effects of high density on animals was done by Christian and his colleagues (Christian, 1955, 1963; Christian & Davis, 1964; Christian, Flyger, & Davis, 1960). Christian believed that the increased stimulation and stress created by the presence of too many animals causes a steady secretion of hormones by the adrenal gland; he also believed that these prolonged periods of stress could result in physiological breakdown and death. In one of his studies (Christian, Flyger, & Davis, 1960) a herd of sika deer was allowed to reproduce unchecked on an isolated island in Chesapeake Bay off the coast of Maryland. The animals were free from predators and provided with an ample supply of food and water. The population grew until it became very large; then it suddenly crashed. Great numbers of animals became ill and died. Autopsies revealed that these animals did indeed have greatly enlarged adrenal glands and other indicators of stress. This phenomenon of population growth followed by a crash has been noted by wildlife biologists in other species as well.

Many other studies confirm that high density is associated with organ damage among animals (Myers, Hale, Mykytowycz, & Hughes, 1971). In rodents, fertility declines dramatically under conditions of high density, and the size and activity of the reproductive organs change when animals are in large groups (Christian, 1955; Davis & Meyer, 1973; Massey & Vandenburgh, 1980; Snyder, 1968; Southwick & Bland, 1959; Thiessen, 1964). Heimstra and McFarling (1978) report that amphetamine was found to be much more lethal when administered to mice kept in groups than when it was given to isolated animals. High density also caused increases in blood pressure readings in animals (Henry, Meehan, & Stephens, 1967; Henry, Stephens, Axelrod, & Mueller, 1971). Research has even shown that pregnant rats who experience crowding give birth to offspring who exhibit disrupted emotional and sexual behavior (Chapman, Masterpasqua, & Lore, 1976).

Behavioral Consequences of High Density

Often more visible than the physiological effects of high density is the disruption of behavior that is observed. The most common discovery is that high density dramatically increases the amount of fighting and aggressive behavior, and this effect has been noted in an impressive variety of species. Some species that exhibit more aggression under high-density conditions include monkeys, fruit flies, cats, hermit crabs, hogs, chickens, wolf spiders, gerbils, dragonflies, and the dreaded Allegheny woodrat (Anderson, Erwin, Flynn, Lewis, & Erwin, 1977; Aspey, 1977; Hazlett, 1968; Hodosh, Ringo, & McAndrew, 1979; Hull, Langan, & Rosselli, 1973; Kinsey, 1976; Moore, 1987; Moss, 1978; Polley, Craig, & Bhagwhat, 1974; Southwick, 1967). High density also may disrupt more "cognitive" behaviors such as learning and task performance (Goeckner, Greenough, & Maier, 1974; Goeckner, Greenough, & Mead, 1973).

Early studies of how high density affects the social behavior of animals were conducted by Calhoun (1957, 1962, 1973). He began his research by observing the behavior of wild rats enclosed in an outdoor quarter-acre pen. As in Christian's study of deer, Calhoun's rats were protected from predators and given unlimited access to food, water, and other resources. Despite these luxuries, during almost three years of observation the population of rats never grew beyond 150 animals. Puzzled by this, Calhoun decided to pursue the problem under more controlled conditions. In follow-up experiments, he studied six different populations of albino rats for 16 months each in a 10-by-14-foot observation room. The room was divided into four equal-sized pens, each containing a drinking fountain, a food hopper, and an elevated artificial burrow containing five nest boxes. A window in the ceiling of the room permitted observation. Figure 7-1 is a sketch of the observation room. The only major difference among the pens was that two of them (pens 1 and 4) were accessible by only one ramp from an adjoining pen. Pens 2

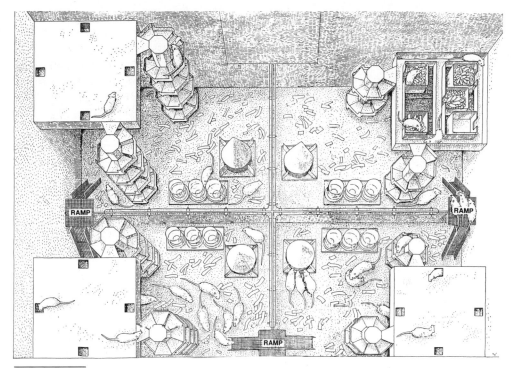

F I G U R E   7·1   Observation room used in Calhoun's studies of crowding in rats (Source: Calhoun, 1962)

and 3, on the other hand, had two different ramps that could be used as entrances or exits, giving the rats easy access to the pen from two other locations. Any rat travelling between pens 1 and 4 was forced to go through both pen 2 and pen 3.

Under ordinary circumstances, male rats assemble a harem of females for mating. The harem tends to stay within a territory guarded by the male. Males mate only with females in their own harem, and females resist attempts by other males to mate with them. In Calhoun's study, this is exactly what happened in pens 1 and 4. A relatively small population of rats came under the protection of a dominant male. The dominant male easily maintained control of his pen and prevented other males from entering by way of the one available ramp, even sleeping at the base of the ramp to discourage intruders. The females in these groups usually made good mothers, and survival rates in pens 1 and 4 were very good.

The situation in pens 2 and 3 was quite different. Since these pens had two means of access, it was impossible for any male to establish dominance and keep intruders out. This resulted in very crowded conditions and a complete breakdown of the normal behaviors of the males and females in these pens. Females no longer built adequate nests, and maternal behavior was completely disrupted. In one of the populations, 96 percent of the pups died before they were weaned. Infants were often abandoned or eaten by the adults. Females in heat were pursued relentlessly by packs of males, and many of them died during pregnancy or when giving birth. Many males developed strange behavior patterns including homosexuality, hyperactivity, or heightened levels of aggression. The disruption of social behavior in pens 2 and 3 was most likely to occur if feeding was arranged to encourage the animals to eat in groups.

Calhoun referred to the extremely disorganized, crowded pens as a **behavioral sink.** A behavioral sink forms when a population distributes itself unevenly, causing population densities in some areas to exceed the capacity of that species to maintain normal social organization. Calhoun's term quickly caught on, and for a while it was used freely to describe human conditions which bore a superficial resemblance to the rats studied by Calhoun.

This brings us to an important question: How much can we generalize from the density studies of animals to human beings? The tendency to do this was very strong in the 1960s and early 1970s, since much was known about the bad effects of crowding on animals and very little direct research on humans had yet been done. As data on the effects of high density on humans began to accumulate, however, it became clear that the relationship is much more complicated for humans than it is for most other animals. Freedman (1979) noted that early researchers on human crowding were overly influenced by dramatic animal studies such as Calhoun's that showed negative consequences and that they tended to ignore other less eye-catching studies indicating that high density may not *always* be harmful to animals. Furthermore, Freedman and others (Baron & Needel, 1980; Baum & Paulus, 1987) propose that even if the relationship between density and negative consequences was consistent in animals, there are many reasons it may not be true for human beings. These include the importance of learning, cognitive processes, and cultural factors in determining spacing requirements and the greater complexity and flexibility of human social interaction. In short, the consensus now is that while animal studies have been extremely useful, their results cannot be applied in a direct and simple way to humans.

THE EFFECTS OF HIGH DENSITY ON HUMANS

Studies of Short-Term Crowding

Research on long-term crowding usually examines the responses of humans in naturally occurring populations living under high-density conditions for prolonged periods of time; ordinarily, these studies are correlational in nature. Before discussing the effects of long-term exposure to high density, I will examine the results of research on the effects of short-term crowding.

Studies of short-term crowding are more likely to be experiments than correlational studies. Typically, the researcher randomly assigns subjects to one of two or more experimental conditions that differ according to the spatial or social density of the setting in which the experiment takes place. The session may be as short as 30 minutes or as long as several hours. Obviously, the brevity of the experiment and the artificial nature of the situation limit the extent to which the results of these studies can be generalized to the problems of people who experience chronic crowding in real environments. Nevertheless, these experiments are valuable because they are the only valid way to "tease out" many of the demographic and situational variables that are hopelessly confounded in most field studies of long-term crowding. Also, a greater variety of different independent and dependent variables can be studied using experimental techniques. The most common dependent variables in experiments on short-term crowding are affective and emotional responses, task performance, and social behaviors such as aggression, helping behavior, and interpersonal attraction.

Experiments on short-term crowding can be conducted in both laboratory and field settings. A good example of a laboratory study on the effects of short-term exposure to high density is one by Mathews, Paulus, and Baron (1979). Their goal was to determine what effects density has on aggressive behavior in situations where subjects would be either competing or cooperating with each other. The subjects in this experiment were male introductory psychology students. They were randomly assigned to either a high-density (four people in a 2.0-by-1.7-meter room) or low-density (four people in a 3.9-by-3.4 meter room) group in which they attempted to complete a very complicated task requiring them to trace through 12 horizontal mazes connected by correct and incorrect vertical alleys. In half the groups, students competed with the other subjects in their group, while in the other half, the students worked together, believing that their group was in competition with other groups. When this was completed, they were told that the second part of the experiment concerned the effects of punishment on physiological responses. The subjects' task in this part of the study was to distract a confederate who was trying to learn a list of nonsense syllables. The subjects were to distract the individual by administering electric shock. (No shock was actually given; subjects only believed that it was.) The intensity and duration of the shocks administered by the subjects were the dependent variables.

In this case, the investigators found that high density actually reduced aggression under competitive conditions. While these results appear to be at odds with some other studies we will discuss, they are consistent with recent research indicating that crowding under competitive conditions leads to withdrawal rather than aggression (Baum &

Valins, 1977; Loo, 1978). Density had no effect on aggression in the cooperating subjects. Mathews, Paulus, and Baron also found that giving the subject a 30-minute break between the first and second part of the study eliminated any crowding effects. They suggested that the results of laboratory crowding studies can be generalized best to short-term crowding experiences such as those that occur on elevators and buses.

Saegert, Mackintosh, and West (1975) conducted two studies that are excellent examples of research on short-term crowding effects in a field setting. The goal in both studies was to investigate the effects of density on a person's ability to efficiently perform tasks that require attentiveness and clear thinking. In the first study, the subjects were female students randomly assigned to participate during periods of high or low density in the shoe department of a mid-Manhattan department store. Each subject focused her attention on the shoes and customers in the shoe department. Afterwards, subjects were asked to describe the different shoes and also the people they had observed. While subjects in the low-density condition provided slightly better descriptions, the striking effect of density showed in their ability to recall other things on which they had not specifically focused their attention. When quizzed later, the women in the high-density group had much poorer memory for incidental items in the shoe department such as furniture and display stands, and they produced much less detailed and accurate cognitive maps of the area. These findings are consistent with the narrowing of attention that occurs in stressful or arousing situations and indicates that the higher arousal levels associated with high density may be responsible.

Their second study was conducted at the Pennsylvania Railroad Station in New York City. The subjects were males and females from various age groups and occupational backgrounds recruited through advertisements. All were relatively unfamiliar with Penn Station. Each was given a list of 42 cognitive tasks to complete during a period of high or low density in the station. The tasks were simple, inconspicuous activities such as locating the ticket counter, looking up a phone number, or buying something at a newsstand. Everyone had to complete the tasks in the same order. Subjects in the high-density group experienced more anxiety and completed fewer tasks than low-density subjects did. Interestingly, males in the high-density group reported more extreme emotions (for example, aggression, elation) than females.

The tradition of studying short-term crowding in the laboratory or field has provided most of the information researchers now have about the effects of density on humans. Although there are some exceptions, instances of short-term exposure to high density are more likely to have negative than positive effects. Increasing density, especially social density, definitely increases levels of physiological arousal (Aiello, Epstein, & Karlin, 1975; Evans, 1979; Saegert, 1978; Singer, Lundberg, & Frankenhaeuser, 1978), and this arousal is often interpreted negatively by the people who experience it. Short-term exposure to high density can also produce negative aftereffects, as people who have recently experienced crowding show a decreased ability to tolerate frustration (Dooley, 1975; Sherrod, 1974).

High density is even more offensive if other people are touching you (Nicosia, Hyman, Karlin, Epstein, & Aiello, 1979). Not surprisingly, subjects in small rooms feel more crowded, confined, uncomfortable, and perceive the room as being hotter and stuffier than subjects placed in large rooms; students in crowded classrooms are more likely to complain about ventilation, room size, and the class they are taking (Stokols, Rall, Pinner, & Schopler, 1973). Simply *expecting* to experience high density causes individuals to cut back involvement with others and to withdraw from interaction (Baum & Greenberg, 1975; Baum & Koman, 1976). Griffit and Veitch (1971) showed that high density caused their subjects to be in worse moods and to dislike strangers more than subjects who experienced low density; the effects of high density became even more pronounced if the room temperature was hot.

Many studies of short-term crowding have been conducted with children. Density may have no effect on aggressive behavior in children when resources are abundant (Loo & Smetana, 1978; Rohe & Patterson, 1974), but in most cases high density has been associated with disruptive and aggressive behavior (Ginsburg, Pollman, Wauson, & Hope, 1977; Hutt & Vaizey, 1966; McGrew, 1972). Loo and Kennelly (1979), in a field study of 5-year-olds, confirmed that high density increased aggression and that it also was associated with more self-reported distress and less playing with toys. Furthermore, they found that boys under high density were more destructive and angry than girls and often broke toys or got into fights. Only a few studies (for example, Loo, 1972) have failed to find a link between higher density and increased aggression in children. Loo (1973) explained these exceptions via mitigating circumstances present in these studies that were not found in others.

Studies also have established that adult males, but not females, often become more aggressive under conditions of high social density (Schettino & Borden, 1976; Stokols et al., 1973). In fact, males and females respond differently to high density in a number of interesting ways (see box p. 152).

High density not only affects our feelings, it can influence our ability to perform tasks effectively as well. While high density does not affect the performance of simple tasks very much, it does affect performance on more complex, difficult tasks requiring problem solving, persistence, and discrimination (Freedman, Klevansky, & Ehrlich, 1971; Klein & Harris, 1979; Nagar & Pandey, 1987; Paulus, Annis, Seta, Schkade, & Matthews, 1976; Sherrod, 1974). Group as well as individual task performance is disrupted by high density, especially when the group is highly structured by having an appointed leader and specific rules of procedure (Worchel & Shackelford, 1991). Several researchers note that high density disrupts complex tasks in much the same way as other environmental factors such as noise. Cohen (1978, 1980) and Sherrod and Cohen (1978) propose that the close presence of strangers can make an environment unpredictable and potentially uncontrollable. Such environments require close monitoring to guard against threat or surprise. This demands additional

---

Do Males and Females Respond Differently to Crowding?

The experience of crowding appears to be very different for males and females. Freedman (1971) points out that density has a relatively small effect on mixed-sex groups, but that crowding in all-male or all-female groups usually produces more of an effect. Laboratory studies consistently show that males rate themselves as more aggressive and competitive and that they show greater deindividuation, experience more stress, and rate themselves and others more negatively in a crowded room as compared to an uncrowded room. For females, exactly the opposite effects often occur (Epstein & Karlin, 1975; Freedman, 1971; Freedman, Levy, Buchanan, & Price, 1972; Nicosia et al., 1979; Ross, Layton, Erickson, & Schopler, 1973; Schettino & Borden, 1976; Stokols et al., 1973). For example, in the study by Ross and his colleagues (Ross et al., 1973), males clearly withdrew from each other when crowded in same-sex groups, while females actually affiliated more with each other and engaged in more eye contact. Similarly, Freedman and colleagues (1972) found that crowding in an experiment made the experience more positive for women but less positive for men. In this study, women crowded in a mock jury situation also gave more lenient sentences to the defendant than less crowded women did; men completely reversed this pattern.

Why these sex differences should appear under high density is not yet clear. There is some evidence that males are more susceptible to sensory overload in high density nonsocial situations than females are (Leventhal & Levitt, 1979). Epstein and Karlin (1975) proposed that sex differences in response to crowding can be traced to the different group processes that occur in male and female groups. They found that in unstructured, high-

density situations, female groups became more cohesive, cooperative, and interacted more. Male groups, on the other hand, interacted less and became fragmented and competitive. Similarly, Karlin, McFarland, Aiello, and Epstein (1976) found that females responded positively to crowding when a lot of interaction was encouraged by the situation, but responded negatively when interaction was discouraged. The only lab study in which men responded more positively than women to crowding (Marshall & Heslin, 1975) confirmed that the nature of the task is an important variable. In this case, the situation was highly structured, and successful task performance depended on the formation of an achievement-oriented team. Thus, crowding seems to be most unpleasant for males in unstructured situations where involvement with other people in the room is not absolutely necessary.

The few field studies on sex differences in response to crowding appear to contradict the laboratory findings. Studies of students living three-to-a-room in dormitories designed for two find that women report being crowded more than men (Aiello, Baum, & Gormley, 1981; Mandel, Baron, & Fisher, 1980). Aiello, Thompson, and Baum (1981) suggest that this may be because men are more likely to cope with crowding by leaving their room, while women spend more time in their rooms even if they feel crowded.

The findings of male/female differences in perceptions of crowding remind us that the relationship between density and crowding is not a simple one; also, they demonstrate that many variables must be considered before drawing conclusions about human reactions to high-density situations.

attentional capacity, diminishing the cognitive resources available for performance of complex, high-information tasks. In this respect, density is no different from other uncontrollable events.

Studies of Long-Term Crowding

For quite some time, studies of the long-term effects of high-density living were limited to examining archival data collected by various agencies for other purposes. While this data base is useful for suggesting hypotheses and as a basis for developing theories, it is usually too piecemeal and haphazard for studying the effects of high-density living in any systematic way. However, researchers continue to make the most of these statistics as they become available. For example, a study by Zuravin (1986) suggests that high-density living is related correlationally to higher rates of child abuse. For the most part, though, research has not found that serious negative effects are reliably related to high-density living, which suggests that socioeconomic and demographic factors may be at least as important (Booth & Edwards, 1976; Ruback & Pandey, 1991).

Studying the long-term effects of density experimentally is very difficult to do. Over the last 20 years or so, environmental psychologists have turned to two residential settings that provide as controlled a look at long-term crowding as is now possible. These settings are prisons and college dormitories.

In many respects, prisons offer a good opportunity for researchers interested in crowding. Prisons provide a wide variety of living arrangements and densities and subjects who, in most cases, have not freely chosen their living arrangements. Additionally, prison crowding is becoming a greater problem, and there is a pressing need to understand its dynamics. As an illustration, consider that inmate populations increased by 45 percent from 1979 to 1984, yet housing space increased by only 29 percent during that same period. Even worse, the highest densities are found in the older, maximum security, male-only facilities (Innes, 1986). Ruback and Innes (1988) report that the inmate populations in state prisons grew by nearly 70 percent from 1978 to 1988. Clearly, many people are living under conditions of high density that are both intense and inescapable. What effects does this have on the hundreds of thousands of people now incarcerated in American prisons?

It is well-established that high blood pressure in prisoners is systematically related to the density of their living conditions (D'Atri, 1975; D'Atri & Ostfeld, 1975; Paulus, McCain, & Cox, 1978), and illness complaints in prisons and county jails alike increase at higher densities (McCain, Cox, & Paulus, 1976; Wener & Keys, 1988). Using archival data as well as data they collected themselves, Paulus, McCain, and Cox (1978) studied inmates in ten different prisons ranging in population from 245 to 2,400. In all cases, higher populations yielded higher death rates and higher rates of psychiatric commitments. The inmates' perceptions of crowding were more strongly related to spatial density than to social density. In a study conducted in two prisons, Ruback, Carr, and Hopper (1986) found that having a sense of some control in the prison environment was strongly related to the amount of stress inmates experienced. Inmates in single rooms had greater feelings of control than other inmates, as did inmates who had been in prison a long time. Both these groups reported relatively lower levels of stress than other inmates.

Policymakers have been slow to consider the results of prison research in implementing prison policy. According to Ruback and Innes (1988), this is probably because psychologists have focused on individuals rather than on larger units of analysis and concentrated on dependent variables like inmate feelings of frustration and control that are not as useful to prison administrators and government officials as other variables might be.

College dormitories also have proven to be useful laboratories for psychologists interested in crowding. While college students certainly have more control over their living arrangements than prisoners (in spite of what you might think), dormitories offer a variety of densities, physical arrangements, and degrees of choice for their residents. These factors enable researchers to study how such conditions affect the people who must spend so much time there. Much of the dormitory research focuses on differences between "suite" dormitories, in which small groups of people are housed in isolated units, and "corridor" dormitories, in which larger groups of people are housed in rooms opening into long, straight hallways. Valins and Baum (1973) found that residents of suite dormitories felt less crowded than residents of corridor dormitories. They hypothesized that this may be due to an increase in unwanted interactions in the corridor dorms and fostering of cohesive groups in the suites. These ideas received some support in a later study by Baum, Harpin, and Valins (1975) in which first-year residents of suites were better able to solve group problems than were the residents of corridor dormitories. The suite groups seemed more cohesive and functioned more smoothly, indicating that a suite arrangement may indeed mediate feelings of being crowded.

Regardless of how the rooms are arranged, it is clear that extremely high densities in college dormitories result in negative reactions and social withdrawal by students (Baron, Mandel, Adams, & Griffin, 1976; Baum & Valins, 1977). Many studies have focused on the common practice of "tripling" in which three students are assigned to a room designed for two. This arrangement is almost always unsatisfactory, and its negative effects are most pronounced when the victims are male and when it occurs in long-corridor dormitories (Mullen & Felleman, 1990). Baum, Shapiro, Murray, and Wideman (1979) have proposed that the crowding experienced in triples is not entirely a function of density and that it is at least partially due to the instability of three-person groups. In three-person groups, it is common for two of the individuals to become friendlier with each other than they are with the third, forming a coalition that leaves the third party feeling like an outsider. A recent study by Lepore, Evans, and Schneider (1991) indicates that students who feel that they are part of a supportive social network within the dormitory withstand crowding better than students who do not have this social support; however, Lepore and his colleagues also found that if the crowding persists for a long time (more than eight months), the accompanying stress eats away at the social support and greatly diminishes its effectiveness as a buffer against crowding.

The effects of long-term crowding have been studied in other settings. For example, Dean, Pugh, and Gunderson (1976) questioned enlisted men aboard 13 naval ships and found a relationship among density, satisfaction, and intentions to remain in the navy. Fleming, Baum, and Weiss (1987) found higher rates of stress and illness in crowded residential neighborhoods. However, there have been too few of these studies, and prisons and dormitories continue to be the most fertile source of information on long-term exposure to high-density living.

Moderators of Density Effects

The gender of the individuals involved is an important consideration in predicting reactions to high density. Many other factors also affect the relationship between density and crowding. In a study of Asian women, Jain (1987) found that a scarcity of resources contributes to feelings of being crowded independent of density. Loo and her colleagues (Loo, 1973; Loo & Smetana, 1978) report that age is an influential factor in how children cope with high density and propose that the extent to which the environment and group activities are structured is also important.

Many psychologists believe that personality is a significant variable in crowding. Khew and Brebner (1985) report that extraverts notice crowding more quickly than introverts; several other studies have found that persons high in the "need for affiliation" tolerate crowding better than those low in this need (Miller & Nardini, 1977; Miller, Rossbach, & Munson, 1981). Stimulus screening (described in Chapter 3) has also been linked to the ability to withstand crowding (Baum, Calesnick, Davis, & Gatchel, 1982).

Naturally, a person's cultural background and personal history of experiences with crowding affect how he or she will respond, although the nature of these relationships is not yet clear. A preliminary-questionnaire study of reactions to high-density situations revealed that, as a group, the British were least tolerant of high density and that a mixed group of Asians was the most tolerant. Southern Europeans in this study, primarily Italians, fell in between (Gillis, Richard, & Hagan, 1986). At the individual level, the research indicates that a person who has experienced a lot of crowding sometimes adapts to high density better than one who has not, but in some cases the reverse is true (Booth, 1976; Gove & Hughes, 1980; Rohe, 1982; Sundstrom, 1978; Walden, Nelson, & Smith, 1981).

Many times, the architectural features of buildings are the primary factors controlling how crowded the people in that environment feel. In dormitory rooms, bunk beds allow more usable floor space than twin beds and usually seem less crowded (Rohner, 1974). Schiffenbauer and colleagues (1977) examined crowding in dormitories and found that many physical factors other than actual floor space contribute to perceived size and crowdedness. Rooms that receive a lot of sunlight are judged as lighter and less crowded, while rooms with more usable floor space and rooms on higher floors are perceived as larger. Savinar (1975) found that higher ceilings are associated with less crowding. A number of studies on the relationship between architecture and crowding have used a projective measure of crowding in which subjects place figures in model rooms, adjusting the number of figures and the distances between them to the room's capacity. Using this technique, Desor (1972) determined that rooms with doors and windows can better accommodate more figures, as can rectangular rooms when compared with square rooms of the same area. Rotton (1987) found that subjects were less tolerant of crowding in rooms with curved (rather than straight) walls, and Baum and Davis (1976) report that more figures were placed in light colored rooms than in dark ones.

Adding pictures to a room or otherwise increasing its visual complexity also affects perceptions of crowding, but this effect is complicated and depends to a great extent on the nature of the other activities taking place in the room (Baum & Davis, 1976; Worchel & Teddlie, 1976).

THEORIES OF CROWDING

Now that you are familiar with how density affects human beings, it is time to consider the theories that attempt to explain these effects. Baum and Paulus (1987) point out that theories of crowding differ from each other in a number of important ways. Some theories focus on the external, situational influences on crowding, and others focus on the responses of the individual. Some look primarily at the physical setting, and others emphasize social variables. However, all theories of crowding must account for the data generated by research and predict the causes and consequences of crowding in specific situations if they are to be taken seriously.

Theories about the nature of crowding are still in their infancy. A variety of theories are competing for attention. Most seem reasonable and have some degree of support but none are completely satisfactory. I will describe the kinds of theories that have been popular with environmental psychologists and briefly explain the most influential models.

Models of crowding belong to one of five categories: **ecological, over-load, density-intensity, arousal,** and **control models.**

Ecological Models

While it is not specifically a theory of crowding, the ecological psychology model of Roger Barker (Barker, 1960, 1963, 1965, 1968; Barker & Wright, 1955; Wicker, 1973) offers a perspective for interpreting many of the behaviors seen under high-density conditions. Barker's model grew out of his observations at the Midwest Psychological Field Station in Oskaloosa, Kansas. According to Barker, behavior settings need just the right number of people to function well. Whether the setting is a ship, a store, or a college classroom, there is an optimal number of people that will cause that setting to function as efficiently as it can. Too few people leads to **understaffing,** which results in instability and greater demands on the people using that environment. **Overstaffing,** on the other hand, occurs when there are many more people than are needed for that setting to function. This leads to competition for the limited resources and a feeling of being crowded.

A more recent theory in the spirit of the ecological model is called **social physics** (Knowles, 1983). This model focuses on the distribution of people throughout a behavior setting rather than just examining interpersonal distances. For example, it is important to know if the people surrounding an individual are merely present or whether they are actively observing or interacting with that person. There also may be visual or auditory barriers in the situation that will affect perceptions of crowding. Social physics is much like the ecological model in that it emphasizes the nature of the behavior setting in dictating when crowding will occur. Knowles (1983) and Freimark, Wener, Phillips, and Korber (1984) have found this perspective useful in predicting when observers will evaluate settings as crowded or uncrowded.

Overload Models

Several researchers (Cohen, 1978; Milgram, 1970; Saegert, 1978) have developed theories that can be thought of as stimulus or information overload models. While these models differ in some respects, they all propose that high-density environments present individuals with sensory information that exceeds their preferred levels of stimulation and also often exceeds their ability to absorb it. In these high-density situations the cognitive, information-processing demands are very high. This can tax a person's attentional capacity and lead to stress and arousal. A person in this situation must focus on relevant information from the environment and screen out and ignore irrelevant information. Milgram (1970) proposed that the overloaded individual withdraws from social involvement with less important people as social demands increase. This may account for many of the seemingly rude, distant, "big city" behaviors that we will consider in a later chapter. Evans, Palsane, Lepore, and Martin (1989) agree that people living under crowded conditions may adopt an interpersonal style of social withdrawal to deal with the overloaded situation. Consequently, these individuals may lack an extensive social support network that would help protect them from the stress that can accompany crowding. In a field study conducted in India, they confirmed that high residential density was associated with more stress *and* less social support and that those individuals reporting large amounts of social support were least likely to report high levels of psychological distress.

The Density-Intensity Model

The density-intensity model, proposed by Freedman (1975), is one of the few theories of crowding to propose that the effects of high density on humans are not always negative. According to this theory, density by itself has neither good nor bad effects on people, but it intensifies whatever the individual's typical reaction to that situation would be. Thus, if a person finds him or herself in a pleasant situation (for example, a party or sporting event), a crowd of other people may in fact make the situation more pleasant. On the other hand, unpleasant situations like last minute Christmas shopping or standing in line to register for classes become even more aversive if crowding occurs. Freedman likens the effect of density to the volume knob on a stereo. Turning up the volume on music you like allows you to enjoy it more; when your neighbor turns up the volume on music you dislike, your disapproval quickly intensifies. A number of studies have supported Freedman's ideas since density has been shown to intensify the feelings people have in both pleasant and unpleasant situations (Freedman, Birsky, & Cavoukian, 1980; Freedman & Perlick, 1979; Schiffenbauer & Schiavo, 1976; Walden & Forsyth, 1981).

Arousal Models

Some theories of crowding (Evans, 1978; Paulus, 1980) rely on evidence that shows that high density is arousing for a number of reasons. These theories propose that the heightened levels of arousal affect task performance and social behaviors. That is, high arousal levels affect complex tasks but not simple ones, and disrupt normal social phenomena such as attraction, aggression, helping behavior, and nonverbal communication. In some respects, arousal models are related to overload models since heightened arousal levels are a by-product of the sensory overload that can occur in high-density situations.

Worchel and Teddlie (1976) believe that the relationship between crowding and arousal is a bit more complicated, and they proposed a "two-factor" theory of crowding. According to Worchel and Teddlie, invasions of personal space cause heightened arousal levels. If the person attributes the increased arousal to the other people in the setting, then that person will feel crowded. Gochman and Keating (1980) report that people often attribute unpleasant feelings aroused by other factors to crowding, even when other explanations are readily available. On the other hand, there is evidence that people do in fact feel less crowded if they believe that their arousal stems from some other source, such as a film they are watching (Worchel & Brown, 1984) or even a nonaudible, subliminal noise (Worchel & Yohai, 1979), rather than to crowding.

Control Models

The last group of crowding theories will be referred to as control models, a perspective that is becoming increasingly influential. Many previously competing theories are being united by the concept of personal control—that is, the freedom that an individual has to pursue the decisions and behaviors of his or her choice. Personal control also can refer to feelings of "cognitive control," meaning that the individual feels that he or she has enough understanding and information in a situation to feel some degree of control over what happens. Control models propose that high density affects human behavior and feelings because it tends to diminish the individual's feelings of control, leading to a perception of crowding.

This perspective grew out of earlier models of crowding. Interference models (Schopler & Stockdale, 1977) said that the presence of too many other people blocks goal-directed activities and causes frustration. Behavioral constraint models (Proshansky, Ittelson, & Rivlin, 1976; Stokols, 1972, 1976) proposed that too many other people put real or perceived restrictions on our behavior. Other researchers (Baron & Rodin, 1978; Baum & Valins, 1979; Schmidt & Keating, 1979; Sherrod & Cohen, 1978) elaborated on these earlier ideas by developing the idea of the importance of predictability and control for human comfort. The close presence of others not only interferes with attaining goals, but when these other people are strangers the environment also becomes less predictable, potentially uncontrollable, and restrictive. Therefore, perceived uncontrollability and not density per se is responsible for the negative effects often found in crowded situations. In many respects, the control model of crowding is similar to the more general learned helplessness theory of Seligman (1975) in that people experiencing high density develop an expectancy that their actions do not really affect what happens to them.

There is evidence that the unwanted interaction resulting from high density does in fact damage feelings of personal control. Montano and Adamopoulos (1984) found that people often identify behavioral constraint and goal-blocking as primary components of the crowding experience, and many other studies have found that increasing a person's feelings of personal control can greatly alleviate the experience of crowding (Burger, Oakman, & Ballard, 1983; Karlin, Katz, Epstein, & Woolfolk, 1979; Langer & Saegert, 1977; Paulus & Matthews, 1980; Rodin, Solomon, & Metcalf, 1978; Sherrod, 1974). One of these studies (Langer & Saegert, 1977) demonstrated the importance of cognitive control in the experience of crowding. Subjects went through a New York City supermarket with a grocery list during crowded or uncrowded periods. Their task was to select the most economical brand for each item on the list. Langer and Saegert found that merely providing subjects with advance information about the effects of crowding improved both task performance and the subjects' emotional reactions under high density.

CHAPTER SUMMARY

It is important to make a distinction between the concepts of density and crowding. Density is an objective measure of the number of individuals per unit of space; crowding refers to a subjective, psychological state that results in negative feelings. While density is usually an important ingredient in crowding, perceptions of crowding are affected by other situational and demographic variables such as architecture, task requirements, and an individual's age and sex.

There is no question that prolonged exposure to high density can have severe negative consequences for the health and social behaviors of many species of animals. While the same may also be true for humans, one must be extremely cautious about generalizing the results of animal studies to human beings in a direct and simple way.

Research on human reactions to high density can be divided into studies of short-term and long-term crowding. Studies of short-term crowding are usually experimental in design and seldom last for more than a few hours. Research on short-term crowding reveals that this experience can have a negative effect on feelings and disrupts performance on complex tasks. Studies of long-term crowding examine naturally occurring populations (usually in prisons or college dormitories) who live under conditions of high density for prolonged periods. While this research is far from complete, indications are that the effects of prolonged exposure to high density in these settings are usually negative, especially in aversive environments such as prisons.

Many theories have been proposed to account for the effects of density on human beings. Ecological models examine behavior settings with an eye toward establishing the optimal number of people needed for that setting to function well. Overload models explain crowding as a response to too much stimulation and environmental information. Freedman's density-intensity model proposes that density in itself is neither positive nor negative, but that it intensifies whatever is going on in the situation. Arousal models describe crowding as a side effect of the heightened levels of arousal present in high-density situations. Control models emphasize the role of the individual's loss of control over the situation as a primary factor in the experience of crowding. All these theories have some support, but a more definitive theory of the nature of human crowding awaits further research.

GLOSSARY

Arousal Models of Crowding   Models that explain crowding as a side effect of the heightened arousal that occurs in high-density situations.

Behavioral Sink   The extremely disorganized conditions that occur when population densities exceed a species' ability to maintain normal social organization.

Control Models of Crowding   Models that emphasize the individual's loss of control over the situation as the primary factor in the experience of crowding.

Crowding   A subjective, psychological reaction to density that results in negative feelings.

Density   An objective measure of the number of individuals per unit of space.

Density-Intensity Model of Crowding   A model proposed by Freedman (1975) that suggests that density in itself is neither positive nor negative; it intensifies whatever feelings are already present in the situation.

Ecological Models of Crowding   Models that focus on the optimal number of people required for a behavior setting to function effectively.

Overload Models of Crowding   Models that explain crowding as a response to too much environmental information and stimulation.

Overstaffing   More people in a behavior setting than the optimal number needed for it to function effectively.

Social Density   Density refers to the number of individuals per unit of space. Changing the number of individuals in a space of constant size is known as a change in social density.

Social Physics   A perspective on crowding developed by Knowles (1983) that focuses on the distribution and relationships of the people present in an environment.

Spatial Density   Density refers to the number of individuals per unit of space. Density differences that occur when the same number of individuals occupy physical spaces of different sizes are known as differences in spatial density.

Understaffing   Too few people present in a behavior setting for that environment to function effectively.

Work
Environments

8

How the ambient environment and human needs for space and privacy affect behavior have been the subjects of the preceding chapters. This chapter and the two that follow will examine the implications of these findings for the design of the built environment in which we live and work.

Two incorrect assumptions are often made about the relationship between architecture and behavior (Heimsath, 1977). On the one hand, many people believe that the structure of buildings and other physical features such as room color completely determine behavior. (This position has been called **architectural determinism.**) These people often have unrealistically high expectations for solving behavioral problems by painting walls with the "right" color of paint or manipulating the physical environment in some other way. On the other hand, it is equally common to find those who believe that architecture has absolutely no effect on behavior. The truth undoubtedly lies somewhere in between. Architecture can be quite important, but it is never the only determinant of behavior in any setting. The physical environment serves primarily to magnify the effects of other factors such as crowding that may already be operating in that situation.

Architects need to be concerned with creating sturdy, safe structures that will be both functional and aesthetically pleasing (Lang, 1987, 1988a). Unfortunately, as Gifford (1987) has pointed out, architects and designers are too often isolated from the people who use their buildings, and they may value beauty more than function, remaining unaware of the emotional and behavioral effects of their decisions. For example, rooms with built-in, inflexible furniture force people to move from one place to another for different activities (High & Sundstrom, 1977), and rooms that are too large will be informally redesigned by residents by partitioning the space with draperies, plants, and furniture (Miller & Schlitt, 1985).

The materials used on the surface of building interiors are important as well. Some materials have strong associations with particular types of buildings and are vital for maintaining an appropriate auditory, visual, and tactile ambience (Lang, 1988b). You probably would agree that inexpensive wood paneling is terribly out-of-place in the lobby of a state capitol building or in a cathedral, but it might be perfectly acceptable in a basement recreation room or in a fraternity house lounge area. Hall and Albert (1976) found that the influence of interior surfaces may go beyond simply contributing to "atmosphere"; soft environmental surfaces actually increased social interaction among autistic children in a playroom.

ROOMS AND FURNISHINGS

Rooms

Before discussing work environments and other built environments that will be considered in later chapters, some attention must be paid to the role of rooms and furniture, as they are the building blocks of any built environment. First of all, rooms must create the impression that they are adequate for the activities that take place there, and the perception of a room's size can be affected by many things. Rectangular rooms appear larger than square rooms of the same area (Sadalla & Oxley, 1984), and light-colored rooms are perceived as being larger and more spacious than darker rooms (Acking & Küller, 1972; Baum & Davis, 1976). A lot of furniture tends to make a room appear smaller (Imamoglu, 1973) as do messiness and signs of disorder (Samuelson & Lindauer, 1976). Pennartz (1986) determined that the arrangement of rooms and the relationship between them may be as important as their size and shape in determining the atmosphere within a building.

Sunlight in indoor spaces can have some negative effects such as glare or overheating (Boubekri, Hull, & Boyer, 1991), but the positive

P H O T O   8·1   An inside window

effects of admitting natural light indoors seem to far outweigh the draw-backs. Consequently, windows are a valuable addition to most rooms. People tend not to like rooms without windows (Collins, 1975; Cuttle, 1983; Finnegan & Solomon, 1981; Gilgen & Barrier, 1976; Heerwagen & Heerwagen, 1986; Hollister, 1968; Ruys, 1970, Wotton & Barkow, 1983); thus, windowless rooms are often decorated with natural scenes and objects to compensate for this lack of access to the outside world (Heer-wagen & Orians, 1986). The smaller a room is, the more important windows become (Butler & Steuerwald, 1991). When it is not possible to have windows to the outside, "inside windows" that give a view of other inside space are well-liked and add to a room's pleasantness (Biner, Butler, & Winsted, 1991). (See Photo 8-1.) The lone exception to this strong preference for windows occurs in areas such as bathrooms where privacy is extremely important (Butler & Biner, 1989).

The impression that rooms convey to us is important for many reasons. Russell and Mehrabian (1978) found that subjects were more willing to affiliate with others when they were in rooms that they found attractive. In another study, Campbell (1979) showed slides of faculty offices to college students and found that neatness, plants, fish, and artwork led these individuals to feel more comfortable and to believe that they would be compatible with that professor. Conversely, when people are uncomfortable because of environmental factors, they have a strong tendency to blame the discomfort on the people they are interacting with rather than on the setting (Aiello & Thompson, 1980).

P H O T O   8-2   The interior architecture of a church clearly communicates the formal nature of the behaviors that occur there.

Furniture

The arrangement of furniture affects the behavior and feelings of people in a room. It is one of the primary facilitators of conversation and establishes interaction boundaries and appropriate interaction distances (Holahan, 1972; Sommer & Ross, 1958). Joiner (1976) described three basic qualities that are important in determining the styles of interaction in a room: the position of the furnishings, the distance between furnishings, and the amount of symbolic decoration that is used. According to Joiner, these qualities indicate the formality of the interactions that occur in that setting and provide cues for behavior. The arrangement of the interior space in a large church is a good example of how position, distance, and symbolic decoration create clear demands on people's behavior in the church (see Photo 8-2). The sanctuary area where the priest or minister stands is physically removed from the congregation by considerable space, usually going well beyond the "formal interaction distance" described by Hall (1966). The sanctuary is separated from the rest of the church by a railing and is elevated above the floor as well. The pews are fastened to the floor and face forward, focusing attention on the sanctuary and making casual interaction among congregation members difficult. Often, high ceilings, impressive paintings, statues, light fixtures, and stained glass windows combine to create a formal atmosphere that inspires feelings of awe and submissiveness. The physical environment of the church clearly communicates to all who enter that they are not

P H O T O S   8-3A and B   Sociofugal environments are designed to keep people apart; socio-petal environments are designed to bring people together.

encouraged to converse or move around and that they should remain quietly seated and pay attention to activities occurring at the front of the church. Similar arrangements of space are found in courtrooms, concert halls, and other formal settings. The less formal distances, positions, and decorations found in lounges, restaurants, and waiting rooms communicate a very different set of behavioral expectations.

Osmond (1959) coined the terms **sociopetal** and **sociofugal** to describe the extent to which environments encourage or discourage social interaction. Sociopetal environments bring people together and promote interaction through face-to-face seating and movable furniture. Sociofugal environments discourage interaction, often through immobile seating arrangements that are designed to make interaction difficult. Sociofugal spatial arrangements are often used in public places like shopping malls and airports (see Photos 8-3A and 8-3B) where people usually do not want interaction with those around them and also where it is in the management's financial interest to keep people moving and browsing in the shops and snack bars. In some such places, furniture and other environmental features have even been designed intentionally to be uncomfortable to prevent people from idly lounging about (Sommer, 1969). One common example is the sharp spikes placed on walls and railings in public places to discourage people from sitting down; a strategy that has also been used to prevent birds from roosting on window ledges (see Photos 8-4A and 8-4B).

Small Group Ecology

In any environment, an individual's seating preference usually indicates either an invitation to interaction or a preference to be left alone. Sommer (1969) describes the positions people take at rectangular tables such as those frequently found in libraries (see Figure 8-1). Generally, a person seated at the center of such a table is advertising a desire to be alone and a wish to have the table completely to him or herself. Others readily

P H O T O S   8-4A and B Sharp edges on spaces in public prevent people and animals from becoming too comfortable and loitering where they are not wanted.

recognize and usually respect this intent. A person seated at a corner position is perceived as being open to having others sit there as well. Other studies by Sommer (1969) and Cook (1970) reveal the consistency with which people select seating positions to match the situation; these preferences are illustrated in Figure 8-2. At rectangular tables, people usually choose a corner-to-corner or face-to-face arrangement for casual conversation. If they are competing with each other, they ordinarily sit across the table, face-to-face, and seldom sit corner-to-corner. Individuals who are cooperating with each other on some task normally choose a side-by-side seating arrangement but sit as far away as possible from the other when working completely independently of that person. Other research by Sommer shows that, even across cultures, side-by-side seating is always rated as the most intimate seating arrangement. This ar-

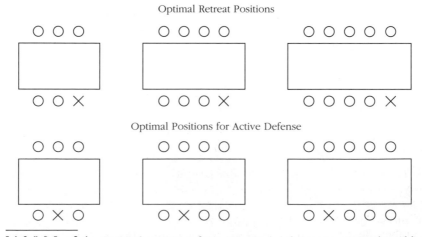

F I G U R E   8-1 Optimal positions for retreat and defense at rectangular tables (Source: Sommer, 1969)

Percentage of Individuals Choosing This Arrangement

Seating Arrangement	Condition 1 (conversing)	Condition 2 (cooperating)	Condition 3 (coacting)	Condition 4 (competing)
(diagram)	42	19	3	7
(diagram)	46	25	32	41
(diagram)	1	5	43	20
(diagram)	0	0	3	5
(diagram)	11	51	7	8
(diagram)	0	0	13	18
Total	100	100	100	99

F I G U R E   8-2 Seating preferences at rectangular tables   (Source: Sommer, 1969)

rangement is very common in children, but its frequency of use decreases with age. Studies also have determined that females are more likely than males to use side-by-side seating (Norum, Russo, & Sommer, 1967; Sommer, 1969).

Although side-by-side seating connotes intimacy, it does not seem to be the preferred arrangement for talking. Mehrabian and Diamond (1971) found that side-by-side seating on a couch inhibited conversation in otherwise sociable people, and other studies reported by Sommer (1969) showed that individuals only choose a side-by-side position for conversation when it was not possible to arrange a face-to-face conversation at a distance of less than 5 1/2 feet. Curiously, people are more likely to direct comments to those seated next to them when they are a member of a group with a strong, directive leader (Hearn, 1957; Sommer, 1969; Steinzor, 1950).

C A R T O O N   The arrangement of furniture often reflects the status of individuals in a group. Reprinted with special permission of King Features Syndicate, Inc.

A rectangular table is used most frequently in our society for business meetings, jury deliberations, and other important group proceedings. A great many studies have discovered an interesting relationship among seating patterns, status, and leadership in groups using these tables. There is a strong tendency for the person sitting at the head of the table to talk more in group discussions and to be elected by the group as a leader (Leavitt, 1951; Strodtbeck & Hook, 1961). Research has also shown that people who are already leaders tend to select the head position at rectangular tables (Sommer, 1961). Malandro, Barker, and Barker (1989) report that status at these tables diminishes with distance from the head of the table, and that even when round tables are used for meetings, other ways can be found to signal status within the group through seating arrangements (see Hagar the Horrible cartoon).

THE PHYSICAL ENVIRONMENT AND WORK PERFORMANCE

Franklin Becker (1991) has identified a number of important trends that work organizations must deal with throughout the 1990s and into the decade following the year 2000. Most of these trends have implications for the physical design of the workplace. Employers will have to contend with a more demanding work force that has higher expectations about all aspects of their jobs, including the physical setting in which they work. Workers will become more involved in decisions about changes in the work environment and will have more control over noise levels, thermal comfort, and the layout of furniture than has traditionally been the case. Rising property and building costs in major cities, coupled with the needs of new information technology, will also create tension between the need for more sophisticated buildings and an overriding concern with cost effectiveness.

Increased global competition and a growing internationalism in corporations also present a challenge to work-space designers, as different cultural attitudes and needs can create conflicting work-space demands within corporations. For example, a sauna is considered a necessity in Finnish office buildings because contracts are often negotiated and even signed in saunas. On the other hand, British companies often consider even air conditioning an unnecessary frill and resist changes that suggest that money is being wasted on luxuries (Becker, 1991).

Problems of design in the workplace are not new to psychologists. A serious interest in the effect of the physical environment on work performance goes back to the famous Hawthorne studies, a series of field experiments conducted over a 12-year period during the 1920s and 1930s at the Western Electric Company's Hawthorne Plant in Cicero, Illinois (Landsberger, 1958; Roethlisberger & Dickson, 1939). These studies began as an effort to determine the effect of illumination on productivity; they ultimately evolved into ground-breaking research on the important role played by workers' perceptions and feelings in determining worker productivity. The researchers set up different assembly workrooms where the intensity of the light varied from very bright to very dim. Surprisingly, the level of illumination had no effect on productivity. Later studies with other tasks and different environmental variables revealed the same thing. From these studies, researchers learned that nonphysical factors such as employee attitudes and the prestige of being singled out for special attention can have powerful effects on behavior. An enduring discovery from this research has become known as the **Hawthorne effect:** Work performance improves following the introduction of any novel factor into a work situation. When the novelty wears off, performance returns to previous levels. While the Hawthorne effect is very common, it is not always possible to explain why it occurs (Adair, 1984). Since the Hawthorne studies, researchers have continued to examine the relationship between work and the physical environment through worker surveys, field studies of many kinds, and laboratory experiments. The research that psychologists conduct has relied particularly heavily on laboratory studies.

According to Sundstrom (1987), laboratory experiments on work performance and the physical environment have focused on five types of tasks:

Clerical tasks, which require identifying or transcribing symbols as in typing or checking numbers.

Motor tasks, which are most common in factories where workers must manipulate controls or objects in response to signals or instructions.

Mental tasks, which include learning, recall, calculation, proofreading, or the transformation of data.

Vigilance tasks, such as monitoring machinery or detecting irregularities in output.

Dual tasks, or simultaneously performing two tasks, one of which is usually a vigilance task.

The distinction between different types of tasks is important, as it is the nature of the task that determines the effects (if any) that the physical environment has on work performance. For example, ambient stressors

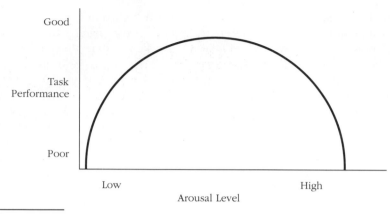

F I G U R E   8-3 The "inverted U" relationship between arousal and task performance (the Yerkes-Dodson Law)

such as heat and noise may be very disruptive to complex mental work but under some circumstances can actually facilitate the performance of repetitive physical or manual work. Ambient stressors affect work performance primarily because they change arousal levels (see Chapter 3). The next section briefly reviews the relationship between arousal and work.

Arousal and Work

Arousal and task performance   The most throughly researched of all the effects that arousal changes can have on human behavior is the relationship between arousal and task performance. As early as 1908, Yerkes and Dodson proposed a model of this relationship. They suggested that it takes the form of an "inverted U" (see Figure 8-3) in which very low or very high arousal levels are associated with relatively poor task performance — with the best performance coming at some moderate level of arousal known as the "optimal" level. This model has withstood the test of time and has been so widely replicated that it is now known as the **Yerkes-Dodson Law** (Hebb, 1955). As time passed, studies indicated that different kinds of tasks showed somewhat different performance–arousal curves. Specifically, what was found is that very simple or well-learned tasks have high optimal levels and that arousal must be extremely high for these tasks to be disrupted. Conversely, very difficult, unfamiliar tasks quickly become disrupted by even moderate levels of arousal. What constitutes efficient task performance or task difficulty is highly dependent on the nature of the task (for example, speed versus accuracy), and researchers must describe precisely what occurs in their studies. As we saw in Chapter 3, many aspects of our physical environment, such as noise and temperature, have a profound impact on task performance because they are arousing.

Although there is little disagreement about the consistency of the

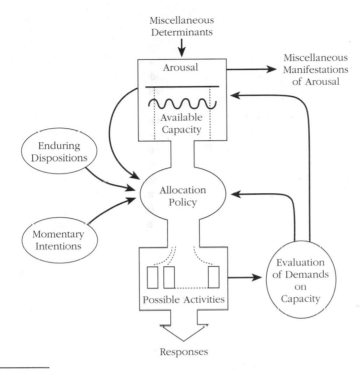

F I G U R E   8·4 A capacity model of attention (Source: Kahneman, 1973)

inverted-U performance–arousal curve, the reason it occurs is still uncertain. Eysenck (1982) concludes that the curvilinear relationship between performance and arousal cannot be explained by a single mechanism; it is a by-product of several different processes that occur as arousal levels change. One of these processes is almost certainly the change in the individual's attentional capacity that occurs as arousal levels fluctuate.

Attention and arousal   Kahneman (1973) developed a capacity model of attention that may explain the effects of arousal on attention, and ultimately, on task performance. His model is a prototypical example of the capacity models of attention now popular in cognitive psychology. A schematic diagram of Kahneman's model is presented in Figure 8-4.

According to Kahneman, all activities that require using conscious attention draw on some limited central processing capacity. Some activities require more attentional capacity than others, and the total amount of capacity available at any given time changes. The individual must have some **allocation policy** to parcel out the available capacity to competing demands. In Figure 8-4 the factors that determine this allocation of resources point toward the center, where the allocation policy is represented. The enduring dispositions of some stimuli force the allocation of a great deal of attention to them. Generally, the more intense and unpredictable a stimulus is, the more it demands attention. The evolutionary significance of very novel stimuli, sudden motion, or personally significant stimuli (for example, hearing one's own name) cause these stimuli to capture our attention in spite of our efforts to prevent it. Momentary intentions, such as an experimenter's instructions to concentrate on a light in the front of the room, also make demands on attention. Additionally, continuous feedback concerning the available capacity and the extent of the demands will influence the allocation of attention.

This brings us back to the problems of arousal. In Figure 8-4 arousal is located in the same box as is available capacity. According to Kahneman's model, the level of arousal is the single most important determinant of how much attentional capacity is available. As arousal levels increase, the amount of attention available for task performance *decreases.* Therefore, difficult, unfamiliar tasks that require great amounts of attention suffer as arousal levels increase. Athletes, musicians, and soldiers must rehearse and practice constantly to make their skills so familiar and automatic that they will not be disrupted by the high arousal levels experienced during real competition, performances, and battles, since familiar tasks require very little attention and will be performed well even when arousal levels are quite high. Within this framework, arousal has an impact on task performance because of the changes it causes in the attention available for completing the task. The capacity model of attention also helps explain people's social behaviors in the overstimulating, information-overload situations that will be discussed in other chapters (Cohen, 1978; Milgram, 1970).

Motivation and arousal   In addition to controlling attention and task performance, arousal levels are also an important part of motivation. Arousal serves as both a **drive** (an internal stimulus that spurs behavior) and as an **incentive** (something that an individual works to attain). Many theories of motivation propose that humans seek some optimal, intermediate level of stimulation from their environment and that much of our behavior constitutes an attempt to increase or decrease our arousal to maintain this ideal degree of stimulation (Berlyne, 1960, 1967, 1971, 1974; Berlyne & Madsen, 1973; Fiske & Maddi, 1961; Wohlwill, 1974). Other theorists (McClelland, Atkinson, Clark, & Lowell, 1953) believe that what people really seek are small discrepancies from expected arousal levels. Schneirla (1959) has confirmed that moderate deviations from the general level of stimulation appear to be rewarding and cause approach behavior in a broad range of animal species, but that drastic deviations are aversive and lead to withdrawal. Russell and Mehrabian (1975, 1977a, 1978) believe that people prefer intermediate levels of arousal only when pleasure is neutral, but in situations very high or low in pleasure, they prefer arousal levels that maximize pleasure or minimize displeasure (see Figure 8-5). In spite of their differences, all these theories agree that arousal is an integral part of human motivation in most situations.

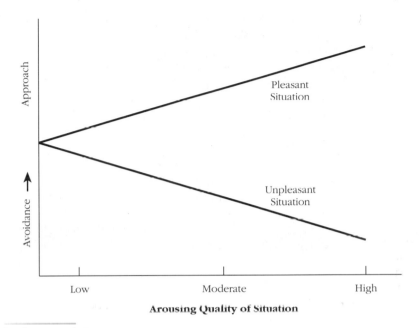

FIGURE 8-5 The pleasure-arousal hypothesis proposes that our tendency to approach pleasant situations and avoid unpleasant situations becomes stronger as arousal levels increase. (Source: Mehrabian, 1976a)

The Physical Environment and Job Satisfaction

A study of 360 office employees in eight different organizations found a significant correlation between job satisfaction and satisfaction with the physical environment (Ferguson & Weisman, 1986). Although a few other studies show similar results, job satisfaction surveys of workers usually find that the physical environment is perceived as being relatively unimportant to job satisfaction (Sundstrom, 1987). However, Sundstrom believes that workers underestimate its importance because they adapt to the environment and because it usually meets at least some minimum level of adequacy. The physical environment may function primarily as what Herzberg identified as a **hygiene factor** in job satisfaction (Herzberg, 1966; Herzberg, Mausner, & Snyderman, 1959). According to Herzberg, when a worker's basic needs for security and comfort are not met, dissatisfaction with work results. When these basic hygiene factors are met, the worker will no longer be dissatisfied, although there is no guarantee that he or she will be satisfied. From this perspective, the physical environment may lead to dissatisfaction in the workplace if it is inadequate, but, in and of itself, it is not sufficient to cause high levels of job satisfaction even if it is quite acceptable. Such a role for the physical environment may explain the elusiveness of a consistent relationship between satisfaction with work and satisfaction with the workplace.

Cherulnik and Koenig's study (1989) suggests that the physical environment may be related to job satisfaction in even more subtle ways. The perceived quality of the workplace influenced the judgments that observers made about the character of the people who worked in that environment. Overall, subjects attributed more favorable personality traits to workers who were associated with high-quality workplaces. Thus, it appears that simply working in a pleasant, high-quality environment increases an individual's sense of self-worth and standing in the eyes of others, leading to greater job satisfaction.

To help you determine how important the physical features of the workplace might be for your own job satisfaction, try it (see box How Important Is the Physical Environment to Your Own Job Satisfaction?).

TRY IT!

How Important Is the Physical Environment to Your Own Job Satisfaction?

Individuals differ according to the value they place on the different rewards that can be acquired through work. Some people are motivated primarily by money, whereas others find that long vacations or the social benefits of their jobs outweigh financial gain in determining how satisfied they are with their occupations. To help you explore the values you place on different rewards and to see how important physical characteristics of the workplace are to you, try the following exercise. (This exercise is similar to one developed by Gibson, Ivancevich, and Donnelly, 1979.)

Imagine that you are a manager in a large corporation. Look at the list of rewards available to your company's employees. From this list, set up a list of those rewards that are directly related to the physical environment of your workplace and a different list of rewards that are not related to the physical environment. Separately rank the items in the two lists (from most important to least important) as to how important you think the items in each list would be to your own personal job satisfaction. After you have ranked both lists, select and rank the eight most important rewards found on either list. How many of these are directly related to the physical work environment?

- Expensive office furniture
- Piped-in music
- Long vacations
- Office with a large window
- Control over office temperature

The Physical Environment and Communication in Work Organizations

Allen, Becker, and Steele (1987) identified three types of face-to-face communication that are especially important in work organizations. The first is **coordination,** or sharing information to coordinate the efforts of different departments or work groups. This type of communication usually is scheduled, formal in nature, and occurs in a meeting place (such as a conference room) designed for that purpose. Some workplace communication is more **informative** in nature. This involves sharing necessary information to stay current in one's profession. This kind of communication may be scheduled and formal, but more often it occurs informally during encounters in corridors or over lunch. A third kind of

---

TRY IT!

- Opportunity to travel
- Feedback on your career progress
- Country club privileges
- Company recreation facilities
- Comfortable lounge or cafeteria
- Private parking space
- Your boss seeking your advice
- Office located near "important" people
- Corner office
- Chance to complete project from beginning to end
- Company picnics
- Challenging work
- Time off for good performance
- Private office
- Salary increase
- Company-wide recognition for your work
- Larger office
- Participation in important decisions
- Quiet office
- Stock options
- Plush carpeting in your office
- Good pension plan
- Private secretary
- Access to "executive washroom"

communication, described as **inspirational,** facilitates creative thinking and the generation of new ideas. Frequent informal contact outside of one's own group enhances inspirational communication.

Each type of communication may require a different kind of meeting area. Designers of workplaces must consider each organization's needs in determining what proportions of space to allocate to different types of areas. The issue of designing space appropriate to workers' communication needs is at the heart of many design problems, especially office design, which will be considered later in this chapter.

The degree to which an employee feels informed and part of an organization's communication network is a significant factor in his or her job satisfaction. Research shows that informal communication in work organizations (the "grapevine") is often more efficient than the formal communication networks of the organization (Davis, 1984). Therefore, the physical design of the workplace can indirectly affect job satisfaction to the extent that it facilitates or inhibits the formation of an informal communication network. In the workplace, individuals gravitate toward settings that bring people together for gossip and other activities (Bechtel, 1977). Most workplaces contain a lounge, cafeteria, or other area where employees can take breaks or have lunch. If these areas are properly designed, they can build cohesiveness among the workers and contribute to overall job satisfaction. Gifford (1988) found that appropriate lighting levels and a comfortable "home-like" decor increased the length and intimacy of conversations. Campbell and Campbell (1988) studied 28 departmental lounges at a large Midwestern university and conducted a nationwide mail survey of lounge usage in academic departments. They concluded that lounges function most effectively as communication centers if several criteria are met. Lounges must contain items that will attract people to them in the first place: mail boxes, vending machines, or coffee pots. Second, a lounge should have built-in features so people will linger once they have arrived. A bulletin board and a small coffee machine that requires people to wait while a fresh pot is brewing work well. Finally, the lounge should have comfortable seating that will encourage communication.

SPECIFIC WORK SETTINGS

Factories

Sundstrom (1987) defined a factory as any facility "devoted to the conversion of raw materials into marketable products" (p. 733). Most of the research on the effects of the physical environment on work performance in factories has focused on the impact of ambient factors such as temperature, noise, and lighting. (Refer to Chapter 3 for more background on this research and details on these factors.) Of these ambient factors, the one most frequently reported as a source of dissatisfaction in factories

P H O T O   8-5 Workers in factories must often perform complex tasks under conditions of high environmental load.

and offices is temperature that is too hot or too cold (Boyce, 1974; Hedge, 1982). Paciuk (1990) has demonstrated that satisfaction with temperature in the workplace is strongly related to perceptions of control. That is, if workers feel that they have some control over the temperature, they are more satisfied with it. Since this is not true in most workplaces, it is not surprising that dissatisfaction with temperature is so common. Another reason for frequent complaints about temperature is undoubtedly the wide disagreement among people as to what constitutes a comfortable temperature (Sundstrom, 1987). However, one must remember that the generally limited range of temperatures found in most work settings is more likely to affect comfort and satisfaction rather than actual work performance.

Mehrabian (1976a) described the special problems faced by the designers of factories. For the most part, factory jobs are low-load, repetitious, and inherently unpleasant. The challenge for the designer, therefore, is to create a physical environment that is arousing and pleasant to compensate for what the work itself lacks. Special attention should be paid to the design of cafeterias and lounges, since the social interaction and change of scenery that occur during breaks and lunch hours may be the high points of the day for many workers. Mehrabian also notes that increasing the flexibility of coffee and lunch breaks, varying workers' tasks, and creating cohesive, autonomous work groups might improve work performance in low-load factory environments.

Music is frequently introduced into the workplace to create a more pleasant environment, and many believe that music boosts productivity. The research to date, however, indicates that although employees like to listen to music while they work, it has little real effect on actual productivity (Fox, 1983; Sundstrom, 1986a).

Offices

More research has been done on office design than on any other work setting for a number of reasons, not the least of which is that an office is the work setting where environmental psychologists spend most of their time. Indeed, over half the work force in the United States is employed in office settings (Giuliano, 1982). Research demonstrates that the physical structure of an office can influence job satisfaction, work performance, and motivation to perform well on the job (Becker, 1981; Sundstrom, 1986a; Wineman, 1986). Poor office design can exacerbate problems inherent in office work such as eyestrain, irritability, and fatigue that are experienced by office workers who must use video display terminals for long periods of time (Kleeman, 1988).

Crouch and Nimran (1989) asked 65 managers to identify the aspects of their offices that they thought facilitated their work performance and those that inhibited it. Factors that promote supportive social interaction and adequate space and lighting were primary facilitators. Factors that increased distraction (such as overhearing other people's conversations) or design features that led to frequent interruptions inhibited work performance.

Privacy in office environments   Of the many things that make an individual feel satisfied with his or her office, none is more important than privacy. Although the complexity and demands of the specific job must be considered when trying to pin down the relationship between the degree of privacy and satisfaction with an office (Hedge, 1982), studies tend to show that satisfaction with office surroundings increases as privacy increases (Sundstrom, 1986b; Wineman, 1982). A survey of college faculty members ranked privacy in offices as more important than other factors such as space, temperature, ventilation, lighting, and furniture (Farrenkopf & Roth, 1980). Similar preferences for privacy were obtained in a recent laboratory study by Block and Stokes (1989). In their study, 169 undergraduates worked on a task in a private office or in an office shared with four other people. In each condition, all subjects worked at an identical desk with exactly the same amount of workspace. The students liked the private office significantly better than the shared office. This was especially true if the subjects were working on a complex task (filling out tax forms) as opposed to a simple one (clipping papers together).

As Justa and Golan (1977) point out, it is often difficult to discriminate between aspects of privacy that can be dealt with through physical

P H O T O 8-6 An open-plan office

design and those that cannot. Privacy in offices is achieved through an interaction of physical features, social norms, and official office policies. In their studies of administrators, accountants, and programmers in four different companies, Justa and Golan found that the ability to regulate interaction is just as important as simply being shielded from noise.

The problem of privacy in offices became apparent with the growth of **open-plan offices** during the 1960s. Typically, they consist of an entire floor of an office building with no internal floor-to-ceiling partitions (see Photo 8-6). Plants, cabinets, or bookcases can be used occasionally to screen neighboring workers from each other, but for the most part there is little visual or auditory privacy in open-plan offices. When the only privacy is afforded by facing all desks in the same direction, the office is sometimes referred to as a "bullpen" or "cabbage patch" office (Mehrabian, 1976b). Open-plan offices offer flexibility, low-cost construction and maintenance. It was thought that they might foster group cohesiveness and communication as well (Heimstra & McFarling, 1978).

Open-plan offices do foster increased social activity, especially among lower-level employees, as long as the area is not too large (Allen & Gertsberger, 1973; Brookes & Kaplan, 1972; Ives & Ferdinands, 1974; Nemecek & Grandjean, 1973; Wells, 1965). Szilagyi and Holland (1980) concluded that if the increase in social and spatial density is only moderate and if the work involved is not too demanding, open-plan offices can increase feedback, interaction with coworkers, and job satisfaction. Some evidence shows that performance of simple tasks may be better in open-plan arrangements, possibly because of social facilitation (Block & Stokes, 1989).

In spite of these advantages, however, research generally does not confirm the expected benefits of open-plan offices; most employee reactions to open-plan offices are negative (Becker, 1981; Ng & Gifford, 1984). Occupants of conventional, private offices express greater satisfaction with their work space than those who work in open-plan offices (Marans & Sprecklemeyer, 1982), and employees who move from a conventional, closed office to an open-plan office exhibit a drop in both satisfaction and motivation (Oldham & Brass, 1979). Open-plan offices lack the boundaries that make a conventional office into a private, defensible space; this prompts frequent complaints about the lack of privacy in open-plan offices and the noise and distractions inherent in this arrangement (Brookes & Kaplan, 1972; Oldham & Brass, 1979; Riland & Falk, 1972; Sundstrom, Burt, & Kamp, 1980; Sundstrom, Town, Brown, Forman, & McGee, 1982). In an unpublished doctoral dissertation by Clearwater (cited by Becker, 1981), communication among employees actually worsened after a move from conventional offices to an open-plan office.

The noise that is a by-product of the lack of privacy in open-plan offices is the most frequently reported problem for workers. As we saw in Chapter 3, uncontrollable and unpredictable noise is the most distracting, annoying, and disruptive to task performance. Unfortunately, this is precisely the type of noise generated by ringing telephones and others' conversations to which workers in open-plan offices are exposed (Boyce, 1974; Hedge, 1982; McCarrey, Peterson, Edwards, & Von Kulmiz, 1974; Sundstrom, 1987). Noise almost always produces unpleasant feelings in workers. Weinstein (1977) showed that workers believe that noise disrupts their job performance even when it does not. The lack of **speech privacy,** which is the freedom to talk without unwanted others overhearing, can be just as disturbing as being one of the "unwanted others" (Cavanaugh, Farrell, Hirtle, & Watters, 1962; Sundstrom, Herbert, & Brown, 1982).

Offices as status symbols and territories   "People in authority frequently manipulate territory in order to impress subordinates symbolically" (Merleman, 1988, p. 580). According to Sundstrom (1987), aside from impressing subordinates, status markers serve several important functions in offices. Status symbols communicate rank and provide visitors with cues for appropriate behavior. Also they serve as incentives or as compensation for job performance (see box p. 183). The importance of advertising rank through offices is so great that many organizations have written policies for the status characteristics to be included in the work spaces of people of different ranks (Konar & Sundstrom, 1986).

Status markers in office buildings are remarkably similar across settings. Universally, higher status is associated with greater floor space and fewer workers per room (Langdon, cited in Sundstrom, 1987), good location (for example, corner offices, offices on higher floors), windows, controlled access (a secretary), paintings and wall decorations, and higher quality office furniture and floor coverings (BOSTI, 1981; Harris & Associates, 1978; Konar, Sundstrom, Brady, Mandel, & Rice, 1982; Mehrabian, 1976b).

Desks are an especially effective way to regulate interaction and advertise status. For example, higher-status office occupants tend to place desks between themselves and the door, rather than against a side or back wall (Joiner, 1971). Studies show that college professors are most likely to sit sideways to their office doors, and business people and government officials almost always sit facing their doors, preferring to interact with visitors across their desks (Korda, 1975; Mehrabian, 1976b; Zweigenhaft, 1976). Even within academia higher-status people tend to interact from behind a desk. Administrators, such as deans and presidents, are more likely than faculty to sit behind a desk facing a door. Zweigenhaft (1976) found that three-quarters of senior faculty members placed their desks between themselves and their students and that fewer than half of junior faculty members did so. Zweigenhaft also noted that the professors who did not interact from behind a desk were perceived as more personable and approachable by students. Thus, research in a variety of settings shows that high-status people tend to use a desk to display dominance, and it is equally clear that their behavior has implications for the comfort of visitors in their offices (Joiner, 1976; Morrow & McElroy, 1981; Zweigenhaft, 1976).

Office Politics

Sommer and Steiner (1988) conducted an interesting study in which they described the politics behind office assignment and decor in the California State Capitol Building. Since there was plenty of actual space available in the building, conflicts were primarily over symbolic things like parking spaces and office furniture. Conflicts over seemingly petty office features actually were tests of power and status since these "perks" were visible signs of the esteem that each legislator had in the eyes of the capitol leadership. Office size in the building generally corresponded to seniority and responsibility and was accompanied by other desirable features, such as a high-quality view and the freedom to personalize interior space. Losers of political battles in the legislature often received undesirable office assignments near bathrooms and in remote corners of the building far removed from centers of visibility and power. In the words of Sommer and Steiner (1988), for these politicians "the office is both a symbol of the self and an indication of how self is regarded by others" (p. 551). The political importance of offices is also an issue at the level of national government; United States senators are assigned private "hideaway" offices in the bowels of the Capitol Building based on seniority (Gugliotta, 1991).

CHAPTER SUMMARY

Architecture plays an important role in people's behavior in work environments. Room design and the arrangement of furniture affect social interaction and the emotional responses of people in these environments. The way in which the ambient environment of the workplace affects workers' arousal levels has a powerful impact on their job performance. A poorly designed physical environment can lead to job dissatisfaction and low work motivation. Privacy and a work environment appropriate to a person's status in the organization are important to most employees, especially office workers. For the most part, open-plan offices, which became popular in the last 30 years, fall short of satisfying employees on either count.

GLOSSARY

Allocation Policy   In capacity models of attention, allocation policy refers to the decision rules by which attention is divided among competing demands.

Architectural Determinism   The belief that behavior is completely determined by the physical environment.

Coordination (Communication)   Sharing information to coordinate the efforts of different departments or work groups.

Drive   An internal stimulus that motivates behavior.

Hawthorne Effect   Improvement of work performance following the introduction of novelty into the work situation.

Hygiene Factors   Herzberg's theory of job satisfaction in which hygiene factors are job features whose absence causes dissatisfaction, but whose presence alone cannot ensure job satisfaction.

Incentive   Any external, motivating stimulus.

Informative Communication   Sharing information needed to stay current in one's profession.

Inspirational Communication   Communication that facilitates creative thinking and the generation of new ideas.

Open-Plan Offices   Extended office areas with no partitions between workers.

Sociofugal   Environmental designs that discourage social interaction.

Sociopetal   Environmental designs that encourage social interaction.

Speech Privacy   The freedom to talk without being overheard by others.

Yerkes-Dodson Law   The "inverted U-shaped" relationship between arousal level and task performance.

Learning Environments

9

SCHOOLS AND CLASSROOMS

Environments that will be familiar to anyone reading this book are the school and classroom settings in which you have spent so much of your life. Gump (1978) calculated that the average person spends about 14,000 hours in school from kindergarten through 12th grade. People who go to preschool or college tack on even more time. In effect, young people spend most of their waking hours in school environments; therefore, it is important that they be pleasant as well as functional and that they facilitate learning experiences.

The Physical Features of School Buildings

The most basic features of the physical environment are ambient variables such as light, color, and the hardness or softness of surfaces.

Research shows that paying attention to these basic ambient factors can lead to a better learning environment. Sometimes, all that is required are simple modifications. Mehrabian (1976a) relates a story about how student use of a drab elementary school library increased dramatically when many tables and chairs were removed and replaced by shaggy, fluffy carpeting and a bunch of pillows. Other, more systematic experiments have confirmed the advantages of a "softer" learning environment. Sommer and Olsen (1980) found that removing the hardness and linearity from college classrooms by using cushions, adjustable lighting, and carpeting increased class participation. Neill (1982b) reported that in a nursery school carpeting alone produced more teacher–student interaction than floors with a "harder" surface.

Much discussion centers on the importance of windows in classrooms, especially in elementary schools. Research confirms that students strongly prefer classrooms with windows, but teachers sometimes feel that windowless rooms are more flexible and less distracting (Ahrentzen, Jue, Skorpanich, & Evans, 1982; Larson, 1965). None of this research, however, has found any difference in student performance between classrooms with windows and those without them.

Color appears to be an especially important dimension in determining children's responses to their physical settings (Cohen & Trostle, 1988); Cohen and Trostle (1990) found that girls preferred even more intense and complex arrangements of shapes, color, and other environmental stimuli than boys did.

The Size of Classes and Schools

One aspect of the school environment that has implications for the physical design of a building and for the kind of education students receive is the class size into which students are grouped. The optimal class size for learning is a persistent problem and a pressing political issue in many school districts. One of the major problems with increasing class size is that usually it increases spatial and social density. The consequences of high density were discussed in Chapter 7, and it is clear that high-density levels promote disruptive behaviors in many situations; the classroom is probably no exception. For example, Rohe and Nuffer (1977) found that increased spatial density in a preschool class decreased cooperative behavior and increased aggression. Even worse, however, is that increasing class size not only increases density but also increases competition for resources such as desks, learning materials, and the teacher's attention. The best critical analysis of the importance of class size in elementary schools is by Glass and colleagues (1982). Not surprisingly, they conclude that smaller classes lead to better learning environments in almost every respect, including teacher and student attitudes, interaction, and actual student achievement. Moreover, they believe that once class size reaches 20 to 25 students, adding others makes relatively little difference. In other words, adding 5 students to a class of 15 brings about a much greater change in the classroom atmosphere than adding 5 to a class of 28.

By extension, setting optimal class sizes has implications for the school's optimal size; this issue is especially troublesome at the high school level. For an in-depth discussion of this controversy, see the following box.

The Ecology of Classroom Seating

Traditional classrooms consist of rows and columns of student desks that face the teacher and the blackboard at the front of the room. The

---

How Big Should a High School Be?

High schools differ from grade schools in the vast array of extracurricular activities and settings they provide. These activities and settings undoubtedly play an important role in the development of adolescent social skills and psychological identity. Given the importance of the high school experience, many researchers have studied the relative merits of large versus small high schools from an ecological perspective that stresses the importance of "staffing" the school with a number of persons that is optimal for the individual student, as well as for the school as a whole.

These studies find that the ratio of students to activities such as athletics, drama, and student government is much smaller in small high schools than at large schools. Schools with small student populations require a greater responsibility on the part of each student to work hard to make the school succeed. Consequently, students in small high schools are more likely to occupy leadership positions and receive recognition for their achievements than are students in large high schools; they more frequently report the satisfaction that grows out of meeting challenges, being part of a productive group, and developing a sense of competence (Baird, 1969; Barker & Gump, 1964; Gump, 1987; Schoggen, 1984). This added responsibility is especially important for academically marginal

students (Willems, 1967). In small schools, students also get to know their teachers and peers extremely well, enriching the depth of these relationships and perhaps enhancing personal development (Gump, 1987). Also, the lack of anonymity in small schools can result in less deviant and criminal behavior (McPartland & McDill, 1977; Plath, 1965).

Small high schools are often at the heart of community life in small towns and urban neighborhoods; school activities and athletics provide a common focus and topic of conversation that is an important part of the community's sense of identity. Often, these communities bitterly oppose cost-cutting initiatives to consolidate schools and make considerable sacrifices to keep their own high schools. Learning that there is strength in numbers, communities have begun to band together to fight the notion that bigger is necessarily better. One such movement, calling itself "the Voice of the Prairie," recently defeated a state effort to consolidate small high schools in rural Illinois.

Now I return to my original question: How big is too big? Research indicates that crucial school size is somewhere between 500 and 700 students. Once enrollments exceed this threshold, further increases seem to have little effect (Garabino, 1980).

relationship between seating position and student performance has interested educators and educational psychologists for many years. Griffith's (1921) classic early study of the relationship between student grades and seating position has been described by Knowles (1982). In this study, the grades of students who had been assigned to seats alphabetically were carefully recorded over many different classes. Griffith ultimately accumulated approximately 20,000 grades and carefully examined the students' grades in relation to their seating positions. He detected a distinct curvilinear relationship between a student's location and the grade received. Significantly, students in the center of the class tended to receive the highest grades, and a steady drop-off occurred as the seating position got further from the center. Recent studies of college students confirm the importance of seating, with students seated near the front of the class usually receiving higher grades than those in the back (Becker, Sommer, Bee, & Oxley, 1973; Brooks & Rebeta, 1991; Levine, O'Neal, Garwood, & McDonald, 1980; Stires, 1980).

A problem with interpreting these studies arises when students are allowed to select their own seats. Studies of high school students indicate that students have definite perceptions of different parts of the classroom and choose seats that are consistent with their goals, academic commitment, and informal social status within the group (MacPherson, 1984).

TRY IT!

Classroom Seating and Class Participation

Research shows that class participation increases as students sit closer to the teacher and to the front of the room. Attempt to verify this phenomenon in one of your classes. Begin by preparing a data sheet containing three columns labeled "front," "middle," and "back." Classify the one-third of the classroom closest to the instructor as the "front," the middle third as "middle," and the final third as "back." For a period of one week, place a check mark under the appropriate column each time a student in the class asks or answers a question or participates in a class discussion. Since you hardly qualify as a naive participant, do not count your own responses. At the end of the week, count the check marks under each column and find out if there was in fact more class participation by the students in the front of the room. If you fail to find this effect, can you think of any moderating variables such as the architecture of the classroom or the class size that might have diminished the participation advantage of those students seated at the front of the room?

MacPherson found that a feeling of being controlled by and being dependent on the teacher was strongly linked with seats in the front of the room. The rear of the room was associated with freedom to interact with peers and freedom from teacher control. Consequently, it is not surprising that a certain amount of self-selection in seating occurs when students are free to sit wherever they choose. Students who take seats near the front of the room tend to be high achievers who enjoy being in class more than those further from the teacher; generally, they report that they like school and work hard. High achievers also score higher on measures of self-esteem (Hillman, Brooks, & O'Brien, 1991; Millard & Simpson, 1980; Walberg, 1969; Wulf, 1977). Brooks and Rebeta (1991) report that women are more likely than men to sit in the front of the classroom. Undoubtedly, part of the relationship between performance and seating position is due to this self-selection process. In studies where students have been assigned to seats, the relationship is not always found (Wulf, 1977). Nevertheless, even in these studies seating position in and of itself appears to have some effect on performance (Koneya, 1976; Levine et al., 1980; Millard & Simpson, 1980).

Research indicates that attitudes toward the course and class participation are more strongly affected by seat location than grades are (Levine et al., 1980; Montello, 1988). The closer students are to the front and center of the room, the more often they interact with the teacher (Adams & Biddle, 1970) and the more attentive they are to classroom tasks (Breed & Colaiuta, 1974; Schwebel & Cherlin, 1972). This seems to hold true from the early elementary grades (Schwebel & Cherlin, 1972) through college (Sommer, 1967). While this effect often can be traced to self-selection, apparently the high levels of eye contact with the instructor and visibility in the class from sitting near the front greatly encourage participation (Caproni, Levine, O'Neal, McDonald, & Garwood, 1977). To see if this effect holds true in your classes, try it (see box Classroom Seating and Class Participation).

Traditional versus Open Classrooms

One of the educational changes that grew out of the 1960s was a move toward **open-plan classrooms.** These classrooms are similar in design to the open-plan offices discussed in Chapter 8. They are large areas of undivided, flexible space, and they offer many of the same advantages (low construction and maintenance costs) found in open-plan offices (see Figure 9-1). Although no necessary relationship exists between classroom design and the educational program carried out there (Bennett, Andreal, Hegarty, & Wade, 1980), Sommer (1967) believes that the way a teacher arranges classroom space reflects his or her philosophy of education. Rivlin and Rothenberg (1976) believe that "open classrooms embody both an educational policy and a setting that departs from traditional forms" (p. 480). Thus, a widely-held belief was that departure

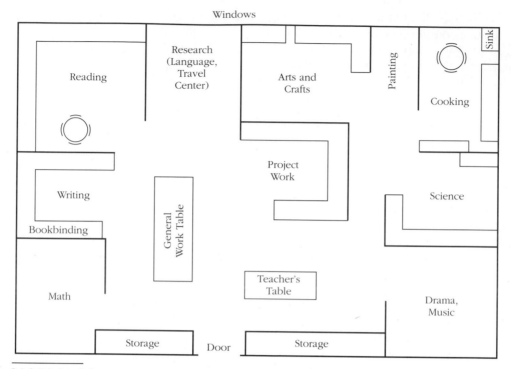

FIGURE 9-1   Sample floor plan for an open classroom (Source: Stephens, 1974)

from the standard "egg carton" design used in traditional classrooms (see Figure 9-2) would be accompanied by new approaches to teaching and learning. The "ecological" perspective in studying behavior settings (Barker, 1968; Wicker, 1979) stressed the importance of a good fit between the physical and psychological/social aspects of a setting, a principle referred to as **synomorphy.** Accordingly, a good fit between the design of the classroom and the style of teaching should be crucial to the success of open-plan classrooms. Traub, Weiss, and Fisher (in Gifford, 1987) found that the fit between teaching style and classroom environment is indeed a good predictor of teacher satisfaction with the classroom environment.

What differences might be expected between teachers in open-plan and those in traditional classrooms? Weinstein and Woolfolk (1981) showed slides of different kinds of classrooms to college students and asked them to make judgments about the teachers and pupils who would use each room. Teachers in open classrooms were thought to be more responsive to students and more creative than teachers in traditional classrooms. Interestingly enough, however, a sample of fifth graders in their study did not differentiate between the two. Since extended open space encourages movement and active play (Loughlin & Suina, 1982) and since children must move around to different activity centers in

Teacher's
Desk

Pupils' Desks

FIGURE 8-2 Seating arrangement of a traditional classroom

open-plan classrooms (Gump, 1974), one would expect teachers with a strong need for order and control to prefer a traditional over an open classroom. This has been confirmed in at least one study (Feitter, Weiner, & Blumberg, cited by Gifford, 1987).

What educational benefits might be expected from an open-plan school? There are many reasons to think that the flexibility and relative freedom of the open-plan classroom might decrease boredom and increase student involvement and motivation. Zifferblatt (1972) found that arrangements that encouraged teachers to move around the room rather than sit in one place resulted in more attentive, less noisy students. Open-plan schools do lead to increased interaction among teachers (Meyer, in Weinstein, 1979). Therefore, there are many indications that an open-plan classroom might have real educational advantages. To answer the question conclusively, a number of studies directly comparing the educational outcomes of the two classroom designs have been undertaken. Unfortunately, field research of this kind is handicapped by the degree to which the physical setting's effects and the educational program are intertwined, making it difficult to separate the two influences (Gump, 1987). The problem is complicated further by the range in the extent to which new approaches to teaching have accompanied a changed classroom environment; in many cases, methods developed in traditional schools simply have been transferred to the new setting. With these limitations in mind, I will review some of the research on the relationship between classroom design and educational performance. For the most part, these findings are not very encouraging for the future of open-plan schools.

Although some research shows more on-task activity in open or circular seating arrangements (Rosenfield, Lambert, & Black, 1985), most studies find that students seated around tables interact with each other more but spend less time focused on the task at hand (Axelrod, Hall, & Tams, 1979; Wheldall, Morris, Vaughan, & Ng, 1981). Students in open-plan classrooms also spend more time in aimless movement (Moore, 1983; Neill, 1982a) and "getting ready" for new tasks but less time actually working on those tasks (Gump, 1984, 1987). There is widespread agreement that open-plan classrooms are noisier (Kyzar, 1977; Walsh, 1975) and more distracting (Ahrentzen, Jue, Skorpanich, & Evans, 1982; Rivlin & Rothenberg, 1976; Stebbins, 1973).

Weinstein (1979) stresses that the quality of the data is suspect in many of these studies because control of other important variables, such as the children's family background and the nature of the educational program, is seldom adequate. She believes that actual *achievement* behaviors are relatively unaffected by the physical environment but that nonachievement behaviors such as attendance, class participation, and satisfaction are more likely to be affected. While it is true that most studies comparing the actual academic achievement of children in open versus traditional schools show no major differences, studies that do report differences tend to favor the traditional over the open-plan school (Angus, Beck, Hill, & McAtee, 1979; Bell, Abrahamsen, & Growse, 1977; Bennett et al., 1980; Gump, 1987; Sanders & Wren, 1975; Traub & Weiss, 1975). Students in traditional schools usually outscore those from open-plan schools on achievement tests although the reason for this is not clear (Wright, 1975). The open-plan classroom seems especially ill-suited for low ability or low motivation students (Grapko, cited by Gump, 1987;

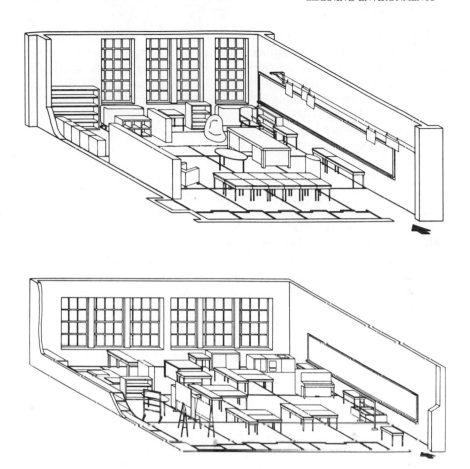

F I G U R E   9-3A and B Classrooms used in Rivlin and Rothenberg (1976) study (Source: Proshansky, Ittelson, & Rivlin, 1976)

Reiss & Dydhalo, 1975) or for students not being instructed in their native language (Traub & Weiss, 1974).

Virtually all this research has occurred in actual educational settings. For example, Moore (1986) believed that well-defined behavior settings with clear boundaries would facilitate attention and decrease classroom interruptions. He tested his hypothesis in a field study of 14 child-care centers that varied according to how well defined their spatial areas were. He found that the well-defined settings were associated with significantly more "developmentally supportive" behaviors such as exploration, cooperation, and child-initiated behavior focused on specific activities. In another field study, Rivlin and Rothenberg (1976) looked at open classrooms in two urban public elementary schools. Diagrams of these classrooms are presented in Figures 9-3A and 9-3B. They traced the location of furniture and equipment in the rooms throughout the school year and constructed a behavior map describing the location and activities of individuals during the observation periods. Throughout the study they also interviewed students and teachers. Despite an apparent freedom of movement, Rivlin and Rothenberg found that activity and movement primarily occurred in a few key sectors of the room, leaving much of the classroom underutilized. There was also a considerable amount of individual work, such as writing, in spite of the stated goal of group projects and interaction.

Lack of privacy was a frequent complaint from both students and teachers in the Rivlin and Rothenberg study. Although the children expressed a strong need for "private spaces," other studies (for example, Weinstein, 1982) indicate that such spaces are seldom used when they are available, posssibly because they engender feelings of isolation or because, in fact, there is less freedom of movement than it would appear. The lack of privacy for teachers is a more serious problem, since teachers who share open space may avoid inviting guest speakers or using musical instruments that might distract other groups in the area (Gump, 1987).

SCHOOLYARDS AND PLAYGROUNDS

Much informal learning of social skills and constructive play ought to occur in the schoolyards and playgrounds where children spend non-school time. Various studies (for example, Becker, 1976; Moore, 1980; Moore & Young, 1978) indicate that between 2 percent to 42 percent of children's outdoor activities take place on public playgrounds, with perhaps an additional 9 percent occurring in schoolyards. The importance of these settings to children is underscored by a study showing that playgrounds and schoolyards are the second most common settings in children's drawings. Yet, in the race to improve schools, schoolyards usually are overlooked. Many of them are still what Lady Allen of Hurtwood (cited in Weinstein & Pinciotti, 1988) called "prison yard playgrounds" consisting of a concrete or asphalt surface surrounded by a chain-link fence.

According to Shaw (1987), playgounds and schoolyards should have a variety of different spaces connected by clear paths arranged to facilitate interaction of all types (verbal and visual as well as physical). Variety and complexity are the ideal in schoolyard landscapes, a stark contrast to what is usually found. Weinstein and Pinciotti (1988) studied changes in the play behavior of kindergarteners through third graders in a schoolyard. They employed a multiple time series design (described in Chapter 1) to examine the children's play before and after construction of a tire playground on what had been a typical fenced-in blacktop lot. The tires used about a third of the blacktop area and consisted of three rectangular towers made from tires connected by tire bridges to three pyramidal piles

P H O T O   8-1   The importance of playgrounds as learning environments is often overlooked.

of tires, two with sliding boards. This entire structure was surrounded by wood or rubber-tire balance beams. There was also another tire "mountain" that could be reached by balance beams or hand over hand rings suspended from poles. Weinstein and Pinciotti found a tremendous increase in active play and "pretend" games after the tire playground was built and fewer organized games, less "roughhousing," and less uninvolved "hanging around." A favorite game on the new playground was the children's attempt to get completely around the area without touching the gravel on the ground, because that meant "the alligators will get you" (p. 369). The children reported that the playground cultivated feelings of competence and success as they progressively conquered more difficult tasks requiring greater physical skill. On the down side, Weinstein and Pinciotti noted that there seemed to be a decrease in talking and focused social interaction and an increase in territorial conflicts over different parts of the apparatus.

Other researchers confirm the relationship between the style of play and the nature of the schoolyard. Children in traditional schoolyards (fenced-in blacktop areas) are more likely to play ball games or other apparatus-free games (Beth-Halachmy & Thayer, 1978), especially in the upper grades (Heusser, Adelson, & Ross, 1986). Undoubtedly, this is due to the limited variety and daily familiarity of the playground equipment found in most schoolyards.

Playgrounds not attached to schools often have more available space and, therefore, more flexibility in their design. Hayward, Rothenberg, and

T A B L E   9·1   **Distribution of Playground Users According to Age Groups**

	Traditional playground	Contemporary playground	Adventure playground
% Preschool	29.48	35.23	1.74
% School-Age	20.84	22.21	44.58
% Teenage	9.80	6.85	32.16
% Adult	39.78	35.71	21.52
Total %	100.00	100.00	100.00
Total Observations (n =)	(4,294)	(9,765)	(2,360)
Days of Behavioral Mapping	10.5	11	11

Source: Hayward, Rothenberg, & Beasley, 1974.

Beasley (1974) distinguished between three types of playgrounds. **Traditional playgrounds** contain familiar, premanufactured equipment such as swings, slides, monkey bars, and see-saws. **Contemporary playgrounds** provide move novel equipment designed to be aesthetically pleasing and functional. Often they provide more flexible play materials, such as sand piles and sprinklers or water fountains. **Adventure playgrounds** (sometimes called "junk" playgrounds) supply children with unconventional equipment such as tires, sheets of plywood, dirt hills, digging utensils, water holes, and paintbrushes. These playgrounds are usually unstructured areas that allow children to plan and change the nature of the playground as they wish.

Hayward and colleagues (1974) studied three urban playgrounds, one of each type, by observing behavior, describing the setting, and recording the location, age, sex, and number of people at the playground during each observation period. Overt behaviors were counted and categorized by trained observers who also tape-recorded descriptions of ongoing activities. Interviews were conducted with people (primarily children) found at the playgrounds. People described their reasons for coming, how often they came, what they liked most about the playground, and whose idea it was to come. They were also asked about other playgrounds that they used. The most striking difference among the playgrounds was in the pattern of use they received (see Table 9-1). Preschoolers were almost never found at the adventure playground but were very often at the traditional and contemporary playgrounds. School-aged children (ages 6 to 13) were a large group at all playgrounds, but especially at the adventure playground. Forty-four percent of all people at the adventure playground were school-aged children, but they made up only about 20 percent of the people on each of the other playgrounds. Teenagers accounted for 32 percent of those found at the adventure playground but less than 10 percent of those at each of the other two.

Not surprisingly, adults concentrated most heavily where preschoolers were found. Adults were the most commonly observed age group at the traditional and contemporary playgrounds. (Many of the adults and teen-agers observed on the playgrounds were play leaders or day-camp coun-selors.) Children at the adventure playground usually came alone or with peers. Adults accompanied children more to the other playgrounds, in part because the children were younger on average at the traditional and contemporary playgrounds but also because these playgrounds provided more comfortable and convenient areas for adults to sit and observe. Related to this, children at the adventure playground were most likely to report that it was their favorite playground and that it was their decision to go there; children at the traditional playground were least likely to say this. The play activities that the children engaged in at the different playgrounds were predictable. Children at the adventure playground built clubhouses and played imaginary games, and children at the other play-grounds rode swings and slides and played in the sand or the wading pool.

Although Hart and Sheehan (1986) found less physical activity on contemporary than on traditional playgrounds, Brown and Burger (1984) believe that contemporary playgrounds are only superficially different from traditional ones. They found, as did Hayward and colleagues (1974), few major differences between them in play behavior. Adventure play-grounds, on the other hand, depart radically from traditional notions of what a playground should be. Hayward and colleagues (1974) feel that the adventure playground is beneficial in that it helps children define themselves better by allowing more creativity in their choice of activities. Spivak (1969) reports that children like adventure playgrounds a great deal but adults hate them because they are unattractive, chaotic places that are full of "junk."

Although adding natural features such as vegetation and water greatly enhances children's evaluations of the playground (Moore, 1989a), these features are rarely included. When natural elements are present on play-grounds, usually they are added for aesthetic rather than play purposes (Bruya & Langendorfer, cited by Moore, 1989b). Moore (1989b) describes many advantages inherent in bringing nature into the playground.

> Natural materials that are alive, ever-changing and renewing themselves have a very high play value. They stimulate imagination and fine-muscle coordina-tion through play with vegetation parts, sticks, and dirt. They engage chil-dren in problem solving when making clubhouses from natural materials. They support large-muscle activities through games like hide-and-go-seek played among bushes and weeds and in climbing rocks and trees. . . . Biotic settings powerfully impact children's untarnished senses, stimulating the creation of a world of fantasy and delight that knows no boundaries of mind and spirit [p. 101].

The research thus far indicates that different types of playgrounds may have advantages for children at different developmental stages: matching the age group and playground type might facilitate the experiences that parents and teachers want for their children. Moore (1989b) lists a number of recommendations for improving playgrounds: They should include formal entrances and exits that serve as convenient drop-off/pick-up locations and also gathering places for hellos, good-byes, and gossip. Primary pathways should provide clear routes to facilities such as restrooms and telephones, and secondary pathways (ideally through vegetation) should encourage exploration and hiding games. A variety of play areas should be available: open, flat areas encourage ball games and other running play; hills are great for climbing, sliding, and rolling. Sand and water-play areas are especially valuable for younger children. Also helpful are clear informational and directional signs employing simple graphics.

MUSEUMS AND ZOOS

Museums

Museums are educational institutions that cater to people of all ages and backgrounds and, unlike most schools, explicitly attempt to combine learning with recreation. According to Mehrabian (1976a), museums (especially art museums) should be designed to maximize interest in the exhibits. Too often, however, the environmental load of the building itself is ignored, which results in large, dark museum rooms that are boring and repetitive. This can impose feelings of submissiveness and displeasure and cause museum visitors to behave in a formal, subdued fashion (Mehrabian, 1976a). Although there may be an intentional effort not to detract from a display's impact, a variety of rooms in which exhibits are placed according to their inherent load is a more effective way of accomplishing this. Very high-load, shocking art should be displayed in relatively sparse surroundings, while more subtle pieces would be lost in an already sterile area.

Museums that are confusing and difficult to find one's way through are less enjoyable than those that are more "legible" (Mehrabian, 1976a; Winkel, Olsen, Wheeler, & Cohen, 1976). Good navigation aids, such as maps and suggested routes for viewing specific types of exhibits, cause people to evaluate their museum experience more positively (Borun, 1977). Very early research in the 1920s and 1930s discovered that people explore museums predictably. Visitors almost always examine the first few exhibits encountered in great detail but then begin skipping exhibits and explore only those with the strongest appeal to them. Typically, they move to the right when exploring rooms and consequently are more likely to use exits to other rooms that are easily seen and to their right. This "pull" exerted by exits is called the **exit gradient** (Melton, 1933).

Museum fatigue (Robinson, 1928), which is a common problem visitors experience, greatly decreases the enjoyment of a museum visit. In part, it is due to the exertion of walking around the museum, but primarily it is a result of the attempt to maintain a high degree of attention in such a highly loaded environment. Such information over-load results in an inability to focus on details. Robinson's early work indicates that a break in the nature of the exhibits may help to alleviate museum fatigue (Thomson, 1986). For example, a natural history mu-seum might interrupt a hallway filled with Native American artifacts with a large display featuring animals of importance to people's lives at that time. Such a "cognitive breather" allows visitors to focus on different items and relieves the strain of attending to highly detailed, similar stimuli for long periods of time.

Zoos

Zoos are perhaps the fastest growing educational/recreational environ-ments in North America. The number of accredited zoos in the United States increased from 55 in 1931 to 135 in 1988 (Martin & O'Reilly, 1989). Annually 110 million people visit zoos in the United States (Boyd, 1988). Originally, zoos were created to entertain humans, but this is slowly changing. Increasingly, the purpose of zoos also includes preserving rare species and maintaining the comfort and security of animals. The trans-action between visitors and exhibits often is more dynamic in zoos than in museums because the animals are alive (Martin & O'Reilly, 1988). Since 1960, zoos have made a great effort to capitalize on this and to develop the educational value of zoo visits. These efforts have ranged from instituting new education departments in zoos and aquaria to cre-ating community outreach programs aimed primarily at schoolchildren (Serrell, 1988). After all, zoos are the only link that most contemporary urban people have to wild animals (Livingston, 1974).

Although zoo visitors have higher than average education levels and socioeconomic status (Hood, 1984; Reed & Mindlin, 1963), Serrell (1988) noted that as a group zoo visitors are not very sophisticated in their knowledge of animals. They have a sentimental, emotional interest in animals rather than one based on factual understanding. Studies show that other groups—bird watchers, hunters, and members of humane/ environmental organizations—score higher than zoo visitors on tests of their knowledge of animals (Kellert, in Serrell, 1988). For many of these people, going to the zoo is a social event to be enjoyed with children and other relatives. Fully 70 percent of zoo visitors are in groups of relatives (Brennan, in Serrell, 1988), and 50 percent of all groups contain children (Rosenfeld, in Serrell, 1988). Aside from socializing, visitors report other benefits from their visit to the zoo: relaxation, informal learning, and aesthetic experiences (Loomis, in Serrell, 1988).

Since the motivations and backgrounds of zoo visitors are quite diverse, designers must be careful not to make the educational compo-nent of the zoo too demanding. Most zoo visitors do not read signs, and they must be short, eye-catching, and very relevant if they are to be read at all (Serrell, 1988). In developing signs and other graphic displays for zoos, there has been a shift away from a purely educational philosophy to one more concerned with making the zoo experience as pleasant as possible (Serrell, 1988). Experiential exhibits in which visitors become actively involved through touching, listening, and playing are more effective than instructional signs for teaching new information about animals. For example, Chicago's Brookfield Zoo's "Flying Walk" exhibit forces visitors to move their upper bodies and arms in a way that simulates the figure-eight motion of a bird's wings in flight. A before-and-after study of adults and children who visited this exhibit showed impressive gains in knowledge about the mechanics of flight (Birney, 1988). Similarly, visitors to the African Rock Kopje exhibit at the San Diego Zoo who took advantage of the exhibit's interactive elements learned significantly more about the rocky ecosystem on the plains of Africa than did those who simply looked at it or read the signs (Derwin & Piper, 1988). Interactive exhibits are more likely to attract people to them (Bruce, in Derwin & Piper, 1988). They provide learning experiences at different cognitive levels and address a wide range of learning styles (Lee, 1985; Plaisance, 1984; Webster, 1985; White, 1986). The value of interactive exhibits in museums has also been strongly supported (Danilov, 1982; Fleming & Levie, 1978; Peart, 1984). The only drawback to interactive exhibits is that they can be expensive to develop and maintain (Derwin & Piper, 1988).

Understanding visitor reactions to zoo exhibits is important for improving them. Poor exhibits may lead visitors to form incorrect impressions of animals and encourage feelings of human superiority and indifference; these attitudes ultimately can work against wildlife preservation (Coe, 1985; Maple, 1983; Sommer, 1972b). Especially important are exhibits that dispel fear and misunderstanding about animals, including any species considered ugly, slimy, or unpredictable and sudden in its movements (Bennett-Levy & Marteau, 1984). Finlay, James, and Maple (1988) demonstrated that the zoo environment can in fact influence visitor perceptions of animals. In this study, subjects viewed slides of animals taken in the wild, in a naturalistic zoo, or in a caged zoo. Their judgments about the animals were compared to each other and to a control group who rated the animals without looking at slides. Animals in any kind of zoo were rated as more restricted, tame, and passive than when seen in the wild or when they were rated by people who did not see them in any context. Zoo settings also sometimes conveyed the impression that the animals are harmless and friendly.

Zoo exhibits have gone through three generations of evolution (Campbell, 1984). **First-generation exhibits** (see Photo 9-2A) began in the mid-18th century and usually are small, side-by-side barred cages or deep, smooth-walled pits. **Second-generation exhibits** (see Photo 9-2B) are the ones most commonly seen in zoos today. They usually are barless, cement enclosures surrounded by a moat. **Third-generation exhibits** (see Photo 9-2C) display animals in species-natural groups with vegetation and landforms similar to the animals' natural habitats.

P H O T O   9-2A   A first-generation zoo exhibit

P H O T O   9-2B   A second-generation zoo exhibit

P H O T O   9-2C   A third-generation zoo exhibit

First-generation exhibits fail to meet virtually all the animals' needs. Second-generation exhibits provide more space and better visitor views but are still relatively sterile and boring for the animals. Third-generation exhibits should be better for the animals and more enjoyable and educational for visitors (Maple, 1983; Maple & Stine, 1982). However, very little actual research on the benefits of third-generation exhibits exists. In one recent study, Shettell-Neuber (1988) compared visitor, staff, and animal responses to second- and third-generation exhibits at the San Diego Zoo. At the time of her study, there were separate second- and third-generation exhibits of both Bornean orangutans and pygmy chimpanzees. She carefully tracked the activity patterns of the animals in the exhibits and of visitors. She timed the length of visitors' stays at the exhibits, gave questionnaires to visitors, and conducted interviews with the zoo staff. She found no real differences in the activity or health of the animals in the two exhibits. Visitors and staff both expressed greater liking for the third-generation exhibits, although the staff admitted that they were more difficult to maintain. The time that visitors spent was to some extent a function of the animals. The more passive, slow-moving orangutans were observed longer in the third-generation exhibit, but the active chimps were just as interesting and perhaps easier to see and follow in the second-generation exhibit.

A more general study of zoo visitors is one by Bitgood, Patterson, and Benefield (1988). They studied visitor behavior in 13 zoos across the United States and were particularly interested in the amount of time that visitors spent looking at any particular animal or exhibit. They summarized their major findings as follows:

1. Active animals were associated with twice as much viewing time as inactive animals.
2. Viewing time was directly correlated with the size of the animals. In general, the larger the species, the longer the viewing time.
3. The presence of an infant [animal] was associated with increased viewing time.
4. Visual competition between exhibits decreased visitor stopping.
5. The proximity of the visitor to the animal influenced visitor stopping: The closer the animal to the visitor, the higher the probability of visitors stopping.
6. Visibility of the animals was correlated with the viewing time of visitors. Thus, low lighting levels, visual obstacles, and visual screens were associated with lower visitor viewing times.
7. The physical features of the exhibit appeared to be related to both percentage of visitors who stopped and the amount of viewing time [p. 489].

Martin and O'Reilly (1989) suggested that exhibits incorporating water are very attractive to visitors, especially children.

The implications of these findings for zoo design are clear. Highly attractive exhibits should not be located too close to each other. This keeps crowding to a minimum and increases the viewing time for visitors at each exhibit. Exhibits should be designed so that some animals are always visible. Hiding places should be constructed so that animals are still visible to visitors without causing stress to the animals. Often, it is possible to shield visitors from the animals' view without the opposite being true. Since the size of the animal is an important factor, viewing small species is most preferable at close range in exhibits scaled down to the size of the animal.

These suggestions may not be appreciated equally by all visitors. For example, Verderber, Gardner, Islam, and Nakanishi (1988) found that senior citizens are less interested in interactive exhibits and tend not to like newer, more "open" zoo exhibits. These individuals are not accustomed to thinking of the zoo in these terms and are uncomfortable with the idea of wild animals in the open, roaming free.

CHAPTER SUMMARY

The physical design of schools and classrooms is an important component in the educational process. Studies show that seating positions and whether the class is organized in a traditional "egg carton" or an open classroom can affect student achievement, participation, and satisfaction. Although the research results are mixed, most studies indicate that students in traditional classrooms outperform those in open classrooms.

The design of schoolyards and playgrounds is often a neglected dimension of learning environments. Recent studies are beginning to show that the type of play that children pursue in these environments is dictated to a great degree by the physical constraints of the playground.

Museums and zoos are educational institutions available to people of all ages and backgrounds. These places should be designed to be legible and pleasant. In museums the environmental load must be adjusted to minimize museum fatigue. Zoos must take into account recent research emphasizing the relationship between the animals on display, the exhibit's physical design, and the characteristics of zoo visitors to make the zoo experience as educational and pleasurable as possible.

GLOSSARY

Adventure Playgrounds Unstructured play areas that allow children to plan and change the nature of the playground as they wish.
Contemporary Playgrounds Playgrounds that provide equipment that is novel in design and aesthetically pleasing.
Exit Gradient The tendency for some exits to be used more frequently than others.

First-Generation Zoo Exhibits   Displays of animals in small, side-by-side cages or deep, smooth-walled pits.

Museum Fatigue   The exhaustion often experienced in museums that results from maintaining a high level of attention in a highly loaded environment.

Open-Plan Classroom   Large classrooms of undivided, flexible space in which students sit in a variety of arrangements and go to different places for different activities.

Second-Generation Zoo Exhibits   Displays of animals in barless, cement enclosures usually surrounded by a moat.

Synomorphy   The congruity or fit among the physical, psychological, and social aspects of a behavior setting.

Third-Generation Zoo Exhibits   Displays of animals in species-natural groups with vegetation and landforms similar to the animals' natural habitats.

Traditional Playgrounds   Playgrounds dominated by familiar, premanufactured equipment such as swings and sliding boards.

Residential Environments

10

ATTACHMENT TO PLACE AND THE CONCEPT OF HOME

Throughout history, humans have made shelter from whatever affordances were available in their immediate location (see Photos 10-1A and
10-1B), and the diversity of housing around the world continues to be
astounding. People live in tents, boats, skyscrapers, mud huts, and suburban ranch houses. Whatever form their dwelling might take, individuals
develop very strong sentimental and emotional attachments to the places
in which they live. These attachments may be generic in nature, as when
individuals become dependent on regions or on certain kinds of environments such as cities, mountains, or deserts. An individual with a **generic
place dependence** can be satisfied in a number of different locations, as
long as those places have the right characteristics. **Geographic place
dependence,** on the other hand, refers to an extremely powerful attachment to a very specific town or house (Stokols & Shumaker, 1981).

P H O T O S   10-1A and B Humans have always made shelter from whatever their environment afforded. For example, dwelling places have been made in hollowed-out spaces in Baobab trees and in rocky cliffs.

Attachment to place has been defined as a positive affective association between individuals and their residential environments (Shumaker & Taylor, 1983), an association that creates feelings of comfort and security (Rivlin, 1982). The affective bond between people and places has also been referred to as **topophilia** (Tuan, 1974). Shumaker and Taylor (1983) note the evolutionary advantage inherent in strong attachments to place. In early human groups, this attachment facilitated defense of familiar areas, reduced unnecessary, dangerous exploration and navigation, and bestowed a "resident advantage" (described in Chapter 6) on individuals operating in their own territories.

Our attachments to the settings in our lives vary in intensity. Rubinstein (1989) described the characteristic features of four different levels of attachment. At the lowest level, people merely know of a place and think of it without experiencing any strong feelings or personal memories. At a slightly more elevated level of attachment, known as **personalized attachment,** the individual has memories of a place that are inseparable from personal experiences. Schools you attended or fields and woods in which you played as a child might represent personalized attachments for you. When places elicit highly emotional memories or are psychologically involving in some other way, the attachment we experience is more intense and is referred to as **extension.** The most intense level of attachment, **embodiment,** blurs the boundaries between the self and the environment. A house where an individual has spent a lifetime or the cemetery plot of a spouse, child, or parent may elicit especially intense feelings of attachment. For such individuals, personal identity and place identity have become fused (Howell, 1983).

Many different factors influence people's attachment to places. Shumaker and Taylor (1983) have identified the congruence between the needs and goals of the individual and the resources of the setting, the perceived choice the individual has to leave or remain in the setting, and the attractiveness of alternatives as important parts of the attachment process. Children, older people, and those with restricted mobility are especially likely to be place-dependent (Saegert, 1985). To help you think about the extent of your own attachment to place, try it (see box A Measurement of Attachment to Place).

A strong attachment to place results in greater satisfaction with one's home and greater expectations of future stability. It is also accompanied by a more detailed knowledge of the history and geography of a locale and a greater investment of time and resources in that place (Shumaker & Taylor, 1983).

Although social networks are an important part of place attachment (Fried, 1982; Shumaker & Conti, 1985), these feelings transcend attachment to other people and represent a genuine affection for the physical location itself. People who have relocated to other parts of the country (or world) often report missing the mountains, ocean, or neighborhoods of their former homes even years after they have left. People who are very attached to a location or house suffer great distress if they are forced to move. People with strong place attachment are more firmly rooted, less motivated to seek change, and more satisfied with their place of residence (Stokols, Shumaker, & Martinez, 1983; Tognoli, 1987).

The passage of time seems to be crucial for the development of feelings of attachment; hence, it is not surprising that older people are often the most strongly attached to their home places (Kasarda & Janowitz, 1974; Norris-Baker & Scheidt, 1990; Rowles, 1980; Taylor, 1988). Norris-Baker and Scheidt (1990) studied elderly residents' attachment to a small dying town in Kansas. A decaying town is a problem for many older people in small towns, especially in the Midwest, since the proportion of older residents increases as the size of a community decreases (Clifford, Heaton, Voss, & Fuguitt, 1985). Many formerly thriving towns have all but disappeared with the exodus of jobs and young people over the last 20 years. In most cases, those left behind are the elderly, many of whom have lived their entire lives in the town. Norris-Baker and Scheidt conducted in-depth interviews with the elderly residents of the Kansas town in an effort to understand their reactions to the steady decay of the behavior settings that marked their lives. The older residents did in fact believe that they had stronger attachments to the buildings and places in town than did younger residents. These strong attachments served a number of functions. Strong place attachment helped to affirm their membership in the social organization of the town and provided psychological continuity between the past and present in the face of an uncertain future. Place-based reminiscence also seemed to be a means of maintaining community pride and spirit.

Several studies indicate that people from lower socioeconomic classes are especially dependent on the development of strong interpersonal relationships with neighbors and, consequently, develop strong attachments to their neighborhoods (Gans, 1962; Fried, 1963; Suttles, 1968). Unfortunately, these people are precisely the ones who are most likely to be relocated involuntarily. Porteous (1978) presents a moving account of the forced relocation of 10,000 Bostonians in the city's West End during the 1950s and 1960s. Residents who were relocated were from a low income, socially cohesive, multigenerational ethnic commu-

TRY IT!

A Measurement of Attachment to Place

Individuals differ in the extent to which they feel attachment to the places they live. Some of this variation is due to demographic factors such as age or socioeconomic status, but undoubtedly some is due to personality differences. While there is no precise way to measure individual attachment to place, you can explore the strength of your predisposition to become strongly attached to the places you live by completing this brief questionnaire. Indicate how much you agree or disagree with each of the statements listed according to the following scale:

5 = Strongly agree
4 = Agree
3 = Neither agree nor disagree
2 = Disagree
1 = Strongly disagree

Fill in the blank after each statement with the number that comes closest to expressing your feelings. Instructions for scoring the questionnaire are presented at the end. (This scale has not been empirically validated. It is intended only as a classroom exercise.)

1. I quickly feel at home wherever I am. _____
2. I am extremely satisfied with my present home. _____
3. I don't know very much about the history of my hometown. _____
4. I could draw a very accurate map of my hometown. _____
5. Moving from place to place is exciting and fun. _____

nity, primarily of Italian descent. The West End had been targeted for urban renewal and construction of high-rent apartment housing, which would bring in more money for the city and possibly prompt more activity by private developers.

The "West Enders" were guaranteed space in the new luxury apartments, but none could realistically afford that option. For the most part, they were dispersed far and wide. The displaced residents of the West End lost a supportive environment they were deeply attached to. Old family and friendship networks were destroyed, and the sense of identity these people shared was shattered. After the demolition of their neighborhoods, many returned to the streets of the old neighborhoods just to walk around. Fried (1963) reported evidence of extreme grief in 73 percent of

TRY IT!

6. I have lived in the same town or city my whole life. _____
7. I could not be happy living in one place for the rest of my life. _____
8. Living close to certain natural features such as the ocean or mountains is very important to me. _____
9. The size of the town or city I live in is unimportant to me. _____
10. My family is very close-knit, and I would be unhappy if I could not see them on a regular basis. _____
11. I like going to places where no one knows me. _____
12. I have several close, lifelong friends whom I never want to lose. _____
13. There is not much of a future for me in my present location. _____
14. My parents still live in the same house or apartment they lived in when I was born. _____

To obtain your "attachment to place" score, add all your responses to the odd-numbered questions. Do the same for the even-numbered questions. After you have obtained these two sums, subtract the sum of the odd-numbered questions from the sum of the even-numberd questions and add 28 to the remainder. This is your "attachment to place" score. The maximum possible score is 56, and the minimum possible score is 0. While there is no firm cut-off point, the closer you are to a score of 56, the more you exhibit the characteristics of a person who has a strong attachment to place.

the women who were relocated. The grief was severe enough to induce physical symptoms such as nausea, depression, intestinal disorders, and vomiting.

Our physical surroundings play an important role in creating a sense of meaning and organization in our lives (Little, 1987). Not surprisingly, a sense of the place in which we live is often closely related to our sense of personal identity, since so much of what we are depends on where we live and the experiences that we have there (Dovey, 1985; Feldman, 1990; Little, 1987; Proshansky, Fabian, & Kaminoff, 1983; Relph, 1976). To be "homeless" is to be a social nonentity; becoming homeless is an emotionally powerful, uncontrollable life event that results in severe psychological trauma. According to Goodman, Saxe, and Harvey (1991), homeless people often display classic symptoms of post-traumatic stress disorder (see Chapter 4). The social isolation, depression, and poor nutrition that accompany homelessness are often exacerbated by mental illness and drug or alcohol abuse. The long-term consequences of homelessness are devastating. It is an especially tragic experience for the growing number of homeless children (Rafferty & Shinn, 1991).

Thus, the word *home* connotes more than just a house (Lawrence, 1987; Saegert, 1985). The concept of home represents an emotionally based, meaningful relationship between people and their dwellings. It represents a predictable, secure place where the individual feels in control and properly oriented in space and time. In short, "home" is the primary connection between the person and the rest of the world (Dovey, 1985). The importance of returning home for the holidays, usually to share at least one large meal, reflects the importance of home places in maintaining the bonds between people. Such homecoming rituals reaffirm and renew a person's place in the family and often are the key factor in preserving the family's social fabric (Saile, 1985). To the Zuni of the American Southwest, home is a living thing; the setting for raising children, communicating with God and the spirit world, and for life itself. An annual ceremony in which some homes are blessed and consecrated (called the **Shalako**) is part of the year-ending winter solstice celebration. Social relationships centered in the home are celebrated during the Shalako ceremony by feeding all who visit the Shalako houses and by symbolically feeding the spirits of ancestors who are believed to visit during the Shalako to reestablish bonds with their families. The ceremony strengthens bonds to the community, to the family (including dead ancestors), and to the spirits and gods by strengthening the bond between each of these parties and the home itself (Werner, Altman, & Oxley, 1985).

For all people, home is the center of the world and a place of order that contrasts with the chaos elsewhere (Duncan, 1985). When asked to draw pictures of "where you live," very young children and adolescents center their drawings around the home, making it the anchor for everything else (Filipovitch, Juliar, & Ross, 1981; Schiavo, 1987). This is especially true for females; girls also give more positive and emotional evaluations of their homes than boys do (Csikszentmihalyi & Rochberg-Halton, 1981; Schiavo, 1988). The Tiwi of Bathurst Island (off the coast of Northern Australia) even believed that their island was the only habitable place in the world. All other places were thought of as the "land of the dead." The Tiwi believed that sailors shipwrecked on their island were dead spirits. They were killed because they did not belong in the land of the living (Hart & Pilling, in Duncan, 1985).

Because the concept of home is subjective, it is often studied through qualitative techniques such as **environmental autobiography** (Boschetti, 1987; Marcus, 1978). An environmental autobiography is a written memoir of events from one's life with an emphasis on the role played by the physical environment. Individuals are asked to recall environments that are important to them, to talk and write about them, and to draw pictures or sketches of them. This technique has provided useful leads for the design of home environments, and it is proving to be especially valuable for studying the feelings that children have for the spaces they inhabit (Boschetti, 1987; Marcus, 1978).

Satisfaction with one's residence is extremely important. It can be influenced by physical features as diverse as the amount of storage space and the quality of the plumbing. Nonphysical features such as adequate privacy and the development of social ties to the neighborhood also play a role in residential satisfaction. The physical design of a house reflects many different factors such as the climate, technology, resources, and cultural values of a society as well as the tastes and resources of the individual (Altman & Chemers, 1980; Rapoport, 1969). Altman and his colleagues (Altman & Chemers, 1980; Altman & Gauvain, 1981) described a number of useful categories for classifying homes. Homes can be described according to whether they are permanent, absolutely fixed structures or portable, temporary dwellings such as tents, igloos, or easily assembled huts. Homes can be classified by how homogenous they are. In this sense, homogeneity refers to how much difference there is among dwellings within a society a well as to how highly specialized the different locations within the home are. Residences also differ in the degree to which they are communal and in the extent to which they signal a willingness to interact with neighbors. Generally, North American homes tend to be permanent, specialized/differentiated, and noncommunal.

About three-fourths of American families own their own homes, and most of these are located in suburban metropolitan areas (Wright, 1981). Many studies in England, Australia, and the United States indicate that the free-standing single-family house with a yard represents the ideal that most people seek, especially if they have children (Cooper, 1976; Michelson, 1968; *Professional Builder,* 1985). (See Photo 10-2.) This strong desire for a single-family home reflects a quest for privacy as well as for territorial needs (discussed in Chapter 6). My discussion of specific residential environments begins with the single-family home.

P H O T O   10-2 The single-family detached home (with dog?) is still the choice of residence expressed by most people.

Single-Family Houses

Given the background of most of you who will read this book, I will emphasize houses typical of those found in Western, industrialized societies. However, I must point out that the norm in Western homes is often extremely different from what is found in other countries. Climate and religion often play more of a role in the structure and arrangement of homes in non-Western cultures, and in many Eastern cultures rooms are not always associated with specific activities as in the West (Canter & Lee, 1974; Kent, 1984; Tagg, 1973). The degree to which a home is partitioned into spaces for specialized functions increases as societies become less nomadic; it also reflects the extent to which activities in the family are age or gender specific (Kent, 1991; Layne, 1987). For more detailed accounts of cross-cultural differences in housing, refer to works by Altman and Chemers (1980), Bochner (1975), Kent (1991), Patterson and Chiswick (1981), Rapoport (1969), Tuan (1974), and Turnbull (1961).

"Houses are warehouses of personal experience" (Lawrence, 1985, p. 118). Consequently, houses can reinforce a sense of self, express qualities of the homeowner to other people, define group membership, and signify social status. In effect, the house becomes a symbol of the self for the people who live there and may help to shape individuals through the behavioral opportunities that it provides (Becker, 1977; Cooper, 1976; Csikszentmihalyi & Rochberg-Halton, 1981). According to Sadalla, Vershure, and Burroughs (1987), houses and their contents are part of the language of gestures that individuals use to communicate with each other and to control the amount and type of information that others receive. The style of a house advertises the personality and socioeconomic status of its residents, and people often buy particular kinds of houses to bolster their images of themselves (Cherulnik & Wilderman, 1986; Cooper, 1976; Nasar, 1989). Using the house as a means of self-expression is probably most characteristic of middle- and upper-middle-income families. In the words of Becker (1977),

> It is primarily for the middle class, where it is accepted as a given that the house is a *safe* place, that more attention is paid to the house as a means of self-expression and self-realization. People concerned about the cold, plumbing, and rats do not have the luxury of worrying about the image of their home [p. 18].

Sadalla, Vershure, and Burroughs (1987) pursued this issue in a study of 12 high-income homeowners in Phoenix, Arizona, and 99 undergraduate students at Arizona State University. They selected high-income homeowners because it was assumed that these people could afford to select and furnish their homes according to their tastes. The homeowners were interviewed and completed a 36-item personality scale. They were asked to evaluate how well their home, its view from the street, and their living room reflected their personality, interests, and lifestyle. The college students viewed slides of the 12 homes and gave their impressions of the owners' personalities by responding to the same 36-item personality scale as they thought the homeowner would. All the homeowners felt that their homes expressed their identity at least "fairly well," and there was significant agreement between the homeowners' ratings of their own personalities and the ratings made by the students who merely saw the slides. Agreement was especially strong if the students saw slides of the living room rather than slides of the exterior of the house. Other studies have confirmed the importance of the living room as the place where families show off wealth and advertise social position to the world at large (Amaturo, Costagliola, & Ragone, 1987).

Goffman (1959) distinguished between "front regions" of a house that are constantly on display and "back regions" that are usually off-limits to visitors and less likely to be rigorously policed by the residents. Obviously, the exterior of the house facing the street is a prime front region. Middle-class suburban American homes usually have a lawn between the home and the street. Altman and Gauvain (1981) describe the time and expense that most homeowners devote to the upkeep of the lawn, shrubberies, and surface of the front of the house. It is in this frontmost of all front regions that the individual publicly expresses his or her individuality and conformity to neighborhood standards of taste and sociability (Altman & Gauvain, 1981; Gauvain, Altman, & Fahim, 1983). While this seems contradictory, it is not. By maintaining the yard, using acceptable colors of paint, and displaying appropriate amounts of holiday decoration, people show that they are "good neighbors" who are willing to be associated with the other residents and observe the rules of the community. On the other hand, the considerable leeway within these general guidelines allows the homeowner to express interests and values that will set him or her apart from the neighbors in ways that are important to self-identity. Typically, much less attention is paid to the back of the house, since this is a back region that is supposedly not accessible to others (Altman & Gauvain, 1981).

Thresholds and entryways at the front of the house receive special attention. Often, they are reserved for visitors, and the family uses the side or rear doors for daily life (Altman & Chemers, 1980; Altman & Gauvain, 1981). Altman and his colleages also noted that these areas are often elaborately decorated with lights, mats, wreaths, and other decorations, and there is still great symbolic importance attached to inviting someone to cross the threshold.

The interiors of homes are a collage of private, individual territories and communal family areas (Altman & Gauvain, 1981; Sebba & Churchman, 1983). These areas can be classified further as front and back regions. In front regions, the residents display a peculiar mix of conformity to community norms (for example, not sleeping in the dining room, not keeping the "wrong" kinds of animals indoors) and an expression of individual interests and values (Altman & Gauvain, 1981). These front regions often contain family pictures, artwork, aquaria, and other displays for the benefit of visitors. The choice of furniture and decoration reflects the homeowner's taste, values, and financial resources and communicates these to others. Traditionally, a home's interior reflects the female, while the male receives the credit (or in some cases the blame) for the condition of the home's exterior (Altman & Chemers, 1980). The home's interior front regions often have a formal living room and dining room that the family seldom use under ordinary circumstances. These rooms serve as symbols of a family's status and values, are frequently framed by a picture window, and are usually reserved for special occasions. The real "living" occurs in the family room, kitchen, and backyard patio (Altman & Chemers, 1980; Altman & Gauvain, 1981). Research confirms that kitchens often are the real center of family activity, and that ceremonial living rooms are often poor places for entertaining because they are poorly lit, drably colored, and too large (Heimstra & McFarling, 1978; Mehrabian, 1976a). Mehrabian (1976a) pointed out that often these rooms are dominated by couches, which have been shown to inhibit comfortable conversation.

Other areas, notably bedrooms, are primary territories and back regions that are off-limits to visitors. Bathrooms are "in-between" areas that visitors sometimes use but are considered intensely private nonetheless. Many writers have noted that, in spite of their importance, bathrooms are seldom designed with human safety and comfort in mind (Kira, 1975; Willis, 1975).

The physical environment of the home is especially important to young children who live there. One- to 3-year-olds spend between 80 percent and 90 percent of their waking hours interacting with the physical (not social) environment (White, Kaban, & Attanucci, 1979). Chawla (1991) reviewed the literature on the effects of physical home environments on children and reached several conclusions. First, variety, complexity, and an absence of physical barriers are positively related to cognitive development. Chawla suggests giving young children many opportunities to explore, even setting aside child-accessible cabinets specfically for this purpose. Second, access to diverse outdoor spaces is important. Chawla concludes that the research to date shows that high levels of noise in the home impairs information processing and retards language development. Thus, if noise in the home is unavoidable, soundproofing at least some rooms is a worthwhile investment.

Apartments and Public Housing

Although the single-family detached home is the ideal residence for most people (Tognoli, 1987), many people live in apartments. Apartments offer less space per family, and the combination of thin walls with neighbors over, under, and alongside often results in embarrassingly little auditory privacy (Kuper, 1953; Prestomon, 1968). Consequently, crowding in apartment buildings is a major source of dissatisfaction (Aiello & Thompson, 1980).

Even when apartments are very close together, the architecture of the building may keep people apart by creating a greater **functional distance.** Functional distance between people refers to the likelihood that individuals will come into frequent contact with each other. It is often dictated by such architectural decisions as the placement of doorways, elevators, and stairways. These architectural features have a profound effect on the social lives of the people who live in apartment complexes. In a classic study, Festinger, Schachter, and Back (1950) looked at friendship patterns in a married student housing complex at the Massachusetts Institute of Technology. They uncovered a powerful relationship between architecture and friendship in that 65 percent of most people's friends lived in the same building as they did (there were 17 buildings in the complex); and two-thirds lived on the same floor of the building. People living next door to each other were especially likely to be friends. Curiously, people on the first floor who were most likely to have friends on the second floor were those living near the stairways where mailboxes were located; presumably they had more frequent exposure to their upstairs neighbors.

As you may know from first-hand experience, apartment living can be very pleasant under the right circumstances. The proximity of other people from similar backgrounds, the nearness of urban attractions, and the relative lack of worries about yard care and physical upkeep can be quite attractive as long as basic security needs are met and urban stressors are not too intrusive. Large apartments and developments with interior play spaces are especially well-liked (MacKintosh, 1982). Although recreation facilities also add to satisfaction with apartment living, residents adapt to them and they become less important as time goes on (Michelson, 1977). Becker (1977) summarized a number of other architectural features that increase the appeal of apartments to people who must live in them. These include pitched roofs (to avoid a "commercial" look), distinct and individually identifiable units, and well-defined porches or balconies. Becker also reports that the opportunity to personalize the exterior of their units increases people's satisfaction and over time reduces maintenance costs.

Much of what designers know about the effects of architecture on apartment living has been discovered through mistakes made in the design of public housing projects in many American cities. Any errors in the design of public housing projects are magnified by the unfortunate circumstances faced by residents of these buildings. Five percent of the renters in the United States live in public housing. Usually, the eligibility requirements ensure that there will be many single-parent families and a majority of low-income and unemployed residents (Rohe & Burby, 1988). Public housing is often located near areas with high crime rates; and being elderly, female, and black are demographic characteristics associated with high vulnerability to crime (Rohe & Burby, 1988; Skogan, Maxfield, & Podolefsky, 1981). Tragically, this is precisely the demographic profile of the people who frequently need public housing.

Much of the fear of crime residents of public housing experience can be traced directly to the architecture of the project. By comparison, older ghettoes and slums seldom were more than a few stories high and were concentrated on streets with relatively light traffic, sidewalks, front steps, and stores. This encouraged people to be out in the neighborhood, and children could play safely outdoors. Residents tended to know each other well, and extended families were common in such neighborhoods. Although they were poor, these neighborhoods were socially very cohesive. Social cohesion leads to greater feelings of social control and a belief that others may help if trouble occurs. The feelings of fear and danger residents experience is inversely related to the extent to which social network exists in the neighborhood (Greenberg & Rohe, 1986; Greenberg, Rohe, & Williams, 1982; Yancey, 1971). When these neighborhoods were leveled to make room for public housing, these positive features were lost. The new buildings tended to be high-rise vertical structures, economically built, expensive to maintain, and dangerous to live in (Newman, 1972).

High-rise public housing buildings completely lack what Newman (1972) has called **defensible space.** There are no semipublic spaces like the steps and sidewalks of the old neighborhoods that are crucial for forming informal social networks. The "small town" environments that had developed within cities were destroyed by densely populated high-rise buildings in which residents were unable to monitor outdoor behavior or recognize strangers. Architectural design can indicate whether or not an area is under the influence of a group and warn intruders that they are likely to be seen, recognized, and questioned. In Newman's (1972) words, the architecture becomes a "physical expression of social fabric" (p. 3). The anonymous "vertical ghetto" (Moore, 1969), on the other hand, packs too many people into an area with no defensible space. The starkness of many public housing projects contrasts sharply with the surrounding area, advertising the isolation and vulnerability of those who live there. The buildings themselves are mazes of unsurveillable hiding places and escape routes that undermine social cohesion. "When people [are forced] to protect themselves as individuals and not as a community, the battle against crime is effectively lost" (Newman, 1972, p. 3).

Studies conducted in more than 15 cities nationwide strongly support Newman's defensible space explanation of crime in high-rise public housing (Newman & Franck, 1982; Normoyle & Foley, 1988). In all cities studied, crime rates and residents' fear of crime were greater in high-rise than in low-rise buildings, even when other relevant variables such as sex, race, and income were controlled. For example, McCarthy and Saegert (1978) compared high-rise and low-rise apartments in low-income housing in New York. Although residents of both kinds of housing were similar in all important demographic characteristics, residents of the high-rise buildings were disadvantaged in a number of ways. They reported feeling less safe, more socially overloaded, less satisfied with the building, and less involved with their neighbors.

The best known account of the breakdown of life in public housing occurred in the Pruitt-Igoe housing project in St. Louis (Yancey, 1971). It provides a classic example of what happens when a poor community with no social cohesion is subjected to architectural design that is completely unsympathetic to developing a sense of community. Pruitt-Igoe (built in 1954) consisted of 43 11-story buildings that had replaced several blocks of 3-story inner-city buildings. Pruitt-Igoe was home to about 12,000 people (see Photo 10-3); the fear, crime, vandalism, and vacancies that plagued it resulted in its demolition 18 years after it was built. Yancey (1971) describes life in Pruitt-Igoe as a fearful world of assaults, rapes, and drugs. People reported that they liked their actual apartments but were terrified to leave them. The stairwells were completely uncontrolled, dangerous spaces, and people seldom knew their neighbors. The things associated with a lack of social control and high levels of fear (for example, vandalism, litter, abandoned apartments, gangs of teenagers hanging out [Hunter, 1978]) were commonplace in Pruitt-Igoe. Cost-cutting measures such as elevators that only stopped on every other floor and a lack of toilet facilities on the ground level added significantly to the unpleasantness of life.

Families with children are least likely to be satisfied with high-rise public housing. Children playing outside cannot be observed, and the desolate stretches of "no-man's land" between buildings are seldom

PHOTO   10·3   The Pruitt-Igoe public housing project

under the control of anyone other than gangs. Several authors (for example, Becker, 1976; Moore, 1969) have noted that high-rises simply do not support a wide variety of activities for children and are more suited to "hanging out" than active play. Planned play areas are rare, and there is no place for children to go. Outside, children are so far from the bathrooms in their apartments that urinating and defecating in hallways and elevators are common. Not surprisingly, many parents keep children inside much of the time. Unfortunately, family tension and conflict increase when children must play inside the apartment (Becker, 1974).

Much suffering has occurred as a result of the generally well-intentioned public housing effort. It is never too late, however, to apply the lessons learned from past mistakes to the design of future projects. Researchers have compiled an impressive list of suggestions to make public housing safer and more livable. Some, such as providing adequate lighting and safe locks, are obvious (Rohe & Burby, 1988). Others, such as increasing interaction among residents, are more subtle. Newman (1972) and Mehrabian (1976a) summarized many of these suggestions; much of what follows is drawn from their discussions. The bottom line for most of the improvements that should be made is returning control of the public areas outside the apartments to the people who live in the building. The most obvious first step in this direction is to avoid a high-rise design whenever possible. Studies show that there is a dramatic rise in crime rates as buildings exceed six floors. Newman (1972) proposes that three- to six-story buildings in which only two or three families share a hallway can accommodate people in the same densities and at the same costs as the high-rises now in use. Also, when there are fewer than six apartments on a floor, the corridor becomes a common space that residents look after and protect, and the families become friendlier and know each other better. Units larger than this produce anonymity and less defense of public space, especially when seemingly endless dark corridors are filled with identical doors (Mehrabian, 1976a).

Internal spaces can be divided to encourage territorial behavior by residents. Using institutional vandal-proof interiors creates a bad atmosphere, reduces residential pride, and discourages people from making any effort to care for their place. Obviously, it should be avoided. Since fewer people in an area fosters an increase in protective attitudes, subdividing space with symbolic barriers like gateways and plants can signify entry into private space and encourage residents to assume responsibility for it. Windows should be positioned to allow residents to survey exterior and interior public areas, and the lobbies of buildings should be visible from outside (Mehrabian, 1976a; Newman, 1972).

Designers should avoid stigmatizing forms and create buildings that blend harmoniously with the surrounding neighborhood. They should also become more aware of the relationship between surveillance, crime, and geographical location. For example, Brill (1972) discovered that locations near parking lots, streets, and recreational areas provide easy escape routes and are associated with higher crime rates. Brantingham and Brantingham (1975) found that blocks at the edges of neighborhoods had higher burglary rates than blocks in the interior. Buildings in these locations should be designed with extra sensitivity to the need for surveillance and defensible space.

In nonurban areas, mobile homes may offer a compromise between an apartment and a single-family home. Paulus, Nagar, and Camacho (1991) studied the reactions of United States Army families living in apartments or mobile homes. They found no overall differences in residents' satisfaction between the two settings, but there were different advantages. The apartment complexes generally were rated as more attractive and were liked because they were closer to facilities such as laundromats and stores. Mobile homes, on the other hand, were perceived as less noisy and crime-prone. Paulus and his colleagues concluded that the degree to which the residents perceived that they had some choice was important to their ultimate satisfaction. Expectations about future housing and experiences with past housing strongly influenced satisfaction with their present accommodations.

Dormitories

A residential environment familiar to many people is the college dormitory. Life there is subject to many of the same architectural influences as is life in apartments or public housing. However, there are important differences. In dormitories, students usually share a room with someone who may have been a complete stranger. Also, it is relatively rare for individual dormitory rooms to have bathroom, cooking, and other facilities. In addition, dormitories must facilitate both studying and socializing — activities often in direct conflict.

Because of these factors, some design problems are specific to dormitories. Stokes (1960) determined that 55 percent to 78 percent of studying occurs in dormitory rooms and that 85 percent of students prefer to study alone. Consequently, privacy is a high priority for most college students (Van Der Ryn & Silverstein, 1967; Wolfe, 1975). This is an especially serious problem when three students are assigned to a room built for two. This practice is increasing in universities experiencing a shortage of space and is a fate first-year students usually suffer. Studies show that three-person dormitory rooms are much more likely to produce tension and negative feelings about roommates than are two-person rooms (Aiello, Baum, & Gormley, 1981; Baron, Mandel, Adams, & Griffin, 1976; Mullen & Felleman, 1990). Some researchers believe that this is due to the unstable relationships inherent in three-person groups as much as it is to a lack of space.

A number of studies have examined student reactions to different dormitory designs. Two of the most common living arrangements are suite and corridor designs. In suites, several individual rooms open into a shared lounge area and a bathroom. The more traditional corridor design consists of long corridors with rooms along both sides, usually accompanied by a large group bathroom. While overall space per person may be the same under both arrangements, suite designs usually decrease the number of people one encounters and shares facilities with. Davis (1976) and Davis and Baum (1975) found a number of differences in students' interaction patterns in suite and corridor dormitories. "Corridor" residents prefer to interact with others in the hallways. They rarely report using lounges in the building for socializing. Apparently, these lounges are too public and serve too many people to be comfortable for informal encounters with friends. "Suite" residents, on the other hand, actually do socialize most frequently in the lounges rather than in hallways. Furthermore, Valins and Baum (1973) report that suite residents generally feel less crowded than corridor residents and are also more sociable.

Not surprisingly, the high-rise designs that cause so many problems in public housing also receive low marks when used in dormitory construction. Students living in high-density residence halls perceive less social support in college and experience higher levels of psychological distress (Lakey, 1989). Students like smaller residence halls better than high-rises, and students report that better social relationships occur in smaller dormitories (Heilweil, 1973; Holahan & Wilcox, 1978; Sommer, 1968). There is more crime and vandalism in high-rise than in low-rise dormitories (Sommer, 1987), and Bickman and colleagues (1973) found that helping behavior is more frequent and doors are less likely to be locked in small residence halls.

Clearly, much can be done to improve dormitory life. Avoiding high-rise designs and locating lounges to serve a relatively small number of students are two apparent improvements. Eigenbrod, cited by Becker (1977), compared students who had complete freedom to manipulate the environment in their dormitory rooms by adding appliances, removing, adding, or changing furniture, and putting unlimited amounts of tape on the wall with those who did not. Greater freedom was significantly related to satisfaction with the residence hall and with roommates. There was also less damage in these residence halls, more lounge decoration, fewer disciplinary problems, and better student maintenance of the dormitory building. Since crowding is often a problem, constructing dormitories to maximize perceptions of space and minimize noise is important. Schiffenbauer and colleagues (1977) found that sunlit dorm rooms with more usable floor space were perceived as being larger; they also found that students were disturbed when the possible furniture arrangements in a room were severely limited. Feller (1968) discovered that the noise in corridors can be decreased significantly simply by dimming the lights!

Housing for the Elderly

In the near future, designing good residential environments for senior citizens will be a major concern. In 1987, 12 percent of the population in the United States was already over 65 years of age, and by 2020 that number will rise to at least 20 percent (Dickson, 1987). Housing for the elderly poses special problems. First, such housing is often associated with a loss of health, independence, and even forced relocation from a home in which the individual may have spent a lifetime. Needless to say, this combination of events is traumatic. Second, advancing age often requires focusing more activities in and around the home (Christensen & Carp, 1987; Rubinstein, 1989), which makes the necessity for entertainment and safety features even more salient. This is especially true in residental complexes for healthy, older people who live alone, although residential-care facilities also must be concerned about these features. Since people age and decline at different rates, residents in most complexes for the elderly are at every stage of need. Consequently, the distinction of design features between "housing" and "institution" are no longer as clear cut as they once were (Lawton, 1987).

Evidence shows that elderly people prefer low-rise buildings and age-segregated housing and treasure the ability to control their day-to-day lives (Devlin, 1980; Grant, 1970; Normoyle & Foley, 1988). Since older people confine most of their shopping to their home neighborhoods (Smith, 1991), residential communities should offer easy access to the services available in the immediate vicinity. Because they offer opportunities for solitude or socializing, outdoor spaces like parks are valuable in communities for the elderly (Gelwicks, 1970). To encourage independence and facilitate daily tasks, the buildings should protect against intruders and fire, and contain safeguards such as handrails and nonslip surfaces to prevent falls (Bell, Fisher, Baum, & Green, 1990; Devlin, 1980). An extensive list of special housing requirements needed to meet the psychological, social, and physical needs of the elderly was compiled by Huttman (1977). One specific need is preventing social isolation. As mobility declines, social networks may shrink in spite of the person's desire to socialize. This is especially prevalent among women, since 40 percent of older women live alone as compared to only 14 percent of older men (Lawton, 1987).

NEIGHBORHOODS

Neighborhoods can be described by physical characteristics such as the type of housing they contain, the pattern of social interaction and organization that they exhibit, and the ethnic, socioeconomic, and demographic makeup of their residents (Holahan & Wandersman, 1987; Taylor, 1982). Rivlin (1987) defines a neighborhood as the residents' acknowledgment that a locality exists, and some agreement as to its name, boundaries, and its distinguishing characteristics. One problem with this definition is that outsiders are frequently more aware of boundaries and recognize the unique ethnic or economic makeup of neighborhoods more than the residents, who may be less aware of how their area contrasts with the rest of the city (Tuan, 1974). Tuan defines a neighborhood simply by saying that it is the district in which one *feels* at home. Some researchers conclude that the concept of *neighborhood* is unsatisfactory precisely because it can mean so many things to different people (Lee, 1968). It is true that the description of a neighborhood as nothing more than an area with distinct geographical boundaries fails to capture the essence of what "neighborhood" means to most people. Equally true is that talking about neighborhoods in terms of demographic characteristics of the residents results in a fuzzy concept that fails to account for the importance of the physical environment. In spite of these difficulties, most social scientists find the concept useful to describe that intermediate level of social organization between home and city that allows individuals to achieve a sense of community and relate to larger society manageably (Holahan & Wandersman, 1987; Nisbet, 1962). Indeed, it is this intangible **sense of community** that may represent best what neighborhoods are all about.

Chavis, Hogge, McMillan, and Wandersman (1986) define a sense of community as "a feeling that members have of belonging and being important to each other, and a shared faith that members' needs will be met by their commitment to be together" (p. 25). Taylor (1988) notes that the streetblock is most often the focus of neighborhood ties, and that communication among households is strongest within streetblocks. Taylor also points out that streetblocks are physically bounded behavior settings that permit joint territorial control of the neigborhood, which results in a greater sense of security and well-being for those living on the block. The appearance and upkeep of the houses and properties on the block clearly signal the extent to which the area is watched and under control, and it also communicates expectations of how people ought to behave. Neighborhood norms develop about what constitutes acceptable behavior, and these norms are enforced. Delinquent behavior and aimless "hanging out" are less likely to occur in clearly controlled neighborhoods (Taylor, 1987).

According to Warren (1978), three basic dimensions characterize neighborhoods: the type and amount of interaction among the residents, the sense of identity that residents have because they live in the neighborhood, and the amount of connection between the residents and the outside world. Warren has identified six types of neighborhoods that reflect these three dimensions. **Integral neighborhoods** are marked by a great deal of face-to-face contact among residents. They are cohesive, active, and also maintain connections to the larger community outside of the neighborhood. **Parochial neighborhoods** are also high in interaction but tend to have little involvement with the outside world and are described by Warren as "protective and insular." **Diffuse neighborhoods** lack informal social interaction, although formal neighborhood organizations may exist. Residents of diffuse neighborhoods vary in their connectedness to the outside. **Stepping-stone neighborhoods** are made up entirely of people whose allegiance is to outside groups. Interaction among stepping-stone neighbors is formal, and there is no commitment to the neighborhood since most expect to move on. **Transitory neighborhoods** are marked by low interaction, a complete lack of identity (something that stepping-stone neighborhoods often have), and high turnover. The residents of stepping-stone and transitory neighborhoods may be quite satisfied with limited contacts with neighbors. **Anomic neighborhoods** are completely disorganized with residents having no connection to each other or to outside groups. There also may be little turnover in anomic neighborhoods.

Ultimately, different types of neighborhoods bestow a completely different sense of community upon their residents. A strong sense of community is positively related to length of residence, satisfaction with the community, and the number of neighbors one can identify by first name (Glynn, 1981). In cohesive neighborhoods, residents can provide support systems, social outlets, and an enhanced sense of security (Unger & Wandersman, 1983). Neighborhood turnover, instability, and lower-quality housing decrease territorial marking, resident satisfaction, and the appearance of control (Taylor, 1987). Not surprisingly, neighborhoods consisting of multistory apartments are less cohesive and have a weaker sense of community than neighborhoods full of single-family dwellings (Weenig, Schmidt, & Midden, 1990).

A strong sense of community enhances satisfaction with the neighborhood for most people. However, the fit between individual needs and the size and nature of the community should not be overlooked. Single, young professionals may not be as happy in a stable, blue-collar neighborhood of single-family houses as they would be in an apartment complex with more similar people. A number of studies have looked at the factors that contribute to neighborhood satisfaction. In suburban neighborhoods, Zehner (1972) found that several factors predict residents' satisfaction. These include the density of the neighborhood (with its implications for noise and privacy), the social compatibility of the neighbors, the neighborhood maintenance level, and its accessibility to shopping, hospitals, schools, and other facilities. In a similar study of urban neighborhoods, Carp, Zawadski, and Shokrkon (1976) found that noise, aesthetic quality, safety (traffic and security from crime), mobility, and neighbors' perceptions were good predictors of satisfaction. Generally, these same factors have been identified in other studies of neighborhood satisfaction (Taylor, 1982; Widgery, 1982).

Rapoport (1980) determined that the extent to which a neighborhood has been freely chosen is often an overlooked but important component of residential satisfaction. At least one study found that younger, better educated, and wealthier households, which presumably have a great freedom of choice, also tend to be the most satisfied with their community (Miller, Tsemberis, Malia, & Grega, 1980). Tuan (1974) reports a positive relationship between church affiliation and neighborhood satisfaction (see box p. 225).

While they are clearly related, remember that neighborhood *satisfaction* is not the same as the concept of neighborhood *attachment* described earlier. The two are distinguishable. Attachment is more strongly related to factors such as home ownership, extensiveness of social networks, and similarity to neighbors that do not always influence satisfaction predictably (Guest & Lee, 1983; Ringel & Finkelstein, 1991).

CITIES

Most of the environmental factors associated with city life such as noise, crowding, pollution, and legibility have been discussed in other chapters. This section specifically considers the city as a place to live.

Cities are a relatively late development in human history. As recently as 1850, only 2 percent of the world's population lived in cities (Fischer, 1976). Much has changed in the last 140 years. The 1990 United States census reveals that Americans are flocking to urban areas in greater numbers than ever before, and for the first time in American history more people live in metropolitan than in rural areas or small towns and cities. As this is also the trend in other countries throughout the world, clearly city living is here to stay. Although people are moving to urban areas in record numbers, they apparently have mixed feelings about it. A 1978 Gallup poll asked Americans whether they preferred to live in a city, suburb, small town, or on a farm. Only 13 percent of all respondents

---

Neighborhood Satisfaction on Skid Row

Being homeless is doubly tragic because it means having neither a physical dwelling to call home nor a neighborhood to give one a sense of community and a buffer between the self and the larger society. Tuan (1974) has described life in a skid row "neighborhood" populated by transients. The following passage is taken directly from Tuan's work.

In physical appearance Skid Row is unmistakable. Near the central business district or heavy transportation facilities of almost every large city spreads a drab mosaic of substandard hotels and rooming houses; taverns, cheap restaurants, second-hand stores and pawn shops; employment agencies offering unskilled jobs and missions offering salvation and a free meal. Listless men, standing in groups or loitering around penny arcades or garbage cans, are a common sight. Their life style is so bizarre to the average citizen that the larger Skid Rows are a tourist attraction. Some see it romantically as a carefree life; most see it as the ultimate in degradation. . . . Marginal people do not verbalize their self-perceptions. They appear content to confirm whatever prejudices outsiders may have of them. . . .

Street life is abundant but gray. Early in the morning, while most of the city is still asleep, the sidewalks begin to fill with men. Shuffling movements up and down the street continue until nine or ten at night; thereafter they gradually taper off. On Saturdays and Sundays sidewalks are packed with pedestrians and loiterers. The purpose is to window shop and socialize. Gazing into windows may take hours; reading the menu and choosing a place to eat is often a major decision for the day. Small knots of people collect at hotel entrances, on street corners and near favorite taverns to meet acquaintances. Such encounters often lead into the tavern. Many lean against the wall to watch the social scene. The Skid Rower's one great wealth is time, and like all great wealth it is a burden. After dark the most popular activity is watching television. Drinking in taverns is second in frequency. Winter in a northern city is an added challenge to survival; it also further isolates the men. The wind-swept and icy streets discourage the sort of activity that in warm weather consumes mercifully so large a portion of the Skid Rower's time. In cold weather televison is more than ever the channel for physical and psychological withdrawal. Skid Rowers also seek out the warmth of library reading rooms and in despair they will even have their souls saved at the missions for a few hours of warmth and a free meal. Next to food, a place to sleep (flop) is the vagrant's most consistent problem. To the respectable citizen, sleep could suggest only a bedroom or, under unusual circumstances, a couch or a sleeping bag. But to the urban nomad of Skid Row it could mean one of a hundred possible flops—furnace room, cotton wagon, stairwell, trash box, scale house, hotel toilet, penny arcade, church, loading dock, and so on. . . .

In Chicago's Skid Row a majority of the residents dislike their environment, but a large minority—perhaps a quarter—claim to like it. Most of the "likes," however, are merely adaptations to the need for survival . . . [pp. 222–223].

chose the city, and only 21 percent of those actually living in cities did so (Sears, Peplau, & Taylor, 1991). A 1985 *ABC News/Washington Post* survey asked the same questions and found that only 9 percent of their respondents preferred to live in a city (Bell, Fisher, Baum, & Green, 1990). The 1990 census figures indicate that people are following these preferences as much as possible, since most of the growth in American metropolitan areas is occurring in suburbs and not in urban centers.

In "The Experience of Living in Cities," Milgram (1970) proposed that much of the behavior of urbanites is a response to the **system overload** found in cities. Because there is so much physical and social stimulation in cities, people must disregard low-priority inputs and, out of necessity, allocate less time to inputs they *do* attend to. Consequently, urban settings frequently enforce norms of noninvolvement, whereby unnecessary interaction is avoided and time-consuming social conventions (for example, politeness) are kept to a minimum. Most of the empirical research on urban social behavior is consistent with Milgram's overload hypothesis. For example, people in urban environments are less likely to do favors for others or to provide help of any kind, especially in nonemergency situations (Korte, 1980). Helping strangers becomes less likely if the immediate location is noisy. Moser (1988) found that people were even less likely to help others or willing to engage in verbal interaction with them near noisy construction sites than at other locations in the city. Newman and McCauley (1977) report that eye contact with strangers is common in rural towns, less common in suburbs, and rare in the city. Furthermore, people actually change their gaze patterns when they go into the city, using less eye contact with strangers than they do when in the suburbs (McCauley, Coleman, & DeFusco, 1978). The differences in social interaction between urban and nonurban people seem to operate almost entirely in interactions with strangers, as city people do *not* have an overload of friends and acquaintances compared to small town residents (McCauley & Taylor, 1976). While there are no differences between city dwellers and others in the number and quality of their relationships, there is some evidence that city dwellers have fewer ties to relatives, neighbors, or church groups and more ties to friends and coworkers (Fischer, 1982).

Social facilitation, coupled with the need to decrease environmental inputs in a highly loaded environment, may result in a faster pace of life in cities. Sadalla, Sheets, and McCreath (1990) found that people do subjectively link a city's size with its perceived tempo. Studies in nine different countries confirm that, at the very least, pedestrians walk faster in bigger cities (Bornstein, 1979; Bornstein & Bornstein, 1976; Martin & Heimstra, 1973; Walmsley & Lewis, 1989) and that other activities, such as purchasing items in a store or cashing a check at a bank, also occur more rapidly in urban areas than in rural areas (Amato, 1983; Lowin, Hottes, Sandler, & Bornstein, 1971).

The stimulation associated with city life is not all negative. The cultural, entertainment, and economic opportunities available only in large cities are irresistible to many people; they can make city living a satisfying experience despite its drawbacks. Overall, the reported levels of happiness for city and small town residents are about the same (Shaver & Freedman, 1976), and the rate of mental disturbance among the populace of cities is no greater than that in small towns (Srole, 1972). Hence, high density and high-load environmental conditions are not necessarily related to increased pathology. In a study of alcoholism, suicide, divorce, and crime among city dwellers, Levine, Miyake, and Lee (1989) found that these problems are most common among new immigrants to urban areas. They believe that several factors may contribute to this phenomenon. Dissatisfied people may be more likely to move, bringing their problems with them. Also, the disruption of social organizations and support systems that accompany a move to a new place might make immigrants especially vulnerable to these problems.

Most of what was described earlier about satisfaction with neighborhoods also applies to urban settings. However, research frequently finds that city dwellers are less satisfied with their neighborhoods than residents of suburbs and small towns, and city dwellers are more likely to complain about schools, housing, taxes, and a lack of safety (Fischer, 1982). In one study, Cook (1988) compared neighborhood satisfaction of urban and suburban single-parent women. She found that for both groups safety for themselves and their children was the most important factor, and that suburban women felt safer in their neighborhoods than did urban women. Consequently, urban women were less satisfied with their neighborhoods. In assessing their neighborhoods, suburban women placed greater emphasis on satisfaction with the home itself, proximity to shopping, and the quality of schools. While these differences are suggestive, it should be noted that the two samples of women also differed on important characteristics such as race, employment status, household size, and car ownership. These factors could have contributed to Cook's findings.

Many sources of satisfaction or dissatisfaction in neighborhoods can be traced directly to the influence of the physical environment. One of the most powerful is the volume of traffic, both pedestrian and vehicular, handled by the neighborhood streets. Appleyard and Lintell (1972) conducted a study which graphically illustrates the effects of heavy automobile traffic on the daily life in residential neighborhoods. They compared three adjacent north–south residential streets in San Francisco that differed in the amount of traffic each had. The first (named "Heavy Street" by Appleyard and Lintell) was a one-way street connected to a freeway. Traffic averaged 15,750 vehicles per day with an average of 900 vehicles per hour during rush hours. There were many trucks and buses on this street, and the noise level was about 65 decibels 45 percent of the time. The second street ("Moderate Street") was a two-way street also connected to a freeway. It averaged 8,700 vehicles per day (550 per hour during rush hour) and 25 percent of the time, decibel levels were above 65. The third street ("Light Street") was not connected to the freeway. Vehicles averaged around 2000 per day (200 per hour during rush hour) and noise levels rarely reached 65 decibels. Data were gathered by systematically observing life on the three streets and through detailed, one-hour interviews with 12 residents from each block.

The results of the study were clear. Heavy traffic was associated with stress, withdrawal, few neighborhood friendships, and little use of the street or front of the houses by the neighborhood residents. Light Street residents reported three times as many neighborhood friends and twice as many acquaintances as residents of Heavy Street; this was especially true for friends and acquaintances living on the other side of the street. Moderate Street was only slightly better than Heavy Street in this regard. Residents of Heavy Street felt less territorial or private in their neighborhood and had the least detailed knowledge of its physical layout. It was rare to see people out on the street or front steps, and children were rarely seen playing outdoors. On all measures, residents of Light Street were clearly the most satisfied of the three groups. Residents of Heavy Street and Moderate Street also complained extensively about noise, fumes, and soot—complaints that were rarely voiced by the residents of Light Street.

The implication of this study is that reducing the volume of traffic flowing through residential neighborhoods increases residential satisfaction. Even if traffic reduction is not possible, slowing traffic with curves or rumble strips and protecting sidewalks with trees, hedges, or walls should make life more pleasant in high-traffic neighborhoods.

Residents of city blocks containing stores report more crowding and less ability to regulate social interaction relative to residents of blocks without stores. They also exhibit more symptoms of stress, depression, and anxiety (Fleming, Baum, & Weiss, 1987). Research by Van Staden (1984) on young adolescents in urban neighborhoods suggests that a perceived loss of control is the real underlying stressor and is a more important component of urban crowding than actual spatial restrictions. Its implication is that maintaining control over the "semipublic" open spaces in urban neighborhoods (sidewalks, yards) is extremely important to the well-being of the people who live there. City sidewalks serve as the main arena of contact among neighbors; they are the playground on which children become assimilated into the community (Jacobs, 1961). Thus, easy access to controlled open space is probably more important for child development than totally public parks and playgrounds which frequently are underused and vandalized (Brower, 1977; Francis, 1987; Hester, 1984; Jackson, 1981; Joardar, 1989; Moore, 1985; Perez & Hart, 1980). Parks are often located too far from the neighborhoods where people actually live. Research shows that the distance people will walk to use a park is remarkably consistent from city to city—about three blocks (Hiss, 1990). Also, these areas are often perceived as unsafe because they contain barriers such as walls or dense vegetation that provide potential hiding places for muggers, rapists, or drug dealing (Nager & Wentworth, 1976; Stoks, 1983).

That urban neighborhoods are now less accessible to the children who live in them has been confirmed in a recent study by Gaster (1991). He interviewed several generations of people living in a New York City neighborhood to reconstruct the use of this public space by children from 1915 to 1976. Gaster found that children's freedom of movement in this neighborhood had diminished significantly over the course of the century, especially since the 1940s. As of 1976, children were older before they were allowed outside without supervision, and they visited fewer places in the neighborhood than did children of previous generations. They were also more likely than their predecessors to participate in supervised activities when they were outside. Many of these changes are due to restrictions imposed by parents who perceive the neighborhood as being less safe than it once was.

CHAPTER SUMMARY

Attachment to place is a positive affective association between individuals and their residential environments. It grows stronger with the passage of time and represents an attachment to the physical location itself as well as to the social networks that have developed there. The location of one's home is a place of especially strong attachment for most people, as the home represents a predictable, secure place in which the individual is in control most of the time.

Single-family detached houses represent the ideal home for most people. Houses reinforce a sense of self, express qualities of the home-owner to other people, define group membership, and signify social status. For a variety of reasons, however, many people live in apartments. While crowding and noise are common problems in apartment buildings, improvements in their design can make them comfortable places to live. Of particular importance is the inclusion of defensible semipublic space that encourages territorial control and maintenance by the residents. The lack of defensible space is one of the key ingredients in the high crime rates and lack of social cohesion found in many public housing projects. College dormitories are similar residential environments that confront designers with the problem of encouraging both study and socializing.

Neighborhoods are intermediate units of social organization between the home and the city that allow individuals to experience a sense of community. Cohesive neighborhoods encourage joint territorial control of the area (and hence, security) and provide a social outlet for their residents. While many factors can influence an individual's satisfaction with his or her neighborhood, it is ultimately the overall fit between the individual's needs and goals and the neighborhood that matters most.

Neighborhoods become increasingly important entities as cities grow in size. Most people prefer not to live in cities if it can be avoided, because, in spite of their rewards, the intense physical and social stimulation in city environments and the abundance of ambient stressors make cities exhausting places to live. The recent growth of suburban populations reflects the attempt by many people to experience the best of both worlds.

GLOSSARY

Anomic Neighborhoods   Disorganized neighborhoods in which residents have no connection to each other or to outside groups.

Attachment to Place   The positive affective association between individuals and their residential environments.

Defensible Space   Public or semipublic space that easily lends itself to surveillance and territorial control.

Diffuse Neighborhoods   Neighborhoods lacking informal social interaction in which residents vary in their degree of connectedness to the outside world.

Embodiment   An intense attachment to place in which the boundaries between the self and the environment become blurred.

Environmental Autobiography   A written memoir of events from one's life with an emphasis on the role played by the physical environment.

Extension   A moderately intense attachment to place in which places evoke highly emotional memories and psychological involvement.

Functional Distance   The effect that architecture has on the likelihood that individuals will come into frequent contact with each other.

Generic Place Dependence   An attachment to place in which individuals become strongly dependent on the presence of certain kinds of environments (for example, cities, mountains).

Geographic Place Dependence   An extremely powerful attachment to a specific place.

Integral Neighborhoods   Cohesive, active neighborhoods with considerable face-to-face contact among the residents; residents also maintain connections to the larger community outside the neighborhood.

Parochial Neighborhoods   High-interaction neighborhoods that have little involvement with the outside world.

Personalized Attachment   An attachment to place in which an individual's memories of a place are inseparable from memories of personal experiences.

Sense of Community   A feeling of belonging to a community, of neighbors being important to each other, and a shared faith that residents' needs will be met by their commitment to be together.

Shalako   An annual Zuni ceremony in which houses are consecrated and blessed.

Stepping-Stone Neighborhoods   Neighborhoods made up entirely of people whose allegiance is to outside groups.

System Overload   An excess of physical and social stimulation which leads people to disregard low-priority sensory inputs.

Topophilia   The affective bond between people and places.

Transitory Neighborhoods   Neighborhoods characterized by low interaction, a complete lack of identity, and high turnover.

The Natural
Environment

11

In previous chapters I discussed the relationship between human-made environments and human behavior. In this chapter, the focus is on how people are affected by the natural environment. Studies of how people perceive and think about the environment show that the degree to which a setting is "natural" is one of the most important characteristics used to distinguish between different environments (Herzog, Kaplan, & Kaplan, 1982; Ward & Russell, 1981). Psychologists have devoted much time to uncovering the specific properties of nature that make it different from other "nonnatural" stimuli in the environment (Wohlwill, 1983). Sebba (1991) listed a number of ways in which natural environments differ from built environments. The shapes encountered in natural environments are softer, rounder, and more varied and ambiguous than shapes found in environments created by human beings. There is a greater range of stimulus intensities (wet/dry, hot/cold) and less human control over the strength of these sensory inputs than is usually the case in built environments. Natural environments are more changeable and often contain moving inanimate objects such as clouds, water, trees, and the sun and moon. In spite of these obvious natural characteristics, it is difficult to find a definition of "natural" to satisfy everyone. Natural environments are often defined by what they are not—environments that are not a product of human activity or intervention (Wohlwill, 1983). While this definition is quite workable in many situations, it implies that city parks filled with trees, flowers, and artificial lakes, no matter how "natural" they appear, would not always qualify as natural environments. Obviously, the concept *natural,* which appears simple and clear-cut, can be quite complicated. As you read, think about the criteria you use to identify an environment as natural.

ATTITUDES TOWARD THE NATURAL ENVIRONMENT

Attitudes are lasting, general evaluations of people, objects, or issues (Petty & Cacioppo, 1985). They have three components: affective, cognitive, and behavioral (Breckler, 1984). The *affective* component is what most people think of when they hear the word *attitude.* It is our positive or negative reaction to something, the feeling part of the attitude that causes us to evaluate the thing in question as good or bad, pleasant or unpleasant. The *cognitive* component refers to knowledge or beliefs held about the attitude object, regardless of our affective reaction to it. The *behavioral* component refers to the behaviors we engage in that are relevant to the attitude object.

It is usually assumed that attitudes are learned through a combination of three processes: classical conditioning, instrumental conditioning, and social learning. We will see later that there is evidence that some attitudes are influenced by genetic predispositions as well. While all of this is true of attitudes toward natural environments, in the latter case the conditioning and social learning processes involved are especially subtle. Our attitudes toward something as broad and omnipresent as "nature" are so often taken for granted that we are completely unaware of the forces that have shaped them. This is especially true of those collective attitudes we share with other members of our society. Many of these can be traced to the very dawn of our culture's history when they developed under conditions very different from those we now face. It is extremely important to understand these attitudes, since they often dictate the way a society deals with the natural world through conservation, agriculture, and developing sources of energy.

While North American societies are becoming increasingly pluralistic and multicultural, the legal, religious, and educational forces that have shaped the growth of Canada and the United States over the last several hundred years have unquestionably been dominated by a Christian, white, and Western European perspective. The impact of this perspective has been especially important in the development of attitudes toward the natural environment in these countries.

Historical Roots of Current Environmental Attitudes

Oil spills spoiling beaches and killing wildlife; rain forests disappearing at an alarming rate; depletion of the ozone layer; smoke blackening the sky as oil wells burn in the aftermath of war—all around us we see the unfortunate side effects of modern attitudes toward the natural world. Many scholars have argued that these attitudes are far from "modern" and that their roots can be found in the earliest stirrings of what eventually would become Western, industrialized society. White (1967) pointed out that both modern technology and modern science are distinctly Western in origin, and both can be traced to the Judeo–Christian tradition that has shaped the growth of Western civilization. According to White, "What people do about their ecology depends on what they think about themselves in relation to other things around them. Human ecology is deeply conditioned by beliefs about our nature and destiny—that is, by religion" (p. 1205). Christianity inherited from Judaism, and then refined, a dualistic way of thinking in which humans are not just an ordinary part of nature—they are made in God's image and are quite different from the rest of creation. According to this view, nature exists to serve human purposes, and it is God's will that it be used however people see fit. This attitude is explicitly stated in the Book of Genesis (1:28): "And God blessed them and God said to them 'Be fruitful and multiply and fill the Earth and subdue it; and have dominion over the fish of the sea and the birds of the air and over every living thing that moves upon the Earth.' "

In his essay "The Curse of Abel," David Crownfield (1973) agrees that we can find the beginnings of our current attitudes toward nature in writings as old as the Book of Genesis. He highlights his argument with the story of Cain and Abel:

> Now Abel was a keeper of sheep, and Cain a tiller of the ground. In the course of time, Cain brought to Yahweh an offering of the fruit of the ground, and Abel brought of the firstlings of his flock and of their fat portions. And Yahweh had regard for Abel and his offering, but for Cain and his offering he had no regard. (Genesis 4:2–5)

Why did Yahweh accept Abel's offering and not Cain's? There is no indication that Cain had done anything wrong; the only apparent difference between the two brothers was that Cain raised grain while Abel raised sheep. According to Crownfield, this story reveals much about ancient Hebrew values and their relationship with the natural world. The Hebrews were a sheep-raising people engaged in a never-ending struggle with the grain-growing peoples who lived in Palestine. Their social organization was tribal, seminomadic, and patriarchical, and their primary allegiance was to the group rather than to the land or to any particular place. From an ecological point of view, this mentality is unfortunate because sheep are the original nonrecycling economy. For herding people, migration is the solution to problems—when the resources in one

P H O T O   11·1 A medieval miniature depicts Adam naming the beasts. The privilege of naming the beasts and the fact that Adam is shown clothed reflect medieval European attitudes of humans as superior to natural things.

area have been depleted, one simply moves on to greener pastures. This migratory approach to life has permeated our thinking about the relationship between nature and humans, and it has had a profound impact on Western attitudes not only toward nature but toward time itself. In Crownfield's words, "The present is to be negated, left behind, abandoned with all of its problems and defects . . . the problems of the present are going to be resolved in a dramatic, interventionist future" (p. 59). Existence becomes a migration through this world to a better future, and having faith means trusting (the tribal leader, the divine shepherd, the messiah, technology) that a way will be found to escape from the deteriorating pasture to a better place. People in this kind of society strongly believe that a miraculous divine force will intervene on their behalf and set things right. Even today, many people cheerfully believe that technology, new energy resources, or even migration to outer space will ultimately solve our ecological problems. It is often incredibly difficult to get people to change environmentally destructive behavior under these circumstances. Burke (1985) has observed that this view of life inevitably leads to a technology that has as its goal, not stability, but constant change.

The perceived gap between humans and the natural world grew as Christianity developed during the early Middle Ages. The most popular philosophy during the final days of the Roman Empire was **Neoplatonism,** which was based primarily on the writings of Plato (427–347 B.C.). Plato's philosophy proposed that what we see in the world is not real, but an imperfect copy of the true reality that existed elsewhere in the "realm of the true forms." To make matters worse, according to Plato, we perceive these imperfect copies of reality through the senses, which distort them even further. Thus, for the Neoplatonist, the only way to true knowledge was to turn away from empirical examination of the physical world and introspect on the innate truths with which we were born. Primarily through the work of Saint Augustine (354–430 B.C.), Neoplatonism absorbed a fragmented collection of early Christian beliefs to form the first coherent system of Christian doctrine, which would guide the development of Europe and the Western world for the next 1000 years.

A by-product of this new doctrine was a reduced interest in everyday life and in the physical world in general. Human beings were *not* natural, physical creatures but spiritual beings imprisoned in shells of flesh. Only the soul was real, and life on earth was nothing more than a migration through unpleasantness that must be endured to attain eternal salvation and "real" life in the hereafter. An excellent chronicling of these attitudes and a description of life during the early Middle Ages can be found in the works of a respected European historian who lived during this time, the Venerable Bede (673–735). Bede (1968) paints a picture of a world in which people prayed for an escape from their "bodily prisons"; a world full of miracles and messages from God. Nothing happened by chance; every event in the natural world was a message from God. And nature existed only to provide a medium for God to communicate with, reward, and punish human beings.

The attitude toward nature generated by this worldview was a peculiar blend of fear, arrogance, and disinterest. In medieval art, one seldom sees nature represented at all; pictures are dominated by human and divine figures. When nature is portrayed, it is only incidentally and never realistically. Idealized or mythical representations of plants or animals are all that one sees; landscapes are never shown. Nature was uninteresting and scary.

The typical European peasant led a precarious life; nature was an adversary to be feared and conquered, not a source of comfort. According to Burke (1985), "Dark age Europe was a land of darkness indeed, of almost impenetrable woods in which roamed wild animals: Boar, bear, wolves, and men too violent to live in the tiny clusters of huts scattered through the forest. . . . Only the well armed, or those protected by spiritual courage, ventured into the woods" (pp. 22–23). Fairy tales and myths originating in 12th- through 15th-century Europe (for example, Little Red Riding Hood, Hansel and Gretel) depict the forest as the home of all that is evil and frightening, a place to be avoided and hurried through at all costs (Altman & Chemers, 1980; Itteson, Proshansky, Rivlin, & Winkel, 1974; Nash, 1967; Tuan, 1979).

Thus, our society has inherited a view that we are not truly part of nature: nature was put here for us to use as we saw fit and that we have no moral obligation to preserve it. This early Christian view encouraged thinking about bodies, earth, and even time as disposable containers — noncylical, nonrenewable, and temporary (Crownfield, 1973). Crownfield believes that these attitudes reached a new peak with the growth of Calvinism, the work ethic, and the conquest of the American frontier. It seemed that people were "... obligated to graze this earthly pasture to

---

Native American Attitudes Toward Nature

By and large, Western industrialized societies have been marked by attitudes towared nature that encourage exploitation and conquest for the benefit of human beings. North American Indians, on the other hand, perceive themselves as part of the natural world; a virtuous life demands living in harmony with nature, treating it respectfully, and being a good citizen of an earth that has a life and a spirit of its own.

T. C. Mcluhan (1971) assembled a collection of stories, speeches, and interviews by and with Native Americans; many poignantly describe the attitudes that are at the heart of Indian culture:

We did not think of the great open plains, the beautiful rolling hills, and winding streams with tangled growth as "wild." Only to the white man was nature a "wilderness" and only to him was the land "infected" with "wild" animals and "savage" people. To us it was tame. Earth was bountiful and we were surrounded with the blessings of the Great Mystery. Not until the hairy man from the East came and with brutal frenzy heaped injustice upon us and the families we loved was it "wild" for us. When the very animals of the forest began fleeing from his approach, then it was for us the "Wild West" began.

Chief Luther Standing Bear of the
Oglala Band of Sioux

The Great Spirit, in placing men on the earth, desired them to take good care of the ground, to do each other no harm.

Young Chief of the Cayuses Indians of the
Pacific Northwest, 1855

The Great Spirit is our Father, but the Earth is our Mother. She nourishes us; that which we put into the ground she returns to us, and healing plants she gives us likewise. If we are wounded, we go to our mother and seek to lay the wounded part against her.

Bedagi of the Wabanakis Nation, 1900

If you took all your books, lay them out under the sun, and let the snow and rain and insects work on them for a while, there will be nothing left. But the Great Spirit has provided you and me with an opportunity for study in nature's university, the forests, the rivers, the mountains, and the animals which include us.

Tatanga Mani, a Stoney Indian
commenting on the white man's
education he received

its roots. Only by the fullest use of this temporary stopping place do we show our readiness to migrate to our true home" (p. 60).

To early American settlers, the wilderness was threatening—a place to be "reclaimed and redeemed" (Tuan, 1974, p. 63). Traditionally Westerners tended to bend nature to human will rather than to adapt their lifestyles to the natural surroundings. Saarinen (1988) chronicled the resistance of Anglo-American settlers to accepting the Arizona desert as it is and their attempts to replicate the more humid eastern environments to which they were accustomed. Similarly, the promotional literature that was developed to lure 19th-century American settlers westward emphasized the adaptability of the land and went to great lengths to calm fears of natural hazards, impenetrable forests, and monotonous prairies (Lewis, 1988).

This linear, noncyclical view of existence contrasts sharply with many non-Western traditions, such as those developed in India (Zimmer, 1951) and by North American Indians (Waters, 1963). Native Americans conceived of their relationship with nature in a dramatically different fashion (see box pp. 236–237).

For Native Americans, sacred power is diffused among humans, animals, places, and spirits; harmony exists in the world only when all the

---

We therefore yield to our neighbors, even our animal neighbors, the same right as ourselves, to inhabit this land.

Sitting Bull, Sioux warrior

The country was made without lines of demarcation, and it is no man's business to divide it . . . the earth and myself are of one mind . . . understand me fully with reference to my affection for the land. I never said the land was mine to do with as I chose. The one who has the right to dispose of it is the one who created it.

Chief Joseph of the Nez Perce Indians

The soil was soothing, strengthening, cleansing, and healing. That is why the old Indian still sits upon the earth instead of propping himself up and away from its life-giving forces. For him, to sit or lie upon the ground is to be able to think more deeply and to feel more keenly; he can see more clearly into the mys-

teries of life and come closer in kinship to other lives about him.

Chief Luther Standing Bear of the Oglala Band of Sioux

The white people never cared for land or deer or bear. . . . But the white people plow up the ground, pull down the trees, kill everything. The tree says, "Don't I am sore. Don't hurt me." But they chop it down and cut it up. The spirit of the land hates them. They blast out trees and stir it up to its depths. . . . They blast rocks and scatter them on the ground. The rock says, "Don't. You are hurting me." But the white people pay no attention. . . . How can the spirit of the earth like the white man? . . . Everywhere the white man has touched it, it is sore.

An old holy woman of the Wintu Indians of California, circa 1955 sources of power work together (Tuan, 1974). Unlike Europeans, Native Americans thought of *places* as sacred. For the Pueblo Indians of the Southwest, natural places, such as mountain peaks and caves that are above and below the earth's surface, were sacred and powerful, since they connect the earth with the upper and lower spirit worlds of the sky and the underworld. Activities that brought people into these levels (for example, excavations and expeditions into the mountains) demanded preparation through prayer and sacred rituals appropriate to the occasion (Saile, 1985). While Native Americans accorded nature a reverence that Europeans did not, they were acutely aware of nature's potential threat to their well-being. For example, the Inuit of the Canadian Arctic have traditionally believed in three deities: the god of the moon, the god of the air, and the god of the sea. However, "only the Moon god was good and well-intentioned toward human beings" (Tuan, 1979, p. 50).

In all fairness, we should note that throughout Western history individuals and groups have attempted to call attention to people's attitudes and effect change. One of the most recent and popular is the environmental movement, whose seminal work is Aldo Leopold's *A Sand County Almanac* (1949). Leopold discusses various ethical positions we can take in dealing with the natural world and proposes what he calls "the land ethic." This ethic states that we should extend the same feeling of moral responsibility we have in our dealings with other people to include soil, water, plants, animals, or collectively, the land. "The land ethic changes the role of *Homo sapiens* from conquerer of the land-community to plain member and citizen of it" (Leopold, 1949, pp. 219–220). Leopold also suggests that we should develop this ecological conscience not because it makes economic sense, but because human beings as important members of the ecosystem have a moral obligation to do so. Leopold's ideas have gathered force and his influence can be seen today in such disparate movements as animal liberation and wilderness conservation. This renewed interest in nature has spawned a new discipline known as "environmental ethics," engaging philosophers in the environmental dialogue with other environmentalists and social scientists (Callicot, 1989; VanDeVeer & Pierce, 1986).

ENVIRONMENTAL PREFERENCES: IN SEARCH OF "THE GREEN EXPERIENCE"

Despite the generally negative attitudes toward nature described in the previous section, people have long sought scenic beauty and outdoor experiences, and this tendency has increased with growing urbanization. One of the benchmarks of the English romantic movement of the early 19th century was the belief that nature had an uplifting, comforting, and beneficial effect on human beings. Romantics sought out natural settings and painted and wrote about the magnificent feelings these settings inspired. However, by 1800 England was the least wooded and "wild" of all Northern European nations (Daniels, 1988), and the romantics were almost all city dwellers whose idea of communing with nature would not measure up to most people's idea of a wilderness experience today.

Human reactions to landscapes undoubtedly involve both innate and learned components (Bourassa, 1990; Tooby & Cosmides, 1990). Therefore, it is not surprising that although some natural features such as trees and running water have always been liked better than others, such as swamps and desert scrubland, preferences for natural environments are also influenced to some degree by the spirit of the times. For example, during the 18th century, the influences of Newton, Descartes and others inspired the Age of Reason in which all of nature was thought of as a finely tuned machine that had been set in motion by a "divine watch-maker" God. Nature was symmetrical, geometric, and mathematically precise and appreciated most when it met these expectations. The rigid geometry of French gardens with their neatly sculpted hedges and precise design was nature at its finest. Later, the English romantic movement reacted against this, and gardens began to have more free-flowing lines and gently curving contours in an attempt to break down the boundaries between garden and countryside (Zube, 1978).

The most dramatic aspects of nature, especially mountains and the sea, have always inspired a mixture of awe, fear, and reverence in human beings. According to Tuan (1974), virtually every society has had a sacred mountain that served as a focal point in its cosmology: Mounts Olympus (Greece), Meru (India), Tabor (Israel), and Fuji (Japan) are but a few examples. The legends from different cultures are particularly revealing. Moses received the Ten Commandments on a mountain top, and it was on a mountain that Abraham prepared to sacrifice his son Isaac to Yahweh. Noah's Ark came to rest on a mountain top, and it was in the mountains that Jesus was tempted by the devil. Prometheus of Greek mythology was shackled to a mountain peak by Zeus, and everyone knows that Mohammed "went to the mountain." The Chinese emperor Wu (140–87 B.C.) sacrificed to heaven in the mountains, and it was in the mountains that Dr. Frankenstein pursued his creature and sought tranquility and refuge from his torments. Clearly, nature in its grandest form has figured prominently in human thinking throughout history.

What about today? What kind of experiences with nature do people prefer and actively seek out? Environmental psychologists have been quite interested in this question and have collected considerable data that can help us understand the psychology behind current environmental preferences.

Rachel Kaplan (1978) describes the encounter with the natural environment as **the green experience.** The drive to seek out nature and have the green experience is very strong in most people; often they will go to considerable trouble to commune with nature in almost any form. As an illustration, Kaplan describes urban assembly-line workers who rush off during their lunch hour, driving madly for several miles, to reach a spot with trees where they can sit and eat their lunch.

Research confirms that the nature one experiences need not be spectacular—even the most common instances of nature, such as an ordinary tree or a small piece of open land, can be quite satisfying (Kaplan, Kaplan, & Wendt, 1972; Little, 1975; Talbot & Kaplan, 1986). Research demonstrates that viewing natural scenes reduces stress (as measured through self-report and physiological indices), promotes more positive moods and feelings, and can facilitate recovery from illness (Parsons, 1991; Ulrich, 1981, 1984; Ulrich & Simons, 1986; Ulrich, Simons, Losito, Fiorito, Miles, & Zelson, 1991). Hendee and Stankey (1973) and Kaplan and Kaplan (1978, 1989) maintain that nature is an example of an intrinsic need, which is sought out for itself and not acquired to be exchanged for something else.

In studies of environmental preference, subjects are shown slides depicting different scenes. They are asked to rate how pleasing each scene is, how much they would like to be there, or to select a favorite scene from a group of scenes. This research consistently shows that people greatly prefer viewing natural over human-made scenes (Evans & Wood, 1981; R. Kaplan, 1975, 1977; Wohlwill, 1976). This effect is even stronger when slides are presented for very brief periods, approximating a view of scenes as seen through a car window; even "sympathetic," tasteful human intrusions into nature can reduce the attractiveness of a scene (R. Kaplan, 1978; Schroeder, 1991). Simply labelling a slide as a "wilderness area" elevates the area's scenic-quality rating, while labels such as "commercial timber stand" reduce it (Anderson, 1981). Intrusions of natural elements in built environments are usually perceived favorably. Sheets and Manzer (1991) found that trees and shrubs along city streets produce positive reactions and lead to positive evaluations of the quality of life in the area.

The lasting impact of natural environments on individuals is illustrated in a recent study by Sebba (1991). She asked 96 architecture students and 102 teachers and principals in Israel to name the place that was most significant to them in their childhoods. Ninety-seven percent identified an outdoor setting such as a park or the seashore as the most significant place of their youth. In a similar study (Marcus, 1978), 86 percent of the environments recalled by American college students were outdoors. This effect is probably due to the emotional, enduring qualities of memories for outdoor places rather than to an accurate reflection of childhood activities. Sebba studied 174 Israeli children (highly similar to the adults in her study on geographic and socioeconomic variables) who did not identify outdoor places as significant in their lives nearly as often as adults reflecting on their own childhoods. She found that boys and rural children were most likely to select outdoor places, whereas urban children actually preferred indoor settings.

Physical Features of Landscapes

One approach to understanding what makes some natural scenes more appealing than others has been to analyze the scene's content to find out which items tend to be reliably related to higher ratings. Although preferences for landscapes depend to some extent on the demographic characteristics of the viewer and the outdoor activities he or she is interested in (Schroeder, 1987), these studies identified some specific natural features that almost always increase the attractiveness of landscapes. Open meadows surrounded by woods are very well liked (Zube, 1976; Zube, Pitt, & Anderson, 1975), and forests (especially deciduous forests) are most strongly preferred when there is little underbrush and an abundance of grass cover (Daniel & Bolster, 1976; Patey & Evans, 1979; Schroeder, 1991). Hull and Harvey (1989) studied emotional responses to suburban parks in Australia and found that the amount of vegetation and wildlife, the size of the trees, and the density of the trees were all positively related to increased feelings of pleasure in that environment. Pathways through the parks only increased pleasure when the underbrush was very dense.

Similarly, Patsfall, Feimer, Buhyoff, and Wellman (1984) studied responses to scenic vistas along a major tourist highway and found that the relative amounts of vegetation in the background, middleground, and foreground were important components of the attractiveness of the view, a finding that agrees with what Shafer, Hamilton, and Schmidt (1969) found in a study of landscapes in New York State. Kaplan, Kaplan, and Brown (1989) determined that weedy fields, scrubland, and agriculture lead to negative judgments about the attractiveness of scenery, while Palmer and Zube (1976) found that the amount of natural water area and the degree of "ruggedness" strongly influence the attractiveness of scenery.

Many other studies confirm that water is a highly preferred part of any natural scene. Studies of waterscapes indicate that it is not just the amount of water that is significant—clarity and freshness seem at least as important. Mountain lakes and rushing water, especially waterfalls, are extremely well-liked, while swampy areas or water covered with algae bloom receive low ratings (Calvin, Dearinger, & Curtain, 1972; Herzog, 1985; R. Kaplan, 1984). Anderson, Mulligan, Goodman, and Regen (1983) showed that even sounds influence the aesthetic evaluation of settings, with the appropriateness of the sound to the setting being an important factor. For example, the sounds of birds and animals enhance the beauty of a forest setting much more than they enhance the beauty of an urban setting.

Some factors outside the landscape influence an individual's reaction to a natural scene. Several studies indicate that a person's age may be one such factor. Zube, Pitt, and Evans (1983) asked 294 subjects ranging in age from 6 to over 70 to sort 56 color photographs on scenic quality. They found that young children rated landscapes differently from adults, and that older adults differ slightly from young and middle-aged adults. Specifically, young children's preferences were less affected by the presence of human influences in landscapes than were young and middle-aged adults, who greatly disliked these. Elderly adults were not as disturbed by human intrusions as younger adults were, but they disliked them more than children did. Young and middle-aged adults were most sensitive to complexity in landscapes, while children exhibited an especially strong attraction to water in landscapes. Bernaldez, Ruiz, and Ruiz (1984) confirmed that children prefer less naturalistic, less complex landscapes than adults; Bernaldez, Benayas, and DeLucio (1987) have confirmed that children are particularly fond of water in landscapes. In another study, Bernaldez and his colleagues compared the landscape preferences of 11- and 16-year-olds in the Canary Islands. They found that landscape features such as darkness and roughness, which could be associated with fear and insecurity, were liked significantly less by the 11-year-olds than by the 16-year-olds (Bernaldez, Gallardo, & Abello, 1987).

Finally, it has also been shown that the season in which subjects judge the pictures can affect how they are rated. Buhyoff and Wellman (1979) found that people like fall foliage better in late summer than in spring, and green foliage better in spring than in late summer.

Psychological Features of Landscapes

A more useful way to understand scenic preferences is to study the general organization of the landscape rather than its individual physical elements. This general organization mediates between the raw physical properties of a scene and the aesthetic response of the person viewing it. These organizational features of a landscape are referred to as its **collative properties.** They operate in our response to natural environments as well as to urban environments (discussed in Chapter 10).

Litton (1968, 1972) has emphasized that the organization of landscape elements determines what in the scene will command attention. He proposes that we prefer landscapes that clearly direct our attention to important parts of the scene, facilitating orderly perception. For Litton, the key collative properties that help us organize our perceptions of scenery include enframement, convergence, and contrast. **Enframement** refers to the extent to which a scene provides its own "picture frame," allowing the viewer to quickly focus on its key aspects. Viewing mountains or a lake through nearby trees that "frame" the picture is an example (see Photo 11-2). **Convergence** refers to a point at which two

P H O T O   11·2 Enframement enhances the attractiveness of a landscape by helping the observer organize his or her perceptions of the scene.

or more lines in a scene come together, dominating the scene because it draws attention to some point on the horizon. One example is a roadway lined with trees disappearing into the distance. **Contrast** refers to obvious differences between various elements of a scene in form, color, or texture. The differences prevent blending of these elements and allow the viewer to structure the scene into a clear background and foreground. Generally, highly preferred scenes contain a focal point—enframement, convergence, and contrast all tend to give scenery greater focus and make it more attractive.

Heat-Moon (1991b) describes how the tall-grass prairie landscape of eastern Kansas, lacking virtually all collative properties, requires more work to comprehend and appreciate:

> I believe now that two years of watching the Atlantic Ocean [while in the navy] had changed the way I viewed landscape, especially levelish, rolling things . . . I began to like the American grasslands, not because they demand your attention, like mountains and coasts, but because they almost defy absorbed attention . . . I liked the clarity of line in a place that seemed to require me to bring something to it and to open it actively: see far, see little. I learned a prairie's secret; take the numbing distance in small doses and gorge on the little details that beckon. The prairie doesn't give up anything easily, unless its horizon and sky . . . I had to begin thinking open and lean, seeing without set points of obvious focus, first noticing the horizion and then drawing my vision back toward middle distance, where so little appears to exist. [p. 48]

A very influential "psychological" model of landscape preference is the **preference framework** developed by Stephen and Rachel Kaplan (R. Kaplan, 1977; S. Kaplan, 1975; Kaplan & Kaplan, 1982). Their work grew out of earlier research on the nature of aesthetic judgments in general, especially that of Berlyne (1960, 1971, 1974). Berlyne proposed that we pay special attention to the collative properties of complexity, novelty, incongruity, and surprisingness when making judgments about the beauty of just about anything. According to Berlyne, we find some- thing most pleasing when it stimulates us and arouses our curiosity, inviting us to achieve a sense of satisfaction by resolving uncertainty through exploration. An object or a setting that is very low in novelty, incongruity, complexity, and surprisingness is boring, unstimulating, and not very attractive. On the other hand, a stimulus that is too highly arousing because it is extremely novel or incongruous is usually not well-liked either. We are most attracted to things that are moderately complex, novel, incongruous, and surprising.

The Kaplans extended Berlyne's ideas and developed a model that specifically deals with aesthetic responses to environments. In the Kap- lans' model, four factors determine our reactions to an environment: coherence, legibility, complexity, and mystery.

Essentially, the Kaplans' model divides environmental features into those currently being experienced and those that only hold out the promise of being experienced in the future (Heath, 1988). Coherence and complexity are the two properties that refer to immediately visible features. **Coherence** is the extent to which a scene is organized and hangs together as a unified whole. Greater coherence leads to greater liking. **Complexity** reflects the number and variety of elements that are found in a scene. As long as it does not become too extreme, greater complexity also leads to greater liking.

Legibility and mystery are properties that require the viewer to con- template possible future experiences with the environment. **Legibility** is the extent to which an environment can be read easily, or the extent to which it looks as if one could explore it extensively without getting lost. More legible environments are preferred over less legible ones. **Mystery** implies that the scene contains more information than can be seen at the moment, and that one could learn much more about the environment by walking through it and exploring. Stephen Kaplan (1987) stresses the importance of inference in the definition of mystery. Many studies have confirmed that people do in fact perceive mystery as a distinct quality of landscapes and that a sense of mystery tremendously increases the attrac- tiveness of natural environments (Gimblett, Itami, & Fitzgibbon, 1985; Herzog, 1984, 1985, 1987, 1989; R. Kaplan, 1973; Kaplan & Kaplan, 1989; Kaplan, Kaplan, & Brown, 1989; Ulrich, 1977). The lone exception occurs when the heightened sense of mystery is accompanied by a sense of danger, as it is in deep narrow canyons and urban alleys (Herzog, 1987; Herzog & Smith, 1988). (See Photo 11-3.)

P H O T O   11·3 Mystery may not enhance the attractiveness of an environment if it is linked with a sense of danger.

   Eliovson (1978) described how the strategic use of these properties, especially mystery, creates the magic that many people experience in Japanese gardens (see Photo 11-4). These gardens are often cultivated in an extremely small space, so the clever use of foliage, trees, rocks, and water is essential to the successful composition of the tranquility and beauty in which the Japanese garden is famous. The illusion of greater distance and depth is attained by placing large trees in the foreground, near the house, and planting the smaller ones further away. This creates the impression that these trees are farther away than they actually are, making the garden appear larger. By arranging features in the foreground with more elaborate detail, the objects in the background become even less prominent, recede into the distance, and increase the illusion of size and distance. Mystery is created in a Japanese garden by using an obscured view. By placing rocks or planting trees strategically, the gardener ensures that the whole area cannot be seen at once, and the viewer is invited to walk through it to discover new perspectives. If a stream, fountain, or waterfall is included, it is often hidden from view (rather than covered with spotlights as one might find in an American garden) so that the sound of bubbling water intrigues visitors, motivating them to ex-

PHOTO 11·4
A Japanese garden

plore the garden to discover the source of the sound. Pathways are usually winding and disappear into shrubbery, creating a sense of mystery and greater distance.

The Origins of Human Environmental Preferences

Having described the consistency with which people exhibit specific preferences for certain types of natural environments, let's examine how these preferences developed. Many scholars assert that environmental preferences are learned responses, shaped by each individual's life experiences and cultural values, such as harmony with nature (Lyons, 1983; Tuan, 1979). Knopf (1987) summarizes the evidence for this position. The issue of whether human environmental preference is an innate or learned response is far from settled. Relatively few cross-cultural studies of landscape preferences have tested this question. One recent study found considerable similarity between native Balinese and Western tourists in evaluating landscapes in Bali (Hull & Revell, 1989).

Zube (1990) notes that although some ethnic and racial differences have been found in studies of landscape preferences, these studies are often confounded by other factors such as educational levels and urban versus rural populations. The consensus at this point is that with age and experience people begin to show stronger preferences for familiar surroundings, but familiarity does not seem to be as strong a predictor of environmental preferences as other factors (Balling & Falk, 1982; Kaplan & Kaplan, 1989). In a review of the literature, Kaplan and Kaplan (1989) concluded that different cultural groups seldom disagree as to *what* they like in natural environments but rather on *how much* they are attracted to different natural features.

In recent years, a perspective that sees environmental preferences as a by-product of human evolution has been growing in popularity (Kaplan & Kaplan, 1989; S. Kaplan, 1987; Ulrich, 1977, 1983). According to this view, human preferences have developed because they have been crucial to our survival as individuals and as a species. Charlesworth (1976) points out that it is not sufficient for a species merely to recognize environments in which it could function well, but it would be highly adaptive for a species to develop a strong preference that motivates the individual to actively seek out that environment. S. Kaplan (1979) describes participants' reactions in his research on environmental preferences — reactions that eventually led him to an evolutionary interpretation.

> Participants made preference judgments rapidly and easily. They even seemed to enjoy the process. The results were not wildly idiosyncratic as folklore seemed to imply, but were remarkably stable and repeatable across groups with widely varying backgrounds   Increasingly, preference came to look like an expression of an intuitive guide to behavior, an inclination to make choices that would lead the individual away from inappropriate environments and toward desirable ones [pp. 14–15].

Put very simply, the evolutionary position states that individuals who preferred the "right" environments survived longer and reproduced more successfully than individuals who did not prefer them as strongly, and the tendency to prefer these same environments has been passed on to us. According to Tuan (1974), "a preference for the stark environment, bare as the desert or the monk's cell, is contrary to the normal human desire for ease and abundance" (p. 51).

Within this framework, human preferences for scenes containing fresh water, vegetation, and light make perfect sense. British geographer Jay Appleton (1975, 1984) clearly thought along these lines when he proposed two characteristics of a habitat that would be adaptive and hence attractive: "prospect" and "refuge." Greenbie (1982) states that these environments offer "the opportunity to see without being seen, to eat without being eaten, to produce offspring that survive" (p. 2). **Refuge** means having a safe place to hide where one can be sheltered from the threatening, dangerous parts of the environment. **Prospect** refers to one's clear, unobstructed view of the landscape. Appleton claims that

P H O T O   11·5 Environments that offer a strong sense of prospect and refuge tend to be very well liked and are popular play spaces with children.

humans prefer environments and scenes that offer prospect and refuge; preliminary research has supported his prediction (Nasar, Julian, Buchman, Humphreys, & Mrohaly, 1983).

Universally, children display a strong preference for playing in enclosed spaces. The concepts of prospect and refuge may help explain the almost magical quality of feelings evoked by memories of favorite spaces from childhood and the unusual richness of detail that can be recalled about these favorite childhood "hiding places" (Boschetti, 1987; Hester, 1979; Marcus, 1978). Eibl-Eibesfeldt (1988) reports a number of situations in which we prefer places that offer protection. In restaurants, diners first occupy tables in corners or nooks. Tables in the center of the room are used only when all others are taken. People prefer seats that allow them to sit with their backs against a wall. Housing sites with unobstructed views are strongly preferred. He agrees that these preferences are the remnants of successful evolutionary strategies that helped our ancestors detect and avoid predators and enemies. Sommer (1969) illustrates the disadvantages of a location that is too central by recounting an interview with a London prostitute:

> This is my favourite table, and here I can sit with my back against the wall, facing the door. Here is a vantage point from which entries and exists can be observed without too much effort. Nobody can get behind me, and there is safety in this. If there is any trouble, if fighting breaks out for any reason . . . a wall position is the best to be in. . . . In the centre of a room, however alert you are you can be knocked out of your chair by scuffling men before the

first blow has landed, and if you are lucky enough to get back on your feet
unharmed you will probably find yourself in the heart of the battle, in which
several outsiders will by this time have involved themselves [p. 47].

The evolutionary perspective fits well with the environmental preference framework developed by Kaplan and Kaplan. Coherence and legibility increase the attractiveness of environments because they enable people to quickly comprehend, remember, and make sense of the
environment, all of which are clearly advantageous for survival. Complexity and mystery, as long as they are not linked with danger, hold out the
promise of an abundance of resources and better prospects for survival
than environments lacking these qualities.

Evolutionary interpretations of human aesthetic preferences are still
controversial, and, admittedly, much of the support for this position is
indirect and after-the-fact. Nevertheless, Eibl-Eibesfeldt (1988) summarizes an impressive history of research indicating that humans have
strong innate standards of beauty that value regularity and symmetry in
what they see. A number of studies indicate that animals including monkeys, raccoons, birds, and chimpanzees have similar aesthetic standards
(Eibl-Eibesfeldt, 1988; Morris, 1962; Rensch, 1957, 1958).

The more specific question of a genetic basis for environment or
habitat preference also relies heavily on animal research. Numerous studies demonstrate a strong genetic basis for habitat selection in many
species of animals (Brockmann, 1979; Drickamer & Vessey, 1982; Jackson, 1988; Partridge, 1974, 1978). In a classic study of habitat selection,
Werker (1964) demonstrated that even within a species that lives in
different environments, a genetic preference for one specific habitat is
passed on from parents to offspring. In his study, deer mice born of
parents captured in open fields or woods showed a strong preference for
their parents' habitat, regardless of the habitat they were exposed to early
in their own lives. Alcock (1984) summarized the research on habitat
selection by concluding that although habitat selection in animals can be
modified somewhat by early experience, that early experience cannot
override the genetically-based developmental program that controls habitat preferences.

While no one has argued that human environmental preferences are
as rigidly fixed as those of some animals, the assumption is that humans
must have acquired a degree of innate preference through the same
forces that shaped these preferences in animals. If human beings did in
fact evolve on the savannas of Africa, the most provocative evidence
would be the apparently universal attraction to savanna-like environments (expanses of grass dotted with trees), especially among children
(Balling & Falk, 1982; Falk, in Hiss, 1990). Falk (cited in Hiss, 1990)
attributes the homeowner's obsession with maintaining grass lawns to
this strong evolutionary attachment. Heat-Moon (1991b) expresses his
love of tall-grass prairies from precisely this perspective:

It was tall grass that made man stand up: to be on all fours, to crouch in a six-foot-high world of thick cellulose, is to be blind and vulnerable. People may prefer the obvious beauty of mountains and seacoasts, but we are bipedal because of savanna; man is man because of tall grass. When I walk the prairies, I like to take along the notion that although my blood may long for the haven of the forest, its apprenticeship in the trees, it also recognizes this grand openness as the kind of place where it became itself [p. 48].

OUTDOOR RECREATION AND THE WILDERNESS EXPERIENCE

When people think of recreation, many think of a natural outdoor setting. Not surprisingly, outdoor activities such as fishing, hiking, and camping consistently rank at the top of the list of North Americans' favorite leisure activities; undoubtedly, many of you count these activities among your favorite pastimes. Alexander, in Altman and Chemers (1980) commented on the steady growth of interest in outdoor recreation:

One of the most remarkable phenomena of the twentieth-century culture is the desire to be outdoors. Throughout history man has endeavored to create shelters that protected him from the elements and to find better methods with which to cook his food. However, now that sturdy, air-conditioned and centrally heated structures are common and cooking facilities are efficient, man increasingly turns toward the outdoors to spend his time and to cook his food over open fires [p. 202].

As environmental psychology has expanded, psychologists increasingly have turned their attention to research on leisure behavior and the people who use natural recreational areas. Much of this research on wilderness and outdoor recreation has been driven by practical concerns. There is an innate tension between the growing number of people using these areas and attempts to preserve the quality of the experience they are seeking. A greater understanding of the users' characteristics, motivations, and preferences is crucial for effectively dealing with this problem in the future. This research has been truly interdisciplinary, and valuable contributions have been made by workers in many other fields such as forestry, geography, economics, and sociology.

Often, research on outdoor recreational experiences must begin with very basic questions. What is recreation, and how is it different from other behaviors? What is it about natural settings that make them so satisfying to the individuals who use them? There are many ways to approach such broad questions. Heimstra and McFarling (1978) emphasize that when talking about outdoor experiences, one must distinguish between temporary and permanent interactions with the natural environment. A person visiting a remote mountain forest will have a very different experience from a person who must live there every day.

Recreation, by definition, implies behavior that represents a *tempo-*

rary rather than a permanent interaction. It also implies behavior that is freely chosen and intrinsically satisfying. A person backpacking in the desert is engaged in recreation; someone stranded there after surviving a plane crash is not. Similarly, a lumberjack or a forest ranger at work is not usually seen as engaging in recreational behavior, while a bus driver or a college professor walking through the same woods probably would be considered at leisure. Clearly, recreation is a fuzzy concept with indistinct boundaries. An outdoor recreational experience must be thought of as something more complex than simply being in a natural setting during leisure hours. (After all, many people even think that ice fishing is fun!) Clawson and Knetsch (1966) describe recreation as an experience that consists of several different phases. The first phase begins when the individual starts to think about, plan, and anticipate the experience. The second phase occurs during travel to the location where the recreational activity will occur. The third phase, the on-site activity, is what most people think of when asked about recreation. Clawson and Knetsch suggest that this conception of outdoor recreation may be a bit too narrow. The fourth phase consists of travel back from the location, and the fifth and final phase of a recreational experience is the recollection and remembrance of it after it is over.

When you think about recreation more comprehensively, it becomes apparent that travelling to and from the site and reminiscing about your experiences are indeed very important. You may even have had vacations in which these turn out to be the most enjoyable parts of the experience! Some have argued that driving for pleasure is the most popular form of outdoor recreation in the United States (Highway Research Board, 1973), and highway developers are beginning to take this into account when planning new roadways through scenic areas.

Since sightseeing is a major part of most outdoor activity, our abilities to recognize and recall our surroundings are important factors in determining how much we understand and enjoy that environment and how much pleasure our encounter with nature provides when we think back on it. Hammitt (1987) conducted a study of the visual recognition and recollection of natural environments in the Great Smoky Mountains National Park of Tennessee. He interviewed 750 hikers at the head of a trail either before they began their hike or after they had finished. Hikers judged their preferences for 32 black-and-white photos of features from the trail. Those who had already completed their hike were asked to judge how familiar the features were and how confident they were that they had actually seen them. There was tremendous agreement among these hikers not only on what visual features they preferred to see on a hike, but also on what features were best remembered. Water, especially waterfalls, was easy to remember, and disturbances such as uprooted trees and notable trail erosion were also confidently recalled. Scenes that were high in "trail mystery"—as when the trail curved out of sight around a bend or over a hill—were also very familiar to subjects. Hammitt found that interpretive redwood signs installed along the trail significantly increased the visitors' recall of key locations.

Characteristics of Users of Wilderness Areas

Studies of the characteristics of people who use national and state parks reveal that certain groups are over-represented among visitors to these areas. The United States Department of the Interior (1979) reports that users of national parks and wilderness areas tend to have higher incomes, be employed in professional and technical occupations, and be from urban areas more than might be anticipated by chance alone. Also, there are disproportionately more college graduates and people with advanced degrees: teachers and students constitute two of the largest

---

TRY IT!

How Much of a "Purist" Are You?

Individuals differ according to how much they prefer wilderness areas to be free from signs of human influence. Explore your own "purism" by completing the brief questionnaire below. Indicate how much you agree or disagree with each of the statements according to the following scale:

> 5 = Strongly agree
> 4 = Agree
> 3 = Neither agree nor disagree
> 2 = Disagree
> 1 = Strongly disagree

Fill in the blank after each statement with the number that comes closest to expressing your feelings. Instructions for scoring the questionnaire are presented at the end. (This scale has not been empirically validated. It is intended as a classroom demonstration only.)

1. I grew up in a rural area. _____
2. When I am camping, it bothers me if I can see or hear other campers. _____
3. I went camping or fishing in a wilderness area many times when I was a young child. _____
4. I like the feeling of being very far from "civilization." _____
5. Camping and hiking are enjoyable ways to meet new people. _____
6. I intend to pursue a graduate or professional degree. _____

groups among visitors. These findings are consistent with what other studies show about the characteristics of users of these natural environments (Gilligan, 1962; Lime, 1986; McDonald & Clark, 1968).

Although the accuracy of this demographic profile is widely accepted, it is not clear why visitors to national parks and wilderness areas have these characteristics. Perhaps a greater interest in natural settings is related to being a professional from an urban background, or it may be that these people have more leisure time and money to take advantage of recreational opportunities. In either case, studies have established that these same characteristics are often related to the kind of wilderness experience a person desires. Stankey (1972) developed a scheme for classifying users of wilderness areas as "purists" or "nonpurists," based on interviews with over 600 visitors to wilderness areas in Montana, Utah,

TRY IT!

7. I prefer recreational areas that can be reached quickly and easily. _____
8. I grew up in a large city. _____
9. The financial welfare of individuals and the nation is more important than the preservation of wilderness areas. _____
10. I get very angry when I see litter in wilderness areas. _____
11. Motorboating is more fun than canoeing. _____
12. Natural areas should always be preserved, even at great economic cost. _____
13. I enjoy natural areas where you can see the best scenery without leaving your car. _____
14. Cross-country skiing is more fun than snowmobiling. _____
15. I could never enjoy an outdoor experience if I were alone. _____
16. I enjoy scenery the most when it is hidden and must be discovered by hiking a long way to get to it. _____

To obtain your "purism" score, add up your responses to the odd-numbered questions. Do the same for the even-numbered questions. After obtaining these two sums, subtract the sum of the odd-numbered questions from the sum of the even-numbered questions and add 32 to the remainder. This is your purism score. The maximum possible score is 64, and the minimum is 0. While there is no firm cut-off point, the closer you come to a score of 64, the more you exhibit the characteristics of people identified as purists in previous research.

Wyoming, and Minnesota. **Purists** have stronger desires for solitude and are more disturbed by signs of human intrusion (campsite wear and tear, litter) into natural environments than **nonpurists** are. Cicchetti (1972) found that men tend to have higher purism scores than women, and that purism scores also increase with the individual's level of education and the urbanity of that person's childhood hometown. In addition, the older individuals are when they have their first wilderness experience, the more strongly they are pushed toward the purism end of the scale. He suggests that growing up in a rural area leads to a more utilitarian view of the wilderness; rural residents are more likely than urbanites to see nature as a source of resources and an unremarkable setting for daily existence. The prevalence of nature-exploitative industries (for example, agriculture, mining, lumbering) in rural areas may contribute to this utilitarian view of nature (Buttel, Murdock, Leistritz, & Hamm, 1987). To help you think about where you fall along the purism continuum, try it (see box How Much of a "Purist" Are You?).

Only a few studies have tried to relate personality traits to patterns of outdoor recreation. Rossman and Ulehla (1977) report that participants in some of the purest wilderness activities, such as stream fishing and primitive camping, score very low in the need for affiliation. In another study, Driver and Knopf (1977) compared the personality profiles of tennis players, campers, and nature walkers. They found that the participants in all these activities scored lower than national norms on affiliation and social recognition but scored higher than national norms on autonomy and consciousness of sensation and feeling. Although Driver and Knopf showed that personality was related to choice of recreational activities and the extent to which people engage in them, they concluded that personality is probably a weaker determinant of recreational behavior than other factors.

Motivations of Users of Wilderness Areas

What is it that people seek from nature? What motivates them to travel, at great expense in time and money, to remote wilderness areas? Knopf (1987) has reviewed the research on nature's value to human beings and concludes that the allure of natural environments can be described in four ways.

First, we can think of nature as a restorer, a place that is more peaceful and subdued than the complex, stimulating environments that surround people in their everyday lives. Stephen Kaplan (1977) proposes that we have been programmed through evolution to respond positively to natural environments. Because the patterns in nature are inherently gripping, we do not have to work as hard to screen out and suppress distracting, irrelevant stimuli. As a result, we find ourselves more relaxed and at ease in natural surroundings. A number of studies are consistent with the idea of nature as restorer. Mandell and Marans (1972) interviewed subjects, all of whom were heads of households, and asked them to rate the importance of 12 different reasons for participating in their favorite outdoor activity. Easily, the most important reason cited was the "relief of tension." Other studies indicate that wilderness use is important because it helps individuals achieve solitude and escape from urban areas. Encountering other people in these surroundings usually diminishes the individual's satisfaction (Cicchetti & Smith, 1973; Rossman & Ulehla, 1977).

Another way to think about nature is as a competence builder. From this perspective, nature provides an opportunity for individuals to enhance their feelings of self-reliance and self-confidence. A person in an extended wilderness experience is forced to master new skills and experiences; this renewed assessment of personal strengths and weaknesses may be therapeutic, producing many benefits for the individual's physical and mental well-being. A great many studies support the notion that wilderness experiences are therapeutic and competence-building (Bernstein, 1972; Burch, 1977; Gibson, 1979; Hanson, 1977; R. Kaplan, 1974). For example, Talbot and Kaplan (1986) conducted research over a 10-year period that was designed specifically to investigate the therapeutic benefits of wilderness experiences. The subjects in their study participated in an outdoor challenge program and spent up to two weeks in an isolated wilderness setting where they acquired wilderness survival skills. Among the benefits these people experienced were a growing awareness of their environment and a greater sense of wonder about nature. They also reported greater insight and became more focused on what they considered valuable. In a similar vein, Slotsky (1973) found that a five-day backpacking trip in the Sierras led to improvement in many areas for a group of psychiatric day-care patients.

A problem with many of these studies is that the investigators had little control over the selection of subjects; therefore it is difficult to determine how much of the positive outcomes are due solely to the wilderness experience. Hartig, Mang, and Evans (1991) randomly assigned subjects to conditions in two experiments, providing a more rigorous test of the therapeutic value of wilderness experiences. In the first experiment, experienced backpackers were randomly assigned to an extended backpacking trip in the wilderness; a nonwilderness vacation such as car touring, sightseeing, or visiting family and friends; or a nonvacation of equal length. After each of these experiences, the participants filled out questionnaires and engaged in a proofreading task similar to one completed before the vacation occurred. Hartig and his colleagues found that even under these more controlled conditions, the wilderness experience enhanced feelings of happiness and well-being relative to the other groups, and it was the only condition which improved performance on the proofreading task. In a second experiment,

Hartig and colleagues (1991) obtained similar results after college students were randomly assigned to participate in a nature walk as opposed to an urban walk or a relaxation session.

In earlier chapters, I discussed human needs for stimulation and change as the motivating force behind behavior in many environments. Knopf's third way to describe nature—nature as diversion—fits nicely within this framework. Natural environments provide a very different kind of sensory input from urban environments. Spending time "getting away from it all" in the wilderness can help eliminate the monotony of too much of the same kind of sensory stimulation. Hull and Harvey (1989) found that people prefer parks that are pleasant and arousing; this perspective might explain what motivates people who engage in highly arousing, risky outdoor activities such as hang gliding, rock climbing, and downhill skiing.

For some people, outdoor recreation expresses a central life interest and communicates to others something very important about themselves (Jacob & Schreyer, 1980). The fourth way to think about nature is as a symbol for something else. For many, nature symbolizes important qualities: life, continuity, spirituality, and mystery. Symbolic nature helps confirm the basic values of the individual who seeks it out.

Thus, people's motivation for outdoor experiences clearly differ, and these differences affect how individuals respond to their environment. Among other things, a wilderness experience can be a way to cope with the stress of everyday life, project a particular self-image, develop and display skills, or affiliate with other people (Driver, 1972). Indeed, research on wilderness users' needs reveals that often there is no common motivation even among people engaged in the same activity (Driver & Brown, 1978; Knopf, 1983). Brown, Hautaluoma, and McPhail (1977) found eight motivationally distinct groups among a population of Colorado deer hunters. These motivational differences were related to differences in hunting style and socioeconomic background. Similar results have been obtained in studies of trail hikers (Bowley, 1979), cross-country skiers (Ballman, 1980), anglers (Driver & Cooksey, 1977), and tourists and wilderness users of many other kinds (Brown & Haas, 1980; Knopf & Barnes, 1980). Differences among groups engaged in different activities are even more pronounced. According to Jackson and Wong (1982), cross-country skiers desire solitude, tranquility, and an undisturbed natural environment, while snowmobilers seek adventure and sociability. Anglers do not fish for food as much as for the opportunity to relax, achieve, and socialize (Knopf, Driver, & Bassett, 1973), just as hunters tend to be more interested in escape, companionship, and exercise than in harvesting or displaying game (More, 1973; Potter, Hendee, & Clark, 1973).

A study of 2000 travellers by the President's Commission on Americans Outdoors (1987) attempted to compile a more systematic profile of

P H O T O   11-8 One-fourth of all outdoor recreation is water dependent.

what Americans really want from outdoor recreation. Like other research, however, this study concluded that motivations vary tremendously. About one-third of those studied were classified as "health conscious sociables." The median age of this group was 49. As a group, health conscious sociables enjoy picnicking, sightseeing, and light exercise without high levels of risk or excitement; they tend to take frequent, short vacations by automobile. Another one-third, "get-away actives" (median age of 35), prefer quiet, secluded activities such as hiking and canoeing. About 16 percent of the population (median age of 32) were identified as "excitement-driven competitives" who liked demanding, risky activities such as kayaking and mountain climbing. Eight percent were "fitness-driven" individuals who pursued extremely arduous activities (for example, triathlons and marathons), and another 8 percent were "unstressed and unmotivated" people completely uninterested in any form of outdoor recreation. The planners of recreation areas should note the shift in interests that accompany aging, since it has strong implications for recreational demands as the "baby boom" generation ages.

The motivation for some people to use wilderness areas can be explained simply; they are there because of social pressure. Cheek and Burch (1976) found that 96 percent of visitors to outdoor areas were members of a group and that the lone individual was relatively rare. More than half of these people admitted that they were there at the wish of someone else, fulfilling a social obligation as much as seeking a natural experience. Similar results were obtained in a study by Kelly (1976).

Environmental Quality and the Wilderness Experience

Dorfman (1979) pointed out that the match between a recreation site and the individual's preferences and expectations is an important part of satisfaction with the outdoor experience; however, a person's wilderness experience is also highly dependent on the actual quality of the environment. Obvious signs of environmental deterioration and overcrowding such as vandalism, littering, or visible air and water pollution dramatically reduce the quality of the outdoor experience for most people. Beyond these obvious factors, there are strong individual differences as to what does and does not decrease the quality of a wilderness experience. This is because so much depends on an individual's perceptions, and the perception of crowding in outdoor recreational settings is not a simple matter (Westover, 1989). A very important variable is the number of people the individual expects to encounter, causing the standards for feeling crowded to be quite different in remote wilderness areas than they might be in a city park or at a beach (Hammitt, 1983; Westover & Collins, 1987).

Haas (1975) found that although solitude is an extremely important element of a positive wilderness experience for many people, for many others part of the excitement comes from the opportunity to meet new people. Generally, people who rate solitude as an important part of their outdoor experience overestimate the number of people they meet and express lower satisfaction after encounters than those who rank solitude lower in importance (Lucas, in Stankey, 1989). Camping is a good example of an outdoor recreational activity that appeals to people at both extremes. For some purists, camping means being alone in the wilderness, miles from any signs of other human beings. They often are critical of campers who enjoy a weekend in their Winnebago at a park equipped with electricity, snack bar, and heated swimming pool. Nevertheless, both groups are engaging in legitimate outdoor recreation.

It seems unfair for one group to make value judgments about the other. Nonetheless, different values can be especially problematic and lead to conflict when people with dissimilar orientations try to use the same wilderness areas simultaneously. Of special concern is the extent to which one of the recreationists is "motorized." Several studies have shown that activities such as motorboating, motorcycling, and snowmobiling greatly disturb the activities of less motorized groups like canoeists and cross-country skiers (Catton, 1983; Culhane, 1981), and the larger the motorized group is, the more unpleasant it becomes to others (Lucas, 1964).

Measuring user satisfaction in wilderness areas has become a pressing problem. Environmental psychologists are involved in efforts to develop techniques to systematically describe and evaluate environmental settings. Most of this work is motivated by the practical needs of environmental managers and planners who assess environmental quality by measuring public preferences in natural environments.

An instrument called a **Perceived Environmental Quality Index (PEQI)** is commonly used to quantitatively measure an individual's evaluation of his or her environment. A very thorough description of the development and use of PEQIs can be found in Kasmar (1970), Craik and Zube (1976), Zube (1980), and Craik and Feimer (1987). PEQIs are self-report measures usually in the form of a questionnaire. While the use of PEQIs in assessing human-made environments is more common, assessing natural environments through PEQIs is growing in popularity. In natural environments, PEQIs are often combined with objective measures of environmental quality such as the degree of air or water pollution, and there is evidence that the two different measures often reach the same conclusion about the quality of the environment (Coughlin, 1976; Moser, 1984).

PEQI assessments of natural environments generally are based on people's responses to photographs or slides rather than on firsthand exposure. Subjects do not give completely unstructured reactions to the environment. They respond according to some format that allows the researcher to convert their evaluations into a numerical scale that can be analyzed statistically and compared to other people's responses. Since PEQIs essentially measure a person's attitude toward the environment, they employ many of the same techniques that have been used to measure other attitudes. One of the most commonly used is the **semantic differential,** described in Chapter 3 (Osgood, Suci, & Tannenbaum, 1957). A semantic differential consists of pairs of **bipolar adjectives** (opposites) arranged along a scale. The individual places a mark along the scale, with the distance of the mark from each adjective reflecting his or her feelings about the environment in question. The subject's responses are then converted to a numerical score. In constructing the PEQI, careful attention must be paid to the adjectives selected and to the number of different dimensions assessed. Semantic differential scales have been successfully used to assess the quality of natural environments (Evans & Wood, 1981).

For quite some time, researchers tried to develop a PEQI that was general enough to be used in almost any environment. However, as Bechtel (1976) pointed out, the environments to be evaluated and the reasons for evaluation are so different that it appears unlikely that one PEQI could ever be satisfactory for all situations. One must also keep in mind that the measures developed so far are far from perfect, since the method of presenting the environment to subjects and the context in which the presentation occurs can affect the judgments made (Brown & Daniel, 1987).

Implications for the Management of Wilderness Areas

One would hope that what has been learned from all this research can be applied to the problems of managing wilderness areas. In an excellent summary of the history and problems of managing natural environments, Pitt and Zube (1987) identify the crucial issue for the future as the accurate assessment of each natural environment's recreational carrying capacity. "Carrying capacity" is a concept used in wildlife management to reflect the limitations placed on an animal population by the availability of resources such as food, water, and shelter (Stankey, 1989). **Recreational carrying capacity** refers to the number of people who can be served before the environment becomes adversely affected.

Accurately determining the carrying capacity of recreational environments is critical for the future. In 1990, 60 million people visited American national parks, and the number is estimated to reach 90 million by the year 2010 (Coates, 1991); national forest use has grown at an annual rate of 5 percent since 1965 (Stankey, 1989). To further complicate the problem, 90 percent of visitor use in wilderness areas is concentrated in just 10 percent of the wilderness (Hendee, Stankey, & Lucas, 1978). Overcrowding in national parks and wilderness areas has been called **greenlock** by public land managers. When the number of "windshield tourists" increases as the population ages, the problem will get even worse. Yosemite National Park already has a 21-cell jail (usually full) to deal with temper flare-ups over traffic jams. Primarily because of engine emissions from its 4 million annual tourists, Acadia National Park in Maine now has air pollution health warnings similar to those issued by the city of Los Angeles (Coates, 1991). The question of accessibility to recreational areas is complicated. Certainly, it is desirable for visitors to be able to get to these areas easily, but if access is too convenient, it is difficult to maintain pristine wilderness qualities for very long.

Machlis (1989) has suggested that effective park management can occur only if it is recognized that human beings (both visitors and locals) are the dominant species in most park ecosystems. Once managers acknowledge this, park ecosystems can be set up to accommodate people since much of the human behavior that occurs in these settings is predictable. Researchers (Hayward, 1989; Heimstra & McFarling, 1978; Hiss, 1990; Stankey, 1989) have summarized a number of valuable suggestions for managers of recreation areas. Much of what follows comes from their discussions. Education to improve visitor behavior and influence the temporal and spatial distribution of visitors will be increasingly important. To maintain solitude, as little usage as possible should be the norm, even if it means scheduling visitors to prevent the environment from becoming overloaded. Managers should know the clientele for each area, since "active recreationists" (for example, hunters, canoeists, and anglers) have very different needs from "passive recreationists" like picnickers and walkers. Trails should be specifically designed as connections between landscapes, and whenever possible artificial features should be eliminated. Those that oversee these areas should also know what features contribute to visitors' aesthetic satisfaction. A study by Shafer and Mietz (1972) found that hikers thought the following items were most important:

1. large rock outcrops for observation;
2. natural openings in forests where there is variability in lighting, color, and visible distance; and
3. trails following streams.

The water resources in recreation areas must be carefully planned, since these are often the most heavily-used part of the wilderness. One-fourth of all outdoor recreation is water-dependent (Pitt, 1989), and "among Americans over 11 years of age, one-third swim, fish, and boat at least once each year and between 10 percent and 20 percent canoe, kayak, or raft on a river, ice skate, hunt waterfowl, or sail once each year" (Lime, cited in Pitt, 1989, p. 217). The type of water recreation available in a given location will dictate the nature of the visitors and hence the needs of the park managers. Groups tend to be larger for river activities, such as rafting and tubing, than for other recreational activities (Lime, 1986). Physically demanding activities such as water skiing are more popular among younger people, while less rigorous activities (for example, fishing) remain popular with older people. Beaches are always very popular with teenagers (Field & Martinson, 1986; Hecock, 1970; Kelly, 1980; McDonough & Field, 1979; Pitt, 1989).

The importance of developing natural areas in urban settings should not be overlooked, as this constitutes a major recreational setting for many people. Aside from recreation, there are many advantages to developing "urban forests." They improve air quality, moderate temperatures, decrease noise levels, control erosion, and enhance the subjective feelings and experiences of urban dwellers (Grey & Deneke, 1986; Schroeder, 1989). Visitors to city forest preserves come from nearby (half within ten-minutes' travel time) and tend to stay for short periods of time (53 percent stay for an hour or less) (Young & Flowers, in Schroeder, 1989). Parks that facilitate long-distance views and contain water and open grassy areas are perceived as safer and more inviting. Dense vegetation, graffiti, and litter make parks seem more dangerous (Schroeder & Anderson, 1984); this is especially true for urban African Americans (Kaplan & Talbot, 1988).

In fact, several studies indicate that African Americans are more likely to prefer recreational environments with greater signs of human influence than do white Americans, and as a group they display less general interest in nature and the outdoors (Kellert, 1984; O'Leary & Benjamin, in Schroeder, 1989; Pitt, 1989; Schroeder, 1989; Spotts & Stynes, 1984). At this point, however, it is not clear to what extent this is due to ethnicity per se or to other factors such as familiarity with natural environments (Kellert, 1984; Schroeder, 1983).

CHAPTER SUMMARY

The degree to which a setting is "natural" is one of the most important judgments people make when distinguishing between different environments. Modern attitudes toward nature in Western societies have evolved from earlier attitudes that were deeply rooted in the Judeo–Christian tradition. For the most part, these attitudes reflect a "subdue and conquer" mentality in which humans are not considered to be part of the natural world. Nature is seen as existing primarily to fulfill human needs. These attitudes contrast sharply with those of some non-Western cultures where humans are seen as part of nature and as having moral obligations to the rest of the ecosystem.

In spite of these attitudes, with growing urbanization Western peoples have increasingly sought out what Rachel Kaplan calls the "green experience"—encounters with the natural environment. Studies of landscape preferences consistently show that people greatly prefer natural scenes over scenes of human-made environments. This research also shows that the attractiveness of a scene may be predicted not only by the physical features of the landscape but by its "psychological" organization as well. Specifically, the more a landscape lends itself to quick comprehension and understanding, and the more it invites the viewer to enter and explore it, the more strongly it is preferred.

Many explanations for the origins of human environmental preferences have been proposed, but one of the most popular theories is an evolutionary perspective that describes human environmental preference as a response that evolved as a survival strategy—people prefer environments that contain an abundance of resources and protection from danger.

For many people, nature provides the setting for most of their leisure activities. These recreational activities are temporary interactions with the natural environment that provide many benefits. Natural settings provide people with opportunities to escape from urban stress, to learn and develop new skills, and to relax. There is ample evidence that wilderness experiences can have great therapeutic value for one's mental well-being. Given the importance of outdoor recreation, research aimed at understanding the characteristics and motivations of the users of wilderness recreational areas is an important step toward preserving and improving these areas for future use. This research reveals that people have many different motives for pursuing outdoor recreation, but that as a group the users of wilderness areas are more likely to be urban and well-educated than would be expected by chance alone. The objective quality of the environment is an important part of the wilderness experience; signs of human intrusion and encounters with other people should be kept to a minimum.

GLOSSARY

Attitude   A lasting, general evaluation of people, objects, or issues.

Bipolar Adjectives   Pairs of adjectives that are opposite in meaning.

Coherence   In the Kaplans' preference framework, coherence refers to the extent to which a scene hangs together as a unified whole.

Collative Properties   General, organizational features of an environment or landscape that are not dependent on specific physical features.

Complexity   In the Kaplans' preference framework, complexity reflects the number and variety of elements in a scene.

Contrast   Obvious differences in form, color, or texture among the elements of a scene.

Convergence   The point at which two or more lines in a scene come together.

Enframement   The extent to which a scene provides its own "picture frame."

The Green Experience   The name used by Rachel Kaplan (1978) to describe encounters with the natural environment.

Greenlock   Overcrowding in national parks and wilderness areas, especially by automobiles.

Legibility   In the Kaplans' preference framework, legibility is the extent to which an environment can be easily understood.

Mystery   In the Kaplans' preference framework, mystery implies that a scene contains more information than can be seen at the moment.

Neoplatonism   A philosophy based on the teachings of Plato (427–347 B.C.). One of its principles was that one could not know truth or perceive reality by relying on the senses and empirical observation of the natural world.

Nonpurist   An individual who is relatively undisturbed by signs of human intrusion in wilderness areas.

Perceived Environmental Quality Index (PEQI)   A quantitative measure of subjective evaluations of an environment.

The Preference Framework   An influential model of landscape preference developed by Stephen and Rachel Kaplan (1975, 1977, 1982).

Prospect   A concept developed by Appleton (1975, 1984) that refers to having a clear, unobstructed view of the landscape.

Purist   An individual who is easily disturbed by signs of human intrusion in wilderness areas.

Recreational Carrying Capacity   The number of people a recreational area can serve before the environment becomes adversely affected.

Refuge   A concept developed by Appleton (1975, 1984) in which a landscape appears to offer a safe place to hide.

Semantic Differential   An attitude measurement technique consisting of pairs of bipolar adjectives arranged along a scale.

Environmental Problems and Behavioral Solutions

12

In the spring of 1970 I was a senior in high school. At that time, there was a growing awareness of the problem of pollution, and the finite limits of natural resources such as oil were becoming painfully apparent. As a way of calling attention to these problems, "Earth Day" was proclaimed to rally public support for environmental values and to bring about lifestyle changes that would result in significant conservation of energy and resources and a reduction in pollution. I vividly remember how our class borrowed a casket from a local funeral home and placed a dummy inside with a globe of the earth as its head. This was displayed in the lobby of our school to dramatize the plight of our planet. Across the country, students and citizen groups engaged in a variety of similar educational and conservation activities (see Photo 12-1).

There was hope that this day would mark the beginning of a new era of environmental consciousness, and that a new "land ethic" (discussed in Chapter 11) was about to emerge.

Unfortunately, the political and economic firestorms of the next few

P H O T O   12·1   Earth Day, 1970

years (the Vietnam War, Watergate, recession) pushed the environment completely out of the public eye and Earth Day was soon nothing more than a quaint memory. Twenty years later, however, the environment is again making headlines: massive oil spills, nuclear accidents, illness and death from chemical waste, disappearance of rain forests, and the shrinking ozone layer have become too much to ignore. A sad sign of the times is the New York City garbage barge, which sailed from country to country looking for someplace—anyplace—to deposit its cargo. Virtually every urban area is experiencing a "landfill crisis," and there is no longer anywhere to put our waste.

Environmental cleanup and protection was a major issue in the 1988 presidential campaign, and Americans now rate environmental problems as one of their chief concerns. Popular magazines ranging from *TV Guide* to *U.S. News and World Report* identified the environment as *the* issue of the 1990s. Earth Day '90 was launched amid great fanfare to grab the attention of a new generation of activists for the environmental struggle of the coming century. There were Earth Day events involving more than 200 million people in 140 countries (Cahn & Cahn, 1990). In the United States, these included tree plantings in Arizona and elephants crushing aluminum cans at the National Zoo in Washington to promote recycling. Only time will tell if Earth Day '90 was successful in ushering in a new environmental movement, but the signs are not encouraging: the 875,000 people who gathered in New York and Washington, D.C. to celebrate Earth Day '90 left 161.3 tons of garbage behind (*U.S. News and World Report,* December 31, 1990–January 7, 1991). Time itself may be an endangered resource. Thomas Lovejoy (quoted by Miller, 1990) is convinced that "the great environmental struggles will either be won or lost in the 1990s, and that by the next century it will be too late to act" (p. 449). Environmental psychologists clearly have a personal as well as a professional interest in dealing with environmental problems. *All* natural resources are disappearing at an alarming rate, and population levels projected for the year 2030 approach the estimated maximum carrying capacity of our planet (Stern & Oskamp, 1987).

Environmental crises are not unique to our times. Earlier civilizations modified the natural environment extensively and relied too heavily on agriculture (for example, Mesopotamian civilizations, the Mayans of Meso-America), eventually straining their ecosystems to the point where the human population was no longer sustainable (Ponting, 1990). A crucial difference between then and now, however, is that earlier crises tended to be regional and localized, while our current crisis is global in scope, and most of our environmental problems are more complicated than they appear on the surface. For example, most people believe that disposable plastic diapers are environmentally unsound because they are not recyclable like cloth diapers and because they take up valuable space in landfills. Although it is true that disposable diapers take up landfill space, *Science News* (1990) reports that disposable diapers require only half as much energy to produce as cloth diapers, half as much water, and produce just half the air pollution and one-seventh of the water pollution resulting from the manufacture of cloth diapers. Thus, the "correct" decision in environmental matters is not always apparent.

Another difficulty is that environmental problems are often thought of as engineering or technical challenges to be handled by engineers, physicists, and other practitioners of "hard science." At its core, however, the environmental crisis is a crisis of maladaptive behavior (Maloney & Ward, 1973). Nevertheless, the social, political, and psychological roots of environmental problems are often overlooked in the search for solutions, and there is a firmly entrenched resistance on the part of federal and state governments to use social science techniques to deal with environmental problems (Stern & Oskamp, 1987). One area in which the political and social aspects of environmental problems are quite obvious is in the conduct of war. For a closer look at the relationship between war and the natural environment, see the box on p. 268.

In this chapter, I will examine possible behavioral solutions to environmental problems. These include problems of aesthetics as well as the more serious health and resource problems that threaten the very existence of life on earth. I will begin with a general description of some of the techniques being used in an attempt to alter environmentally destructive behavior.

BEHAVIORAL TECHNOLOGY AND ENVIRONMENTAL PROBLEMS

"The term **behavioral technology** refers to the science, art, skill, or craft of influencing socially important human behavior" (Cone & Hayes, 1980, p. 5). The goal of behavioral technology as it relates to the environment is to increase the frequency of environmentally protective behav-

---

War and the Environment

War, even preparations for war, pose dangerous threats to the environment. The environmental degradation accompanying war-related activities in itself poses a threat to national security (Deudney, 1991). This is not a recent development, as the environment has been an integral part of warfare since the beginning of human history. Struggles over natural resources and mineral and water rights have been the precipitating factors in many conflicts, and such resources have been strategic goals in times of war (Gleick, 1991; Roberts, 1991). The environment has also been used as a weapon throughout history. In 146 B.C. the Romans destroyed the fields of the Carthaginians by covering them with salt. Genghis Khan wrecked Mesopotamian irrigation systems, and medieval European armies poisoned water supplies with the bodies of diseased animals (Mathews, 1991). The United States relied heavily on the use of poisonous herbicides during the Vietnam War.

What is new is the unprecedented scale of environmental damage possible in modern warfare. During the 1991 war in the Persian Gulf, the United States threatened to cut off the flow of the Euphrates River into Iraq, and while this threat was never realized, the Iraqis wreaked environmental havoc during the course of the war. An oil spill covering 600 square miles blackened 300 miles of coastline; it was the largest spill the world has ever seen (Canby, 1991). While some of the spill resulted from blasting pipelines and storage facilities, much of the oil was intentionally dumped into the ocean. The Iraqis also set fire to hundreds of Kuwaiti oil wells (see

P H O T O   12-2 Kuwaiti oil wells burning following the war in the Persian Gulf

Photo 12-2). Five million barrels of oil burned each day, releasing more than half a million tons of aerial pollutants into the atmosphere daily (Canby, 1991). These pollutants included fumes, soot, carbon monoxide, nitrogen dioxide, and sulphuric dioxide (Roberts, 1991). Airborne toxic metals released by the oil slick, the fires, and the explosives used during the war will enter the food chain, posing an inestimable hazard to human and animal populations alike (Canby, 1991).

The fragile ecosystem of the Gulf region was virtually destroyed. Wildlife, especially turtles, dolphins, and seabirds, died by the thousands, and the shrimp populaton was decimated to the point where it will be of no commercial benefit for at least ten years. Some experts believe that traces of the disaster will linger in the Gulf ecosystem for 100 years.

iors, such as recycling, cleaning up litter, and conserving energy, and decrease the frequency of environmentally destructive behaviors. The techniques used fall roughly into one of three categories: environmental education, reminders (prompts or cues of some sort), and reinforcement techniques.

Environmental education and the use of reminders are often referred to as **antecedent strategies** because they are used before the relevant behavior occurs and are aimed at encouraging or preventing its occur-rence. **Consequence strategies,** of which reinforcement is the most common example, manipulate the consequences of behavior so that pleasant or unpleasant events result from the target behavior (Russell & Snodgrass, 1987; Stern & Oskamp, 1987). The research has generally shown that consequence strategies are more effective than antecedent strategies, and that environmental education is the least effective of all these strategies (Cone & Hayes, 1980). I will briefly summarize what is known about the general effectiveness of each of these approaches, and subsequent parts of the chapter will deal with their application to specific environmental problems.

Environmental Education

Probably the most common way of trying to change environmental be-haviors has been through educational campaigns. These usually take the form of billboard advertisements or ad campaigns on television and radio. Many educational programs designed to cultivate proenvironment behav-iors are aimed at children in elementary schools. Whether these are antilittering or energy conservation campaigns, they are popular because they are relatively inexpensive and seem to offer the most convenient means of reaching large numbers of people. The rationale behind these programs is that information will lead to greater awareness about envi-ronmental problems, causing individuals to change their attitudes and, ultimately, their behavior.

The weak link in this chain of reasoning is that the connection between expressed attitudes about the environment and actual behavior in the environment is tenuous at best, unless the attitudes being mea-sured are extremely specific (Diamond & Loewy, 1991; Fishbein & Ajzen, 1975; Heberlein, 1971; Heberlein & Black, 1976; Robinson, 1976; Weigel, 1983; Weigel, Tognacci, & Vernon, 1974). Samuelson and Biek (1991) conducted an energy conservation attitude survey of 1000 people in Texas. They concluded that conservation campaigns must address the issues of consumer comfort and health, the legitimacy of the national energy problem, and beliefs about the role of individual behavior in energy conservation because attitudes about these specific factors were related to actual conservation behaviors. Very general questions about attitudes toward energy conservation were not very useful. In other words, how people say they behave and how they actually behave can be two very different things. For example, Bickman (1972) planted trash on a path and watched the behavior of college students walking by. Ninety-nine percent of the students walked past the litter without picking it up, yet 94 percent of them agreed with the statement, "It should be everyone's responsibility to pick up litter when they see it" (p. 324). Aside from the weak link between attitudes and behavior, there may be other reasons environmental education programs do not work well. Pitt and Zube (1987) point out that information and education programs can only deter litter and vandalism that are the result of ignorance. These programs have no effect on behaviors with more aggressive or purposive origins. In a study of 167 German adults, Schahn and Holzer (1990) demonstrated the lack of correspondence between environmental knowledge and proenvironment behavior. In their study, women were more concerned about environmental issues and were more likely to engage in proenvironment behavior than were men, but men actually knew more about environmental problems.

In a study of the effect of antilittering leaflets on littering behavior, Marler (1971) concluded that another reason educational programs don't work is because people simply do not read leaflets or pay attention to ads.

Although educational campaigns have had an impact on environmental behavior in some cases (Sutton, 1976; Thompson & Stoutemeyer, 1991), most researchers are pessimistic about the prospects of changing environmentally destructive behaviors through education alone (Clark, Hendee, & Burgess, 1972; Cone & Hayes, 1980; O'Riordan, 1976). In spite of this, Fisher, Bell, and Baum (1984) feel that even if education does not really change behavior, it may still be useful for reinforcing attitudes and behaviors of people who are already behaving in desirable ways. Other researchers have suggested that education can be made more effective by explicitly linking environmental behaviors (such as littering and recycling) to morality, inducing feelings of guilt and shame in those who violate moral standards of environmental behavior (Grasmick, Bursik, & Kinsey, 1991; Hopper & Nielsen, 1991).

Reminders: The Effects of Prompts or Cues

Like education, the use of prompts or cues to remind people about environmentally desirable behavior is an antecedent strategy. These reminders are presented to people before they have an opportunity to act, and it is hoped that they will influence individual behavior. Most prompts are written, graphic, or verbal messages that draw attention to things people already know: they shouldn't litter, or they should turn off lights when they leave a room. While research results are mixed, under some conditions prompts have been shown to be effective in curbing environmentally destructive behavior (Geller, 1980; Geller, Winett, & Everett, 1982; Geller, Witmer, & Tuso, 1977); many of these studies will be discussed in some detail later in this chapter. Generally, prompts seem to be most effective when they are polite, when they give very specific instructions (for example, "put litter in trashcan near front door" versus "dispose of properly"), and when they give positively worded advice rather than telling people what *not* to do (Geller, Witmer, & Orebaugh, 1976; Reich & Robertson, 1979). Durdan, Reeder, and Hecht (1985) propose that prompts may be effective in some situations because they reduce uncertainty about what behaviors are socially desirable under those circumstances.

Sometimes, other people's behavior may serve as a prompt for our own behavior. A study by Jason, Zolik, and Matese (1979) found that giving a "pooper scooper" to Chicago dog owners and demonstrating its use led to a reduction in dog feces in the area and eventually led to a city ordinance requiring owners to carry a scooper when walking their dogs.

Applied Behavior Analysis: The Effects of Rewards and Punishments

Applied behavior analysis, the most widely used behavioral science technique, is commonly used to solve environmental problems (Geller, 1987). It grew out of the radical behaviorism of B. F. Skinner (1938, 1958) and is a consequence strategy in which environmental behaviors are altered by making rewards or punishments contingent upon these behaviors. Thus, applied behavior analysis is essentially application of the principles of operant conditioning to human beings in real-life situations.

The concept of reinforcement is central to an understanding of operant conditioning. Reinforcing stimuli, or *reinforcers,* are stimuli which, when they follow a behavior, strengthen that behavior and increase the probability of its future occurrence. You probably are accustomed to thinking about things such as food, money, grades, and other tangible rewards as reinforcers. However, a reinforcer can be literally anything that increases the frequency of a target behavior.

Presenting a person with a satisfying, rewarding stimulus following a behavior is called **positive reinforcement.** Positive reinforcement techniques have been used to decrease high levels of environmental noise (Meyers, Artz, & Craighead, 1976; Schmidt & Ulrich, 1969; Wilson & Hopkins, 1973) and to encourage behaviors such as car pooling and using public transportation, which reduce traffic congestion and air pollution (Deslauriers & Everett, 1977; Everett, Hayward, & Meyers, 1974; Katzev & Bachman, 1982). Reinforcement also has proven effective in getting motorists to wear seat belts (Geller, 1984; Geller, Kalsher, Rudd, & Lehman, 1989).

Negative reinforcement occurs when an aversive, unpleasant stimulus is removed following the performance of a target behavior. While positive reinforcement entails delivery of a pleasant stimulus, negative reinforcement is the removal of an unpleasant stimulus; in both cases, the behavior preceding the reinforcement is strengthened. **Punishment,**

on the other hand, is often confused with negative reinforcement but actually has the opposite effect. In punishment, an aversive, unpleasant stimulus is delivered to the person following the target behavior. The effect of punishment is to weaken, not strengthen, a behavior and it reduces the likelihood that the behavior will occur again.

Using fines as punishment for environmentally destructive behaviors such as littering and air or water pollution is the most common strategy governments use to control environmental behaviors. However, Geller (1987) reviewed the effectiveness of different approaches to changing behavior and concluded that positive reinforcement programs work better, are more socially acceptable, and are more cost-effective in the long run than punishment-based strategies are. Many of these successful programs deal with cleaning up litter. Rewards commonly involve financial incentives such as money, raffle tickets, or tickets redeemable for food and drink (Bacon-Prue, Blount, Pickering, & Drabman, 1980; Chapman & Risley, 1974; Couch, Garber, & Karpus, 1979; Hayes, Johnson, & Cone, 1975; Kohlenberg & Phillips, 1973; McNees, Schnell, Gendrich, Thomas, & Beagle, 1979; Powers, Osborne, & Anderson, 1973).

The schedule established to deliver a reinforcer to an individual is an important determinant of the effectiveness of that reinforcer. While many different schedules are possible, the most important distinction is between **continuous reinforcement** and **intermittent reinforcement.** In continuous reinforcement, the person is reinforced following each and every occurrence of the target behavior. In intermittent reinforcement, only some responses are rewarded, according to a predetermined schedule. While each has certain advantages, intermittent reinforcement usually is more desirable to use with environmental behaviors because it is cheaper to administer and more resistant to extinction. When reinforcers are withheld from someone who has been on a continuous reinforcement schedule, the behavior quickly reverts to its naturally occurring frequency. When an intermittent reinforcement schedule is removed, however, the behavior takes much longer to return to previous levels.

Several intermittent reinforcement schedules have been developed specifically to control environmentally relevant behavior (Geller, 1987; Hayes & Cone, 1977). One is known as the **variable person ratio (VPR).** With the VPR, positive reinforcers are delivered after a particular response occurs among a number of persons making the target response. For example, if people are being rewarded for turning in litterbags full of trash, rewards might be given to one out of every five people returning a bag to the redemption center. Delivering reinforcements to individuals from a larger group differs from the traditional behaviorist reinforcement schedules used with single individuals. Other schedules developed to encourage proenvironment behaviors include the **fixed person ratio (FPR)** and **variable** and **fixed person interval** schedules (**VPI** and **FPI**). On the interval schedules, the amount of time that has passed since the last reinforcement, not the number of responses, is the crucial variable in maintaining the schedule. For example, if a VPI schedule is used to control litter pickup, rewards might be given on the average of once per hour, regardless of the number of people who have turned in their trash bags since the last reinforcement.

Whenever reinforcement is used to control behavior, it is crucial for the administrator to know if the reinforcer is having an effect. While there is no surefire way to determine the effectiveness of reinforcers, several techniques are available that can increase confidence in their utility. To determine the effectiveness of a reinforcer, the researcher must have considerable control over the situation; the target behavior must be clearly defined; and the naturally occurring frequency of the behavior (the **baseline**) must be clearly established. For meaningful conclusions, a stable baseline is important. A wildly fluctuating baseline or one showing a steadily increasing or decreasing tendency makes it difficult to reliably detect changes caused by the reinforcer. Once a stable baseline has been established, one of several procedures can be used to evaluate the reinforcer. One is known as the **withdrawal design:** the reinforcer is introduced, withdrawn to see if behavior returns to baseline levels, then reintroduced and withdrawn again. If the behavior consistently changes concomitantly with the presence or absence of the reinforcer, it is reasonable to assume that the reinforcer is responsible for the changes. For example, suppose a city sanitation department wants to encourage homeowners to separate their trash into recyclable and nonrecyclable items by providing free passes to the community golf course or swimming pool whenever it is done correctly. To see how well this works, a baseline rate of the number of people who normally separate their trash must be determined. After establishing an acceptable baseline, the city could introduce the reinforcement program. On pickup days, sanitation workers would deposit a pass, good for one week, in mailboxes of homeowners who separated their trash; the number of homeowners separating their trash would then be measured for a three-week period. After three weeks of reinforcement, the program would be withdrawn for three weeks to see if the frequency of trash separation returned to normal. If it did, the program would be reinstated for three weeks and then withdrawn again. If the number of people separating their trash fluctuates with the presence or absence of the free passes, the city could reasonably conclude that it has discovered an effective reinforcer. If there is no relationship whatever, the city should look elsewhere for a more compelling reinforcer.

Sometimes, practical or ethical problems are involved in withdrawing a potentially effective reinforcer. In these cases, the researcher can avoid the risks associated with removing reinforcement and still assess the effectiveness of the reinforcer by using a **multiple baseline procedure.** In this procedure, the same reinforcer is tested with a series of different target behaviors. For example, if the city did not want to risk having its residents revert to their earlier, nonrecycling behaviors, it might introduce free passes to encourage other behaviors such as energy conservation, car pooling, or picking up litter in public parks. If introducing the reinforcement program in each of these settings coincided with changes in the frequencies of the target behaviors, confidence in the efficacy of that particular reinforcer would certainly increase. Some researchers have criticized these techniques on the grounds that the results cannot always be generalized to other situations (Kiesler, 1971), but this may not be a serious problem if the technique works well in a specific, desired setting.

PROBLEMS OF ENVIRONMENTAL AESTHETICS

Many current environmental problems are all too readily apparent; their most prominent features are their ugliness. Urban sprawl and burgeoning populations are destroying scenery and natural environments at a steady pace, and the deterioration of older urban areas ruins any aesthetic qualities that may have survived the initial onslaught. Scenery contaminated with litter and vandalism should be an avoidable problem, but governmental concern for aesthetic qualities is relatively recent. For the first hundred years, United States land management existed solely to facilitate disposal of public lands (Pitt & Zube, 1987). The National Park Service was not created until 1916, and it was well into the 20th century before legislation was passed that was aimed at preservation and conservation. The tension between economic development and environmental preservation is one of the thorniest political issues of our times: problems of land use and resource development go beyond aesthetics. For example, deforestation not only destroys scenery but ultimately destroys topsoil, pollutes streams, and contributes to global warming. I will discuss resource and health problems later in the chapter. For now, the primary focus will be on the aesthetic problems of littering and vandalism.

Littering

Americans annually generate one ton of solid waste for every man, woman, and child in the country (Forester, 1988); many millions of these tons end up as litter. Not only is litter unsightly but it poses a health hazard to animals and humans alike, and the annual cost of cleanup is staggering. Many factors contribute to the problem. Perhaps the most powerful facilitator of littering is the presence of other litter. People seem less inhibited about littering in littered areas, and many studies confirm that "litter begets litter" (Finnie, 1973; Geller, Witmer, & Tuso, 1977; Iso-Ahola & Niblock, 1981; Krauss, Freedman, and Whitcup, 1978; Reiter & Samuel, 1980; Robinson & Frisch, 1975). One exception to this occurs in outdoor recreational areas, such as campgrounds, where people are more likely than usual to pick up litter left by others (Crump, Nunes, & Crossman, 1977; Geller, Winett, & Everett, 1982).

Whether a person litters or not is also related to a number of demographic characteristics. Young people litter more than older people, men litter more than women, people living in rural areas litter more than urban residents, and people who are alone litter more than people in groups (Cialdini, Reno, & Kallgren, 1990; Osborne & Powers, 1980; Robinson, 1976). Heberlein (1971) observed a relationship between littering and participation in various outdoor recreational behaviors. He found that bird watchers, nature walkers, and canoeists were very responsive to antilittering messages and of the recreational groups he studied were the least likely to litter. On the other hand, the hunters, fishermen, campers, motorboaters, and water-skiers in his study littered heavily. Golfers, picnickers, and touring motorists were somewhere between the two extremes and were equally likely to litter or not litter.

As previously noted, educational programs alone have not been effective in decreasing littering behavior or increasing cleanup of existing litter. Nevertheless, E. Scott Geller and his colleagues have not given up in their efforts to prevent littering through antecedent strategies; research spearheaded by them shows that using prompts may be a more effective way to reduce litter than education is (Geller, 1975; Geller, Witmer, & Orebaugh, 1976; Geller, Witmer, & Tuso, 1977; Tuso & Geller, 1976). Geller and his colleagues (1982) have described the situations in which prompts are most effective. As is true of prompts in general, specific antilittering prompts are better than general prompts; they are especially helpful when trash disposal is convenient, can be done soon after the prompt, and when polite language is used. Research also shows that positively worded prompts (for example, Please be helpful!) are more effective than negatively worded prompts (for example, Please don't litter!) (Durdan, Reeder, & Hecht, 1985; Reich & Robertson, 1979). The mere presence of a trashcan serves as a prompt for litter disposal, and increasing the number of trashcans in a location helps reduce litter, although they are more effective in clean than in dirty areas (Finnie, 1973; O'Neill, Blanck, & Joyner, 1980).

Many clever techniques have been developed to study the effect of prompts on littering behavior. Baltes and Hayward (1976) studied littering in a football stadium using unwitting football fans as experimental subjects. Upon entering the stadium, each fan received a clear plastic litterbag. There were five different experimental conditions, and each experimental group was located in a separate part of the stadium. In one condition, fans were given bags containing a number. If they turned in a full bag of litter, they were eligible for a prize drawing. Two other groups received bags with prompts printed on them. One was positively worded: "Pitch in. You will be a model for other people." The other group received a bag with a negative prompt: "Pitch in. Don't be a litterbug;

others will disapprove." A fourth group received a plain bag with no message or number, and a control group did not receive a bag or any instructions. The weight of the litter left in each part of the stadium after the game was the dependent variable. In this case, there was no difference among any of the groups who received a litterbag, but subjects in all the bag conditions littered significantly less than the control groups without bags, indicating that having a convenient way to dispose of litter does decrease littering.

Geller, Witmer, and Orebaugh (1976) conducted a classic study of the effects of prompts when they observed littering by grocery store patrons. Subjects were given a handbill advertising the day's specials (see Figure 12-1) as they entered one of two grocery stores at opposite ends of town in Blacksburg, Virginia. Three 20-gallon trashcans were placed at different locations in the store. A silver metal one was positioned at the front of the aisle where most customers shopped first. A green plastic can was located in the middle of the shopping aisle across the back of the store, and a second silver can was positioned in the last aisle, not far from the checkout counter. From 5 to 7 P.M. on 40 consecutive weekdays, two research assistants stood inside the door and distributed handbills to incoming customers. On some days, special instructions circled in red were at the bottom of the handbill. The nature of these instructions was the independent variable. The dependent variable was the location where the customer disposed of the handbill. There were five conditions in the experiment. There was a baseline condition in which no antilitter prompt was included on the handbill. In the other conditions, one of four kinds of prompts was used:

> General prompt: *Please* don't litter. *Please* dispose of properly.
> Specific prompt: *Please* don't litter. *Please* dispose in *green* trashcan located at rear of store.
> Demand prompt: You *must* not litter, you *must* dispose in *green* trashcan located at rear of store.
> Recycle prompt: *Please* help us *recycle*. *Please* dispose for *recycling* in green trashcan located at rear of store.

Prompts were varied daily so that each condition occurred on each day of the week. After the initial 40-day period, for six consecutive weekdays one of two avoidance prompts was used:

> Specific prompt: *Please don't* dispose of in *carts*. *Please* dispose of in *green* trashcan located at rear of store.
> General prompt: *Please don't* dispose of in *carts*. *Please* dispose of properly.

During the seventh week of the study, just for fun, a handbill was distributed with the prompt "*Please* litter. Dispose of on *floor*."

The results of the Geller, Witmer, and Orebaugh study were straightforward. At both grocery stores, significantly more handbills were found

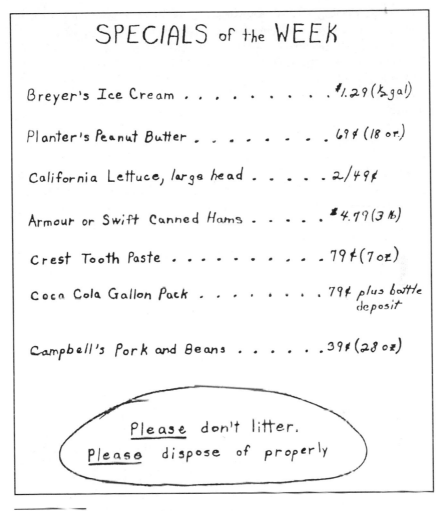

FIGURE 12-1 Typical handbill used in the littering study of Geller, Witmer, and Orebaugh (1976)

in the green can during the demand, specific, and recycle prompt conditions than in either the baseline or general prompt conditions. For the avoidance prompts, specific instructions were more effective than general instructions. Oh, yes; people did throw more paper on the floor when the prompt asked them to! In this study, the general prompts were also effective at reducing litter over baseline conditions, but specific prompts were needed to guide disposal to particular locations.

One setting that suffers from a particularly stubborn littering problem is the movie theater. In an anonymous, dark theater, many otherwise respectable, law-abiding people feel that it is perfectly acceptable to throw anything on the floor. Burgess, Clark, and Hendee (1971) explored solutions to this problem by studying theater littering during Saturday children's matinees. Normally, only 11 percent to 24 percent of the trash at this theater was thrown into containers; the rest was on the floor. Burgess and his colleagues found that simply giving litterbags to children and telling them to use them increased the percent of trash in the containers to 31 percent. Giving them bags coupled with a specific intermission announcement ("Put trash in the litterbags and put the bag in one of the trashcans in the lobby before leaving the theater.") increased the amount of litter deposited to 57 percent. Telling them that they would receive a dime (remember, this occurred before 1971!) for bringing a full bag of litter to the lobby resulted in a 94 percent rate of trash return. In all cases, the use of a withdrawal design verified that the effect was due to the prompts and incentives. Doubling the number of trashcans or showing a Walt Disney cartoon entitled *Litterbugs* had no effect. However, being able to redeem a full bag for a free movie ticket increased litter pickup to 95 percent. Other studies in movie theaters with children and adults reached the same conclusion: rewards work, but pep talks and lectures do not (Lahart & Bailey, 1974; Zane, 1974, both cited in Cone & Hayes, 1980).

Besides clarifying social norms (Cialdini, Reno, & Kallgren, 1990), prompts sometimes work because they remind people to behave in a manner consistent with their self-image. Miller, Brickman, and Bolen (1975) found that children litter less when they see themselves as people who are neat and tidy.

Prompts are much better at getting people to dispose of their own litter than they are at getting them to pick up other's litter (Geller, 1976; Geller, Brasted, & Mann, 1980); as the experiments just described suggest, prompts can be especially effective when they are combined with reinforcement (Byers & Cone, 1976; Kohlenberg & Phillips, 1973). Designing trashcans that are rewarding to approach and use increases their effectiveness as a prompt for litter disposal. Attractive, brightly colored trashcans reduce nearby litter, and trashcans that "talk," resemble animals, or are novel in other ways also attract litter (Finnie, 1973; Miller, Albert, Bostick, & Geller, 1976; O'Neill, Blanck, & Joyner, 1980; Silver, 1974).

Reinforcement alone can be extremely effective in reducing litter when it is administered properly (Clark, Hendee, & Burgess, 1972; Geller, Winett, & Everett, 1982). However, most studies have been short term, seldom lasting more than a few months, and they sometimes have unforeseen side effects such as inducing people to move litter around rather than actually clean it up (Stern & Oskamp, 1987). Nevertheless, some of the gains made through reinforcement are impressive. One of the more successful experimental techniques is the **item-marking technique** in which "marked" pieces of litter are planted in a littered area. The person turning in the marked item along with other trash receives a reward (Bacon-Prue et al., 1980; Hayes, Johnson, & Cone, 1975).

Adults picked up litter in a United States Forest Service recreational area when it gave them a chance in a $20.00 drawing (Powers, Osborne, & Anderson, 1973); rewarding children for litter pickup in national parks also works well (Clark, Burgess, & Hendee, 1972). Casey and Lloyd (1977) found that children picking up litter in exchange for free amusement park rides actually did a better job of cleaning the park than the paid maintenance people did. They concluded that routine maintenance procedures were two and one-half times more expensive as well. Similarly, Chapman and Risley (1974) found that rewarding children with money decreased litter around public housing complexes only as long as the rewards continued. It did not change long-term behaviors, and verbal appeals alone were completely ineffective.

While reinforcement programs can take a lot of time to administer, they may prove to be well worth the effort. These programs are becoming more common in campgrounds and outdoor recreational areas.

Vandalism

Vandalism is an especially troublesome environmental problem because it seems so senseless and unnecessary and yet is so pervasive. The annual cost of vandalism in the United States alone was estimated at $1 billion to $4 billion in 1976, and costs are increasing every year (Fisher, Bell, & Baum, 1984). Often vandalism has little to do with the environment per se. It is highly dependent on the psychological and sociological contexts of the individuals involved (Christensen & Clark, 1978). Vandalism may be a way of exerting control over an environment and a symptom of a poor fit between an environment and the people who use it (Allen & Greenburger, 1980; Warzecha, Fisher, & Baron, 1988). Fisher and Baron (1982) have proposed one of the few theoretical models of vandalism. They suggest that vandalism is a way for people who feel unfairly treated in some way to restore equity when they cannot do it any other way. Many authors have also pointed out that vandalism is often a side effect of other behaviors, such as play, territorial behavior, or financial gain, rather than an end in itself (Cohen, 1973; Miller, 1976; Pitt & Zube, 1987; Sokol, 1976; Williams, 1976). Often, the vandalized object or place is a means to an end or just in somebody's way.

Some characteristics of environments may make them more or less likely to be vandalized. As you recall from the discussion of "defensible space" in earlier chapters, vandalism is most likely to occur in places not obviously under the control of others. Ugly, uninteresting places are more likely to be vandalized than attractive ones (Pablant & Baxter, 1975), and some objects are simply more fun to break than others (Allen & Greenburger, 1980; Greenburger & Allen, 1980). As with litter, places full of graffiti and other damage seem to invite more of the same (Sharpe, 1976). Vandalism is also more common in cities than in small towns (Zimbardo, 1969).

There has been very little empirical research on ways to discourage vandalism. Studies do show that improved lighting (Einolander, 1976) and designing environments to improve visibility and surveillance by others is helpful (Magill, 1976). Magill also recommends designing places to facilitate rather than frustrate the behaviors of the people who will use them. Samdahl and Christensen (1985) studied carving on 190 picnic tables located at three campgrounds in the state of Washington. As expected, they found that previous carvings on a table encouraged more carving. They also found that campgrounds with an authority figure such as a park ranger in residence inhibited carving to some extent.

HEALTH-RELATED ENVIRONMENTAL PROBLEMS

Unfortunately, our environmental problems go far beyond aesthetics. Poisoning the environment through pollution of all kinds produces side effects that are potentially deadly.

Noise often leads the list of complaints by residents of urban neighborhoods (Cohen et al., 1981). It is estimated that over 3 million Americans suffer from noise-induced hearing loss (Environmental Protection Agency, 1972); industrial and community surveys report that prolonged exposure to noise is associated with everything from sexual impotence and anxiety to ulcers and cardiovascular problems. The behavioral and health effects of noise were discussed in earlier chapters. Here, the emphasis is on the threat we face from air and water pollution.

Air and water pollution are a direct result of human behavior. Rivers, lakes, and, increasingly, oceans, are polluted by pesticide runoff, sewage, industrial waste, oil spills, and outright garbage dumping. Entire communities have been destroyed by seepage of toxic waste (Edelstein, 1988). A 1991 study conducted by economists at the University of Tennessee estimated that the costs of cleaning up all kinds of toxic waste in the United States could exceed $1 *trillion* over the next three decades. The radiation and carcinogens found in our air and water are killing us at a rate that we are only beginning to appreciate. According to Miller (1990), one out of three Americans will eventually get some form of cancer, and every 66 seconds someone in the United States dies from cancer. According to the World Health Organization, 80 percent to 90 percent of these cancers can be traced to environmental factors.

The health effects of environmental pollution can be categorized as either acute or chronic. **Acute effects of pollution** appear quickly and range from headaches, rashes, and irritation to convulsions and death. **Chronic effects** take longer to appear and are usually quite serious. Cancer, lung and heart disease, genetic defects, and nervous disorders are all chronic in nature. The terrible health problems experienced by many Vietnam War veterans who were exposed to the defoliant "agent orange" presents a classic example of these effects.

There is much more information about air pollution than water pollution at this point in time. Air pollution affects the majority of the population of the United States, and health costs run into the hundreds of millions of dollars (Evans & Jacobs, 1981). Although there are no firm figures, it is widely believed that the situation is even worse in other parts of the world. There are literally hundreds of kinds of air pollutants, including gases such as carbon monoxide, suspended particles of dust, soot, asbestos, and lead, and a number of radioactive substances. Not surprisingly, there are at least as many different health effects as there are pollutants. Respiratory problems are the most common, but cardiovascular problems also have been firmly linked to air pollution (Coffin & Stokinger, 1977; Goldsmith & Friberg, 1977; Lebowitz, Cassell, & McCarroll, 1972; Sterling, Phair, Pollack, Schumsky, & DeGroot, 1966; Zeidberg, Prindle, & Landau, 1964). At a minimum, in the United States 140,000 deaths per year are attributable to air pollution (Mendelsohn & Orcutt, 1979). Even low levels of ambient air pollution can have a negative impact on mood, reaction time, and the ability to concentrate (Bullinger, 1989). Evans and Jacobs (1981) reviewed the literature on the health effects of air pollution and concluded that although the link between air pollution and ill health is undeniable, environmental psychologists cannot say for sure which pollutants or their combinations are responsible for which disorders.

Air pollution also can affect work and social behavior. A two-year study in a Midwestern city indicated that there was a link between higher smog levels and an increase in the number of family disturbances reported to the police (Rotton & Frey, 1985). Laboratory studies have demonstrated that foul odors lead to more negative feelings about the surroundings and other people encountered there (Rotton, Frey, Barry, Milligan, & Fitzpatrick, 1979). On the other hand, pleasant odors have enhanced performance on clerical tasks in laboratory studies and prompted people to set higher performance goals for themselves (Baron, 1990).

Carbon monoxide, which is the primary component of automobile exhaust, has been linked with decreased attentional and learning capacities (Evans & Jacobs, 1981; National Academy of Sciences, 1977). Other abilities impaired by carbon monoxide include time judgment, reaction time, manual dexterity, and vigilance (Beard & Grandstaff, 1970; Beard & Wertheim, 1967; Breisacher, 1971; Gliner, Raven, Horvath, Drinkwater, & Sutton, 1975). Research conducted in England showed that task performance was negatively affected when subjects breathed air that was collected 15 inches above a busy road, and air pollution has also been associated with slower times by high school cross-country runners (Evans & Jacobs, 1981; Wayne, Wehrle, & Carroll, 1967).

Another serious atmospheric problem is depletion of the ozone layer due to the use of **chlorofluorocarbons (CFCs).** CFCs are used as coolants in air conditioners and refrigerators and as propellants in aero-

P H O T O 12-3 Although air pollution is a serious health hazard, people adapt to it and tend not to notice it after a while.

sol cans (this use was banned in the U.S. but not in other countries). They are also used in the manufacture of Styrofoam and other polystyrene plastics. When CFCs escape into the atmosphere and are exposed to ultraviolet radiation, they speed up the breakdown of ozone into oxygen gas. National Aeronautics and Space Administration (NASA) studies published in 1988 showed that worldwide depletion of the ozone layer is approaching 5 percent. This will result ultimately in increased rates of skin and eye cancers, cataracts, immune system deficiencies, smog, and damage to crops and aquatic plant life. Thus far, the greatest detectable damage to the ozone layer has been over Antarctica where unique weather conditions create a whirlpool of frigid air that traps CFCs in the atmosphere. The leader of a recent expedition to the South Pole compared it to standing under a "huge ultraviolet sunlamp for 24 hours a day." The men in his expedition had to keep their bodies completely covered at all times. One team member forgot and left his skin exposed for a few hours; he suffered severe burns and was nauseated for days (Gorner, 1990).

Depletion of the ozone layer also contributes to the **greenhouse effect.** The greenhouse effect is exacerbated by the heavy use of fossil fuels and is more pronounced when the amount of carbon dioxide in the atmosphere increases, trapping heat and causing global warming. There is evidence that the polar ice caps are already melting at an alarming rate (Brownstein & Easton, 1982). If the greenhouse effect continues unchecked, the earth's climate will change dramatically; coastal areas will flood and vast new deserts will appear.

Not all air pollution problems are found outdoors. Increasingly, people are concerned about the quality of the indoor air they breathe. A logical outcome of this concern is the fight over the rights of smokers and nonsmokers in public places, such as offices and restaurants. Evidence continues to show that passive smoking, which occurs when a nonsmoker shares air space with a smoker, may be a serious health risk (Baron & Byrne, 1987). The research overwhelmingly indicates that nonsmokers react negatively to cigarette smoke at an emotional and behavioral level as well. Nonsmokers feel more irritable, anxious, aggressive, and fatigued when they are in close contact with cigarette smoke (Jones, 1978). Individuals on a public bench are more likely to leave, and leave faster, when their personal space is invaded by a smoker rather than a nonsmoker (Bleda & Bleda, 1978). Nonsmokers report more negative feelings when forced to interact with smokers, even when the smoker tries to be courteous. These interactions often result in depression and hostility (Bleda & Sandman, 1977; Zillman, Baron, & Tamborini, 1981). Smokers argue that they have a right to smoke; nonsmokers reply that they have a right to be free from exposure to cigarette smoke. At this point, the problem of indoor air pollution seems to be as difficult to deal with as more conventional air pollution problems.

Given the magnitude of our global emergency, one wonders why we are so slow to change dangerous behavior. It is not because of insufficient knowledge. Miller (1990), among others, has provided a very detailed set of steps that can be taken now. In a way, air pollution is a sneaky problem because people tend to adapt to it over time and not notice it after a while (Evans, Jacobs, & Frager, 1982). Sommer (1972) pointed out that people are most likely to notice air pollution when it is new to them — when they move to a new location or when pollution levels suddenly increase. Even then, people are aware of pollution only if they can see it, smell it, or if it causes damage (Barker, 1976). Despite a recent Gallup poll showing that two out of three Americans say that pollution is a very serious threat (*U.S. News and World Report,* April 23, 1990), few people complain spontaneously about air pollution or list it as a problem unless they are specifically asked about it (Barker, 1976; Heimstra & McFarling, 1978). People also tend to believe that their own immediate geographic area is less polluted than adjacent areas, especially if they don't travel much and accept their conditions as normal (DeGroot, 1967; Rankin, 1969; Swan, 1970).

Since automobiles account for about 50 percent of urban air pollution, an approximate estimate of air pollution can be obtained by measuring the concentration of automobiles in a given area (Hummel, Loomis, & Hebert, in Bell et al., 1990); this is one way researchers can alert residents to pollution problems in their community. Unfortunately, public concern does not usually lead to political activity or attempts to solve air pollution problems (Sharma, Kivlin, & Fliegel, 1975). People often feel that nothing can be done and accept it fatalistically (Campbell, 1983; Wohlwill, 1974). To make matters worse, people frequently resist legislative attempts to change behaviors that contribute to air and water pollution, reacting strongly against having personal habits dictated by outside agencies (Mazis, 1975).

RESOURCE PROBLEMS: RECYCLING AND CONSERVATION

The Tragedy of the Commons

The fuels that fill most of our current energy needs (oil, coal, and natural gas) are in short supply and dwindling rapidly. Other resources such as water, trees, and metals also will become scarce in the near future if present trends continue. We all know this, yet little changes in our day-to-day behavior. Why do people knowingly persist in what is ultimately self-destructive behavior?

Our inability to manage natural resources efficiently may be traced to what Hardin (1968) called the **tragedy of the commons.** Originally, the commons referred to public land areas on which anyone could graze livestock with no cost to themselves. The tendency was to exploit the commons by grazing one's sheep on the public land, thereby preserving resources on one's own land. The tragedy lies in the fact that the commons is a limited resource used by individuals acting in their own self-interest. Such a community consumes resources at a rate that endangers the very existence of the resource itself. The story of the commons is an apt metaphor for all the problems of limited resources that we now face.

The conflict between individual and group interests is called a **commons dilemma** (Dawes, 1973). It is exacerbated by the tendency to choose immediate rewards even though they have serious long-term costs, which is a decision Platt (1973) refers to as a **social trap.** Dawes (1980) proposed the more general term **social dilemma** to encompass all these maladaptive, resource-related behaviors.

Most of the empirical research on human behavior in social dilemmas has been done in the laboratory using simulation games to observe how people manage common resources (Edney, 1979; Mintz, 1951). Edney's (1979) "Nuts Game" is a good example of such a simulation. In the game, three or more subjects sit around a shallow, nonbreakable, open bowl containing ten hardware hexagonal nuts. Each player's goal is to get as many nuts as possible. Players can take nuts from the bowl at any time after the game starts, knowing that the experimenter will double the number of nuts remaining in the bowl after each ten-second interval. The game continues until some time limit is reached or the bowl is empty. The wise strategy, of course, is to show restraint—take one or two nuts out during each period, and gradually accumulate a stockpile. Edney reports, however, that approximately 65 percent of the groups never even make it to the first replenishment stage! Usually a greedy frenzy of grabbing instantly destroys what would otherwise be a self-replenishing resource.

According to Edney, the nuts in the bowl symbolize any limited resource pool (whales or oil, for example). In spite of the fact that people know the limits of the resources, social pressures in the situation encourage resource-destructive behavior. Studies such as these demonstrate that the tendency toward self-interest increases with the size of the group (Dawes, 1980) and that as the value of the resources increases, cooperation in its management decreases (Bonacich, 1976; Kelley, Condry, Dahlke, & Hill, 1965). Cooperation does increase with experience in dealing with commons situations (Allison & Messick, 1985) and with communication (Cass & Edney, 1978).

Next, I examine possible solutions to some of our resource problems. In keeping with psychological tradition, I will emphasize two approaches that can be studied at the level of individual behaviors: recycling and conservation.

Recycling

One step individuals can take to combat dwindling resources is to do their part in recovering as many as possible of the resources that have already been used. Resource recovery takes two basic forms: reclamation and recycling (Cone & Hayes, 1980; Geller, Winett, & Everett, 1982). **Reclamation** refers to the use of old products in new ways. For example, old automobile tires can be used as an ingredient in paving materials for roadways, as an energy source (30 percent more efficient than coal), and in construction of artificial reefs to benefit marine life. **Recycling** refers to the recovery and reuse of materials for their original purpose. You are probably most familiar with recycling aluminum cans and wastepaper used for manufacturing new aluminum cans and paper.

The benefits of recycling are obvious. The cost of disposing of solid wastes in the United States alone is over $4 billion per year (Purcell, 1981), and Cone and Hayes (1980) have pointed out that recycling not only decreases waste but also increases the pool of resources and eases pollution. Miller (1990) has described the magnitude of the problem presented by aluminum cans alone. Every day, Americans purchase nearly 200 million aluminum cans of beer or soda. As of 1988, 56 percent of these were being recycled. While this may sound encouraging, it means that 44 percent of these cans are simply thrown away—this is more aluminum than most countries in the world use for *all* purposes. If the cans Americans throw away in one year were laid end to end, they would circle the earth's equator 164 times! Paper poses a similar problem. While some countries recycle about 50 percent of their wastepaper, the United States now recycles only about 29 percent. Making paper from the recycled paper rather than from wood takes less energy, reduces air pollution from paper mills by 60 percent to 73 percent, and results in less solid waste and water pollution (Turner, Grace, & Pearce, 1977).

Research on recycling behavior is less common than litter-control studies (Stern & Oskamp, 1987). Environmental psychologists are just beginning to understand the reasons people don't recycle more than they do. The issue is complicated by the fact that there appears to be little relationship between an individual's expressed attitudes toward recycling and the likelihood that he or she actively engages in recycling behaviors (Diamond & Loewy, 1991). Unfortunately, there is little financial incentive for consumers to recycle, since tax structures and governmental regulations are set to actively discourage recycling. Even the White House ignores the District of Columbia's paper recycling law (Atlas, 1990). Consequently, the recycling process actually can cost more than making paper and other goods from scratch (Bidwell, 1977; Cone & Hayes, 1980; Miller, 1990). Much of the expense in recycling comes from separating recyclable items from other waste. The tremendous growth of community programs now making this mandatory should have a very beneficial impact on recycling.

Not surprisingly, making recycling convenient and easy increases its frequency (Reid, Luyben, Rawers, & Bailey, 1976), and under some conditions using prompts at checkout counters can increase the purchase of returnable bottles (Geller, Farris, & Post, 1973; Geller, Wylie, & Farris, 1971). Several studies show that contests and raffles with prizes are effective in increasing the recycling of paper in much the same way that they work in litter cleanup (Couch, Garber, & Karpus, 1978; Geller, Chaffee, & Ingram, 1975; Ingram & Geller, 1975; Witmer & Geller, 1976). In fact, a recent study by Diamond and Loewy (1991) found that college students are more likely to recycle glass and newspaper in exchange for a lottery ticket with a potentially large cash payoff than for a certain but smaller cash reward. A study by Burns (1991) demonstrated that neighborhoods in which a specific individual is assigned as a "recycling block leader" (the person who distributes instructions and recycling bags) recycle significantly more than neighborhoods in which bags and instructions are left anonymously at front doors.

Perhaps the most successful stimuli for recycling are the "bottle bills" in force in about a dozen states as of 1991. These laws require a deposit on each aluminum beverage can or bottle purchased in the state, and although the beverage industry strongly opposes them, bottle bills really work. Ninety percent of cans and bottles are turned in as long as the refund is at least five cents per container. These laws save consumers money, reduce litter by 65 percent to 75 percent, save energy, decrease mining of aluminum, and increase local employment (Knapp, 1982; Levitt & Leventhal, 1984; Miller, 1990; Osborne & Powers, 1980).

Energy Conservation

Ultimately, most of our resource and pollution problems can be traced to industrial society's insatiable appetite for energy. While this appetite is not likely to diminish in the near future, much can be done to ease its impact on the earth's resources. Socolow (1978) estimated that it is possible to reduce residential energy costs by 50 percent through technological improvements in the home and through conservation. Conservation alone can result in significant savings and can be thought of as a source of energy in its own right (Stern & Oskamp, 1987). Stern and Oskamp point out, however, that households are not the predominant energy users in the United States and should not be expected to be the predominant energy savers. It is crucial that business, industry, and government take a more active role in conserving energy.

Behavior changes by individuals and groups are one of the paths society must follow in response to the energy crisis (Oskamp, 1984), but resistance to behavioral technology in energy conservation is strong (Winett, 1976). Many oppose any energy conservation for the simple reason that they make their livelihood through the production and sale of energy.

As with littering, there is little evidence that education or well-intentioned appeals have any real effect on residential energy consumption (Cone & Hayes, 1980; Geller, Winett, & Everett, 1982; Heberlein, 1975; Palmer, Lloyd, & Lloyd, 1978). The use of energy saving prompts is only slightly more effective, and these work best when they are highly specific and presented very close in time and space to the target behavior (Ester & Winett, 1982; Geller, Winett, & Everett, 1982). A few well-developed programs that combine education with modeling and detailed feedback have produced worthwhile results (Winett, Hatcher, Fort, Leckliter, Love, Riley, and Fishback, 1982). Getting an individual to make a public commitment to save energy seems to work better than education or prompting, and just talking about energy with neighbors and coworkers increases the adoption of energy-efficient technology in the home (Becker, 1978; Darley, 1978; Leonard-Barton, 1980; Pallak, Cook, & Sullivan, 1980; Pallak & Cummings, 1976). Modeling and conformity pressures that occur when entire neighborhoods become involved with conservation are also important (Florin & Wandersman, 1983; Nielsen & Ellington, 1983).

Economic factors may be the most effective catalyst for energy conservation (Winkler & Winett, 1982). If individuals are constantly reminded that they are saving money as well as energy, energy consumption tends to be lower. Feedback is an important part of this process and is most effective when given in terms of dollar amounts rather than in energy units (Kempton & Montgomery, 1982). Giving people some sort of signal when home energy consumption exceeds a certain level is effective in reducing energy use, and it works even better when coupled with incentives such as refunds on power bills for attaining specific conservation goals (Kohlenberg, Phillips, & Proctor, 1976; Zarling & Lloyd, cited by Cone & Hayes, 1980). A good example of feedback in residential energy conservation is provided in a study by Becker and Seligman (1978). New Jersey homeowners were given a device that turned on a light in their kitchens whenever the outside air temperature dropped to a point where they could cool their houses effectively by turning off air conditioners and opening windows. This simple device resulted in substantial energy savings.

Several reviews of the literature have summarized the conditions under which feedback about energy consumption is most effective (Cone & Hayes, 1980; Stern & Oskamp, 1987). Frequent feedback is important because it crystallizes for the consumer the relationship between his or her behavior and the consequences of that behavior. It is also important to have a specific standard or goal to measure feedback against, be it past performance or some future goal. Feedback also works best when household energy costs are fairly high to begin with, which motivates the consumer to make reductions.

Some experimental programs have explored using straightforward financial rewards for energy conservation. Such reward systems clearly work, but so far their costs have been greater than the value of the energy they saved (Geller, Winett, & Everett, 1982; Stern & Oskamp, 1987).

So far I have concentrated on conservation of energy in the home. However, transportation accounts for 30 percent to 40 percent of the fuel use in the United States (Everett, cited by Cone & Hayes, 1980); anything that reduces the amount of motorized travelling will save energy. Commoner (1972) has noted that mass transit is 300 percent to 600 percent more energy efficient than private automobiles for moving people. Many reinforcement programs have tried to encourage people to abandon their cars in favor of mass transportation. These programs usually offer small amounts of money or tokens good for free rides to those who use buses or trains. Although some programs in specific areas have increased the use of mass transportation, their overall success has been limited (Deslauriers & Everett, 1977; Everett, Hayward, & Meyers, 1974). Americans seem to love the sense of control and convenience that driving their own cars provides and are apparently willing to endure added expense for this privilege. Another approach to this problem has been to encourage commuters to carpool by offering toll-free passage, express lanes, and reduced fares to cars carrying multiple passengers. These programs also have had limited success, and they have led to interesting behaviors such as riding with inflatable dummies and "pirating" people from bus stops as a way to get rewards without giving up one's car (Cone & Hayes, 1980).

Individual Differences in Environmental Concern and Action

Why do some people go to such lengths to protect the environment while others seem unwilling to make even the smallest changes in their lifestyles in response to environmental concerns? In considering answers to this question, it is important to distinguish between expressed concerns about the environment and actual behavior (Manzo & Weinstein, 1987). The two do not always go together, and even the most concerned individuals usually pursue the easiest course of action (Black, Stern, & Elworth, 1985; Kantola, Syme, & Campbell, 1984; Olsen, 1981; Simmons, Talbot, & Kaplan, 1984–1985).

At first, research painted what seemed to be a coherent demographic portrait of people who actively engaged in proenvironment behaviors. Generally, individuals expressing the most environmental concern in these studies tended to be young, female, well-educated, and urban (Arbuthnot, 1977; Buttel & Flinn, 1974, 1978; Milbrath, 1984; Mohai & Twight, 1986). However, as research continued, this profile failed to hold up consistently. Now researchers think that most of these demographic findings are artifacts of the times in which the data were collected and the methodologies that were used (Samdahl & Robertson, 1989). It is fairly well-established that blacks show less environmental concern and action than whites, and there are a variety of plausible explanations why this may be true (Kellert, 1984; Kreger, 1973; Mitchell, 1980). Many blacks may feel alienated from the upper-class, white professionals who usually dominate environmental-action organizations (Taylor, 1989). Manzo and Weinstein (1987) tried to find some systematic differences between active and nonactive members of the Sierra Club (a national conservation organization) and could only conclude that the active members were more socially involved with other members of the club and enjoyed the organization's activities more than nonactive members.

A few studies have examined the relationship of personal characteristics to very specific environmental behaviors such as recycling or energy conservation. Labay and Kinnear (1981) found that very high- or very low-income earners were most likely to actively conserve energy, although presumably for different reasons. Belk, Painter, and Semenik (1981) discovered that persons who blame the energy crisis on others are less likely to take any action on their own. It is also known that people who have an internal locus of control and believe that their behavior has

CARTOON   Environmental problems increasingly engage our attention. *Frank & Ernest* reprinted by permission of NEA, Inc.

real consequences are more likely to engage in antipollution activities as long as they remain optimistic about future pollution levels (Trigg, Perlman, Perry, and Janisse, 1976). The most recent recycling studies have failed to find any demographic or personality differences between recyclers and nonrecyclers (Oskamp, Harrington, Edwards, Sherwood, Okuda, & Swanson, 1991). However, these studies have determined that nonrecyclers tend to be more concerned about convenience and financial incentives than recyclers, and that recyclers are more knowledgeable about the ins and outs of recycling in their local area (Arbuthnot, 1977; Oskamp et al., 1991; Vining & Ebreo, 1990).

DO IT!

Change Your Behavior to Save the Earth

After reading this chapter, you should be more aware of and sensitive to the ecological problems we face on our planet. Make a personal commitment to do something to improve the situation. Select an ecologically responsible behavior that you are not currently engaged in. It need not be large—if each individual makes just one minor change in his or her own behavior patterns, the ecosystem will benefit tremendously. Recycle newspaper or aluminum cans; ride a bicycle or walk rather than driving short distances; join an environmental organization or volunteer your time in a community litter pickup program. To help yourself further appreciate the impact of your behavior, do a cost/benefit analysis of the financial, health, or energy conservation gains made for just one year as a result of the changes you have made in your life. Who knows, you may just become a good influence on those around you!

CHAPTER SUMMARY

Problems of environmental pollution and depletion of the earth's natural resources promise to be the most pressing issues of the next decade and beyond. Environmental psychologists are studying a variety of ways in which environmentally destructive behavior might be changed. So far, it appears that education alone is ineffective and that prompts are effective in a limited set of circumstances. Behavior modification based on reinforcement has been more successful, but in practice these programs can be expensive and difficult to administer.

The most headway has been made in understanding problems of environmental aesthetics, such as littering and vandalism. Problems of pollution and resource management are much more complicated because of their entanglement with other economic and societal factors. Nevertheless, problems of air and water pollution and depletion of resources pose serious threats to the health of human beings and the planet and must be dealt with in the near future.

Attempts to curb air pollution have focused on urban air pollution caused by automobile exhaust and industrial waste. Research on resource problems has concentrated on behaviors that can be adopted by individuals alone such as recycling and energy conservation.

GLOSSARY

Acute Effects of Pollution   Pollution effects that appear quickly.

Antecedent Strategies of Behavior Change   Behavior change techniques that are used before a target behavior occurs.

Applied Behavior Analysis   The application of operant conditioning to the behavior of human beings in real situations.

Baseline   The naturally occurring frequency of a behavior.

Behavioral Technology   The science, art, skill, or craft of influencing socially important human behavior.

Carbon Monoxide   A gas that is a primary component of automobile exhaust.

Chlorofluorocarbons (CFCs)   Air pollutant used as a coolant, a propellant, and in the manufacture of Styrofoam, which seriously damages the ozone layer when released into the atmosphere.

Chronic Effects of Pollution   Pollution effects that take a long time to appear.

Commons Dilemma   Conflict between individual and group self-interests.

Consequence Strategies of Behavior Change   Behavior change techniques that are used after a target behavior has occurred.

Continuous Reinforcement   A reinforcement schedule in which each and every occurrence of a behavior is reinforced.

Fixed Person Interval (FPI)   A reinforcement schedule in which an individual from a larger group is reinforced for a behavior following the passage of a fixed interval of time since the last reinforcement.

Fixed Person Ratio (FPR)   A reinforcement schedule in which an individual from a larger group is reinforced for a behavior following a fixed number of responses by other people.

The Greenhouse Effect   Global warming caused by an increased concentration of carbon dioxide in the atmosphere.

Intermittent Reinforcement   Any schedule of reinforcement in which each and every response is not reinforced.

Item-Marking Technique   A technique in which marked items of litter are planted in larger areas of trash; a person returning the marked item along with other litter receives a reward.

Multiple Baseline Procedure   A technique for assessing the effectiveness of a reinforcer by using it with a series of different target behaviors.

Negative Reinforcement   Removal of an aversive stimulus following the occurrence of a target behavior.

Positive Reinforcement   Delivery of a rewarding stimulus following the occurrence of a target behavior.

Punishment   Delivery of an aversive stimulus following the occurrence of a target behavior.

Reclamation   Using old products in new ways.

Recycling   Recovery and reuse of materials for their original purpose.

Social Dilemma   A general term that refers to any maladaptive, resource-related behavior.

Social Trap   The tendency to choose immediate rewards even when they have long-term negative consequences.

Tragedy of the Commons   Exploitation of group resources by individuals acting only in their own self-interest.

Variable Person Interval (VPI)   A schedule of reinforcement in which an individual from a larger group is reinforced for a response following the passage of time intervals averaging around some particular interval length since the last reinforcement.

Variable Person Ratio (VPR)   A schedule of reinforcement in which an individual from a larger group is reinforced for a response following some average number of responses by other people.

Withdrawal Design   A technique for assessing the effectiveness of a reinforcer by removing the reinforcer to see if the target behavior returns to baseline levels, and then reintroducing it to see if the behavior changes correspondingly.

References

ACKING, C. A., & KÜLLER, R. (1972). The perception of an interior as a function of its color. *Ergonomics, 15,* 645–654.

ACREDOLO, L. P. (1978). Development of spatial orientation in infancy. *Developmental Psychology, 13,* 1–8.

ACREDOLO, L. P. (1982). The familiarity factor in spatial research. In R. Cohen (Ed.), *Children's conception of spatial relationships.* San Francisco: Jossey-Bass.

ACREDOLO, L. P., & EVANS, D. (1980). Developmental changes in the effects of landmarks on infant spatial behavior. *Developmental Psychology, 16,* 312–318.

ACREDOLO, L. P., PICK, H. L., & OLSEN, M. G. (1975). Environmental differentiation and familiarity as determinants of children's memory for spatial location. *Developmental Psychology, 11,* 495–501.

ADAIR, J. G. (1984). The Hawthorne Effect: A reconsideration of the methodological artifact. *Journal of Applied Psychology, 69,* 334–345.

ADAMS, P. R., & ADAMS, G. R. (1984). Mount Saint Helen's ashfall: Evidence for a disaster stress reaction. *American Psychologist, 39,* 252–260.

ADAMS, R. S., & BIDDLE, B. J. (1970). *Realities of teaching: Explorations with videotape.* New York: Holt, Rinehart, & Winston.

AHMED, S. M. S. (1979). Invasion of personal space: A study of departure time as affected by sex of the intruder and saliency condition. *Perceptual and Motor Skills, 49,* 85–86.

AHRENTZEN, S., JUE, G. M., SKORPANICH, M. A., & EVANS, G. W. (1982). School environments and stress. In G. W. Evans (Ed.), *Environmental stress.* New York: Cambridge University Press.

AHRENTZEN, S., LEVINE, D. W., & MICHELSON, W. (1989). Space, time, and activity in the home: A gender analysis. *Journal of Environmental Psychology, 9,* 89–101.

AIELLO, J. R. (1987). Human spatial behavior. In D. Stokols & I. Altman (Eds.), *Handbook of environmental psychology* (Vol. 1). New York: John Wiley and Sons.

AIELLO, J. R., & AIELLO, T. D. (1974). Development of personal space: Proxemic behavior of children six to sixteen. *Human Ecology, 2,* 177–189.

AIELLO, J. R., BAUM, A., & GORMLEY, F. B. (1981). Social determinants of residential crowding stress. *Personality and Social Psychology Bulletin, 7,* 643–649.

AIELLO, J. R., & COOPER, R. E. (1979). *Personal space and social affect: A developmental study.* Paper presented at the meeting of the Society for Research in Child Development, San Francisco.

AIELLO, J. R., EPSTEIN, Y. M., & KARLIN, R. (1975). Effects of crowding on electrodermal activity. *Sociological Symposium, 14,* 42–57.

AIELLO, J. R., & JONES, S. E. (1971). A field study of the proxemic behavior of young school children in three subcultural groups. *Journal of Personality and Social Psychology, 19,* 351–356.

AIELLO, J. R., & THOMPSON, D. E. (1980). Personal space, crowding, and spatial behavior in a cultural context. In I. Altman, J. F. Wohlwill, & A. Rapoport (Eds.), *Human behavior and evironment* (Vol. 4). New York: Plenum.

AIELLO, J. R., THOMPSON, D. E., & BAUM, A. (1981). The symbiotic relationship between social psychology and environmental psychology: Implications from crowding, personal space, and intimacy regulation research. In J. H. Harvey (Ed.), *Cognition, social behavior, and the environment.* Hillsdale, NJ: Erlbaum.

ALCOCK, J. (1984). *Animal behavior: An evolutionary approach* (3rd ed.). Sunderland, MA: Sinnaver Associates.

ALDWIN, C., & STOKOLS, D. (1988). The effects of environmental change on individuals and groups: Some neglected issues in stress research. *Journal of Environmental Psychology, 8,* 57–75.

ALEXANDER, C., DAVIS, H., MARTINEZ, J., & CORNER, D. (1985). *The production of houses.* New York: Oxford University Press.

ALEXANDER, M., & ISAAC, W. (1965). Effect of illumination and d-amphetamine on the activity of the *Rhesus macaque. Psychological Reports, 16,* 311–313.

ALEXANDER, W. (1968). Some harmful effects of noise. *Canadian Medical Association Journal, 99,* 27–31.

ALLEN, V. L., & GREENBERGER, D. B. (1980). Destruction and perceived control. In A. Baum and J. E. Singer (Eds.), *Advances in environmental psychology* (Vol. 2). Hillsdale, NJ: Erlbaum.

ALLEN, T. J., BECKER, F. D., & STEELE, F. (1987). *The Steelcase CDC: Building for innovation.* Grand Rapids, MI: Steelcase, Inc.

ALLEN, T. J., & GERTSBERGER, P. G. (1973). A field experiment to improve communication in a product engineering department: The nonterritorial office. *Human Factors, 15,* 487–498.

ALLGEIER, A. R., & BYRNE, D. (1973). Attraction toward the opposite sex as a determinant of physical proximity. *Journal of Social Psychology, 90,* 213–219.

ALLISON, S. T., & MESSICK, D. M. (1985). Effects of experience in a replenishable resource trap. *Journal of Personality and Social Psychology, 49,* 943–948.

ALLPORT, G., & PETTIGREW, T. (1957). Cultural influence on the perception of movement: The trapezoidal illusion among the Zulus. *Journal of Abnormal and Social Psychology, 55,* 104–113.

ALTMAN, I. (1975). *Environment and social behavior: Privacy, personal space, territory, and crowding.* Pacific Grove, CA: Brooks/Cole.

ALTMAN, I. (1976a). Environmental psychology and social psychology. *Personality and Social Psychology Bulletin, 2,* 96–113.

ALTMAN, I. (1976b). A response to Epstein, Proshansky, and Stokols. *Personality and Social Psychology Bulletin, 2,* 364–370.

ALTMAN, I., & CHEMERS, M. M. (1980). *Culture and environment.* Pacific Grove, CA: Brooks/Cole.

ALTMAN, I., & GAUVAIN, M. (1981). A cross-cultural and dialectical analysis of homes. In L. Liben, A. Patterson, & N. Newcombe (Eds.), *Spatial representation across the life span.* New York: Academic Press.

ALTMAN, I., & HAYTHORN, W. W. (1967). The ecology of isolated groups. *Behavioral Science, 12,* 168–182.

ALTMAN, I., TAYLOR, D. A., & WHEELER, L. (1971). Ecological aspects of group behavior in social isolation. *Journal of Applied Social Psychology, 1,* 76–100.

ALTMAN, I., & VINSEL, A. M. (1977). Personal space: An analysis of E. T. Hall's proxemics framework. In I. Altman & J. F. Wohlwill (Eds.), *Human behavior and environment: Advances in theory and research* (Vol. 1). New York: Plenum.

AMATO, P. (1983). The effects of urbanization on interpersonal behavior. *Journal of Cross-Cultural Psychology, 14,* 353–367.

AMATO, P. R., & MCINNES, I. R. (1983). Affiliative behavior in diverse environments: A consideration of pleasantness, information rate, and arousal-eliciting quality of settings. *Basic and Applied Social Psychology, 4,* 109–122.

AMATURO, E., COSTAGLIOLA, S., & RAGONE, G. (1987). Furnishing and status attributes: A sociological study of the living room. *Environment and Behavior, 19,* 228–249.

ANDERSEN, J. F., ANDERSEN, P. A., & LUSTIG, M. W. (1987). Opposite sex touch avoidance: A national replication and extension. *Journal of Nonverbal Behavior, 11,* 89–109.

ANDERSON, C. A. (1987). Temperature and aggression: Effects on quarterly, yearly, and city rates of violent and nonviolent crime. *Journal of Personality and Social Psychology, 52,* 1161–1173.

ANDERSON, C. A. (1989). Temperature and aggression: Ubiquitous effects of heat on occurrence of human violence. *Psychological Bulletin, 106,* 74–96.

ANDERSON, C. A., & ANDERSON, D. C. (1984). Ambient temperature and violent crime: Tests of the linear and curvilinear hypotheses. *Journal of Personality and Social Psychology, 46,* 91–97.

ANDERSON, J. R. (1978). Arguments concerning representations for mental imagery. *Psychological Review, 85,* 249–277.

ANDERSON, L. M. (1981). Land use designations affect perception of scenic beauty in forest landscapes. *Forest Science, 27,* 392–400.

ANDERSON, L. M., MULLIGAN, B. E., GOODMAN, L. S., & REGEN, H. Z. (1983). Effects of sounds on preferences for outdoor settings. *Environment and Behavior, 15,* 539–566.

ANDERSON, T. W., ERWIN, N., FLYNN, D., LEWIS, L., & ERWIN, J. (1977). Effects of short-term crowding on aggression in captive groups of pigtail monkeys. *Aggressive Behavior, 3,* 33–46.

ANGUS, M. J., BECK, T. M., HILL, P. W., & MCATEE, W. A. (1979, April). *A summary report of the Australian Open Area Schools Project.* Paper presented at the annual convention of the American Education Research Association, San Francisco.

ANOOSHIAN, A. J., & WILSON, K. L. (1977). Distance distortions in memory for spatial locations. *Child Development, 48,* 1704–1707.

ANTES, J. R., MCBRIDE, R. B., & COLLINS, J. D. (1988). The effect of a new city traffic route on the cognitive maps of its residents. *Environment and Behavior, 20,* 75–91.

APPLETON, J. (1975). *The experience of landscape.* London: John Wiley and Sons.

APPLETON, J. (1984). Prospects and refuges revisited. *Landscape Journal, 8,* 91–103.

APPLEYARD, D. (1969). Why buildings are known. *Environment and Behavior, 1,* 131–156.

APPLEYARD, D. (1970). Styles and methods of structuring a city. *Environment and Behavior, 2,* 100–117.

APPLEYARD, D. (1973). Notes on urban perception and knowledge. In R. M. Downs and D. Stea (Eds.), *Image and the environment: Cognitive mapping and spatial behavior.* Chicago: Aldine.

APPLEYARD, D. (1976). *Planning a pluralistic city.* Cambridge, MA: M.I.T. Press.

APPLEYARD, D., & LINTELL, M. (1972). The environmental quality of city streets: The resident's viewpoint. *Journal of the American Institute of Planners, 38,* 84–101.

ARAGONES, J. I., & ARREDONDO, J. M. (1985). Structure of urban cognitive maps. *Journal of Environmental Psychology, 5,* 197–212.

ARBUTHNOT, J. (1977). The roles of attitudinal and personality variables in the prediction of environmental behavior and knowledge. *Environment and Behavior, 9,* 217–232.

ARDREY, R. (1966). *The territorial imperative.* New York: Dell.

ARGYLE, M., & COOK, M. (1976). *Gaze and mutual gaze.* Cambridge, England: Cambridge University Press.

ARGYLE, M., & DEAN, J. (1965). Eye-contact, distance, and affiliation. *Sociometry, 28,* 289–304.

ARGYLE, M., & INGHAM, R. (1972). Gaze, mutual gaze, and proximity. *Semiotica, 6,* 32–49.

ARONSON, S. J. (1976, April). *Reactions to invasions of marked seats at a race track.* Paper presented at the meeting of the Eastern Psychological Association, New York.

ASHCRAFT, N., & SCHEFLEN, A. E. (1976). *People space: The making and breaking of human boundaries.* Garden City, NY: Anchor Books.

ASHTON, N. L., SHAW, M. E., & WORSHAM, A. P. (1980). Affective reactions to interpersonal distances by friends and strangers. *Bulletin of the Psychonomic Society, 15,* 306–308.

ASPEY, W. P. (1977). Wolf spider sociobiology: II. Density parameters influencing agonistic behavior in *Schizocosa crassipes. Behaviour, 62,* 143–163.

ATLAS, T. (1990, May 20). White House slow to recycle paper. *Chicago Tribune,* p. 5.

AULICIENS, A. (1972). Some observed relationships between the atmospheric environment and mental work. *Environmental Research, 5,* 217–240.

AXELROD, S., HALL, R. V., & TAMS, A. (1979). Comparison of two common classroom seating arrangements. *Academic Therapy, 15,* 29–37.

BACHELARD, G. (1964). *The poetics of space.* New York: Orion Press.

BACHRACH, A. J. (1982). The human in extreme environments. In A. Baum and J. E. Singer (Eds.), *Advances in environmental psychology: Vol. 4. Environment and health.* Hillsdale, NJ: Erlbaum.

BACKSTROM, T., SANDERS, D., LEASK, R., DAVIDSON, D., WARNER, P., & BANCROFT, J. (1983). Mood, sexuality, hormones, and the menstrual cycle: II. Hormone levels and their relationship to the premenstrual syndrome. *Psychosomatic Medicine, 45,* 503–507.

BACON-PRUE, A., BLOUNT, R., PICKERING, D., & DRABMAN, R. (1980). An evaluation of three litter control procedures—trash receptacles, paid workers, and the marked item technique. *Journal of Applied Behavior Analysis, 13,* 165–170.

BAILEY, K. G., HARTNETT, J. J., & GIBSON, F. W. JR. (1972). Implied threat and the territorial factor in personal space. *Psychological Reports, 30,* 263–270.

BAIRD, L. L. (1969). Big school, small school: A critical examination of the hypothesis. *Journal of Educational Psychology, 60,* 286–303.

BAKOS, M., BOZIC, R., CHAPIN, D., & NEUMAN, S. (1980). Effects of environmental changes on elderly residents' behavior. *Hospital and Community Psychiatry, 31,* 677–682.

BALLING, J. D., & FALK, J. H. (1982). Development of visual preference for natural environments. *Environment and Behavior, 14,* 5–28.

BALLMAN, G. (1980). Operationalizing the cross-country skiing opportunity spectrum. In T. B. Knopp and L. C. Merriam (Conference Coordinators), *Proceedings, North American Symposium on Dispersed Winter Recreation.* St. Paul: University of Minnesota, Office of Special Programs.

BALTES, M. M., & HAYWARD, S. C. (1976). Application and evaluation of strategies to reduce pollution: Behavior control of littering in a football stadium. *Journal of Applied Psychology, 61,* 501–506.

BARABASZ, A. F. (1991a). A review of Antarctic behavioral research. In A. A. Harrison, Y. A. Clearwater, & C. P. McKay (Eds.), *From Antarctica to outer space: Life in isolation and confinement.* New York: Springer-Verlag.

BARABASZ, A. F. (1991b). Effects of isolation on states of consciousness. In A. A. Harrison, Y. A. Clearwater, & C. P. McKay (Eds.), *From Antarctica to outer space: Life in isolation and confinement.* New York: Springer-Verlag.

BARABASZ, A. F., & BARABASZ, M. (1985). Effects of restricted environmental stimulation: Skin conductance, EEG alpha and temperature responses. *Environment and Behavior, 17,* 239–253.

BARABASZ, M. (1991). Imaginative involvement in Antarctica: Applications to life in space. In A. A. Harrison, Y. A. Clearwater, & C. P. McKay (Eds.), *From*

Antarctica to outer space: Life in isolation and confinement. New York: Springer-Verlag.

BARASH, D. P. (1973). Human ethology: Personal space reiterated. *Environment and Behavior, 5,* 67–73.

BARASH, D. P. (1982). *Sociobiology and behavior* (2nd ed.). New York: Elsevier.

BAREFOOT, J. C., HOOPLE, H., & MCCLAY, D. (1972). Avoidance of an act which would violate personal space. *Psychonomic Science, 28,* 205–206.

BARKER, M. L. (1976). Planning for environmental indices: Observer appraisal of air quality. In K. Craik and E. H. Zube (Eds.), *Perceiving environmental quality: Research and applications.* New York: Plenum.

BARKER, R. G. (1960). Ecology and motivation. *Nebraska Symposium on Motivation, 8,* 1–50.

BARKER, R. G. (1963). On the nature of the environment. *Journal of Social Issues, 19,* 17–38.

BARKER, R. G. (1965). Explorations in ecological psychology. *American Psychologist, 20,* 1–14.

BARKER, R. G. (1968). *Ecological psychology: Concepts and methods for studying the environment of human behavior.* Stanford, CA: Stanford University Press.

BARKER, R. G. (1990). Settings of a professional lifetime. In I. Altman and K. Christensen (Eds.), *Environment and behavior studies: Emergence of intellectual traditions.* New York: Plenum.

BARKER, R. G., & GUMP, P. V. (1964). *Big school, small school.* Stanford, CA: Stanford Universtiy Press.

BARKER, R. G., & WRIGHT, H. F. (1955). *Midwest and its children: The psychological ecology of an American town.* New York: Row, Peterson.

BARON, R. A. (1978). Invasions of personal space and helping: Mediating effects of invader's apparent need. *Journal of Experimental Social Psychology, 14,* 304–312.

BARON, R. A. (1987a). Effects of negative ions on cognitive performance. *Journal of Applied Psychology, 72,* 131–137.

BARON, R. A. (1987b). Effects of negative ions on interpersonal attraction: Evidence for intensification. *Journal of Personality and Social Psychology, 52,* 547–553.

BARON, R. A. (1990). Environmentally induced positive affect: Its impact on self-efficacy, task performance, negotiation, and conflict. *Journal of Applied Social Psychology, 20,* 368–384.

BARON, R. A., & BELL, P. A. (1975). Aggression and heat: Mediating effects of prior provocation and exposure to an aggressive model. *Journal of Personality and Social Psychology, 31,* 825–832.

BARON, R. A., & BELL, P. A. (1976). Aggression and heat: The influence of ambient temperature, negative affect, and a cooling drink on physical aggression. *Journal of Personality and Social Psychology, 33,* 245–255.

BARON, R. A., & BYRNE, D. (1987). *Social psychology: Understanding human interaction.* Boston: Allyn and Bacon.

BARON, R. A., RUSSELL, G. W., & ARMS, R. L. (1985). Negative ions and behavior: Impact on mood, memory, and aggression among Type A and Type B persons. *Journal of Personality and Social Psychology, 48,* 746–754.

BARON, R. M., MANDEL, D. R., ADAMS, C. A., & GRIFFIN, L. M. (1976). Effects of social density in university residential environments. *Journal of Personality and Social Psychology, 34,* 434–446.

BARON, R. M., & NEEDEL, S. P. (1980). Toward an understanding of the differences in the responses of humans and other animals to density. *Psychological Review, 87,* 320–326.

BARON, R. M., & RODIN, J. (1978). Personal control as a mediator of crowding. In A. Baum, J. E. Singer, & S. Valins (Eds.), *Advances in environmental psychology* (Vol. 1). Hillsdale, NJ: Erlbaum.

BAUM, A., CALESNICK, L. E., DAVIS, G. E., & GATCHEL, R. J. (1982). Individual differences in coping with crowding: Stimulus screening and social overload. *Journal of Personality and Social Psychology, 43,* 821–830.

BAUM, A., & DAVIS, G. E. (1976). Spatial and social aspects of crowding perception. *Environment and Behavior, 8,* 527–544.

BAUM, A., FLEMING, R., & SINGER, J. E. (1983). Coping with technological disaster. *Journal of Social Issues, 39,* 117–138.

BAUM, A., GATCHEL, R. J., & SCHAEFFER, M. A. (1983). Emotional, behavioral, and physiological effects of chronic stress at Three Mile Island. *Journal of Consulting and Clinical Psychology, 51,* 565–572.

BAUM, A., & GREENBERG, C. I. (1975). Waiting for a crowd: The behavioral and perceptual effects of anticipated crowding. *Journal of Personality and Social Psychology, 32,* 667–671.

BAUM, A., HARPIN, R. E., & VALINS, S. (1975). The role of group phenomena in the experience of crowding. *Environment and Behavior, 7,* 185–198.

BAUM, A., & KOMAN, S. (1976). Differential response to anticipated crowding: Psychological effects of social and spatial density. *Journal of Personality and Social Psychology, 34,* 526–536.

BAUM, A., O'KEEFE, M. K., & DAVIDSON, L. M. (1990). Acute stressors and chronic response: The case of traumatic stress. *Journal of Applied Social Psychology, 20,* 1643–1654.

BAUM, A., & PAULUS, P. B. (1987). Crowding. In D. Stokols & I. Altman (Eds.), *Handbook of environmental psychology* (Vol 1). New York: John Wlley and Sons.

BAUM, A., REISS, M., & O'HARA, J. (1974). Architectural variants of reaction to spatial invasion. *Environment and Behavior, 6,* 91–100.

BAUM, A., SHAPIRO, A., MURRAY, D., & WIDEMAN, M. V. (1979). Interpersonal mediation of perceived crowding and control in residential dyads and triads. *Journal of Applied Social Psychology, 9,* 491–507.

BAUM, A., SINGER, J. E., & BAUM, C. (1982). Stress and the environment. In G. W. Evans (Ed.), *Environmental stress.* New York: Cambridge University Press.

BAUM, A., & VALINS, S. (1977). *Architecture and social behavior: Psychological studies of social density.* Hillsdale, NJ: Erlbaum.

BAUM, A., & VALINS, S. (1979). Architectural mediation of residential density and control: Crowding and the regulation of social contact. In L. Berkowitz (Ed.), *Advances in experimental social psychology* (Vol. 12). New York: Academic Press.

BAUM, D. R., & JONIDES, J. (1977, November). *Cognitive maps: Comparative judgments of imagined vs. perceived distance.* Paper presented at the meeting of the Psychonomic Society, Washington, DC.

BAUMEISTER, R. F., & STEINHILBER, A. (1984). Paradoxical effects of supportive audiences on performance under pressure: The home field disadvantage in sports championships. *Journal of Personality and Social Psychology, 47,* 85–93.

BAXTER, J. C. (1970). Interpersonal spacing in natural settings. *Sociometry, 33,* 444–456.

BAXTER, J. C., & ROZELLE, R. M. (1975). Nonverbal expression as a function of crowding during a simulated police-citizen encounter. *Journal of Personality and Social Psychology, 32,* 40–54.

BEARD, R. R., & GRANDSTAFF, N. (1970). Carbon monoxide exposure and cerebral function. *Annals of the New York Academy of Sciences, 174,* 385–395.

BEARD, R. R., & WERTHEIM, G. A. (1967). Behavioral impairment associated with small doses of carbon monoxide. *American Journal of Public Health, 57,* 2012–2022.

BECHTEL, R. B. (1976). Perception of environmental quality: Some new wineskins for old wine. In K. H. Craik & E. H. Zube (Eds.), *Perceiving environmental quality: Research and applications.* New York: Plenum.

BECHTEL, R. B. (1977). *Enclosing behavior.* Stroudsburg, PA: Dowden, Hutchinson, and Ross.

BECK, R. J., & WOOD, D. (1976). Cognitive transformation of information from urban geographic fields to mental maps. *Environment and Behavior, 8,* 199–238.

BECKER, F. D. (1973). A study of spatial markers. *Journal of Personality and Social Psychology, 26,* 439–445.

BECKER, F. D. (1974). *Design for living: The residents' view of multi-family housing.* Ithaca, NY: Center for Urban Development Research.

BECKER, F. D. (1976). Children's play in multifamily housing. *Environment and Behavior, 8,* 545–574.

BECKER, F. D. (1977). *Housing messages.* Stroudsburg, PA: Dowden, Hutchinson, and Ross.

BECKER, F. D. (1981). *Workspace: Creating environments in organizations.* New York: Praeger.

BECKER, F. D. (1991). Workplace planning, design, and management. In E. H. Zube & G. T. Moore (Eds.), *Advances in environment, behavior, and design* (Vol. 3). New York: Plenum.

BECKER, F. D., & MAYO, C. (1971). Delineating personal distance and territoriality. *Environment and Behavior, 3,* 375–381.

BECKER, F. D., SOMMER, R., BEE, J., & OXLEY, B. (1973). College classroom ecology. *Sociometry, 36,* 514–525.

BECKER, L. J. (1978). The joint effect of feedback and goal setting on performance: A field study of residential energy conservation. *Journal of Applied Psychology, 63,* 428–433.

BECKER, L. J., & SELIGMAN, C. (1978). Reducing air conditioning waste by signalling it is cool outside. *Personality and Social Psychology Bulletin, 4,* 412–415.

BEDE (1968). *A history of the English church and people.* New York: Penguin Books.

BELK, R., PAINTER, J., & SEMENIK, R. (1981). Preferred solutions to the energy crisis as a function of causal attributions. *Journal of Consumer Research, 8,* 306–312.

BELL, A. E., ABRAHAMSEN, D. S., & GROWSE, R. (1977). Achievement and self-reports of responsibility for achievement in informal and conventional classrooms. *British Journal of Educational Psychology, 47,* 258–267.

BELL, P. A. (1981). Physiological, comfort, performance, and social effects of heat stress. *Journal of Social Issues, 37,* 71–94.

BELL, P. A. (1982, August). *Theoretical interpretations of heat stress.* Paper presented at the annual meeting of the American Psychological Association, Washington, DC.

BELL, P. A., & BARON, R. A. (1976). Aggression and heat: The mediating role of negative affect. *Journal of Applied Social Psychology, 6,* 18–30.

BELL, P. A., & BARON, R. A. (1977). Aggression and ambient temperature: The facilitating and inhibiting effects of hot and cold environments. *Bulletin of the Psychonomic Society, 9,* 443–445.

BELL, P. A., & BARON, R. A. (1981). Ambient temperature and human violence. In P. F. Brain & D. Benton (Eds.), *A multidisciplinary approach to aggression research.* Amsterdam: Elsevier/North Holland Biomedical Press.

BELL, P. A., FISHER, J. D., BAUM, A., & GREENE, T. E. (1990). *Environmental psychology.* Fort Worth, TX: Holt, Rinehart, & Winston.

BELL, P. A., & FUSCO, M. E. (1989). Heat and violence in the Dallas field data: Linearity, curvilinearity, and heteroscedasticity. *Journal of Applied Social Psychology, 19,* 1479–1482.

BELL, P. A., & GREENE, T. L. (1982). Thermal stress: Physiological, comfort, performance, and social effects of hot and cold environments. In G. W. Evans (Ed.), *Environmental stress.* London: Cambridge University Press.

BENNETT, C. (1977). *Space for people. Human factors in design* Englewood Cliffs, NJ: Prentice-Hall.

BENNETT, N., ANDREAE, J., HEGARTY, P., & WADE, B. (1980). *Open plan schools.* Atlantic Highlands, NJ: Humanities.

BENNETT, R., RAFFERTY, J. M., CANIVEZ, G. L., & SMITH, J. M. (1983, May). *The effects of cold temperature on altruism and aggression.* Paper presented at the meeting of the Midwestern Psychological Association, Chicago.

BENNETT LEVY, J., & MARTEAU, T. (1984). Fear of animals: What is prepared? *British Journal of Psychology, 75,* 37–42.

BENTON, A. L. (1980). The neuropsychology of facial recognition. *American Psychologist, 69,* 77–110.

BERKOWITZ, W. R. (1967). Use of the sensation-seeking scale with Thai subjects. *Psychological Reports, 20,* 635–641.

BERLYNE, D. E. (1960). *Conflict, arousal, and curiosity.* New York: McGraw-Hill.

BERLYNE, D. E. (1967). Arousal and reinforcement. In D. Levine (Ed.), *Nebraska symposium on motivation* (Vol. 15). Lincoln, NE: University of Nebraska Press.

BERLYNE, D. E. (1971). *Aesthetics and psychobiology.* New York: Appleton-Century-Crafts.

BERLYNE, D. E. (1974). *Studies in the new experimental aesthetics: Steps toward an objective psychology of aesthetic appreciation.* New York: Halsted Press.

BERLYNE, D. E., & MADSEN, K. B. (1973). *Pleasure, reward, preference: Their nature, determinants, and role in behavior.* New York: Academic Press.

BERNALDEZ, F. G., BENAYAS, J., & DELUCIO, J. V. (1987). Changes in environmental attitudes as revealed by activity preferences and landscape tastes. *The Environmentalist, 7,* 21–30.

BERNALDEZ, F. G., GALLARDO, D., & ABELLO, R. P. (1987). Children's landscape preferences: From rejection to attraction. *Journal of Environmental Psychology, 7,* 169–176.

BERNALDEZ, F. G., RUIZ, J. P., & RUIZ, M. (1984). Landscape perception and appraisal: Ethics, aesthetics, and utility. *8th International Conference on Environment and Human Action,* Berlin, IAPS.8.

BERNARD, J. (1991, January). Places in space. *Ambassador Magazine,* pp. 54–59.

BERNSTEIN, A. (1972). Wilderness as a therapeutic behavior setting. *Therapeutic Recreation Journal, 6,* 160–161, 185.

BERNSTEIN, D. A. (1991, January). *Research methods: Drawing inferences from archival data.* Paper presented at the Thirteenth Annual National Institute on the Teaching of Psychology, St. Petersburg Beach, Florida.

BEST, C. L., & KILPATRICK, D. G. (1977). Psychological profiles of rape crisis counselors. *Psychological Reports, 40,* 1127–1134.

BETH-HALACHMY, S., & THAYER, R. L. (1978). Play behavior and space utilization in an elementary school play yard. *Man-Environment Systems, 8,* 191–201.

BICKMAN, L. (1972). Environmental attitudes and actions. *Journal of Social Psychology, 87,* 323–324.

BICKMAN, L., TEGER, A. GABRIELE, T., MCLAUGHLIN, C., & SUNDAY, E. (1973). Dormitory density and helping behavior. *Environment and Behavior, 5,* 465–490.

BIDWELL, R. (1977). Recycling policy: An international perspective. In D. W. Pearce & I. Walter (Eds.), *Resource conservation: Social and economic dimensions of recycling.* New York: New York University Press.

BIEL, A. (1982). Children's spatial representation of their neighborhood: A step towards a general spatial competence. *Journal of Environmental Psychology, 2,* 193–200.

BINER, P. M., BUTLER, D. L., FISCHER, A. R., & WESTERGREN, A. J. (1989). An arousal optimization model of lighting level preferences: An interaction of social situation and task demands. *Environment and Behavior, 21,* 3–16.

BINER, P. M., BUTLER, D. L., & WINSTED, D. E. (1991). Inside windows: An alternative to conventional windows in offices and other settings. *Environment and Behavior, 23,* 359–382.

BIRNEY, B. A. (1988). Brookfield Zoo's "Flying Walk" exhibit: Formative evaluation aids in the development of an interactive exhibit in an informal learning setting. *Environment and Behavior, 20,* 416–434.

BIRREN, F. (1965). *Color psychology and color therapy.* New Hyde Park, NY: University Books.

BITGOOD, S., PATTERSON, D., & BENEFIELD, A. (1988). Exhibit design and visitor behavior: Empirical relationships. *Environment and Behavior, 20,* 474–491.

BLACK, J. S., STERN, P. C., & ELWORTH, J. T. (1985). Personal and contextual influences on household energy adaptations. *Journal of Applied Psychology, 70,* 3–21.

BLACKWELL, O. M., & BLACKWELL, H. R. (1971). Visual performance data for 156 normal observers of various ages. *Journal of Illuminating Engineering Society, 1,* 3–13.

BLADES, M., & SPENCER, C. (1987). Young children's strategies when using maps with landmarks. *Journal of Environmental Psychology, 7,* 201–217.

BLAIR, S. M. (1991). The Antarctic experience. In A. A. Harrison, Y. A. Clearwater, & C. P. McKay (Eds.), *From Antarctica to outer space: Life in isolation and confinement.* New York: Springer-Verlag.

BLAUT, J. M., & STEA, D. (1974). Mapping at the age of three. *Journal of Geography, 73,* 5–9.

BLEDA, P. R., & BLEDA, S. (1978). Effects of sex and smoking on reaction to spatial invasion at a shopping mall. *Journal of Social Psychology, 104,* 311–312.

BLEDA, P. R., & SANDMAN, P. H. (1977). In smoke's way: Socioemotional reactions to another's smoking. *Journal of Applied Psychology, 62,* 452–458.

BLOCK, L. K., & STOKES, G. S. (1989). Performance and satisfaction in private versus nonprivate work settings. *Environment and Behavior, 21,* 277–297.

BOCHNER, S. (1975). The house form as a cornerstone of culture. In R. W. Brislin (Ed.), *Topics in culture learning* (Vol. 3). Honolulu: East-West Center.

BOMBARD, A. (1953). *The voyage of the Heretique.* New York: Simon and Schuster.

BONACICH, P. (1976). Secrecy and solidarity. *Sociometry, 39,* 200–208.

BOORAEM, C. D., FLOWERS, J., BODNER, G., & SATTERFIELD, D. (1977). Personal space variations as a function of criminal behavior. *Psychological Reports, 41,* 1115–1121.

BOOTH, A. (1976). *Urban crowding and its consequences.* New York: Praeger.

BOOTH, A., & EDWARDS, J. N. (1976). Crowding and family relations. *American Sociological Review, 41,* 308–321.

BORAY, P. F., GIFFORD, R., & ROSENBLOOD, L. (1989). Effects of warm white, cool white, and full-spectrum fluorescent lighting on simple cognitive performance, mood, and ratings of others. *Journal of Environmental Psychology, 9,* 297–308.

BORDEN, R. J., & FRANCIS, J. L. (1978). Who cares about ecology—Personality and sex differences in environmental concern. *Journal of Personality, 46,* 190–203.

BORNSTEIN, M. H. (1979). The pace of life revisited. *International Journal of Psychology, 14,* 83–90.

BORNSTEIN, M. H., & BORNSTEIN, H. G. (1976). The pace of life. *Nature, 259,* 557–558.

BORUN, M. (1977). *Measuring the unmeasurable.* Washington, DC: Association for Science Technology Centers.

BOSCHETTI, M. A. (1987). Memories of childhood homes: Some contributions of environmental autobiography to interior design education and research. *Journal of Interior Design Education and Research, 13,* 27–36.

BOSTI (Buffalo Organization for Social and Technological Innovation). (1981). *The impact of office environment on productivity and quality of working life: Comprehensive findings.* Buffalo, NY: BOSTI.

BOUBEKRI, M., HULL, R. B., & BOYER, L. L. (1991). Impact of window size and sunlight penetration on office workers' mood and satisfaction. *Environment and Behavior, 23,* 474–493.

BOURASSA, S. C. (1990). A paradigm for landscape aesthetics. *Environment and Behavior, 22,* 787–812.

BOWER, G. H. (1981). Mood and memory. *American Psychologist, 36,* 129–148.

BOWLEY, C. S. (1979). *Motives, managment, preferences, and perceptions of crowding of backcountry trail users in the Allegheny National Forest of Pennsylvania.* Unpublished master's thesis, Pennsylvania State University.

BOYCE, P. R. (1974). Users' assessments of a landscaped office. *Journal of Architectural Research, 3,* 44–62.

BOYCE, P.R. (1975). The luminous environment. In D. Canter & P. Stringer (Eds.), *Environmental interaction: Psychological approaches to our physical surroundings*. New York: International Universities Press.

BOYD, L. (ED.) (1988). *Zoological parks and aquariums in the Americas* (1988–1989 ed.). Wheeling, WV: American Association of Zoological Parks and Aquariums.

BOYLE, G. J. (1985). The paramenstrum and negative moods in normal young women. *Personality and Individual Differences, 6,* 649–652.

BRADY, A. T., & WALKER, M. B. (1978). Interpersonal distance as a function of situationally induced anxiety. *British Journal of Social and Clinical Psychology, 17,* 127–133.

BRANDEIS, H. N. (1972). The psychology of scatological privacy. *Journal of Biological Psychology, 14,* 30–35.

BRANDT, R. M. (1972). *Studying behavior in natural settings*. New York: Holt, Rinehart, & Winston.

BRANTINGHAM, P. J., & BRANTINGHAM, P. L. (1975). The spatial patterning of burglary. *Howard Journal of Penology and Crime Prevention, 14,* 11–24.

BRECKLER, S. J. (1984). Empirical validation of affect, behavior, and cognition as distinct components of attitudes. *Journal of Personality and Social Psychology, 47,* 1191–1205.

BREED, G. (1972). The effect of intimacy: Reciprocity or retreat? *British Journal of Social and Clinical Psychology, 11,* 135–142.

BREED, G., & COLAIUTA, V. (1974). Looking, blinking, and sitting: Non-verbal dynamics in the classroom. *Journal of Communication, 24,* 75–81.

BREISACHER, P. (1971). Neuropsychological effects of air pollution. *American Behavioral Scientist, 14,* 837–864.

BREMNER, J. G. (1978). Egocentric versus allocentric spatial coding in nine-month-old infants: Factors influencing the choice of code. *Developmental Psychology, 14,* 346–355.

BREMNER, J. G., & BRYANT, P. E. (1977). Place versus response as the basis of spatial errors made by young infants. *Journal of Experimental Child Psychology, 23,* 162–171.

BRILL, W. H. (1972, May). Security in public housing: A synergistic approach. In *Deterrence of crime in and around residences*. Paper presented at the 4th National Symposium on Law Enforcement Science and Technology, University of Maryland, College Park, Maryland.

BROADBENT, D. E. (1958). Effects of noise on an "intellectual" task. *Journal of the Acoustical Society of America, 30,* 824–827.

BROADBENT, D. E. (1978). The current state of noise research: Reply to Poulton. *Psychological Bulletin, 85,* 1052–1067.

BROADBENT, D. E., & LITTLE, E. (1960). Effects of noise reduction in a work situation. *Occupational Psychology, 34,* 133–140.

BROCKMANN, H. J. (1979). Nest-site selection in the great golden digger wasp, *Sphex ichneumoneus L. (Sphecidae)*. *Ecological Entomology, 4,* 11–24.

BROMET, E. J. (1990). Methodological issues in the assessment of traumatic events. *Journal of Applied Social Psychology, 20,* 1719–1724.

BRONZAFT, A. L. (1981). The effect of a noise abatement program on reading ability. *Journal of Environmental Psychology, 1,* 215–222.

BRONZAFT, A. L., & MCCARTHY, D. P. (1975). The effects of elevated train noise on reading ability. *Environment and Behavior, 7,* 517–527.

BROOKES, M., & KAPLAN, A. (1972). The office environment: Space planning and affective behavior. *Human Factors, 14,* 373–391.

BROOKS, C. I., & REBETA, J. L. (1991). College classroom ecology: The relation of sex of student to classroom performance and seating preference. *Environment and Behavior, 23,* 305–313.

BROWER, S. (1977). *The design of neighborhood parks.* Baltimore: City Planning Commission.

BROWER, S. (1980). Territory in urban settings. In I. Altman, A. Rapoport, & J. Wohlwill (Eds.), *Human behavior and environment.* New York: Plenum.

BROWN, B. B. (1987). Territoriality. In D. Stokols & I. Altman (Eds.), *Handbook of environmental psychology* (Vol. 1). New York: John Wiley and Sons.

BROWN, B. B., & ALTMAN, I. (1983). Territoriality, defensible space, and residential burglary: An environmental analysis. *Journal of Environmental Psychology, 3,* 203–220.

BROWN, B. B., & HARRIS, P. B. (1989). Residential burglary victimization: Reactions to the invasion of a primary territory. *Journal of Environmental Psychology, 9,* 119–132.

BROWN, B. B., & WERNER, C. M. (1985). Social cohesiveness, territoriality, and holiday decorations: The influence of cul-de-sacs. *Environment and Behavior, 17,* 539–561.

BROWN, J. G., & BURGER, C. (1984). Playground designs and preschool children's behaviors. *Environment and Behavior, 16,* 599–626.

BROWN, J. M., HENDERSON, J., & ARMSTRONG, M. P. (1987). Children's perceptions of nuclear power stations as revealed through their drawings. *Journal of Environmental Psychology, 7,* 189–199.

BROWN, L. T., RUDER, V. G., RUDER, J. H., & YOUNG, S. D. (1974). Stimulation seeking and the change seeker index. *Journal of Consulting and Clinical Psychology, 42,* 311.

BROWN, P. J., & HAAS, G. E. (1980). Wilderness recreation experiences: The Rawah case. *Journal of Leisure Research, 12,* 229–241.

BROWN, P. J., HAUTALUOMA, J. E., & MCPHAIL, S. (1977). Colorado deer hunting experiences. In *Transactions, 42nd North American Wildlife and Natural Resources Conference.* Washington, DC: Wildlife Management Institute.

BROWN, T. C., & DANIEL, T. C. (1987). Context effects in perceived environmental quality assessment: Scene selection and landscape quality ratings. *Journal of Environmental Psychology, 7,* 233–250.

BROWNFIELD, C. A. (1966). Optimal stimulation levels of normal and disturbed subjects in sensory deprivation. *Psychologia, 9,* 27–38.

BROWNSTEIN, R., & EASTON, N. (1982). The greenhouse effect: A doomsday scenario? *Amicus Journal, 3,* 10–11.

BRUNSWIK, E. (1956). *Perception and the representative design of psychological experiments.* Berkeley and Los Angeles: University of California Press.

BRYANT, K. J. (1982). Personality correlates of sense of direction and geographical orientation. *Journal of Personality and Social Psychology, 43,* 1318–1324.

BUCHANAN, D. R., GOLDMAN, M., & JUHNKE, R. (1977). Eye contact, sex, and the violation of personal space. *Journal of Social Psychology, 103,* 19–25.

BUCHANAN, D. R., JUHNKE, R., & GOLDMAN, M. (1976). Violation of personal space as a function of sex. *Journal of Social Psychology, 99,* 187–192.

BUCK, J. R., & MCALPINE, D. B. (1981). The effects of atmospheric conditions on people. Technical report, School of Industrial Engineering, Purdue University.

BUDZYNSKI, T. (1985, March). *A brain lateralization model for REST.* Presented at the Second International Conference on Restricted Environmental Stimulation, New Orleans.

BEUCHLEY, R., VAN BRUGGEN, J., & TRUPPI, L. (1972). Heat Island = Death Island? *Environmental Research, 5,* 85–92.

BUHYOFF, G. J., & WELLMAN, J. D. (1979). Seasonality bias in landscape preference research. *Leisure Sciences, 2,* 181–190.

BULLINGER, M. (1989). Psychological effects of air pollution on healthy residents—a time-series approach. *Journal of Environmental Psychology, 9,* 103–118.

BUNTING, T. E., & COUSINS, L. R. (1983). Development and applications of the Children's Environmental Response Inventory. *Journal of Environmental Education, 15,* 3–10.

BURCH, W. R., JR. (1977). Urban children and nature: A summary of research on camping and outdoor recreation. In *Children, nature, and the urban environment.* Upper Darby, PA: U.S. Department of Agriculture, Forest Service, Northeastern Forest Experiment Station.

BURGER, J. M., OAKMAN, J. A., & BALLARD, N. G. (1983). Desire of control and the perception of crowding. *Personality and Social Psychology Bulletin, 9,* 475–479.

BURGESS, J. W. (1981). Development of social spacing in normal and mentally retarded children. *Journal of Nonverbal Behavior, 6,* 89–95.

BURGESS, J. W. (1983). Developmental trends in proxemic spacing behavior between surrounding companions and strangers in casual groups. *Journal of Nonverbal Behavior, 7,* 158–169.

BURGESS, R. L., CLARK, R. N., & HENDEE, J. C. (1971). An experimental analysis of anti-litter procedures. *Journal of Applied Behavior Analysis, 4,* 71–75.

BURGOON, J. K. (1978). A communication model of personal space violations: Explication and an initial test. *Human Communication Research, 4,* 129–142.

BURGOON, J. K. (1983). Nonverbal violations of expectations. In J. M. Wieman & R. P. Harrison (Eds.), *Nonverbal interaction.* Beverly Hills: Sage.

BURGOON, J. K. (1985). Nonverbal signals. In M. L. Knapp & G. R. Miller (Eds.), *Handbook of interpersonal communication.* Beverly Hills: Sage.

BURGOON, J. K., & JONES, S. B. (1976). Toward a theory of personal space expectations and their violations. *Human Communication Research, 2,* 131–146.

BURKE, J. (1985). *The day the universe changed.* Boston: Little, Brown and Co.

BURNS, S. M. (1991). Social psychology and the stimulation of recycling behaviors: The block leader approach. *Journal of Applied Social Psychology, 21,* 611–629.

BURTON, I. (1972). Cultural and personality variables in the perception of natural hazards. In J. F. Wohlwill & D. H. Carson (Eds.), *Environment and the social sciences: Perspectives and applications.* Washington, DC: American Psychological Association.

BURTON, I., KATES, R. W., & WHITE, G. F. (1978). *The environment as hazard.* New York: Oxford University Press.

BUSS, A. H. (1961). *The psychology of aggression.* New York: John Wiley and Sons.

BUTLER, D. L., & BINER, P. M. (1987). Preferred lighting levels: Variability among settings, behaviors, and individuals. *Environment and Behavior, 19,* 695–721.

BUTLER, D. L., & BINER, P. M. (1989). Effects of setting on window preferences and factors associated with those preferences. *Environment and Behavior, 21,* 17–31.

BUTLER, D. L., & STEUERWALD, B. L. (1991). Effects of view and room size on window size preferences made in models. *Environment and Behavior, 23,* 334–358.

BUTLER, R. A., & ALEXANDER, H. M. (1955). Daily patterns of visual exploratory behavior in monkeys. *Journal of Comparative and Physiological Psychology, 48,* 247–249.

BUTTEL, F. H., & FLINN, W. L. (1974). The structure of support for the environmental movement, 1968–1970. *Rural Sociology, 39,* 56–69.

BUTTEL, F. H., & FLINN, W. L. (1978). Social class and mass environmental beliefs: A reconsideration. *Environment and Behavior, 10,* 433–450.

BUTTEL, F. H., MURDOCK, S. H., LEISTRITZ, F. L., & HAMM, R. R. (1987). Rural environments. In E. Zube & G. T. Moore (Eds.), *Advances in environment, behavior, and design* (Vol 1). New York: Plenum.

BUTTERS, N., & BARTON, M. (1970). Effect of parietal lobe damage on the performance of reversible operations in space. *Neuropsychologia, 8,* 205–214.

BYERS, E. S., & CONE, J. D. (1976). Problem: How to reduce student litter. Solution: Use signs and a reward. *Food Management, 11,* 65.

BYRNE, D. (1971). *The attraction paradigm.* New York: Academic Press.

BYRNE, D., ERVIN, C. R., & LAMBERTH, J. (1970). Continuity between the study of attraction and real life computer dating. *Journal of Personality and Social Psychology, 16,* 157–165.

BYRNE, R. W., & SALTER, E. (1983). Distances and directions in the cognitive maps of the blind. *Canadian Journal of Psychology, 37,* 293–299.

CAHN, R., & CAHN, P. (1990). Did Earth Day change the world? *Environment, 32,* No. 7, 16–20, 36–43.

CALHOUN, J. B. (1957). Social welfare as a variable in population dynamics. *Journal of Mammalogy, 33,* 139–159.

CALHOUN, J. B. (1962). Population density and social pathology. *Scientific American, 206,* 139–148.

CALHOUN, J. B. (1973). Death squared: The explosive growth and demise of a mouse population. *Proceedings of the Royal Society of Medicine, 66,* 80–88.

CALLICOT, J. B. (1989). *In defense of the land ethic: Essays in environmental philosophy.* Albany, NY: SUNY Press.

CALVIN, J. S., DEARINGER, J. A., & CURTAIN, M. E. (1972). An attempt at assessing preferences for natural landscapes. *Environment and Behavior, 4,* 447–470.

CAMERON, P., ROBERTSON, D., & ZAKS, J. (1972). Sound pollution, noise pollution, and health: Community parameters. *Journal of Applied Psychology, 56,* 67–74.

CAMPBELL, D. E. (1979). Interior office design and visitor response. *Journal of Applied Psychology, 64,* 648–653.

CAMPBELL, D. E., & BEETS, J. L. (1978). Lunacy and the moon. *Psychological Bulletin, 85,* 1123–1129.

CAMPBELL, D. E., & CAMPBELL, T. A. (1988). A new look at informal communication: The role of the physical environment. *Environment and Behavior, 20,* 211–226.

CAMPBELL, D. T., & STANLEY, J. C. (1966). *Experimental and quasi-experimental designs for research.* Chicago: Rand McNally.

CAMPBELL, J. (1983). Ambient stressors. *Environment and Behavior, 15,* 355–380.

CAMPBELL, S. (1984). A new zoo? *Zoonooz, 55,* 4–7.

CANBY, T. Y. (1986). Are the Soviets ahead in space? *National Geographic, 170* (4), 420–459.

CANBY, T. Y. (1991). After the storm. *National Geographic, 180*(2), 2–35.

CANTER, D., & LEE, K. H. (1974). A non-reactive study of room usage in modern Japanese apartments. In D. Canter & T. Lee (Eds.), *Psychology and the built environment.* New York: Halsted Press.

CAPPELLA, J. N., & GREENE, J. O. (1982). A discrepancy-arousal explanation of mutual influence in expressive behavior in adult and infant-adult interaction. *Communication Monographs, 49,* 89–114.

CAPRONI, V., LEVINE, D., O'NEAL, E., MCDONALD, P., & GARWOOD, G. (1977). Seating position, instructor's eye contact availability, and student participation in a small seminar. *Journal of Social Psychology, 103,* 315–316.

CARP, F. M., ZAWADSKI, R. T., & SHOKRKON, H. (1976). Dimensions of urban environmental quality. *Environment and Behavior, 8,* 239–264.

CARR, A. (1965). The navigation of the green turtle. *Scientific American, 212,* 79–86.

CARR, S. J., & DABBS, J. M. JR. (1974). The effects of lighting, distance, and intimacy of topic on verbal and visual behavior. *Sociometry, 37,* 592–600.

CARRÈRE, S., EVANS, G. W., & STOKOLS, D. (1991). Winter-over stress: Physiological and psychological adaptation to an Antarctic isolated and confined environment. In A. A. Harrison, Y. A. Clearwater, & C. P. McKay (Eds.), *From Antarctica to outer space: Life in isolation and confinement.* New York: Springer-Verlag.

CARROLL, E. N., ZUCKERMAN, M., & VOGEL, W. H. (1982). A test of the optimal level of arousal theory of sensation seeking. *Journal of Personality and Social Psychology, 42,* 572–575.

CASEY, L., & LLOYD, M. (1977). Cost and effectiveness of litter removal procedures in an amusement park. *Environment and Behavior, 9,* 535–546.

CASEY, M. W. (1978). Cognitive mapping by the blind. *Journal of Visual Impairment and Blindness, 72,* 297–301.

CASS, R. C., & EDNEY, J. J. (1978). The commons dilemma: A simulation testing resource visibility and territorial division. *Human Ecology, 6,* 371–386.

CATTON, W. R. JR. (1983). Social and behavioral aspects of carrying capacity in natural environments. In I. Altman & J. F. Wohlwill (Eds.), *Human behavior and environment: Vol. 6. Behavior and the natural environment.* New York: Plenum.

CAVANAUGH, W. J., FARRELL, W. R., HIRTLE, P. W., & WATTERS, B. G. (1962). Speech privacy in buildings. *Journal of the Acoustical Society of America, 34,* 475–492.

CHAIKIN, A. (1984). Sick in space. *Science, 84,* 51–55.

CHAPMAN, C., & RISLEY, T. R. (1974). Anti-litter procedures in an urban high-density area. *Journal of Applied Behavior Analysis, 7,* 377–384.

CHAPMAN, R., MASTERPASQUA, F., & LORE, R. (1976). The effects of crowding during pregnancy on offspring emotional and sexual behavior in rats. *Bulletin of the Psychonomic Society, 7,* 475–477.

CHARLESWORTH, W. R. (1976). Human intelligence as adaptation: An ethological approach. In L. B. Resnick (Ed.), *The nature of intelligence.* Hillsdale, NJ: Erlbaum.

CHARRY, J. M., & HAWKINSHIRE, F. B. (1981). Effects of atmospheric electricity on some substrates of disordered social behavior. *Journal of Personality and Social Psychology, 41,* 185–197.

CHAVIS, D. M., HOGGE, J. H., MCMILLAN, D. W., & WANDERSMAN, A. (1986). Sense of community through Brunswik's lens: A first look. *Journal of Community Psychology, 14,* 24–40.

CHAWLA, L. (1991). Homes for children in a changing society. In E. H. Zube and G. T. Moore (Eds.), *Advances in environment, behavior, and design* (Vol. 3). New York: Plenum.

CHEEK, W. H., & BURCH, W. R. (1976). *The social organization of leisure in human society.* New York: Harper & Row.

CHERULNIK, P. D. (1983). *Behavioral research: Assessing the validity of research findings in psychology.* New York: Harper & Row.

CHERULNIK, P. D., & BAYLESS, J. K. (1986). Person perception in environmental context: The influence of residential settings on impressions of their occupants. *Journal of Social Psychology, 126,* 667–673.

CHERULNIK, P. D., & KOENIG, R. L. (1989). *Perceptions of the workplace and perceptions of the worker: A potentially practical example of the influence of environmental setting on personal identity.* Paper presented at the 20th annual meeting of the Environmental Design Research Association, Black Mountain, North Carolina.

CHERULNIK, P. D., & SOUDERS, S. B. (1984). The social contents of place schemata: People are judged by the places they live and work. *Population and Environment, 7,* 211–233.

CHERULNIK, P. D., & WILDERMAN, S. K. (1986). Symbols of status in urban neighborhoods: Contemporary perceptions of nineteenth-century Boston. *Environment and Behavior, 18,* 604–622.

CHILD, I. L., HANSEN, J. A., & HORNBECK, F. W. (1968). Sex differences in children's color preferences. *Child Development, 39,* 237–247.

CHILD, I. L., & IWAO, S. (1969). Comparison of color preferences in college students of Japan and the United States. *Proceedings of the 77th Annual Convention of the American Psychological Association, 4,* 469–470.

CHOI, S. C., MIRJAFARI, A., & WEAVER, H. B. (1976). The concept of crowding: A critical review and proposal of an alternative approach. *Environment and Behavior, 8,* 345–362.

CHRISTENSEN, D. L., & CARP, F. M. (1987). PEQI-based environmental predictors of the residential satisfaction of older women. *Journal of Environmental Psychology, 7,* 45–64.

CHRISTENSEN, H. H., & CLARK, R. N. (1978). Understanding and controlling vandalism and other rule violations in urban recreation areas. In *Proceedings of the National Urban Forestry Conference.* Washington, DC: U.S. Department of Agriculture, Forest Service.

CHRISTIAN, J. J. (1955). Effect of population size on the adrenal glands and reproductive organs of male white mice. *American Journal of Physiology, 181,* 477–480.

CHRISTIAN, J. J. (1963). The pathology of overpopulation. *Military Medicine, 128,* 571–603.

CHRISTIAN, J. J., & DAVIS, D. E. (1964). Endocrines, behavior, and population. *Science, 146,* 1550–1560.

CHRISTIAN, J. J., FLYGER, V., & DAVIS, D. E. (1960). Factors in the mass mortality of a herd of sika deer, *Cervus nippon. Chesapeake Science, 1,* 79–95.

CHRISTIE, D. J., & GLICKMAN, C. D. (1980). The effects of classroom noise on children: Evidence for sex differences. *Psychology in the Schools, 17,* 405–408.

CIALDINI, R. B., RENO, R. R., & KALLGREN, C. A. (1990). A focus theory of normative conduct: Recycling the concept of norms to reduce littering in public places. *Journal of Personality and Social Psychology, 58,* 1015–1026.

CICCHETTI, C. J. (1972). A multivariate statistical analysis of wilderness users in the United States. In J. V. Krutilla (Ed.), *Natural environments: Studies in theoretical and applied analysis.* Baltimore: Johns Hopkins University Press.

CICCHETTI, C. J., & SMITH, V. K. (1973). Congestion, quality deterioration, and optimal use: Wilderness recreation in the Spanish Peaks primitive area. *Social Science Research, 2,* 15–30.

CLARK, R. N., BURGESS, R. L., & HENDEE, J. C. (1972). The development of anti-litter behavior in a forest campground. *Journal of Applied Behavior Analysis, 7,* 377–383.

CLARK, R. N., HENDEE, J. C., & BURGESS, R. L. (1972). The experimental control of littering. *Journal of Environmental Education, 4,* 2.

CLAWSON, M., & KNETSCH, J. L. (1966). *Economics of outdoor recreation.* Baltimore: Johns Hopkins University Press.

CLEARWATER, Y. A., & COSS, R. G. (1991). Functional esthetics to enhance well-being in isolated and confined settings. In A. A. Harrison, Y. A. Clearwater, & C. P. McKay (Eds.), *From Antarctica to outer space: Life in isolation and confinement.* New York: Springer-Verlag.

CLIFFORD, W., HEATON, T., VOSS, P., & FUGUITT, G. (1985). The rural elderly in demographic perspective. In R. Coward & G. Lee (Eds.), *The elderly in rural society: Every fourth elder.* New York: Springer-Verlag.

COATES, J. (1991, April 21). Crowds threaten U.S. park system. *Chicago Tribune, 1,* pp. 1, 14.

COCHRAN, C. D., HALE, W. D., & HISSAM, C. P. (1984). Personal space requirements in indoor vs. outdoor locations. *Journal of Personality, 111,* 137–140.

COCHRAN, C. D., & URBANCZYK, S. (1982). The effect of availability of vertical space on personal space. *Journal of Psychology, 111,* 137–140.

COE, J. C. (1985). Design and perception: Making the zoo experience real. *Zoo Biology, 4,* 197–208.

COFFIN, D., & STOKINGER, H. (1977). Biological effects of air pollutants. In A. C. Stern (Ed.), *Air pollution* (3rd ed.). New York: Academic Press.

COHEN, R. (ED.) (1985). *The development of spatial cognition.* Hillsdale, NJ: Erlbaum.

COHEN, S. (1973). Property destruction: Motives and meanings. In C. Ward (Ed.), *Vandalism.* New York: Van Nostrand Reinhold.

COHEN, S., & TROSTLE, S. L. (1988). Choice and stability of young children's preferences for physical-environmental setting characteristics. *Perceptual and Motor Skills, 66,* 187–191.

COHEN, S., & TROSTLE, S. L. (1990). Young children's preferences for school-related physical-environmental setting characteristics. *Environment and Behavior, 22,* 753–766.

COHEN, S. A. (1978). Environmental load and the allocation of attention. In A. Baum, J. E. Singer, & S. Valins (Eds.), *Advances in environmental psychology* (Vol. 1). Hillsdale, NJ: Erlbaum.

COHEN, S. A. (1980). Aftereffects of stress on human performance and social behavior: A review of research and theory. *Psychological Bulletin, 88,* 82–108.

COHEN, S. A., EVANS, G. W., KRANTZ, D. S., & STOKOLS, D. (1980). Physiological, motivational, and cognitive effects of aircraft noise on children. *American Psychologist, 35,* 231–243.

COHEN, S. A., EVANS, G. W., KRANTZ, D. S., STOKOLS, D., & KELLY, S. (1981). Aircraft noise and children: Longitudinal and cross-sectional evidence on adaptation to noise and the effectiveness of noise abatement. *Journal of Pesonality and Social Psychology, 40,* 331–345.

COHEN, S. A., EVANS, G. W., STOKOLS, D., & KRANTZ D. (1986). *Behavior, health, and environmental stress.* New York: Plenum.

COHEN, S. A., GLASS, D. C., & SINGER, J. E. (1973). Apartment noise, auditory discrimination, and reading ability in children. *Journal of Experimental Social Psychology, 9,* 407–422.

COHEN, S. A., & SPACAPAN, S. (1978). The aftereffects of stress: An attentional interpretation. *Environmental Psychology and Nonverbal Behavior, 3,* 43–57.

COHEN, S. A., TYRRELL, D. A. J., & SMITH, A. P. (1991). Psychological stress and susceptibility to the common cold. *New England Journal of Medicine, 325,* 606–612.

COHEN, S. A., & WEINSTEIN, N. (1980). Nonauditory effects of noise on behavior and health. *Journal of Social Issues, 37,* 36–70.

COHEN, S. A., & WEINSTEIN, N. (1982). Nonauditory effects of noise on behavior and health. In G. W. Evans (Ed.), *Environmental Stress.* New York: Cambridge University Press.

COHEN, S. A., & WILLIAMSON, G. M. (1991). Stress and infectious disease in humans. *Psychological Bulletin, 109,* 5–24.

COHEN, S. A., & WILLS, T. A. (1985). Stress, social support, and the buffering hypothesis. *Psychological Bulletin, 98,* 310–357.

COHEN, S. L., & COHEN, R. (1985). The role of activity in spatial cognition. In R. Cohen (Ed.), *The development of spatial cognition.* Hillsdale, NJ: Erlbaum.

COLLIGAN, M. J., & MURPHY, L. R. (1982). A review of mass psychogenic illness in work settings. In M. J. Colligan, J. W. Pennebaker, & L. R. Murphy (Eds.), *Mass psychogenic illness.* Hillsdale, NJ: Erlbaum.

COLLINS, B. L. (1975). Windows and people: A literature survey. Psychological reaction to environments with and without windows. *NSB Building Science Series, 70,* 88.

COLLINS, D. L., BAUM, A., & SINGER, J. E. (1983). Coping with chronic stress at Three Mile Island: Psychological and biochemical evidence. *Health Psychology, 2,* 149–166.

COLMAN, R., FRANKEL, F., RITVO, E., & FREEMAN, B. (1976). The effects of fluorescent and incandescent illumination upon repetitive behavior in autistic children. *Journal of Autism and Childhood Schizophrenia, 6,* 157–162.

COMMONER, B. (1972). *The closing circle: Nature, man, and technology.* New York: Knopf.

CONE, J. D., & HAYES, S. C. (1980). *Environmental problems/Behavioral solutions.* Pacific Grove, CA: Brooks/Cole.

CONNERS, M. M., HARRISON, A. A., & AKINS, F. R. (1986). Psychology and the resurgent space program. *American Psychologist, 41,* 906–913.

CONROY, J., & SUNDSTROM, E. (1977). Territorial dominance in a dyadic conversation as a function of similarity of opinion. *Journal of Personality and Social Psychology, 35,* 570–576.

COOK, C. C. (1988). Components of neighborhood satisfaction: Responses from urban and suburban single-parent women. *Environment and Behavior, 20,* 115–149.

COOK, M. (1970). Experimentation on orientation and proxemics. *Human Relations, 23,* 61–76.

COOK, T., & CAMPBELL, D. (1979). *Quasi-experimentation.* Boston: Houghton Mifflin.

COOPER, C. (1976). The house as symbol of the self. In H. M. Proshansky, W. H. Ittelson, & L. G. Rivlin (Eds.), *Environmental psychology: People and their physical settings.* New York: Holt, Rinehart, & Winston.

CORCORAN, D. W. J. (1962). Noise and loss of sleep. *Quarterly Journal of Experimental Psychology, 14,* 178–182.

CORNELIUS, P. E. (1991). Life in Antarctica. In A. A. Harrison, Y. A. Clearwater, & C. P. McKay (Eds.), *From Antarctica to outer space: Life in isolation and confinement.* New York: Springer-Verlag.

COTTERELL, J. L. (1991). The emergence of adolescent territories in a large urban lesiure environment. *Journal of Environmental Psychology, 11,* 25–41.

COTTON, J. L. (1986). Ambient temperature and violent crime. *Journal of Applied Social Psychology, 16,* 786–801.

COUCH, J. V., GARBER, T., & KARPUS, L. (1978). Response maintenance and paper recycling. *Journal of Environmental Systems, 8,* 302–310.

COUGHLIN, R. E. (1976). The perception and valuation of water quality: A review of research method and findings. In K. H. Craik & E. H. Zube (Eds.), *Perceiving environmental quality: Research and applications.* New York: Plenum.

COURNEYA, K. S., & CARRON, A. V. (1991). Effects of travel and length of home stand/road trip on the home advantage. *Journal of Sport and Exercise Psychology, 13,* 42–49.

COURSEY, R. D., BUCHSBAUM, M., & FRANKEL, B. L. (1975). Personality measures and evoked responses in chronic insomniacs. *Journal of Abnormal Psychology, 84,* 239–249.

COUSINS, J. H., SIEGEL, A. W., & MAXWELL, S. E. (1983). Way finding and cognitive mapping in large scale environments: A test of a developmental model. *Journal of Experimental Child Psychology, 35,* 1–20.

COUTTS, L. M., & LEDDEN, M. (1977). Nonverbal compensatory reactions to changes in interpersonal proximity. *Journal of Social Psychology, 102–103,* 283–290.

COX, V. C., PAULUS, P. B., MCCAIN, G., & KARLOVAC, M. (1982). The relationship between crowding and health. In A. Baum & J. Singer (Eds.), *Advances in environmental psychology* (vol. 4). Hillsdale, NJ: Erlbaum.

COZBY, P. C. (1989). *Methods in behavioral research* (4th ed.). Mountain View, CA: Mayfield Publishing.

CRAIK, K. H. (1983). The psychology of the large scale environment. In N. R. Feimer & E. S. Geller (Eds.), *Environmental psychology: Directions and perspective.* New York: Praeger.

CRAIK, K. H., & FEIMER, N. R. (1987). Environmental assessment. In D. Stokols & I. Altman (Eds.), *Handbook of environmental psychology* (Vol. 2). New York: John Wiley and Sons.

CRAIK, K. H., & ZUBE, E. H. (1976). The development of perceived environmental quality indices. In K. H. Craik & E. H. Zube (Eds.), *Perceiving environmental quality: Research and applications.* New York: Plenum.

CRITCHLEY, M. (1955). The idea of a presence. *Acta Psychiatrica et Neurologica Scandinavia, 30,* 155–168.

CROOK, M.A., & LANGDON, F. J. (1974). The effects of aircraft noise on schools in the vicinity of the London Airport. *Journal of Sound and Vibration, 34,* 241–248.

CROUCH, A., & NIMRAN, V. (1989). Perceived facilitators and inhibitors of work performance in an office environment. *Environment and Behavior, 21,* 206–226.

CROWNFIELD, D. (1973). The curse of Abel: An essay in biblical ecology. *The North American Review,* Summer, 58–63.

CRUMP, S. L., NUNES, D. L. & CROSSMAN, E. K. (1977). The effects of litter on littering behavior in a forest environment. *Environment and Behavior, 9,* 137–146.

CSIKSZENTMIHALYI, M., & ROCHBERG-HALTON, E. (1981). *The meaning of things: Domestic symbols and the self.* Cambridge, England: Cambridge University Press.

CULHANE, P. J. (1981). *Public land politics.* Baltimore: Johns Hopkins University Press.

CUNNINGHAM, M. R. (1979). Weather, mood, and helping behavior: Quasi experiments with the sunshine Samaritan. *Journal of Personality and Social Psychology, 37,* 1947–1956.

CURRAN, J. P., & CATTELL, R. B. (1976). Manual for the Eight State Questionnaire. *Multivariate Experimental Clinical Research, 7,* 113–132.

CUTTLE, K. (1983). *People and windows in workplaces.* Paper presented at the Conference on People and the Physical Environment Research, Wellington, New Zealand.

DABBS, J. M. (1971). Physical closeness and negative feelings. *Psychonomic Science, 23,* 141–143.

DABBS, J. M., FULLER, J. P. H., & CARR, T. S. (1973). Personal space when "cornered": College students and prison inmates. *Proceedings of the 81st Annual Convention of the American Psychological Association, 8,* 213–214.

DABBS, J. M. JR., & STOKES, N. A. (1975). Beauty is power: The use of space on the sidewalk. *Sociometry, 38,* 551–557.

DAITZMAN, R. J., ZUCKERMAN, M., SAMMELWITZ, T., & GANJAM, V. (1978). Sensation seeking and gonadal hormones. *Journal of Biosocial Science, 10,* 401–408.

DANIEL, T. C., & BOLSTER, R. S. (1976). *Measuring landscape aesthetics: The scenic beauty estimation method.* (Research paper No. RM–167). Ft. Collins, CO: U.S. Department of Agriculture, Rocky Mountain Forest and Range Experiment Station.

DANIELS, S. (1988). The political iconography of woodland in later Georgian England. In D. Cosgrove & S. Daniels (Eds.), *The iconography of landscape.* Cambridge, England: Cambridge University Press.

DANILOV, V. J. (1982). Chicago's fountain of discovery. *Children Today, 11,* 14–16.

DARLEY, J. M. (1978). Energy conservation techniques as innovations and their diffusion. *Energy and Buildings, 1,* 339–343.

DART, F. E., & PRADHAM, P. L. (1967). The cross-cultural teaching of science. *Science, 155,* 649–656.

D'ATRI, D. A. (1975). Psychophysiological responses to crowding. *Environment and Behavior, 7,* 237–251.

D'ATRI, D. A., & OSTFELD, A. (1975). Crowding: Its effects on the elevation of blood pressure in a prison setting. *Preventive Medicine, 4,* 550–566.

DAVES, W. F., & SWAFFER, P. W. (1971). Effect of room size on critical interpersonal distance. *Perceptual and Motor Skills, 33,* 926.

DAVIDSON, L. M., BAUM, A., & COLLINS, D. L. (1982). Stress and control-related problems at Three Mile Island. *Journal of Applied Social Psychology, 12,* 349–359.

DAVIES, N. B. (1982). Territory. In D. McFarland (Ed.), *The Oxford companion to animal behavior.* Oxford: Oxford University Press.

DAVIS, G. E. (1976, April). *Designing for high density.* Paper presented at the meeting of the Eastern Psychological Association, New York.

DAVIS, G. E., & BAUM, A. (1975). Role of social interaction in tall buildings. In S. Margolis (Chair), *Social-psychological research on high rise residential environments.* Symposium presented at the meeting of the American Psychological Association, Chicago.

DAVIS, G. J., & MEYER, R. K. (1973). FSH and LH in snowshoe hare during the increasing phase of the 10 year cycle. *General Comparative Endocrinology, 20,* 53–60.

DAVIS, T. R. V. (1984). The influence of the physical environment in offices. *Academy of Management Review, 9,* 271–283.

DAWES, R. M. (1973). The commons dilemma game: An N-person mixed-motive game with a dominating strategy for defection. *ORI Research Bulletin, 13,* 1–12.

DAWES, R. M. (1980). Social dilemmas. *Annual Review of Psychology, 31,* 169–193.

DEAN, L. M., PUGH, W. M., & GUNDERSON, E. K. E. (1976). Spatial and perceptual components of crowding: Effects on health and satisfaction. In S. Saegert (Ed.), *Crowding in real environments.* Beverly Hills: Sage.

DEAN, L. M., WILLIS, F. N., & LAROCCO, J. M. (1976). Invasion of personal space as a function of age, sex, and race. *Psychological Reports, 38,* 959–965.

DEFRONZO, J. (1984). Climate and crime: Tests of an FBI assumption. *Environment and Behavior, 16,* 185–210.

DEGROOT, I. (1967). Trends in public attitudes toward air pollution. *Journal of the Air Pollution Control Association, 17,* 679–681.

DELLINGER, R. W. (1979). Jet roar: Health problems take off near airports. *Human Behavior, 8,* 50–51.

DERWIN, C. W., & PIPER, J. B. (1988). The African Rock Kopje Exhibit: Evaluation and interpretive elements. *Environment and Behavior, 20,* 435–451.

DESLAURIERS, B. C., & EVERETT, P. B. (1977). Effects of intermittent and continuous token reinforcement on bus ridership. *Journal of Applied Psychology, 62,* 369–375.

DESOR, J. A. (1972). Toward a psychological theory of crowding. *Journal of*

Personality and Social Psychology, 21, 79–83.

DEUDNEY, D. (1991). Environment and security: Muddled thinking. *The Bulletin of the Atomic Scientists, 47,* No. 3, 17–21.

DEVLIN, A. S. (1980). Housing for the elderly: Cognitive considerations. *Environment and Behavior, 12,* 451–466.

DEW, M. A., BROMET, E. J., & SCHULBURG, H. C. (1987). Mental health effects of the Three Mile Island nuclear reactor restart. *American Journal of Psychiatry, 144,* 1074–1077.

DIAMOND, W. D., & LOEWY, B. Z. (1991). Effects of probabilistic rewards on recycling attitudes and behavior. *Journal of Applied Social Psychology, 21,* 1590–1607.

DICKSON, D. (1987). Adjusting to an aging population. *Science, 236,* 772–773.

DIGON, E., & BLOCK, H. (1966). Suicides and climatology. *Archives of Environmental Health, 12,* 279–286.

DITTON, R. B., FEDLER, A. J., & GRAEFE, A. R. (1983). Factors contributing to perceptions of recreational crowding. *Leisure Sciences, 5,* 273–287.

DONNERSTEIN, E., & WILSON, D. W. (1976). The effects of noise and perceived control upon ongoing and subsequent aggressive behavior. *Journal of Personality and Social Psychology, 34,* 774–781.

DOOLEY, B. B. (1975). Crowding stress: The effects of social density on men with "close" or "far" personal space. *Man-Environment Systems, 5,* 306.

DORFMAN, P. W. (1979). Measurement and meaning of recreation satisfaction. *Environment and Behavior, 11,* 483–510.

DOSEY, M., & MEISELS, M. (1969). Personal space and self-protection. *Journal of Personality and Social Psychology, 11,* 93–97.

DOVEY, K. (1985). Home and homelessness. In I. Altman & C. Werner (Eds.), *Home environments.* New York: Plenum.

DOWNS, R. M., & STEA, D. (1973). Cognitive maps and spatial behavior: Process and products. In R. M. Downs & D. Stea (Eds.), *Image and environment: Cognitive mapping and spatial behavior.* Chicago: Aldine.

DOWNS, R. M., & STEA, D. (1977). *Maps in minds: Reflections on cognitive mapping.* New York: Harper & Row.

DRICKAMER, L. C., & VESSEY, S. H. (1982). *Animal behavior: Concepts, processes, and methods.* Boston: Willard Grant Press.

DRIVER, B. L. (1972). Potential contributions of psychology to recreation resource management. In J. Wohlwill and D. H. Carson (Eds.), *Environment and the social sciences: Perspectives and applications.* Washington, DC: American Psychological Association.

DRIVER, B. L., & BROWN, P. J. (1978). The opportunity spectrum concept and behavioral information in outdoor recreation resource supply inventories: A rationale. In H. G. Lund, V. J. LaBau, P. F. Folliott, & D. W. Robinson (Technical Coordinators), *Proceedings, Integrated Inventories of Renewable Natural Resources Workshop.* Ft. Collins, CO: U.S. Department of Agriculture, Forest Service, Rocky Mountain Forest and Range Experiment Station.

DRIVER, B. L., & COOKSEY, R. W. (1977). Preferred psychological outcomes of recreational fishing. In *Catch-and-release fishing as a management tool: A national sport fishing symposium.* Arcata, CA: Humboldt State University.

DRIVER, B. L., & KNOPF, R. C. (1977). Personality, outdoor recreation, and expected consequences. *Environment and Behavior, 9,* 169–193.

DUBROV, A. P. (1978). *The geomagnetic field and life: Geomagnetobiology.* New York: Plenum.

DUKE, M. P., & NOWICKI, S. JR. (1972). A new measure and social-learning model for interpersonal distance. *Journal of Experimental Research in Personality, 6,* 119–132.

DUNCAN, J. S. (1985). The house as symbol of social structure. In I. Altman & C. M. Werner (Eds.), *Home environments.* New York: Plenum.

DURDAN, C. A., REEDER, G. D., & HECHT, P. R. (1985). Litter in a university cafeteria: Demographic data and the use of prompts as an intervention strategy. *Environment and Behavior, 3,* 387–404.

EDELSTEIN, M. R. (1988). *Contaminated communities: The social and psychological impacts of residential toxic exposure.* San Diego: Westview.

EDNEY, J. J. (1972). Property, possession, and permanence: A field study in human territoriality. *Journal of Applied Social Psychology, 2,* 275–282.

EDNEY, J. J. (1975). Territoriality and control: A field experiment. *Journal of Personality and Social Psychology, 31,* 1108–1115.

EDNEY, J. J. (1979). The nuts game: A concise commons dilemma analog. *Environmental Psychology and Nonverbal Behavior, 3,* 252–254.

EDNEY, J. J., & JORDAN-EDNEY, N. L. (1974). Territorial spacing on a beach. *Sociometry, 37,* 92–104.

EDNEY, J. J., WALKER, C. A., & JORDAN, N. L. (1976). Is there reactance in personal space? *Journal of Social Psychology, 100,* 207–217.

EDWARDS, D. J. A. (1972). Approaching the unfamiliar: A study of human interaction distances. *Journal of Behavioral Sciences, 1,* 249–250.

EFRAN, M. G., & CHEYNE, J. A. (1974). Affective concomitants of the invasion of shared space: Behavioral, physiological, and verbal indicators. *Journal of Personality and Social Psychology, 29,* 219–226.

EIBL-EIBESFELDT, I. (1988). The biological foundations of aesthetics. In I. Rentschler, B. Herzberger, & D. Epstein (Eds.), *Beauty and the brain: Biological aspects of aesthetics.* Boston: Birkhauser Verlag.

EINOLANDER, J. C. (1976). Vandalism at "Red Rock." In *Vandalism and outdoor recreation.* Berkeley, CA: U.S. Department of Agriculture, Pacific Southwest Forest and Range Experiment Station.

EISER, J. R., & HOEPFNER, F. (1991). Accidents, disease, and the greenhouse effect: Effects of response categories on estimates of risk. *Basic and Applied Social Psychology, 12,* 195–210.

ELIOVSON, S. (1978). The Japanese garden. In S. Kaplan & R. Kaplan (Eds.), *Humanscape: Environments for people.* North Scituate, MA: Duxbury Press.

ELLIS, L. (1991). Monoamine oxidase and criminality: Identifying an apparent biological marker for antisocial behavior. *Journal of Research in Crime and Delinquency, 28,* 227–251.

ELLSWORTH, P. C., & CARLSMITH, J. M. (1968). Effects of eye contact and verbal content on affective response to a dyadic interaction. *Journal of Personality and Social Psychology, 10,* 15–20.

ELLSWORTH, P. C., FRIEDMAN, H. S., PERLICK, D., & HOYT, M. E. (1978). Some effects of gaze on subjects motivated to seek out or to avoid social comparison. *Journal of Experimental Social Psychology, 14,* 69–87.

EMLEN, S. T. (1975). The stellar-orientation system of a migratory bird. *Scientific American, 233,* 102–111.

ENVIRONMENTAL PROTECTION AGENCY (EPA) (1972). *Report to the presi-*

dent and congress on noise. Washington, DC: U.S. Government Printing Office.

EPSTEIN, Y. M., & KARLIN, R. A. (1975). Effects of acute experimental crowding. *Journal of Applied Social Psychology, 5,* 34–53.

ESTER, P. A., & WINETT, R. A. (1982). Toward more effective antecedent strategies for environmental programs. *Journal of Environmental Systems, 11,* 201–221.

EVANS, G. W. (1978). Human spatial behavior: The arousal model. In A. Baum & Y. M. Epstein (Eds.), *Human response to crowding.* Hillsdale, NJ: Erlbaum.

EVANS, G. W. (1979). Behavioral and physiological consequences of crowding in humans. *Journal of Applied Social Psychology, 9,* 27–46.

EVANS, G. W. (1980). Environmental cognition. *Psychological Bulletin, 88,* 259–287.

EVANS, G. W., BRENNAN, P. L., SKORPANICH, M. A., & HELD, D. (1984). Cognitive mapping and elderly adults: Verbal and location memory for urban landmarks. *Journal of Gerontology, 39,* 452–457.

EVANS, G. W., & CARRÈRE, S. (1991). Traffic congestion, perceived control, and psychological stress among urban bus drivers. *Journal of Applied Psychology, 76,* 658–663.

EVANS, G. W., & COHEN, S. A. (1987). Environmental stress. In D. Stokols & I. Altman (Eds.), *Handbook of environmental psychology* (Vol. 1). New York: John Wiley and Sons.

EVANS, G. W., & HOWARD, R. B. (1973). Personal space. *Psychological Bulletin, 80,* 334–344.

EVANS, G. W., & JACOBS, S. V. (1981). Air pollution and human behavior. *Journal of Social Issues, 37,* 95–125.

EVANS, G. W., JACOBS, S. V., & FRAGER, N. B. (1982). Behavioral responses to air pollution. In A. Baum & J. E. Singer (Eds.), *Advances in environmental psychology* (Vol. 4). Hillsdale, NJ: Erlbaum.

EVANS, G. W., MARRERO, D. G., & BUTLER, P. A. (1981). Environmental learning and cognitive mapping. *Environment and Behavior, 13,* 83–104.

EVANS, G. W., PALSANE, M. N., LEPORE, S. J., & MARTIN, J. (1989). Residential density and psychological health: The mediating effects of social support. *Journal of Personality and Social Psychology, 57,* 994–999.

EVANS, G. W., & PEZDEK, K. (1980). Cognitive mapping: Knowledge of real-world distance and location information. *Journal of Experimental Psychology: Human Learning and Memory, 6,* 13–24.

EVANS, G. W., & TAFALLA, R. (1987). Measurement of environmental annoyance. In H. S. Koelega (Ed.), *Environmental annoyance: Characterization, measurement, and control.* Amsterdam: Elsevier Science Publishers.

EVANS, G. W., & WOOD, D. (1981). Assessment of environmental aesthetics in scenic highway corridors. *Environment and Behavior, 12,* 255–273.

EVERETT, P. B., HAYWARD, S. C., & MEYERS, A. W. (1974). The effects of a token reinforcement procedure on bus ridership. *Journal of Applied behavior Analysis, 7,* 1–9.

EWERT, J. P. (1974). The neural basis of visually guided behavior. *Scientific American, 230,* 34–42.

EWERT, J. P. (1980). *Neuro-ethology.* New York: Springer-Verlag.

EYSENCK, H. J. (1967). *The biological basis of personality.* Springfield, IL: Charles C Thomas.

EYSENCK, M. W. (1982). *Attention and arousal.* New York: Springer-Verlag.

FARRENKOPF, T., & ROTH, V. (1980). The university faculty office as an environment. *Environment and Behavior, 12,* 467–477.

FATHY, H. (1973). *Architecture for the poor.* Chicago: University of Chicago Press.

FELDMAN, R. A. (1990). Settlement identity: Psychological bonds with home places in a mobile society. *Environment and Behavior, 22,* 183–229.

FELIPE, N., & SOMMER, R. (1966). Invasions of personal space. *Social Problems, 14,* 206–214.

FELLER, R. A. (1968). Effect of varying corridor illumination on noise level in a residential hall. *Journal of College Student Personnel, 9,* 150–152.

FERGUSON, G. S., & WEISMAN, G. D. (1986). Alternative approaches to the assessment of employee satisfaction with the office environment. In J. D. Wineman (Ed.), *Behavioral issues in office design.* New York: Van Nostrand Reinhold.

FESTINGER, L. (1957). *A theory of cognitive dissonance.* Evanston, IL: Row, Peterson.

FESTINGER, L., SCHACHTER, S., & BACK, K. (1950). *Social pressures in informal groups.* Stanford, CA: Stanford University Press.

FIELD, D. R., & MARTINSON, K. (1986). Water-based recreation participation. In the President's Commission on Americans Outdoors (Ed.), *A literature review.* Washington, DC: U.S. Government Printing Office.

FIGLER, M. H., & EVENSEN, J. (1979). Experimentally produced prior residence effect in male convict cichlids: The role of initial proximity to territorial markers. *Bulletin of the Psychonomic Society, 13,* 130–132.

FILIPOVITCH, A. J., JULIAR, K., & ROSS, K. D. (1981). Children's drawings of their home environment. In A. E. Ostberg, C. P. Tiernan, & R. A. Findlay (Eds.), *Design research interactions.* Washington, DC: Environmental Design Research Association.

FINE, T. E., & TURNER, J. W. (1982). The effect of brief restricted environmental stimulation therapy in the treatment of essential hypertension. *Behavior Research and Therapy, 20,* 567–570.

FINLAY, T., JAMES, L. R., & MAPLE, T. L. (1988). People's perceptions of animals: The influence of zoo environment. *Environment and Behavior, 20,* 508–528.

FINNEGAN, M. C., & SOLOMON, L. Z. (1981). Work attitudes in windowed vs. windowless environments. *Journal of Social Psychology, 115,* 291–292.

FINNIE, W. C. (1973). Field experiments and litter control. *Environment and Behavior, 5,* 123–143.

FISCHER, C. S. (1976). *The urban experience.* New York: Harcourt, Brace, Jovanovich.

FISCHER, C. S. (1982). *To dwell among friends: Personal networks in town and city.* Chicago: University of Chicago Press.

FISCHOFF, B., SVENSON, O., & SLOVIC, P. (1987). Active responses to environmental hazards: Perceptions and decision making. In D. Stokols & I. Altman (Eds.), *Handbook of environmental psychology* (Vol. 2). New York: John Wiley and Sons.

FISHBEIN, M., & AJZEN, I. (1975). *Belief, attitude, intention, and behavior.* Reading, MA: Addison-Wesley.

FISHER, J. D., & BARON, R. M. (1982). An equity-based model of vandalism. *Population and Environment, 5,* 182–200.

FISHER, J. D., BELL, P. A., & BAUM, A. (1984). *Environmental psychology* (2nd ed.). New York: Holt, Rinehart, & Winston.

FISHER, J. D., & BYRNE, D. (1975). Too close for comfort: Sex differences in response to invasions of personal space. *Journal of Personality and Social Psychology, 32,* 15–21.

FISKE, D. W., & MADDI, S. R. (1961). *Functions of varied experience.* Homewood, IL: Dorsey Press.

FLEMING, I., BAUM, A., & WEISS, L. (1987). Social density and perceived control as mediators of crowding stress in high-density residential neighborhoods. *Journal of Personality and Social Psychology, 52,* 899–906.

FLEMING, M., & LEVIE, W. H. (1978). *Instructional message design: Principles from the behavioral sciences.* Bloomington, IN: Indiana University Educational Technology Publications.

FLETCHER, J. F. (1980). Spatial representation in blind children, 1: Development compared to sighted children. *Journal of Visual Impairment and Blindness, 74,* 381–385.

FLETCHER, J. F. (1981a). Spatial representation in blind children, 2: Effects of task variations. *Journal of Visual Impairment and Blindness, 75,* 1–3.

FLETCHER, J. F. (1981b). Spatial representation in blind children, 3: Effects of individual differences. *Journal of Visual Impairment and Blindness, 75,* 46–49.

FLORIN, P., & WANDERSMAN, A. (1983). A psychosocial perspective on neigh borhood conservation. In N. R. Feimer & E. S. Geller (Eds.), *Environmental psychology: Directions and perspectives.* New York: Praeger.

FOLEY, J. E., & COHEN, A. J. (1984). Working mental representations of the environment. *Environment and Behavior, 16,* 713–729.

FOLK, G. E. (1974). *Textbook of environmental physiology.* Philadelphia: Lea and Febiger.

FOLKMAN, S., LAZARUS, R., PIMLEY, S., & NOVACEK, J. (1987). Age differences in stress and coping processes. *Psychology and Aging, 2,* 171–184.

FOOT, H. C., CHAPMAN, A. J., & SMITH, J. R. (1977). Friendship and social responsiveness in boys and girls. *Journal of Personality and Social Psychology, 35,* 401–411.

FORD, J. G., & GRAVES, J. R. (1977). Differences between Mexican-American and white children in interpersonal distance and social touching. *Perceptual and Motor Skills, 45,* 779–785.

FORESTER, W. S. (1988). Solid waste: There's a lot more coming. *Environmental Protection Agency Journal, 14,* 11–12.

FORGAYS, D. G., & BELINSON, M. J. (1986). Is flotation isolation a relaxing environment? *Journal of Environmental Psychology, 6,* 19–34.

FORGAYS, D. G., FORGAYS, D. K., PUDVAH, M., & WRIGHT, D. (1991). A direct comparison of the 'wet' and 'dry' flotation environments. *Journal of Environmental Psychology, 11,* 179–187.

FORSTON, R. F., & LARSON, C. V. (1968). The dynamics of space: An experimental study in proxemic behavior among Latin Americans and North Americans. *Journal of Communication, 18,* 109–116.

FOSTER, H. D. (1980). *Disaster planning: The preservation of life and property.* New York: Springer-Verlag.

FOUSHEE, H. C. (1982, November). The role of communications, sociophysiological, and personality factors in the maintenance of crew coordination. *Aviation, Space, and Environmental Medicine, 53,* 1062–1066.

FOX, J. G. (1983). Industrial music. In D. J. Osborne & M. M. Gruneberg (Eds.), *The physical environment at work.* New York: John Wiley and Sons.

FOX, W. F. (1967). Human performance in the cold. *Human Factors, 9,* 203–220.

FRANCIS, M. (1987). Urban open spaces. In E. H. Zube & G. T. Moore (Eds.), *Advances in environment, behavior, and design* (Vol. 1). New York: Plenum.

FREEDMAN, J. L. (1971). The crowd—maybe not so madding after all. *Psychology Today, 9,* 58–62.

FREEDMAN, J. L. (1975). *Crowding and behavior.* New York: Viking Press.

FREEDMAN, J. L. (1979). Reconciling apparent differences between the responses of humans and other animals to crowding. *Psychological Review, 86,* 80–85.

FREEDMAN, J. L., BIRSKY, J., & CAVOUKIAN, A. (1980). Environmental determinants of behavioral contagion: Density and number. *Basic and Applied Social Psychology, 1,* 155–161.

FREEDMAN, J. L., KLEVANSKY, S., & EHRLICH, P. I. (1971). The effect of crowding on human task performance. *Journal of Applied Social Psychology, 1,* 7–26.

FREEDMAN, J. L., LEVY, A., BUCHANAN, R., & PRICE, J. (1972). Crowding and human aggressiveness. *Journal of Experimental Social Psychology, 8,* 528–548.

FREEDMAN, J. L., & PERLICK, D. (1979). Crowding, contagion, and laughter. *Journal of Experimental Social Psychology, 15,* 295–303.

FREIMARK, S., WENER, R., PHILLIPS, D., & KORBER, E. (1984, August). *Estimation of crowding, number and density for human and non-human stimuli.* Poster at the annual meeting of the American Psychological Association, Toronto.

FREUDENBURG, W. R., & JONES, T. R. (1991). Attitude and stress in the presence of technological risk: A test of the Supreme Court hypothesis. *Social Forces, 69,* 1143–1168.

FRIED, M. (1963). Grieving for a lost home. In L. J. Duhl (Ed.), *The urban condition.* New York: Simon and Schuster.

FRIED, M. (1982). Residential attachment: Sources of residential and community satisfaction. *Journal of Social Issues, 38,* 107–119.

FRISANCHO, A. R. (1979). *Human adaptation.* St. Louis: Mosby.

FRY, A. M., & WILLIS, F. N. (1971). Invasion of personal space as a function of the age of the invader. *Psychological Record, 21,* 385–389.

FULKER, D., EYSENCK, S. B. G., & ZUCKERMAN, M. (1980). A genetic and environmental analysis of sensation seeking. *Journal of Research in Personality, 14,* 261–281.

FURBY, L. (1978). Possessions: Toward a theory of their meaning and function throughout the life cycle. In P. B. Baltes (Ed.), *Life span development and behavior* (Vol. 1). New York: Academic Press.

FURST, P. T. (1977). "High states" in culture-historical perspective. In N. W. Zinberg (Ed.), *Alternate states of consciousness.* New York: The Free Press.

GALE, N., GOLLEDGE, R. G., PELLEGRINO, J. W., & DOHERTY, S. (1990). The acquisition and integration of route knowledge in an unfamiliar neighborhood. *Journal of Environmental Psychology, 10,* 3–25.

GALLE, O. R., GOVE, W. R., & MCPHERSON, J. M. (1972). Population density and pathology: What are the relationships for man? *Science, 176,* 23-30.

GALTON, F. (1883). *Inquiries into human faculty and its development.* London: Macmillan.

GANS, H. J. (1962). *The urban villagers.* New York: The Free Press.

GANZHORN, J. U. (1990). Towards the map of the homing pigeon? *Animal Behaviour, 40,* 65–78.

GARABINO, J. (1980). Some thoughts on school size and its effects on adolescent development. *Journal of Youth and Adolescence, 9,* 19–31.

GÄRLING, T., BÖÖK, A., & LINDBERG, E. (1985). Adults' memory representations of the spatial properties of their everyday physical environment. In R. Cohen (Ed.), *The development of spatial cognition.* Hillsdale, NJ: Erlbaum.

GÄRLING, T., BÖÖK, A., & LINDBERG, E. (1986). Spatial orientation and wayfinding in the designed environment: A conceptual analysis and some suggestions for postoccupancy evaluation. *Journal of Architectural Planning Research, 3,* 55–64.

GÄRLING, T., BÖÖK, A., LINDBERG, E., & ARCE, C. (1990). Is elevation encoded in cognitive maps? *Journal of Environmental Psychology, 10,* 341–351.

GÄRLING, T., BÖÖK, A., LINDBERG, E., & NILSSON, T. (1981). Memory for the spatial layout of the everyday physical environment: Factors affecting the rate of acquisition. *Journal of Environmental Psychology, 1,* 263–277.

GÄRLING, T., & GOLLEDGE, R. G. (1989). Environmental perception and cognition. In E. H. Zube and G. T. Moore (Eds.), *Advances in environment, behavior, and design* (Vol. 2). New York: Plenum.

GÄRLING, T., LINDBERG, E., CARREIRAS, M., & BÖÖK, A. (1986). Reference systems in cognitive maps. *Journal of Environmental Psychology, 6,* 1–18.

GARRETT, G. A., BAXTER, J. C., & ROZELLE, R. M. (1981). Training university police in black-American nonverbal behavior. *Journal of Social Psychology, 113,* 217–229.

GASTER, S. (1991). Urban children's access to their neighborhood: Changes over three generations. *Environment and Behavior, 23,* 86–114.

GAUVAIN, M., ALTMAN, I., & FAHIM, H. (1983). Homes and social change: A cross-cultural analysis. In N. R. Feimer & E. S. Geller (Eds.), *Environmental psychology: Directions and perspectives.* New York: Praeger.

GEEN, R. G., & O'NEAL, E. C. (1969). Activation of cue-elicited aggression by general arousal. *Journal of Personality and Social Psychology, 11,* 289–292.

GELLER, E. S. (1975). Increasing desired waste disposals with instructions. *Man-Environment Systems, 5,* 125–128.

GELLER, E. S. (1976). *Behavioral approaches to environmental problem solving: Littering and recycling.* Symposium presentation at the meeting of the Association for the Advancement of Behavior Therapy, New York, NY.

GELLER, E. S. (1980). Applications of behavioral analysis for litter control. In D. Glenwick & L. Jason (Eds.), *Behavioral community psychology: Progress and prospects.* New York: Praeger.

GELLER, E. S. (1984). Motivating safety belt use with incentives: A critical review of the past and a look to the future. In *Advances in belt restraint systems: Design, performance, and usage* (No. 141). Society of Automotive Engineers, Inc, 400 Commonwealth Drive, Warrendale, PA 15096.

GELLER, E. S. (1987). Applied behavior analysis and environmental psychology: From strange bedfellows to a productive marriage. In D. Stokols & I. Altman (Eds.), *Handbook of environmental psychology* (Vol. 1). New York: John Wiley and Sons.

GELLER, E. S., BRASTED, W., & MANN, M. (1980). Waste receptacle designs as interventions for litter control. *Journal of Environmental Systems, 9,* 145–160.

GELLER, E. S., CHAFFEE, J. F., & INGRAM, R. E. (1975). Promoting paper recycling on a university campus. *Journal of Environmental Systems, 5,* 39–57.

GELLER, E. S., FARRIS, J. C., & POST, D. S. (1973). Promoting a consumer behavior for pollution control. *Journal of Applied Behavior Analysis, 6,* 367–376.

GELLER, E. S., KALSHER, M. J., RUDD, J. R., & LEHMAN, G. R. (1989). Promoting safety belt use on a university campus: An integration of commitment and incentive strategies. *Journal of Applied Social Psychology, 19,* 3–19.

GELLER, E. S., WINETT, R. A., & EVERETT, P. B. (1982). *Preserving the environment: Strategies for behavior change.* New York: Pergamon.

GELLER, E. S., WITMER, J. F., & OREBAUGH, A. L. (1976). Instructions as a determinant of paper disposal behaviors. *Environment and Behavior, 8,* 417–440.

GELLER, E. S., WITMER, J. F., & TUSO, M. E. (1977). Environmental interventions for litter control. *Journal of Applied Psychology, 62,* 344–351.

GELLER, E. S., WYLIE, R. G., & FARRIS, J. C. (1971). An attempt at applying prompting and reinforcement toward pollution control. *Proceedings of the 79th Annual Convention of the American Psychological Association, 6,* 701–702.

GELWICKS, L. (1970). Home range and the use of space by an aging population. In L. A. Pastalan & D. H. Carson (Eds.), *Spatial behavior of older people.* Ann Arbor: University of Michigan Press.

GERARD, R. (1958). *Differential effects of colored lights on psychophysiological functions.* Unpublished doctoral dissertation, University of California, Los Angeles.

GERGEN, K. J., GERGEN, M. M., & BARTON, W. H. (1973, October). Deviance in the dark. *Psychology Today,* pp. 129–130.

GIBSON, E. J., & WALK, R. D. (1960). The "visual cliff." *Scientific American, 202,* 64–71.

GIBSON, J. J. (1957a). Optical motions and transformations as stimuli for visual perception. *Psychological Review, 64,* 288–295.

GIBSON, J. J. (1957b). Review of E. Brunswik's *Perception and the representative design of psychological experiments. Contemporary Psychology, 2,* 33–35.

GIBSON, J. J. (1958). Visually controlled locomotion and visual orientation in animals. *British Journal of Psychology, 49,* 182–194.

GIBSON, J. J. (1960). Perception. In *Encyclopedia of science and technology.* New York; McGraw-Hill.

GIBSON, J. J. (1966). *The senses considered as perceptual systems.* Boston: Houghton Mifflin.

GIBSON, J. J. (1979). *An ecological approach to visual perception.* Boston: Houghton Mifflin.

GIBSON, J. L., IVANCEVICH, J. M., & DONNELLY, J. H. (1979). *Organizations* (3rd ed.). Dallas, TX: Business Publications Inc.

GIBSON, P. M. (1979). Therapeutic aspects of wilderness programs: A comprehensive literature review. *Therapeutic Recreation Journal, 13,* 21–33.

GIFFORD, R. (1980). Environmental dispositions and the evaluation of architectural interiors. *Journal of Research in Personality, 14,* 386–399.

GIFFORD, R. (1982). Projected interpersonal distance and orientation choices:

Personality, sex, and social situation. *Social Psychology Quarterly, 45,* 145–152.

GIFFORD, R. (1987). *Environmental psychology: Principles and practice.* Boston: Allyn and Bacon.

GIFFORD, R. (1988). Light, decor, arousal, comfort, and communication. *Journal of Environmental Psychology, 8,* 177–189.

GILGEN, A., & BARRIER, A. (1976). Sunlight and natural light indoors. In E. Grandjean & A. Gilgen (Eds.), *Environmental factors in urban planning.* London: Taylor and Francis.

GILLIGAN, J. P. (ED.). (1962). *Wilderness and recreation.* Washington, DC: Outdoor Recreation Resources Review Commission.

GILLIS, A. R., RICHARD, M. A., & HAGAN, J. (1986). Ethnic susceptibility to crowding: An empirical example. *Environment and Behavior, 18,* 683–706.

GIMBLETT, R. H., ITAMI, R. M., & FITZGIBBON, J. E. (1985). Mystery in an information-processing model of landscape preference. *Landscape Journal, 4,* 87–95.

GINSBURG, H. J., POLLMAN, V. A., WAUSON, M. S., & HOPE, M. L. (1977). Variation of aggressive interaction among male elementary school children as a function of changes in spatial density. *Environmental Psychology and Nonverbal Behavior, 2,* 67–75.

GIULIANO, V. E. (1982). The mechanization of office work. *Scientific American, 247,* 149–164.

GLASER, D. (1964). *The effectiveness of a prison and parole system.* Indianapolis: Bobbs-Merrill.

GLASS, A. L., & HOLYOAK, K. J. (1986). *Cognition* (2nd ed.). New York: Random House.

GLASS, D. C., & SINGER, J. E. (1972). *Urban stress.* New York: Academic Press.

GLASS, D. C., SINGER, J. E., & FRIEDMAN, L. W. (1969). Psychic cost of adaptation to an environmental stressor. *Journal of Personality and Social Psychology, 12,* 200–210.

GLASS, G. V., CAHEN, L. S., SMITH, M. L., & FILBY, N. N. (1982). *School class size: Research and policy.* Beverly Hills: Sage.

GLEICK, P. H. (1991). Environment and security: The clear connections. *The Bulletin of the Atomic Scientists, 47,* No. 3, 17–21.

GLINER, J., RAVEN, P., HORVATH, S., DRINKWATER, B., & SUTTON, J. (1975). Man's physiological response to long-term work during thermal and pollutant stress. *Journal of Applied Physiology, 39,* 628–632.

GLYNN, T. J. (1981). Psychological sense of community: Measurement and application. *Human Relations, 34,* 780–818.

GOCHMAN, I. R., & KEATING, J. P. (1980). Misattributions to crowding: Blaming crowding for nondensity-caused events. *Journal of Nonverbal Behavior, 4,* 157–175.

GOECKNER, D., GREENOUGH, W., & MAIER, S. (1974). Escape learning deficit after overcrowded rearing in rats: Tests of a helplessness hypothesis. *Bulletin of the Psychonomic Society, 3,* 54–57.

GOECKNER, D., GREENOUGH, W., & MEAD, W. (1973). Deficit in learning tasks following overcrowding in rats. *Journal of Personality and Social Psychology, 28,* 256–261.

GOFFMAN, E. (1959). *The presentation of self in everyday life.* New York: Doubleday.

GOLDBERG, G., KIESLER, C., & COLLINS, B. (1969). Visual behavior and face-to-face distance during interaction. *Sociometry, 32,* 43–53.

GOLDHABER, M. K., HOUTS, P. S., & DISABELLA, R. (1983). Moving after the crisis: A prospective study of Three Mile Island area mobility. *Environment and Behavior, 15,* 93–120.

GOLDSMITH, J., & FRIBERG, L. (1977). Effects of air pollution on human health. In A. C. Stern (Ed.), *Air pollution* (3rd ed.). New York: Academic Press.

GOLDSTEIN, K. (1942). Some experimental observations concerning the influence of colors on the functions of the organism. *Occupational Therapy, 21,* 147–151.

GOLLEDGE, R. G. (1978). Learning about urban environments. In T. Carlstein, D. Parkes, & N. Thrift (Eds.), *Timing space and spacing time* (Vol. 1). London: Edward Arnold.

GOLLEDGE, R. G. (1987). Environmental cognition. In D. Stokols & I. Altman (Eds.), *Handbook of environmental psychology* (Vol. 1). New York: John Wiley and Sons.

GOODCHILD, B. (1974). Class differences in environmental perception. *Urban Studies, 11,* 59–79.

GOODMAN, L., SAXE, L., & HARVEY, M. (1991). Homelessness as psychological trauma. *American Psychologist, 46,* 1219–1225.

GORNER, P. (1990, May 20). Antarctic team found adventure, ozone peril. *Chicago Tribune,* p. 3.

GOUGH, H. G. (1975). *Manual for the California Psychological Inventory* (Revised ed.). Palo Alto, CA: Consulting Psychologists Press.

GOULD, J. L. (1982). *Ethology: The mechanisms and evolution of behavior.* New York: Norton.

GOVE, W. R., & HUGHES, M. (1980). In pursuit of preconceptions: A reply to the claim of Booth and his colleagues that household crowding is not an important variable. *American Sociological Review, 45,* 878–886.

GRANT, D. P. (1970). Architect discovers the aged. *Gerontologist, 10,* 275–281.

GRASMICK, H. G., BURSIK, R. J., & KINSEY, K. A. (1991). Shame and embarrassment as deterrents to noncompliance with the law: The case of an anti-littering campaign. *Environment and Behavior, 23,* 233–251.

GREEN, B. L. (1990). Defining trauma: Terminology and generic stressor dimensions. *Journal of Applied Social Psychology, 20,* 1632–1642.

GREEN, B. L., GRACE, M. C., LINDY, J. D., GLESER, G. C., LEONARD, A. C., & KRAMER, T. L. (1990). Buffalo Creek survivors in the second decade: Comparison with unexposed and nonlitigant groups. *Journal of Applied Social Psychology, 20,* 1033–1050.

GREENBAUM, P. E., & GREENBAUM, S. D. (1981). Territorial personalization: Group identity and social interaction in a Slavic-American neighborhood. *Environment and Behavior, 13,* 574–589.

GREENBERG, S., & ROHE, W. (1986). Informal social control and crime prevention in modern urban neighborhoods. In R. Taylor (Ed.), *Urban neighborhoods: Research and policy.* New York: Praeger.

GREENBERG, S., ROHE, W., & WILLIAMS, J. (1982). Safety in urban neighborhoods: A comparison of physical characteristics and informal territorial control in high and low crime neighborhoods. *Population and Environment, 5,* 144–165.

GREENBERGER, D. B., & ALLEN, V. C. (1980). Destruction and complexity: An application of aesthetic theory. *Personality and Social Psychology Bulletin, 6,* 479–483.

GREENBIE, B. B. (1982). The landscape of social symbols. *Landscape Research, 7,* 2–6.

GREENE, T. C., & BELL, P. A. (1980). Additional considerations concerning the effects of "warm" and "cool" colours on energy conservation. *Ergonomics, 23,* 949–954.

GREENFIELD, P. (1984). *Media and the mind of a child: From print to television, video games, and computers.* Cambridge: Harvard University press.

GREER, D. L. (1983). Spectator booing and the home advantage: A study of social influence in the basketball arena. *Social Psychology Quarterly, 46,* 252–261.

GREY, G. W., & DENEKE, F. J. (1986). *Urban forestry* (2nd ed.). New York: John Wiley and Sons.

GRIFFIT, W. (1970). Environmental effects on interpersonal affective behavior: Ambient effective temperature and attraction. *Journal of Personality and Social Psychology, 15,* 240–244.

GRIFFIT, W., & VEITCH, R. (1971). Hot and crowded: Influence of population density and temperature on interpersonal affective behavior. *Journal of Personality and Social Psychology, 17,* 92–99.

GRIFFITH, C. R. (1921). A comment upon the psychology of the audience. *Psychological Monographs, 30,* 36–47.

GUARDO, C. J. (1976). Personal space, sex differences, and interpersonal attraction. *Journal of Psychology, 92,* 9–14.

GUENTER, C. A., JOERN, A. T., SHURLEY, J. T., & PIERCE, C. M. (1970). Cardio-respiratory and metabolic effects in men on the South Polar Plateau. *Archives of Internal Medicine, 125,* 630–637.

GUEST, A. M., & LEE, B. A. (1983). Sentiment and evaluation as ecological variables. *Sociological Perspectives, 26,* 158–184.

GUGLIOTTA, G. (1991). Hidden pleasures in the senate. *Washington Post National Weekly Edition, 8,* 11.

GUMP, P. V. (1974). Operating environments in open and traditional schools. *School Review, 84,* 575–593.

GUMP, P. V. (1978). School environments. In I. Altman & J. F. Wohlwill (Eds.), *Children and the environment.* New York: Plenum.

GUMP, P. V. (1987). School and classroom environments. In D. Stokols & I. Altman (Eds.), *Handbook of environmental psychology* (Vol. 1). New York: John Wiley and Sons.

GUMP, P. V. (1990). A short history of the Midwest Psychological Field Station. *Environment and Behavior, 22,* 436–457.

GUNDERSON, E. K. E. (1973). Individual behavior in confined or isolated groups. In J. E. Easmussen (Ed.), *Man in isolation and confinement.* Chicago: Aldine.

HAAS, G. (1975). *Relationships among campers in Shenandoah National Park as related to social interaction, activity patterns, camping style, and descriptive characteristics.* Unpublished master's thesis, Pennsylvania State University.

HAGGARD. L. M., & WERNER, C. M. (1990). Situational support, privacy regulation, and stress. *Basic and Applied Social Psychology, 11,* 313–337.

HAINES, R. F. (1991). Windows: Their importance and functions in confining environments. In A. A. Harrison, Y. A. Clearwater, & C. P. McKay (Eds.), *From*

Antarctica to outer space: Life in isolation and confinement. New York: Springer-Verlag.

HALE, J. L., & BURGOON, J. K. (1984). Models of reactions to changes in nonverbal immediacy. *Journal of Nonverbal Behavior, 8,* 287–314.

HALL, D. K., & ALBERT, B. F. (1976, April). *The influence of environmental softness on social interaction among autistic children.* Paper presented at the meeting of the Eastern Psychological Association, New York.

HALL, F. T. (1966). *The hidden dimension.* New York: Doubleday.

HALL, R. A., RAPPAPORT, M., HOPKINS, H. K., GRIFFIN, R. B., & SILVERMAN, J. (1970). Evoked response and behavior in cats. *Science, 170,* 998–1000.

HAMMITT, W. E. (1983). Toward an ecological approach to perceived crowding in outdoor recreation. *Leisure Sciences, 5,* 309–320.

HAMMITT, W. E. (1987). Visual recognition capacity during outdoor recreation experiences. *Environment and Behavior, 19,* 651–672.

HANSEN, W. B., & ALTMAN, I. (1976). Decorating personal places: A descriptive analysis. *Environment and Behavior, 8,* 491–504.

HANSON, R. A. (1977). An outdoor challenge program as a means of enhancing mental health. In *Children, nature, and the urban environment.* Upper Darby, PA: U.S. Department of Agriculture, Forest Service, Northeastern Forest Experiment Station.

HARDIE, G. J. (1989). Environment and behavior research for developing countries. In E. H. Zube & G. T. Moore (Eds.), *Advances in environment, behavior, and design* (Vol. 2). New York: Plenum.

HARDIN, G. (1968). The tragedy of the commons. *Science, 162,* 1243–1248.

HARRIES, K. D., & STADLER, S. J. (1988). Heat and violence: New findings from Dallas field data, 1980–1981. *Environment and Behavior, 18,* 346–368.

HARRIS, B., LUGINBUHL, J. E. R., & FISHBEIN, J. E. (1978). Density of personal space in a field setting. *Social Psychology, 41,* 350–353.

HARRIS, L., & ASSOCIATES, INC. (1978). *The Steelcase national study of office environments: Do they work?* Grand Rapids, MI: Steelcase.

HARRIS, P. B., & MCANDREW, F. T. (1986). Territoriality and compliance: The influence of gender and location on willingness to sign petitions. *Journal of Social Psychology, 126,* 657–662.

HARRIS, P. R. (1991). Personnel deployment systems: Managing people in polar and outer space settings. In A. A. Harrison, Y. A. Clearwater, & C. P. McKay (Eds.), *From Antarctica to outer space: Life in isolation and confinement.* New York: Springer-Verlag.

HARRISON, A. A., STRUTHERS, N. J., & PUTZ, B. J. (1989). Individual differences, mission parameters, and spaceflight environment habitability. In C. Stoker (Ed.), *The case of Mars III: Strategies for exploration.* San Diego: Univelt.

HARRISON, A. A., STRUTHERS, N. J., & PUTZ, B. J. (1991). Mission destination, mission duration, gender, and student perceptions of space habitat acceptability. *Environment and Behavior, 23,* 221–232.

HART, C. H., & SHEEHAN, R. (1986). Preschoolers' play behavior in outdoor environments: Effects of traditional and contemporary playgrounds. *American Educational Research Journal, 23,* 669–678.

HART, R. A. (1979). *Children's experience of place.* New York: Irvington.

HART, R. A. (1981). Children's spatial representation of the landscape: Lessons and questions from a field study. In L. S. Liben, A. H. Patterson, & N. Newcombe (Eds.), *Spatial representation and behavior across the life span.* New York: Academic Press.

HART, R. A., & MOORE, G. T. (1973). The development of spatial cognition: A review. In R. M. Downs & D. Stea (Eds.), *Image and environment: Cognitive mapping and spatial behavior.* Chicago: Aldine.

HART, T., & HARDIE, G. J. (1987). State sanctioned self-help and self-help home-builders in South Africa. *Environment and Behavior, 19,* 353–370.

HARTIG, T., MANG, M., & EVANS, G. W. (1991). Restorative effects of natural environment experiences. *Environment and Behavior, 23,* 3–26.

HARTNETT, J. J., BAILEY, K. G., & GIBSON, F. W. JR. (1970). Personal space as influenced by sex and type of movement. *Journal of Psychology, 76,* 139–144.

HASLER, A. D., & LARSEN, J. A. (1955, August). The homing salmon. *Scientific American,* pp. 20–23.

HATHAWAY, S. R., & MCKINLEY, J. C. (1951). *The Minnesota Multiphasic Inventory manual* (Revised ed.). New York: Psychological Corporation.

HATWELL, Y. (1966). *Privation sensorielle et intelligence.* Paris: Presses Universitaires de France.

HAYDUK, L. A. (1981). The shape of personal space: An experimental investigation. *Canadian Journal of Behavioural Science, 123,* 87–93.

HAYDUK, L. A. (1983). Personal space: Where we now stand. *Psychological Bulletin, 94,* 293–335.

HAYES, S. C., & CONE, J. D. (1977). Reducing residential electrical use: Payments, information, and feedback. *Journal of Applied Behavior Analysis, 14,* 81–88.

HAYES, S. C., JOHNSON, V. W., & CONE, J. D. (1975). The marked item technique: A practical procedure for litter control. *Journal of Applied Behavior Analysis, 8,* 381–386.

HAYWARD, D. G., ROTHENBERG, M., & BEASLEY, R. R. (1974). Children's play and urban playground environments: A comparison of traditional, contemporary, and adventure playground types. *Environment and Behavior, 6,* 131–168.

HAYWARD, J. (1989). Urban parks: Research, planning, and social change. In I. Altman & E. H. Zube (Eds.), *Public places and spaces.* New York: Plenum.

HAZEN, N., LOCKMAN, J., & PICK, H. (1978). The development of children's representations of large-scale environments. *Child Development, 49,* 623–636.

HAZLETT, B. A. (1968). Effects of crowding on the agonistic behavior of the hermit crab *Pargus bernhardus. Ecology, 49,* 573–575.

HEARN, G. (1957). Leadership and the spatial factor in small groups. *Journal of Abnormal and Social Psychology, 104,* 269–272.

HEATH, T. F. (1988). Behavioral and perceptual aspects of the aesthetics of urban environments. In J. L. Nasar (Ed.), *Environmental aesthetics.* New York: Cambridge University Press.

HEAT-MOON, W. L. (1991a). *PrairyErth: A deep map.* New York: Houghton Mifflin.

HEART-MOON, W. L. (1991b). PrairyErth: Portraits from Chase County, Kansas. *Atlantic Monthly, 268,* 45–74.

HEATON, A. W., & SIGALL, H. (1989). The "championship choke" revisited: The role of fear of acquiring a negative identity. *Journal of Applied Social Psychology, 19,* 1019–1033.

HEBB, D. O. (1955). Drives and the C.N.S. (central nervous system). *Psychological Review, 62,* 243–254.

HEBB, D. O. (1972). *Textbook of psychology* (3rd ed.). Philadelphia: Saunders.

HEBERLEIN, T. A. (1971). *Moral norms, threatened sanctions, and littering behavior*. Doctoral dissertation, University of Wisconsin-Madison. (University Microfilms No. 72–2639).

HEBERLEIN, T. A. (1975). Conservative information: The energy crisis and electricity consumption in an apartment complex. *Energy Systems and Policy, 1,* 105–117.

HEBERLEIN, T. A., & BLACK, J. S. (1976). Attitudinal specificity and the prediction of behavior in a field setting. *Journal of Personality and Social Psychology, 33,* 474–479.

HECOCK, R. D. (1970). Recreation behavior patterns as related to site characteristics of beaches. *Journal of Leisure Research, 2,* 237–250.

HEDGE, A. (1982). The open-plan office: A systematic investigation of employee reactions to their work environment. *Environment and Behavior, 14,* 519–542.

HEDIGER, H. (1950). *Wild animals in captivity*. London: Buttersworth.

HEDIGER, H. (1955). *Studies of the psychology and behavior of captive animals in zoos and circuses*. London: Buttersworth.

HEERWAGEN, J. H. (1990). Affective functioning, "light hunger," and room brightness preferences. *Environment and Behavior, 22,* 608–635.

HEERWAGEN, J. H., & HEERWAGEN, D. R. (1986). Lighting and psychological comfort. *Lighting, Design, and Application, 16,* 47–51.

HEERWAGEN, J. H., & ORIANS, G. H. (1986). Adaptations to windowlessness: A study of the use of visual decor in windowed and windowless offices. *Environment and Behavior, 18,* 623–639.

HEFFRON, M. H. (1972). The naval ship as an urban design problem. *Naval Engineers Journal, 12,* 49–64.

HEFT, H. (1979). The role of environmental features in route-learning: Two exploratory studies of way-finding. *Environmental Psychology and Nonverbal Behavior, 3,* 172–185.

HEFT, H., & WOHLWILL, J. F. (1987). Environmental cognition in children. In D. Stokols & I. Altman (Eds.), *Handbook of environmental psychology* (Vol. 1). New York: John Wiley and Sons.

HEIDER, F. (1958). *The psychology of interpersonal relations*. New York: John Wiley and Sons.

HEILWEIL, M. (1973). The influence of dormitory architecture on resident behavior. *Environment and Behavior, 5,* 377–412.

HEIMSATH, C. (1977). *Behavior architecture: Toward an accountable design process*. New York: McGraw-Hill.

HEIMSTRA, N. W., & MCFARLING, L. H. (1978). *Environmental psychology* (2nd ed.). Pacific Grove, CA: Brooks/Cole.

HELLEKSON, C. J., KLINE, J. A., & ROSENTHAL, N. E. (1986). Phototherapy for seasonal affective disorder in Alaska. *American Journal of Psychiatry, 143,* 1035–1037.

HENDEE, J. C., & STANKEY, G. H. (1973). Biocentricity in wilderness management. *Bioscience, 23,* 535–538.

HENDEE, J. C., STANKEY, G. H., & LUCAS, R. C. (1978). *Wilderness management*. Washington, DC: U.S. Government Printing Office.

HENDRICKS, M., & BOOTZIN, R. (1976). Race and sex as stimuli for negative affect and physical avoidance. *Journal of Social Psychology, 98,* 111–120.

HENLEY, N. M. (1977). *Body politics*. Englewood Cliffs, NJ: Prentice-Hall.

HENRICK, C., GIESEN, M., & COY, S. (1974). The social ecology of free seating arrangements in a small group interaction context. *Sociometry, 37,* 262–274.

HENRY, J. P., MEEHAN, J. P., & STEPHENS, P. M. (1967). The use of psychosocial stimuli to induce prolonged systolic hypertension in mice. *Psychosomatic Medicine, 29,* 408–432.

HENRY, J. P., STEPHENS, P. M., AXELROD, J., & MUELLER, R. A. (1971). Effect of psychosocial stimulation on the enzymes involved in the biosynthesis and metabolism of noradrenaline and adrenaline. *Psychosomatic Medicine, 33,* 227–237.

HERMAN, J. F., MILLER, B. S., & SHIRAKI, J. H. (1987). The influence of affective associations on the development of cognitive maps of large environments. *Journal of Environmental Psychology, 7,* 89–98.

HERMAN, J. F., & SIEGEL, A. W. (1978). The development of cognitive mapping of the large-scale environment. *Journal of Experimental Child Psychology, 26,* 389–406.

HERZBERG, F. (1966). *Work and the nature of man.* Cleveland: World Publishing.

HERZBERG, F., MAUSNER, B., & SNYDERMAN, B. (1959). *The motivation to work.* New York: John Wiley and Sons.

HERZOG, T. R. (1984). A cognitive analysis of preference for field-and-forest environments. *Landscape Research, 9,* 10–16.

HERZOG, T. R. (1985). A cognitive analysis of preferences for waterscapes. *Journal of Environmental Psychology, 5,* 225–241.

HERZOG, T. R. (1987). A cognitive analysis of preference for natural environments: Mountains, canyons, deserts. *Landscape Journal, 6,* 140–152.

HERZOG, T. R. (1989). A cognitive analysis of preference for urban nature. *Journal of Environmental Psychology, 9,* 27–43.

HERZOG, T. R., KAPLAN, S., & KAPLAN, R. (1982). The prediction of preference for unfamiliar places. *Population and Environment, 5,* 43–59.

HERZOG, T. R., & SMITH, G. A. (1988). Danger, mystery, and environmental preference. *Environment and Behavior, 20,* 320–344.

HESHKA, S., & NELSON, Y. (1972). Interpersonal speaking distance as a function of age, sex, and relationship. *Sociometry, 35,* 491–498.

HESTER, R. (1979). A womb with a view: How spatial nostalgia affects the designer. *Landscape Architecture, 69,* 475–481, 528.

HESTER, R. (1984). *Planning neighborhood space with people.* New York: Van Nostrand Reinhold.

HEUSSER, C. P., ADELSON, M., & ROSS, D. (1986). How children use their elementary school playgrounds. *Children's Environments Quarterly, 3,* 3–11.

HIGH, T., & SUNDSTROM, E. (1977). Room flexibility and space use in a dormitory. *Environment and Behavior, 9,* 81–90.

HIGHWAY RESEARCH BOARD, NATIONAL RESEARCH COUNCIL (1973). *Environmental considerations in planning, design, and construction* (Special Report 138). Washington, DC: National Academy of Sciences.

HILLMANN, R. B., BROOKS, C. I., & O'BRIEN, J. (1991). Differences in self-esteem among college freshmen as a function of classroom seating-row preference. *The Psychological Record, 41,* 315–320.

HISS, T. (1990). *The experience of place.* New York: Knopf.

HOCKEY, G. R. J., & HAMILTON, P. (1970). Arousal and information selection in short-term memory. *Nature, 226,* 866–867.

HODOSH, R. J., RINGO, J., & MCANDREW, F. T. (1979). Density and lek displays in *Drosophila grimshawi. Zeitschrift fur Tierpsychologie, 49,* 164–172.

HOLAHAN, C. J. (1972). Seating patterns and patient behavior in an experimental dayroom. *Journal of Abnormal Psychology, 80,* 115–124.

HOLAHAN, C. J. (1978). *Environment and Behavior.* New York: Plenum.

HOLAHAN, C. J. (1982). *Environmental psychology.* New York: Random House.

HOLAHAN, C. J., & DOBROWOLNY, M. B. (1978). Cognitive and behavioral correlates of the spatial environment: An interactional analysis. *Environment and Behavior, 10,* 317–334.

HOLAHAN, C. J., & WANDERSMAN, A. (1987). The community psychology perspective in environmental psychology. In D. Stokols & I. Altman (Eds.), *Handbook of environmental psychology* (Vol. 1). New York: John Wiley and Sons.

HOLAHAN, C. J., & WILCOX, B. L. (1978). Environmental satisfaction in high and low-rise student housing. *Journal of Educational Psychology, 70,* 237–241.

HOLLISTER, F. D. (1968). *Greater London Council: A report on the problems of windowless environments.* London: Hobbs.

HOLLYFIELD, R. L., & FOULKE, E. (1983). The spatial cognition of blind pedestrians. *Journal of Visual Impairment and Blindness, 77,* 204–209.

HOLMES, T. H., & RAHE, R. H. (1967). The Social Readjustment Rating Scale. *Journal of Psychosomatic Research, 11,* 213–218.

HOOD, M. (1984). The role of audience development in strategic planning. *Annual Proceedings of the American Association of Zoological Parks and Aquariums.* Wheeling, WV: American Association of Zoological Parks and Aquariums.

HOPPER, J. R., & NIELSEN, J. M. (1991). Recycling as altruistic behavior: Strategies to expand participation in a community recycling program. *Environment and Behavior, 23,* 195–220.

HOROWITZ, M. J., DUFF, D. F., & STRATTON, L. O. (1964). Body-buffer zone: Exploration of personal space. *Archives of General Psychiatry, 11,* 651–656.

HOWARTH, E., & HOFFMAN, M. S. (1984). A multidimensional approach to the relationship between mood and weather. *British Journal of Psychology, 75,* 15–23.

HOWELL, S. C. (1983). The meaning of place in old age. In G. Rowles & R. Ohta (Eds.), *Aging and milieu: Environmental perspectives on growing old.* New York: Academic Press.

HUBEL, D. H., & WIESEL, T. N. (1962). Receptive fields, binocular interaction, and functional architecture in the cat's visual cortex. *Journal of Physiology, 160,* 106–154.

HUGHES, J., & GOLDMAN, M. (1978). Eye contact, facial expression, sex, and the violation of personal space. *Perceptual and Motor Skills, 46,* 579–584.

HUGHES, P. C., & MCNELIS, J. F. (1978, August). *Lighting, productivity, and the work environment.* Paper presented at the annual Illuminating Engineering Society technical meeting, Denver.

HULL, E. M., LANGAN, C. J., & ROSSELLI, L. (1973). Population density and social, territorial, and physiological measures in the gerbil, *Meriones unquiculatus. Journal of Comparative and Physiological Psychology, 84,* 414–422.

HULL, R. B., & HARVEY, A. (1989). Explaining the emotion people experience in suburban parks. *Environment and Behavior, 21,* 323–345.

HULL, R. B., & REVELL, G. R. B. (1989). Cross-cultural comparison of landscape scenic beauty evaluations: A case study in Bali. *Journal of Environmental Psychology, 9,* 177–191.

HUNT, M. E. (1984). Environmental learning without being there. *Environment and Behavior, 16,* 307–334.

HUNTER, A. (1978, November). *Symbols of incivility: Social disorder and fear of crime in urban neighborhoods.* Paper presented at the annual meeting of the American Society of Criminology, Dallas, TX.

HUNTINGTON, E. (1915). *Civilization and climate.* New Haven: Yale University Press.

HUNTINGTON, E. (1945). *Mainsprings of civilization.* New York: John Wiley and Sons.

HUTCHINS, G. L., & NORRIS, F. H. (1989). Life change in the disaster recovery period. *Environment and Behavior, 21,* 33–56.

HUTT, C., & VAIZEY, J. (1966). Differential effects of group density on social behavior. *Nature, 209,* 1371–1372.

HUTTMAN, E. D. (1977). *Housing and social services for the elderly: Social policy trends.* New York: Praeger.

HYMBAUGH, K., & GARRETT, J. (1974). Sensation seeking among skydivers. *Perceptual and Motor Skills, 38,* 118–119.

IMAMOGLU, V. (1973). The effect of furniture density on the subjective evaluation of spaciousness and estimation of size of rooms. In R. Kuller (Ed.), *Architectural Psychology: Proceedings of the Lund Conference.* Stroudsburg, PA: Dowden, Hutchinson, and Ross.

INGRAM, R. E., & GELLER, E. S. (1975). A community-integrated, behavior modification approach to facilitating paper recycling. *JSAS Catalog of Selected Documents in Psychology, 5,* 327. (Ms. No. 1097).

INNES, C. A. (1986). *Population density in state prisons.* Washington, DC: Bureau of Justice Statistics. (Bureau of Justice Statistics Bulletin No. NCJ–103204).

ISAAC, W., & DEVITO, J. L. (1958). Effect of sensory stimulation on the activity of normal and prefrontal-lobectomized monkeys. *Journal of Comparative and Physiological Psychology, 51,* 172–174.

ISAAC, W., & KENDALL, N. P. (1967). Sensory stimulation and timing behavior. *Psychonomic Science, 8,* 41–42.

ISAAC, W., & REED, W. G. (1961) The effect of sensory stimulation on the activity of cats. *Journal of Comparative and Physiological Psychology, 54,* 677–678.

ISO-AHOLA, S. E., & NIBLOCK. L. A. (1981). Reducing litter through the signed petition: A field experiment in the campground. In *Abstracts from the 1981 Symposium on Leisure Research.* Washington, DC: National Recreation and Parks Association.

ITTELSON, W. H. (1976). Environment perception and contemporary perceptual theory. In H. Proshansky, W. Ittelson, & L. Rivlin (Eds.), *Environmental psychology: People and their physical settings* (2nd ed.). New York: Holt, Rinehart, & Winston.

ITTELSON, W. H. (1989). Notes on theory in environment and behavior research. In E. H. Zube & G. T. Moore (Eds.), *Advances in environment, behavior, and design* (Vol. 2). New York: Plenum.

ITTELSON, W. H., PROSHANSKY, H. M., RIVLIN, L. G., & WINKEL, G. H. (1974). *Introduction to environmental psychology.* New York: Holt, Rinehart, & Winston.

IVES, R. S., & FERDINANDS, R. (1974). Working in a landscaped office. *Personnel Practice Bulletin, 30,* 126–141.

JACKSON, E. L. (1981). Responses to earthquake hazard: The west coast of North America. *Environment and Behavior, 13,* 387–416.

JACKSON, E. L., & WONG, R. A. G. (1982). Perceived conflict between urban cross-country skiers and snowmobilers in Alberta. *Journal of Leisure Research, 14,* 47–62.

JACKSON, J. B. (1981). The public park needs reappraisal. In L. Taylor (Ed.), *Urban open spaces.* New York: Rizzoli.

JACKSON, J. F. (1988). Crevice occupation by musk turtles: Taxonomic distribution and crevice attributes. *Animal Behaviour, 36,* 793–801.

JACOB, G. R., SCHREYER, R. (1980). Conflict in outdoor recreation: A theoretical perspective. *Journal of Leisure Research, 12,* 368–380.

JACOBS, G. D., HEILBRONNER, R. L., & STANLEY, J. M. (1984). The effects of short term flotation REST on relaxation: A controlled study. *Health Psychology, 3,* 99–112.

JACOBS, J. (1961). *The death and life of great American cities.* New York: Random House.

JACOBS, K. W., & KOEPPEL, J. C. (1974). Psychological correlates of the mobility decision. *Bulletin of the Psychonomic Society, 3,* 330–332.

JACOBSEN, F. M., MURPHY, D. L., & ROSENTHAL, N. E. (1989). The role of serotonin in seasonal affective disorder and the antidepressant response to phototherapy. In N. E. Rosenthal & M. C. Blehar (Eds.), *Seasonal affective disorders and phototherapy.* New York: Springer-Verlag.

JAIN, V. (1987). Effects of population density and resources on the feeling of crowding and personal space. *Journal of Social Psychology, 127,* 331–338.

JAMES, S. P., WEHR, T. A., SACK, D. A., PARRY, B. L., & ROSENTHAL, N. E. (1985). Treatment of seasonal affective disorder with light in the evening. *British Journal of Psychiatry, 147,* 424–428.

JAMES, W. (1890). *Principles of psychology.* New York: Holt, Rinehart & Winston.

JANNEY, J., MINORU, M., & HOLMES, T. (1977). Impact of a natural catastrophe on life events. *Journal of Human Stress, 3,* 22–34.

JASON, L. A., REICHLER, A., & RUCKER, W. (1981). Territorial behavior on beaches. *Journal of Social Psychology, 114,* 43–50.

JASON, L. A., ZOLIK, E. S., & MATESE, F. (1979). Prompting dog owners to pick up dog droppings. *American Journal of Community Psychology, 7,* 339–351.

JAYNES, J. (1976). *The origin of consciousness in the breakdown of the bicameral mind.* Toronto: University of Toronto Press.

JILEK, W. G. (1974). *Salish Indian mental health and culture change: Psychohygienic and therapeutic aspects of the Guardian Spirit Ceremonial.* Toronto: Holt, Rinehart, & Winston.

JILEK, W. G. (1982). *Indian healing: Shamanistic ceremonialism in the Pacific Northwest today.* Surrey, BC: Hancock House.

JOARDAR, S. D. (1989). Use and image of neighborhood parks: A case of limited resources. *Environment and Behavior, 21,* 734–762.

JOINER, D. (1971). Office territory. *New Society, 7,* 660–663.

JOINER, D. (1976). Social ritual and architectural space. In H. M. Proshansky, W. H. Ittelson, & L. G. Rivlin (Eds.), *Environmental psychology: People and their physical settings* (2nd ed.). New York: Holt, Rinehart, & Winston.

JONES, A. (1969). Stimulus-seeking behavior. In J. P. Zubek (Ed.), *Sensory deprivation: Fifteen years of research.* New York: Appleton-Century-Crofts.

JONES, B. (1975). Spatial perception in the blind. *British Journal of Psychology, 66,* 461–472.

JONES, J. W. (1978). Adverse emotional reactions of nonsmokers to secondary cigarette smoke. *Environmental Psychology and Nonverbal Behavior, 3,* 125–127.

JONES, S. E. (1971). A comparative proxemic analysis of dyadic interaction in selected subcultures of New York City. *Journal of Social Psychology, 84,* 35–44.

JORALEMON, D. (1984). The role of hallucinogenic drugs and sensory stimuli in Peruvian ritual healing. *Culture, Medicine, and Psychiatry, 8,* 399–430.

JOURARD, S. M., & FRIEDMAN, R. (1970). Experimenter-subject "distance" and self-disclosure. *Journal of Personality and Social Psychology, 15,* 278–282.

JUSTA, F. C., & GOLAN, M. B. (1977). Office design: Is privacy still a problem? *Journal of Architectural Research, 6,* 5–12.

KAHNEMAN, D. (1973). *Attention and effort.* Englewood Cliffs, NJ: Prentice-Hall.

KAMINSKI, G. (1989). The relevance of ecologically oriented conceptualizations to theory building in environment and behavior research. In E. H. Zube & G. T. Moore (Eds.), *Advances in environment, behavior, and design* (Vol. 2). New York: Plenum.

KANT, G. J., EGGLESTON, T., LANDMAN-ROBERTS, L., KENION, C. C., DRIVER, G. C., & MEYERHOFF, J. L. (1985). Habituation to repeated stress is stressor specific. *Pharmacology, Biochemistry, and Behavior, 22,* 631–634.

KANTOLA, S. J., SYME, G. J., & CAMPBELL, N. A. (1984). Cognitive dissonance and energy conservation. *Journal of Applied Psychology, 69,* 416–421.

KAPLAN, R. (1973). Predictors of environmental preference: Designers and clients. In W. F. E. Preiser (Ed.), *Environmental design research.* Stroudsburg, PA: Dowden, Hutchinson, and Ross.

KAPLAN, R. (1974). Some psychological benefits of an outdoor challenge program. *Environment and Behavior, 6,* 101–116.

KAPLAN, R. (1975). Some methods and strategies in the prediction of preference. In E. H. Zube, R. O. Brush, & J. G. Fabos (Eds.), *Landscape assessment: Values, perceptions, and resources.* Stroudsburg, PA: Dowden, Hutchinson, and Ross.

KAPLAN, R. (1977). Patterns of environmental preference. *Environment and Behavior, 9,* 195–215.

KAPLAN, R. (1978). The green experience. In S. Kaplan & R. Kaplan (Eds.), *Humanscape: Environments for people.* North Scituate, MA: Duxbury Press.

KAPLAN, R. (1984). Wilderness perception and psychological benefits: An analysis of a continuing program. *Leisure Sciences, 6,* 271–290.

KAPLAN, R., & KAPLAN, S. (1989). *The experience of nature: A psychological perspective.* New York: Cambridge University Press.

KAPLAN, R., KAPLAN, S., & BROWN, T. (1989). Environmental preference: A comparison of four domains of predictors. *Environment and Behavior, 21,* 509–530.

KAPLAN, R., & TALBOT, J. F. (1988). Ethnicity and preference for natural settings: A review and recent findings. *Landscape and Urban Planning, 15,* 107–117.

KAPLAN, S. (1975). An informal model for the prediction of preference. In E. H. Zube, J. G. Fabos, & R. O. Brush (Eds.), *Landscape assessment: Values, perceptions, and resources.* Stroudsburg, PA: Dowden, Hutchinson, and Ross.

KAPLAN, S. (1976). Adaptation, structure, and knowledge. In G. Moore & R.

Golledge (Eds.), *Environmental knowing*. Stroudsburg, PA: Dowden, Hutchinson, and Ross.

KAPLAN, S. (1977). Tranquility and challenge in the natural environment. In *Children, nature, and the urban environment*. Upper Darby, PA: U.S. Department of Agriculture, Forest Service, Northeastern Forest Experiment Station.

KAPLAN, S. (1978a). Perception of an uncertain environment. In S. Kaplan & R. Kaplan (Eds.), *Humanscape: Environments for people*. North Scituate, MA: Duxbury Press.

KAPLAN, S. (1978b). Attention and fascination: The search for cognitive clarity. In S. Kaplan & R. Kaplan (Eds.), *Humanscape: Environments for people*. North Scituate, MA: Duxbury Press.

KAPLAN, S. (1979). Perception and landscape: Conceptions and misconceptions. In *Proceedings of our National Landscape Conference*. USDA Forest Service General Technical Report PSW–35.

KAPLAN, S. (1987). Aesthetics, affect, and cognition: Environmental preference from an evolutionary perspective. *Environment and Behavior, 19,* 3–32.

KAPLAN, S., & KAPLAN, R. (1978). *Humanscape: Environments for people*. North Scituate, MA: Duxbury Press.

KAPLAN, S., & KAPLAN, R. (1982). *Cognition and environment*. New York: Praeger.

KAPLAN, S., KAPLAN, R., & WENDT, J. S. (1972). Rated preferences and complexity for natural and urban visual material. *Perception and Psychophysics, 12,* 354–356.

KARABENICK, S., & MEISELS, M. (1972). Effects of performance evaluation on interpersonal distance. *Journal of Personality, 40,* 257–286.

KARAN, P. P., BLADEN, W. A., & SINGH, G. (1980). Slum dwellers' and squatters' images of the city. *Environment and Behavior, 12,* 81–100.

KARLIN, R. A., KATZ, S., EPSTEIN, Y. M., & WOOLFOLK, R. L. (1979). The use of therapeutic interventions to reduce crowding-related arousal: A preliminary investigation. *Environmental Psychology and Nonverbal Behavior, 3,* 219–227.

KARLIN, R. A., MCFARLAND, D., AIELLO, J. R., & EPSTEIN, Y. M. (1976). Normative mediation of reactions to crowding. *Environmental Psychology and Nonverbal Behavior, 1,* 30–40.

KASARDA, J. P., & JANOWITZ, M. (1974). Community attachment in mass society. *American Sociological Review, 39,* 328–339.

KASMAR, J. V. (1970). The development of a usable lexicon of environmental descriptors. *Environment and Behavior, 2,* 153–170.

KASPER, S., ROGERS, S. L. B., YANCEY, A., SKWERER, R. G., SCHULZ, P. M., & ROSENTHAL, N. E. (1989). Psychological effects of light therapy in normals. In N. E. Rosenthal & M. C. Blehar (Eds.), *Seasonal affective disorders and phototherapy*. New York: Guilford.

KASSOVER, C. J. (1972). Self-disclosure, sex, and the use of personal distance. *Dissertation Abstracts International, 32,* 442B.

KATES, R. W. (1962). *Hazard and choice perception in flood plain management*. Chicago: University of Chicago Press.

KATES, R. W. (1976). Experiencing the environment as hazard. In H. M. Proshansky, W. H. Ittelson, & L. G. Rivlin (Eds.), *Environmental psychology: People and their physical settings* (2nd ed.). New York: Holt, Rinehart, & Winston.

KATZEV, R., & BACHMAN, W. (1982). Effects of deferred payment and fare manipulations on urban bus ridership. *Journal of Applied Psychology, 67,* 83–88.

KEANE, T. M., & WOLFE, J. (1990). Comorbidity in post-traumatic stress disorder: An analysis of community and clinical studies. *Journal of Applied Social Psychology, 20,* 1776–1788.

KEETON, W. T. (1974). The mystery of pigeon homing. *Scientific American, 231,* 96–107.

KEGEL-FLOM, P. (1976). Identifying the potential rural optometrist. *American Journal of Optometry and Physiological Optics, 53,* 479–482.

KELLERT, S. R. (1984). Urban American perceptions of animals and the natural environment. *Urban Ecology, 8,* 209–228.

KELLEY, H. H., CONDRY, J. C., DAHLKE, A. E., & HILL, A. H. (1965). Collective behavior in a simulated panic situation. *Journal of Experimental Social Psychology, 1,* 20–54.

KELLY, J. R. (1976). *Two orientations of leisure choices.* Paper presented at the annual American Sociological Association convention, New York.

KELLY, J. R. (1980). Outdoor recreation participation: A comparative analysis. *Leisure Sciences, 3,* 129–154.

KEMPTON. W., & MONTGOMERY, L. (1982). Folk quantification of energy. *Energy, 7,* 817–827.

KENRICK, D. T., & MACFARLANE, S. W. (1986). Ambient temperature and horn honking: A field study of the heat/aggression relationship. *Environment and Behavior, 18,* 179–191.

KENT, S. (1984). *Analyzing activity areas: An ethnoarchaeological study of the use of space.* Albuquerque: University of New Mexico.

KENT, S. (1991). Partitioning space: Cross-cultural factors influencing domestic spatial segmentation. *Environment and Behavior, 23,* 438–473.

KERR, N. H. (1983). The role of vision in "visual imagery" experiments: Evidence from the congenitally blind. *Journal of Experimental Psychology: General, 112,* 265–277.

KHEW, K., & BREBNER, J. (1985). The role of personality in crowding research. *Personality and Individual Differences, 6,* 641–643.

KIESLER, D. J. (1971). Experimental designs in psychotherapy research. In A. E. Bergin & S. L. Garfield (Eds.), *Handbook of psychotherapy and behavior change: An empirical analysis.* New York: John Wiley and Sons.

KING, G. E. (1976a). Socioterritorial units and interspecific competition: Modern carnivores and early hominids. *Journal of Anthropological Research, 32,* 276–284.

KING, G. E. (1976b). Society and territory in human evolution. *Journal of Human Evolution, 5,* 323–332.

KINSEY, K. P. (1976). Social behavior in confined populations of the Allegheny woodrat, *Neotoma Floridana magister. Animal Behaviour, 24,* 181–187.

KINZEL, A. F. (1970). Body buffer zone in violent prisoners. *American Journal of Psychiatry, 127,* 59–64.

KIRA, A. (1975). *The bathroom* (2nd ed.). New York: Viking Press.

KIRASIC, K. C., & MATHES, E. A. (1990). Effects of different means for conveying environmental information on elderly adults spatial cognition and behavior. *Environment and Behavior, 22,* 591–607.

KISH, G. B., & DONNENWERTH, G. V. (1969). Interests and stimulus seeking. *Journal of Counseling Psychology, 16,* 551–556.

KISH, G. B., & DONNENWERTH, G. V. (1972). Sex differences in the correlates of stimulus seeking. *Journal of Consulting and Clinical Psychology, 38,* 42–49.

KISH, G. B., & LEAHY, L. (1970). Stimulus seeking, age, interests, and attitudes: An amplification. *Perceptual and Motor Skills, 30,* 670.

KLEEMAN, W. B. JR. (1988). The politics of office design. *Environment and Behavior, 20,* 537–549.

KLEIN, R., & HARRIS, B. (1979). Disruptive effects of disconfirmed expectancies about crowding. *Journal of Personality and Social Psychology, 37,* 769–777.

KLEINHESSELINK, R. R., & ROSA, E. A. (1991). Cognitive representation of risk perceptions: A comparison of Japan and the United States. *Journal of Cross-Cultural Psychology, 22,* 11–28.

KLEINKE, C. L., & POHLEN, P. D. (1971). Affective and emotional responses as a function of other person's gaze and cooperativeness in a two-person game. *Journal of Personality and Social Psychology, 17,* 308–313.

KNAPP, D. (1982). *Resource recovery: What recycling can do.* Berkeley, CA: Materials World Publishing.

KNAPP, M. L. (1980). *Essentials of nonverbal communication.* New York: Holt, Rinehart, & Winston.

KNOPF, R. C. (1983). Recreational needs and behavior in natural settings. In I. Altman & J. F. Wohlwill (Eds.), *Human behavior and environment: Vol. 6. Behavior and the natural environment.* New York: Plenum.

KNOPF, R. C. (1987). Human behavior, cognition, and affect in the natural environment. In D. Stokols & I. Altman (Eds.), *Handbook of environmental psychology, Vol. 1.* New York: John Wiley and Sons.

KNOPF, R. C., & BARNES, J. D. (1980). Determinants of satisfaction with a tourism resource: A case study of visitors to Gettysburg National Military Park. In D. E. Hawkins, E. L. Shafer, & J. M. Rovelstad (Eds.), *Tourism, marketing, and management issues.* Washington, DC: George Washington University Press.

KNOPF, R. C., DRIVER, B. L., & BASSETT, J. R. (1973). Motivations for fishing. In *Transactions, 38th North American Wildlife and Natural Resources Conference.* Washington, DC: Wildlife Management Institute.

KNOWLES, E. S. (1980). Convergent validity of personal space measures: Consistent results with low intercorrelations. *Journal of Nonverbal Behavior, 4,* 240–248.

KNOWLES, E. S. (1982). A comment on the study of classroom ecology: A lament for the good old days. *Personality and Social Psychology Bulletin, 8,* 357–361.

KNOWLES, E. S. (1983). Social physics and the effects of others: Tests of the effects of audience size and distance on social judgments and behavior. *Journal of Personality and Social Psychology, 45,* 1263–1279.

KOHLENBERG, R. J., & PHILLIPS, T. (1973). Reinforcement and rate of litter depositing. *Journal of Applied Behavior Analysis, 6,* 391–396.

KOHLENBERG, R. J., PHILLIPS, T., & PROCTOR, W. (1976). A behavioral analysis of peaking in residential electricity energy consumption. *Journal of Applied Behavior Analysis, 9,* 13–18.

KONAR, E., & SUNDSTROM, E. (1986). Status demarcation in the office. In J. Wineman (Ed.), *Behavioral issues in office design.* New York: Van Nostrand Reinhold.

KONAR, E., SUNDSTROM, E., BRADY, C., MANDEL, D., & RICE, R. (1982). Status markers in the office. *Environment and Behavior, 14,* 561–580.

KONECNI, V. J. (1975). Annoyance, type and duration of post-annoyance activity, and aggression: The "cathartic" effect. *Journal of Experimental Psychology: General, 104,* 76–102.

KONECNI, V. J., LIBUSER, L., MORTON, H., & EBBESEN, E. B. (1975). Effects of a violation of personal space on escape and helping responses. *Journal of Experimental Social Psychology, 11,* 288–299.

KONEYA, M. (1976). Location and interaction in the row and column seating arrangements. *Environment and Behavior, 8,* 265–282.

KORDA, M. (1975). *Power! How to get it, how to use it.* New York: Random House.

KOROSEC-SERFATY, P., & BOLITT, D. (1986). Dwelling and the experience of burglarly. *Journal of Environmental Psychology, 6,* 329–344.

KORTE, C. (1980). Urban-nonurban differences in social behavior and social psychological models of urban impact. *Journal of Social Issues, 36,* 29–51.

KOSSLYN, S. M., PICK, H. L., & FARIELLO, G. R. (1974). Cognitive maps in children and men. *Child Development, 45,* 707–716.

KOZLOWSKI, L. T., & BRYANT, K. J. (1977). Sense of direction, spatial orientation, and cognitive maps. *Journal of Experimental Psychology: Human Perception and Performance, 3,* 590–598.

KRAIL, K., & LEVENTHAL, G. (1976). The sex variable in the intrusion of personal space. *Sociometry, 39,* 170–173.

KRAUSS, R. M., FREEDMAN, J. L., & WHITCUP, M. (1978). Field and laboratory studies of littering. *Journal of Experimental Social Psychology, 14,* 109–122.

KREGER, J. (1973). Ecology and black student opinion. *Journal of Environmental Education, 4,* 3.

KRIPKE, D. F., GILLIN, J. C., MULLANEY, D. J., RISCH, S. C., & JANOWSKY, D. S. (1987). Treatment of major depressive disorders by bright white light for five days. In A. Halaris (Ed.), *Chronobiology and neuropsychiatric disorders.* New York: Elsevier.

KRIPKE, D. F., RISCH, S. C., & JANOWSKY, D. (1983). Bright white light alleviates depression. *Psychiatric Research, 10,* 105–112.

KRYTER, K. D. (1970). *The effects of noise on man.* New York: Academic Press.

KRYTER, K. D. (1976). Extra-auditory effects of noise. In D. Henderson, R. P. Hamernik, S. Dosanjh, & J. H. Miller (Eds.), *Effects of noise on hearing.* New York: Raven Press.

KRYTER, K. D. (1980). Physiological acoustics and health. *Journal of the Acoustical Society of America, 68,* 10–14.

KUETHE, J. L. (1962a). Social schemas. *Journal of Abnormal and Social Psychology, 65,* 31–38.

KEUTHE, J. L. (1962b). Social schemas and the reconstruction of social object displays from memory. *Journal of Abnormal and Social Psychology, 65,* 71–74.

KEUTHE, J. L. (1964). Pervasive influence of social schemata. *Journal of Abnormal and Social Psychology, 68,* 248–254.

KUPER, L. (Ed.). (1953). *Living in towns.* London: Cresset Press.

KUSHNIR, T. (1982). Skylab effects: Psychological reactions to a human-made environmental hazard. *Environment and Behavior, 14,* 84–93.

KYZAR, K. (1977). Noise pollution and the schools: How much is too much? *Council of Educational Facility Planners Journal, 4,* 10–11.

LABAY, D. G., & KINNEAR, T. C. (1981). Exploring the consumer decision process in the adoption of solar energy systems. *Journal of Consumer Research, 8,* 271–278.

LACEY, J. I. (1967). Somatic response patterning and stress: Some revisions of activation theory. In M. H. Appley & R. Trumbull (Eds.), *Psychological stress.* New York: Appleton-Century-Crofts.

LACOSTE, V., & WIRZ-JUSTICE, A. (1989). Seasonal variation in normal subjects: An update of variables current in depression research. In N. E. Rosenthal & M. C. Blehar (Eds.), *Seasonal affective disorders and phototherapy.* New York: Guilford Press.

LAFRANCE, M., & MAYO, C. (1976). Racial differences in gaze behavior during conversations: Two systematic observational studies. *Journal of Personality and Social Psychology, 33,* 547–552.

LAIRD, J. D., WAGENER, J. J., HALAL, M., & SZEGDA, M. (1982). Remembering what you feel: Effects of emotion on memory. *Journal of Personality and Social Psychology, 42,* 646–657.

LAKEY, B. (1989). Personal and environmental antecedents of perceived social support developed at college. *American Journal of Community Psychology, 17,* 503–519.

LANDSBERGER, H. A. (1958). *Hawthorne revisited: Management and the worker, its critics, and developments of human relations in industry.* Ithaca, NY: New York State School of Industrial and Labor Relations.

LANG, J. (1987). *Creating architectural theory: The role of behavioral sciences in environmental design.* New York: Van Nostrand Reinhold.

LANG, J. (1988a). Understanding normative theories of architecture. *Environment and Behavior, 20,* 601–632.

LANG, J. (1988b). Symbolic aesthetics in architecture: Toward a research agenda. In J. L. Nasar (Ed.), *Environmental aesthetics.* Cambridge, England: Cambridge University Press.

LANGER, E. U., & SAEGERT, S. (1977). Crowding and cognitive control. *Journal of Personality and Social Psychology, 35,* 175–182.

LANPHIER, E. H. (1974). Medical aspects of diving: Underwater psychology. In B. E. Empleton, E. H. Lanphier, J. E. Young, & L. G. Goff (Eds.), *The new science of skin and scuba diving* (Revised ed.). Chicago: Follett.

LARSON, C. T. (1965). *The effect of windowless classrooms on elementary school children.* Ann Arbor: Architectural Research Laboratory, University of Michigan.

LAWRENCE, R. J. (1985). A more humane history of homes. In I. Altman & C. M. Werner (Eds.), *Home environments.* New York: Plenum.

LAWRENCE, R. J. (1987). What makes a house a home? *Environment and Behavior, 19,* 154–168

LAWTON, M. P. (1987). Housing for the elderly in the mid-1980s. In G. Lesnoff-Caravaglia (Ed.), *Handbook of applied gerontology.* New York: Human Sciences Press.

LAYNE, L. (1987). Village-Bedouin: Patterns of change from mobility to sedentism in Jordan. In S. Kent (Ed.), *Method and theory for activity area research: An ethnoarchaeological approach.* New York: Columbia Univeristy Press.

LAZARUS, R. S. (1966). *Psychological stress and the coping process.* new York: McGraw-Hill.

LAZARUS, R. S., & COHEN, J. (1977). Environmental stress. In J. Wohlwill & I. Altman (Eds.), *Human behavior and environment.* New York: Plenum.

LAZARUS, R. S., & LAUNIER, R. (1978). Stress related transactions between person and environment. In L. Pervin & M. Lewis (Eds.), *Perspectives in interactional psychology.* New York: Plenum.

LEAVITT, H. J. (1951). Some effects of certain communications patterns on group performance. *Journal of Abnormal and Social Psychology, 46,* 38–50.

LEBO, C. P., & OLIPHANT, K. P. (1968). Music as a source of acoustical trauma. *Laryngoscope, 78,* 1211–1218.

LEBOWITZ, M. D., CASSELL, E. J., & MCCARROLL, J. R. (1972). Health and the urban environment: XV. Acute respiratory episodes as reactions by sensitive individuals to air pollution and weather. *Environmental Research, 5,* 135–141.

LECOMPTE, W. F., & ROSENFELD, H. M. (1971). Effects of minimal eye contact in the instruction period on impressions of the experimenter. *Journal of Experimental Social Psychology, 7,* 211–220.

LEE, M. C. (1985). Sense-sational marine education. *American Association of Zoological Parks and Aquariums 1985 Annual Proceedings,* pp. 414–418.

LEE, T. R. (1962). Brennan's law of shopping behavior. *Psychological Reports, 11,* 662.

LEE, T. R. (1968). Urban neighborhood as a socio-spatial schema. *Human Relations, 21,* 662.

LEE, T. R. (1978). A theory of socio-spatial schemata. In S. Kaplan & R. Kaplan (Eds.), *Humanscape: Environments for people.* North Scituate, MA: Duxbury Press.

LEGGETT, W. C. (1973). The migrations of the shad. *Scientific American, 228,* 92–98.

LEHMAN, D. R., & TAYLOR, S. E. (1987). Date with an earthquake: Coping with a probable unpredictable disaster. *Personality and Social Psychology Bulletin, 13,* 546–555.

LEISER, D., & ZILBERSHATZ, A. (1989). The traveller: A computational model of spatial network learning. *Environment and Behavior, 21,* 435–463.

LEONARD, J. A., & NEWMAN, R. C. (1967). Spatial orientation in the blind. *Nature, 215,* 1413–1414.

LEONARD-BARTON, D. (1980, September). *The role of interpersonal communication networks in the diffusion of energy conserving practices and technologies.* Paper presented at the International Conference of Consumer Behavior and Energy Policy, Banff, Alberta, Canada.

LEOPOLD, A. (1949). *A Sand County almanac.* New York: Oxford University Press.

LEPORE, S. J., EVANS, G. W., & SCHNEIDER, M. L. (1991). Dynamic role of social support in the link between chronic stress and psychological distress. *Journal of Personality and Social Psychology, 61,* 899–909.

LEVENSON, M. R. (1990). Risk taking and personality. *Journal of Personality and Social Psychology, 58,* 1073–1080.

LEVENTHAL, G., & LEVITT, L. (1979). Physical, social, and personal factors in the perception of crowding. *Journal of Nonverbal Behavior, 4,* 40–55.

LEVESQUE, M. (1991). An experiential perspective on conducting social and behavioral research at Antarctic research stations. In A. A. Harrison, Y. A. Clearwater, & C. P. McKay (Eds.), *From Antarctica to outer space: Life in isolation and confinement.* New York: Springer-Verlag.

LEVINE, A. S. (1991). Psychological effects of long-duration space missions and stress amelioration techniques. In A. A. Harrison, Y. A. Clearwater, & C. P. McKay (Eds.), *From Antarctica to outer space: Life in isolation and confinement.* New York: Springer-Verlag.

LEVINE, D., O'NEAL, E., GARWOOD, S. G., & MCDONALD, P. (1980). Classroom ecology: The effects of seating position on grades and participation. *Personality and Social Psychology Bulletin, 6,* 409–416.

LEVINE, R. D., MIYAKE, K., & LEE, M. (1989). Places rated revisited: Psycho-social pathology in metropolitan areas. *Environment and Behavior, 21,* 734–762.

LEVITT, L., & LEVENTHAL, G. (1984, August). *Litter reduction: How effective is the New York State bottle bill?* Paper presented at the meeting of the American Psychological Association, Toronto.

LEVY-LEBOYER, C., & NATUREL, V. (1991). Neighborhood noise annoyance. *Journal of Environmental Psychology, 11,* 75–86.

LEWIN, K. (1943). Defining the field at a given time. *Psychological Review, 50,* 292–310.

LEWIS, C. A. (1973). People-plant interaction: A new horticultural perspective. *American Horticulturist, 52,* 18–25.

LEWIS, G. M. (1988). Rhetoric of the western interior: Modes of environmental description in American promotional literature of the nineteenth century. In D. Cosgrove & S. Daniels (Eds.), *The iconography of landscape.* Cambridge, England: Cambridge University Press.

LEWIS, O. (1961). *The children of Sanchez.* New York: Random House.

LEY, D., & CYBRIWSKY, R. (1974). Urban graffiti as territorial markers. *Annals of the Association of American Geographers, 64,* 491–505.

LIBEN, L. S., MOORE, M. L., & GOLBECK, S. L. (1982). Preschoolers' knowledge of their classroom environment: Evidence from small-scale and life-size spatial tasks. *Child Development, 53,* 1275–1284.

LIME, D. W. (1986). River recreation and natural resource management: A focus on river running and boating. In the President's Commission on Americans Outdoors (Ed.), *A literature review.* Washington, DC: U.S. Government Printing Office.

LINDSLEY, D. B. (1961). Common factors in sensory deprivation, sensory distortion, and sensory overload. In P. Solomon, P. E. Kubzansky, P. H. Leiderman, J. Mendelson, & D. Wexler (Eds.), *Sensory deprivation.* Cambridge: Harvard University Press.

LITTLE, B. R. (1987). Personality and the environment. In D. Stokols & I. Altman (Eds.), *Handbook of environmental psychology* (Vol. 1). New York: John Wiley and Sons.

LITTLE, C. E. (1975). Some methods and strategies in the prediction of preference. In E. H. Zube, R. O. Brush, & J. G. Fabos (Eds.), *Landscape assessment.* Stroudsburg, PA: Dowden, Hutchinson, and Ross.

LITTLE, K. B. (1965). Personal space. *Journal of Experimental Social Psychology, 1,* 237–247.

LITTLE, K. B. (1968). Cultural variations in social schemata. *Journal of Personality and Social Psychology, 10,* 1–7.

LITTON, R. B. (1968). *Forest landscape description and inventories — a basis for land planning and design.* Berkeley, CA: Pacific Southwest Forest and Range Experiment Station. (USDA Forest Service Research Paper PSW–49).

LITTON, R. B. (1972). Aesthetic dimensions of the landscape. In J. V. Krutilla

(Ed.), *Natural environments: Studies in theoretical and applied analysis.* Baltimore: Johns Hopkins University Press.

LIVINGSTON, B. (1974). *Animals, people, places.* New York: Arbor House.

LLOYD, E. L. (1981). Hallucinations and misinterpretations in hypothermia and cold stress. In B. Harvald & H. Hansen (Eds.), *Circumpolar 81: Proceedings of the Fifth International Symposium on Circumpolar Health, Copenhagen.* Oulu, Finland: Nordic Council for Arctic Medical Research.

LOCKARD, J. S., MCVITTIE, R. I., & ISAAC, L. M. (1977). Functional significance of the affiliative smile. *Bulletin of the Psychonomic Society, 9,* 367–370.

LOMBARDO, J. P. (1986). Interaction of sex and sex role in response to violations of preferred seating arrangements. *Sex Roles, 15,* 173–183.

LOMBARDO, T. J. (1987). *The reciprocity of perceiver and environment.* Hillsdale, NJ: Erlbaum.

LONG, G. T., SELBY, J. W., & CALHOUN, L. G. (1980). Effects of situational stress and sex on interpersonal distance preference. *Journal of Psychology, 105,* 231–237.

LOO, C. M. (1972). The effects of spatial density on the social behavior of children. *Journal of Applied Social Psychology, 2,* 372–381.

LOO, C. M. (1973). Important issues in researching the effects of crowding on humans. *Representative Research in Social Psychology, 4,* 219–226.

LOO, C. M. (1978). Density, crowding, and preschool children. In A. Baum & Y. Epstein (Eds.), *Human response to crowding.* Hillsdale, NJ: Erlbaum.

LOO, C. M., & KENNELLY, D. (1979). Social density: Its effects on behaviors and perceptions of preschoolers. *Environmental Psychology and Nonverbal Behavior, 3,* 131–146.

LOO, C. M., & SMETANA, J. (1978). The effects of crowding on the behavior and perception of 10-year-old boys. *Environmental Psychology and Nonverbal Behavior, 2,* 226–249.

LORENZ, K. A. (1966). *On aggression.* New York: Bantam Books.

LOTT, B. S., & SOMMER, R. (1967). Seating arrangements and status. *Journal of Personality and Social Psychology, 7,* 90–95.

LOUGHLIN, L. E., & SUINA, J. H. (1982). *The learning environment: An instructional strategy.* New York: Teacher's College, Columbia Unversity.

LOVE, K. D., & AIELLO, J. R. (1980). Using projective techniques to measure interaction distance: A methodological note. *Personality and Social Psychology Bulletin, 6,* 102–104.

LOWIN, A., HOTTES, J. H., SANDLER, B. E., & BORNSTEIN, M. (1971). The pace of life and sensitivity to time in urban and rural settings: A preliminary study. *Journal of Social Psychology, 83,* 247–253.

LUCAS, R. C. (1964). *The recreational capacity of the Quetico-Superior* (Research Paper 5–15). Washington, DC: Lake State Forest Experiment Station, Forest Service, USDA.

LUKAS, J. H., & SIEGEL, J. (1977). Cortical mechanisms that augment or reduce evoked potentials in cats. *Science, 196,* 73–75.

LUTZ, W. J., & SHEIRER, C. J. (1974). Coding processes for pictures and words. *Journal of Verbal Learning and Verbal Behavior, 13,* 316–320.

LYMAN, S. M., & SCOTT, M. B. (1967). Territoriality: A neglected sociological dimension. *Social Problems, 15,* 236–249.

LYNCH, K. (1960). *The image of the city.* Cambridge, MA: MIT Press.

LYNCH, K. (1965). The city as environment. *Scientific American, 213,* 209–219.

LYNCH, K. (1977). *Growing up in cities.* Cambridge, MA: MIT Press.

LYONS, E. (1983). Demographic correlates of landscape preference. *Environment and Behavior, 15,* 487–511.

MACDERMOTT, V. (1971). *The cult of the seer in the ancient Middle East.* Berkeley, CA: University of California Press.

MACDONALD, J. E., & GIFFORD, R. (1989). Territorial cues and defensible space theory: The burglar's point of view. *Journal of Environmental Psychology, 9,* 193–205.

MACHLIS, G. E. (1989). Managing parks as human ecosystems. In I. Altman & E. H. Zube (Eds.), *Public places and spaces.* New York: Plenum.

MACKINTOSH E. (1982). High in the city. In P. Bart, A. Chen, & G. Francescato (Eds.), *Knowledge for design: Proceedings of the 13th Environmental Design Research Association conference* (pp. 424–434). Washington, DC: Environmental Design Reserach Association.

MACPHERSON, J. C. (1984). Environments and interaction in row-and-column classrooms. *Environment and Behavior, 16,* 481–502.

MAGILL, A. W. (1976). The message of vandalism. In *Vandalism and outdoor recreation.* Berkeley, CA: U.S. Department of Agriculture, Pacific Southwest Forest and Range Experiment Station.

MALANDRO, L. A., BARKER, L., & BARKER, D. A. (1989). *Nonverbal communication* (2nd ed.). New York: Random House.

MALMBERG, T. (1980). *Human territoriality.* New York: Mouton.

MALONEY, M. P., & WARD, M. P. (1973). Ecology: Let's hear from the people. *American Psychologist, 30,* 787–790.

MALTZMAN, I., & RASKIN, D. C. (1965). Effects of individual differences in the orienting reflex on conditioning and complex processes. *Journal of Experimental Research in Personality, 1,* 1–16.

MANDEL, D. R., BARON, R. M., & FISHER, J. D. (1980). Room utilization and dimensions of density: Effects of height and view. *Environment and Behavior, 12,* 308–319.

MANDELL, L., & MARANS, R. (1972). *Participation in outdoor recreation: A national perspective.* Ann Arbor, MI: Institute for Social Research.

MANZO, L. C., & WEINSTEIN, N. D. (1987). Behavioral commitment to environmental protection: A study of active and nonactive members of the Sierra Club. *Environment and Behavior, 19,* 673–694.

MAPLE, T. (1983). Environmental psychology and great ape reproduction. *International Journal for the Study of Animal Problems, 4,* 295–299.

MAPLE, T., & STINE, W. (1982). Environmental variables and great ape husbandry. *American Journal of Primatology Supplement, 1,* 67–76.

MARANS, R. W., & SPRECKELMEYER, K. F. (1982). Evaluating open and conventional office design. *Environment and Behavior, 14,* 333–351.

MARCUS, C. C. (1978). Remembrance of landscapes past. *Landscape, 22,* 34–43.

MARCUS, C. C. (1990). From the pragmatic to the spiritual: An intellectual autobiography. In I. Altman & K. Christensen (Eds.), *Environment and behavior studies.* New York: Plenum.

MARKHAM, S. (1947). *Climate and the energy of nations.* New York: Oxford University Press.

MARKUS-KAPLAN, M., & KAPLAN, K. J. (1984). A bidimensional view of distancing:

Reciprocity vs. compensation, intimacy vs. social control. *Journal of Nonverbal Behavior, 8,* 315–326.

MARLER, L. (1971). A study of anti-litter messages. *Journal of Environmental Education, 3,* 51–53.

MARSHALL, J., & HESLIN, R. (1975). Boys and girls together. *Journal of Personality and Social Psychology, 31,* 952–961.

MARSHALL, M. (1972). Privacy and environment. *Human Ecology, 1,* 93–110.

MARTIN, D. W. (1985). *Doing psychology experiments* (2nd ed.). Pacific Grove, CA: Brooks/Cole.

MARTIN, G. L., & HEIMSTRA, N. W. (1973). The perception of hazard by children. *Journal of Safety Research, 5,* 238–246.

MARTIN, J., & O'REILLY, J. (1988). Editor's introduction: Contemporary environment-behavior research in zoological parks. *Environment and Behavior, 20,* 387–395.

MARTIN, J., & O'REILLY, J. (1989). The emergence of environment-behavior research in zoological parks. In I. Altman & E. H. Zube (Eds.), *Public places and spaces,* New York: Plenum.

MARTINDALE, D. A. (1971). Territorial dominance behavior in dyadic verbal interactions. *Proceedings of the Annual Convention of the American Psychological Association, 6,* 305–306.

MASSEY, A., & VANDENBURGH, J. G. (1980). Puberty delay by a urinary cue from female house mice in feral populations. *Science, 209,* 821–822.

MATHEWS, J. (1991). Acts of war and the environment. *The Washington Post National Weekly Edition, 8,* 27.

MATHEWS, K. E., & CANON, L. K. (1975). Environmental noise level as a determinant of helping behavior. *Journal of Personality and Social Psychology, 32,* 571–577.

MATHEWS, R. W., PAULUS, P. B., & BARON, R. A. (1979). Physical aggression after being crowded. *Journal of Nonverbal Behavior, 4,* 5–17.

MATLIN, M. W. (1989). *Cognition.* New York: Holt, Rinehart, & Winston.

MATTHEWS, M. H. (1985). Young children's representation of the environment: A comparison of techniques. *Journal of Environmental Psychology, 5,* 261–278.

MAYRON, L. W., OTT, J. N., NATIONS, R., & MAYRON, E. L. (1974). Light, radiation, and academic behavior. *Academic Therapy, 10,* 441–448.

MAZIS, M. B. (1975). Antipollution measures and psychological reactance theory: A field experiment. *Journal of Personality and Social Psychology, 31,* 654–660.

MCANDREW, F. T. (1984). Comparative psychology, ethology, and external validity: Does it always matter if the snark is a boojum? *Comparative Psychology Newsletter, 4,* 1–4.

MCANDREW, F. T. (1992, April). *The home advantage also operates in individual sports: A study of high school wrestlers.* Paper presented at the meeting of the Eastern Psychological Association, Boston, MA.

MCANDREW, F. T., & CLARK, J. D. (1983, April). *Situational preferences of individuals differing in arousability.* Paper presented at the meeting of the Eastern Psychological Association, Philadelphia.

MCANDREW, F. T., GOLD, J. A., LENNEY, E., & RYCKMAN, R. M. (1984). Explorations in immediacy: The nonverbal system and its relationship to affective and situational factors. *Journal of Nonverbal Behavior, 8,* 210–228.

MCANDREW, F. T., RYCKMAN, R. M., HORR, W., & SOLOMON, R. (1978). The effects of invader placement of spatial markers on territorial behavior in a college population. *Journal of Social Psychology, 104,* 149–150.

MCANDREW, F. T., & THORNTON, B. G. (1987, April). *Approach and avoidance tendencies of screeners and nonscreeners.* Paper presented at the meeting of the Eastern Psychological Association, Arlington, VA.

MCANDREW, F. T., & WARNER, J. E. (1986). Arousal seeking and the maintenance of mutual gaze in same and mixed-sex dyads. *Journal of Nonverbal Behavior, 10,* 168–172.

MCBRIDE, G., KING, M. G., & JAMES, J. W. (1965). Social proximity effects on galvanic skin responses in adult humans. *Journal of Psychology, 61,* 153–157.

MCCAIN, G., COX, V. C., & PAULUS, P. B. (1976). The relationship between illness complaints and degree of crowding in a prison environment. *Environment and Behavior, 8,* 283–290.

MCCARREY, M. W., PETERSON, L., EDWARDS, S., & VON KULMIZ, P. (1974). Landscape office attitudes: Reflections of perceived degree of control over transactions with the environment. *Journal of Applied Psychology, 59,* 401–403.

MCCARTHY, D. P., & SAEGERT, S. (1978). Residential density, social overload, and social withdrawal. *Human Ecology, 6,* 253–272.

MCCAULEY, C., COLEMAN, G., & DEFUSCO, P. (1978). Commuters' eye contact with strangers in city and suburban train stations: Evidence of short-term adaptation to interpersonal overload in the city. *Environmental Psychology and Nonverbal Behavior, 2,* 215–225.

MCCAULEY, C., & TAYLOR, J. (1976). Is there an overload of acquaintances in the city? *Environmental Psychology and Nonverbal Behavior, 1,* 41–55.

MCCLELLAND, D. C., ATKINSON, J. W., CLARK, R. A., & LOWELL, E. L. (1953). *The achievement motive.* New York: Appleton-Century-Crofts.

MCCORMICK, E. J., & SANDERS, E. J. (1982). *Human factors in engineering and design.* New York: McGraw-Hill.

MCDONALD, A. L., & CLARK, N. (1968). *Evaluation of the interpretive program for Yellowstone National Park.* Washington, DC: National Park Service.

MCDONOUGH, M. H., & FIELD, D. R. (1979). *Coulee Dam National Recreation Area: Visitor use patterns and preferences.* Seattle, WA: University of Washington Press.

MCGREW, P. L. (1970). Social and spatial density effects on spacing behavior in preschool children. *Journal of Child Psychology and Psychiatry, 11,* 197–205.

MCGREW, W. G. (1972). *An ethological study of children's behavior.* New York: Academic Press.

MCGUINESS, D., & SPARKS, J. (1979). Cognitive style and cognitive maps: Sex differences in representations of familiar terrain. *Journal of Mental Imagery, 7,* 101–118.

MCKECHNIE, G. E. (1974). *ERI manual: Environmental Response Inventory.* Berkeley, CA: Consulting Psychologists Press.

MCKECHNIE, G. E. (1977). The Environmental Response Inventory in application. *Environment and Behavior, 9,* 255–276.

MCLEARN, G. E. (1959). Genetics of mouse behavior in novel situations. *Journal of Comparative and Physiological Psychology, 52,* 62–67.

MCLUHAN, T. C. (1971). *Touch the earth: A self-portrait of Indian existence.* New York: Simon and Schuster.

MCNAIR, D. M., LORR, M., & DROPPLEMAN, L. F. (1971). *Manual: Profile of mood states.* San Diego: Educational and Industrial Testing service.

MCNEES, M. P., SCHNELLE, J. F., GENDRICH, J., THOMAS, M. M., & BEAGLE, G. P. (1979). McDonald's litter hunt: A community litter control system for youth. *Environment and Behavior, 11,* 131–138.

MCPARTLAND, J. M., & MCDILL, E. L. (1977). *Violence in schools.* Lexington, MA: Lexington Books.

MECHANIC, D. (1978). *Medical sociology.* New York: The Free Press.

MEHRABIAN, A. (1967). Orientation behaviors and nonverbal attitude communication. *Journal of Communication, 16,* 324–332.

MEHRABIAN, A. (1969a). Significance of posture and position in the communication of attitude and status relationships. *Psychological Bulletin, 71,* 359–372.

MEHRABIAN, A. (1969b). Some referents and measures of nonverbal behavior. *Behavior Research Methods and Instrumentation, 1,* 203–207.

MEHRABIAN, A. (1973). A measure of arousal seeking tendency. *Environment and Behavior, 5,* 315–333.

MEHRABIAN, A. (1975). Affiliation as a function of attitude discrepancy with another and arousal seeking tendency. *Journal of Personality, 43,* 582–590.

MEHRABIAN, A. (1976a). *Manual for the questionnaire measure of stimulus screening and arousability.* Los Angeles: Albert Mehrabian.

MEHRABIAN, A. (1976b). *Public places and private spaces.* New York: Basic Books.

MEHRABIAN, A. (1977a). A questionnaire measure of individual differences in stimulus screening and associated differences in arousability. *Environmental Psychology and Nonverbal Behavior, 1,* 89–103.

MEHRABIAN, A. (1977b). Individual differences in stimulus screening and arousability. *Journal of Personality, 45,* 237–250.

MEHRABIAN, A. (1978). Characteristic individual reactions to preferred and unpreferred environments. *Journal of Personality, 46,* 717–731.

MEHRABIAN, A. (1980). *Basic dimensions for a general psychological theory.* Cambridge, MA: Oelgeschlager, Gunn, & Hain.

MEHRABIAN, A., & DIAMOND, S. G. (1971). Effects of furniture arrangement, props, and personality on social interaction. *Journal of Personality and Social Psychology, 20,* 18–30.

MEHRABIAN, A., & RUSSELL, J. A. (1974a). *An approach to environmental psychology.* Cambridge, MA: MIT Press.

MEHRABIAN, A., & RUSSELL, J. A. (1974b). A verbal measure of information rate for studies in environmental psychology. *Environment and Behavior, 6,* 233–252.

MEHRABIAN, A., & WIXEN, W. J. (1986). Preferences for individual video games as a function of their emotional effects on players. *Journal of Applied Social Psychology, 16,* 3–15.

MELICK, M. (1978). Life change and illness: Illness behavior of males in the recovery period of a natural disaster. *Journal of Health and Social Behavior, 19,* 335–342.

MELLSTROM, M., CICALA, G. A., & ZUCKERMAN, M. (1976). General versus specific trait anxiety measures in the prediction of fear of snakes, heights, and darkness. *Journal of Consulting and Clinical Psychology, 44,* 83–91.

MELTON, A. (1933). Some behavior characteristics of museum visitors. *Psychological Bulletin, 30,* 720–721.

MENDELSOHN, R., & ORCUTT, G. (1979). An empirical analysis of air pollution dose-response curves. *Journal of Environmental Economics and Management, 6,* 85–106.

MERLEMAN, R. M. (1988). The political uses of territoriality. *Environment and Behavior, 20,* 576–600.

MEYERS, A. W., ARTZ, L. M., & CRAIGHEAD, W. E. (1976). The effects of instructions, incentives, and feedback on a community problem: Dormitory noise. *Journal of Applied Behavior Analysis, 9,* 445–457.

MICHELSON, W. (1968). Most people don't want what architects want. *Transaction, 5,* 37–43.

MICHELSON, W. (1977). *Environmental choice, human behavior, and residential satisfaction.* New York: Oxford University Press.

MIDDLEMIST, R. D., KNOWLES, E. S., & MATTER, C. F. (1976). Personal space invasions in the lavatory: Suggestive evidence for arousal. *Journal of Personality and Social Psychology, 33,* 541–546.

MILBRATH, L. W. (1984). *Environmentalist: Vanguard for a new society.* Albany, NY: State University of New York Press.

MILGRAM, S. (1970). The experience of living in cities. *Science, 167,* 1461–1468.

MILGRAM, S. (1977). *The individual in a social world: Essays and experiments.* Reading, MA: Addison-Wesley.

MILGRAM, S., & JODELET, D. (1976). Psychological maps of Paris. In H. R. Proshansky, W. Ittelson, & L. Rivlin (Eds.), *Environmental psychology: People and their physical settings.* New York: Holt, Rinehart, & Winston.

MILLARD, R., & SIMPSON, D. (1980). Enjoyment and productivity as a function of classroom seating location. *Perceptual and Motor Skills, 50,* 439–444.

MILLER, F. D., TSEMBERIS, S., MALIA, G. P., & GREGA, D. (1980). Neighborhood satisfaction among urban dwellers. *Journal of Social Issues, 36,* 101–117.

MILLER, G. T. (1990). *Living in the environment* (6th ed.). Belmont, CA: Wadsworth.

MILLER, M., ALBERT, M., BOSTICK, D., & GELLER, E. S. (1976). *Can the design of a trash can influence litter-related behavior?* Paper presented at the meeting of the Southeastern Psychological Association.

MILLER, R. L., BRICKMAN, P., & BOLEN, D. (1975). Attribution vs. persuasion as a means of modifying behavior. *Journal of Personality and Social Psychology, 31,* 430–441.

MILLER, S., & NARDINI, K. M. (1977). Individual differences in the perception of crowding. *Environmental Psychology and Nonverbal Behavior, 2,* 3–13.

MILLER, S., ROSSBACH, J., & MUNSON, R. (1981). Social density and affiliative tendency as determinants of dormitory residential outcomes. *Journal of Applied Social Psychology, 11,* 356–365.

MILLER, S., & SCHLITT, J. K. (1985). *Interior space: Design concepts for personal needs.* New York: Praeger.

MILLER, T. (1976). Vandalism in California state parks. In *Vandalism and outdoor recreation.* Berkeley, CA: U.S. Department of Agriculture, Pacific Southwest Forest and Range Experiment Station.

MINTZ, A. (1951). Nonadaptive group behavior. *Journal of Abnormal and Social Psychology, 46,* 150–159.

MITCHELL, R. C. (1980). *Public opinion on environmental issues, results of a national public opinion survey, CEQ, DOA, DOE, and EPA.* Washington, DC: U.S. Government Printing Office.

MOAR, I., & BOWER, G. H. (1983). Inconsistency in spatial knowledge. *Memory and Cognition, 11,* 107–113.

MOCELLIN, J. S. P., & SUEDFELD, P. (1991). Voices from the ice: Diaries of polar explorers. *Environment and Behavior, 23,* 704–722.

MOCELLIN, J. S. P., SUEDFELD, P., BERNALDEZ, J. P., & BARBARITO, M. E. (1991). Levels of anxiety in polar environments. *Journal of Environmental Psychology, 11,* 265–275.

MOESER, S. D. (1988). Cognitive mapping in a complex building. *Environment and Behavior, 20,* 21–49.

MOHAI, P., & TWIGHT, B. W. (1986). *Rural-urban differences in environmentalism revisited.* Paper presented at the annual meeting of the Rural Sociological Society, Salt Lake City, Utah.

MONEY, K. E. (1981). Biological effects of space travel. *Canadian Aeronautics and Space Journal, 27,* 195–201.

MONTANO, D., & ADAMOPOULOS, J. (1984). The perception of crowding in interpersonal situations: Affective and behavioral responses. *Environment and Behavior, 16,* 643–666.

MONTELLO, D. R. (1988). Classroom seating location and its effect on course achievement, participation, and attitudes. *Journal of Environmental Psychology, 8,* 149–157.

MONTELLO, D. R. (1991). Spatial orientation and the angularity of urban routes: A field study. *Environment and Behavior, 23,* 47–69.

MOOK, D. G. (1983). In defense of external invalidity. *American Psychologist, 38,* 379–387.

MOORE, A. J. (1987). The behavioral ecology of *Libellula luctosa* (Burmeister) (Anisoptera: Libellulidae): 1. Temporal changes in the population density and the effects on male territorial behavior. *Ethology, 75,* 246–254.

MOORE, G. T. (1974). Developmental variations between and within individuals in the cognitive representation of large-scale spatial environments. *Man-Environment Systems, 4,* 55–57.

MOORE, G. T. (1979). Knowing about environmental knowing: The current state of theory and research on environmental cognition. *Environment and Behavior, 11,* 33–70.

MOORE, G. T. (1983, April). *Some effects of the organization of the social-physcial environment on cognitive behavior in child-care settings.* Paper presented at the meeting of the Society for Research on Child Development, Detroit.

MOORE, G. T. (1985). State of the art in play environment research and applications. In J. Frost (Ed.), *When children play.* Wheaton, MD: Association for Childhood Education International.

MOORE, G. T. (1986). Effects of the spatial definition of behavior settings on children's behavior: A quasi-experimental field study. *Journal of Environmental Psychology, 6,* 205–231.

MOORE, R. C. (1969). *The vertical ghetto: Everyday life in an urban project.* New York: Random House.

MOORE, R. C. (1980). Collaborating with young people to assess their landscape values. *Ekistics, 281,* 128–135.

MOORE, R. C. (1986). *Children's domain: Play and space in child development.* London: Croom Helm.

MOORE, R. C. (1989a). Before and after asphalt: Diversity as a measure of ecological quality in children's play environments. In M. Bloch & T. Pellegrini (Eds.), *The ecological context of children's play.* Norwood, NJ: Ablex Publishing.

MOORE, R. C. (1989b). Playgrounds at the crossroads: Policy and action research needed to ensure a viable future for public playgrounds in the United States. In I. Altman & E. H. Zube (Eds.), *Public places and spaces.* New York: Plenum.

MOORE, R. C., & YOUNG, D. (1978) Children outdoors: Toward a social ecology of the landscape. In I. Altman & J. F. Wohlwill (Eds.), *Children and the environment.* New York: Plenum.

MOOS, W. S. (1964). The effects of "Foehn" weather on accident rates in the city of Zurich (Switzerland). *Aerospace Medicine, 35,* 643–645.

MORE, T. A. (1973). Attitudes of Massachusetts hunters. In J. C. Hendee & C. Schoenfeld (Eds.), *Human dimensions in wildlife programs.* Rockville, MD: Mercury.

MORRIS, D. (1962). *The biology of art.* London: Methuen.

MORROW, P. C., & MCELROY, J. C. (1981). Interior office design and visitor response. *Journal of Applied Psychology, 66,* 630–646.

MOSER, G. (1984). Water quality perception: A dynamic perspective. *Journal of Environmental Psychology, 4,* 210.

MOSER, G. (1988). Urban stress and helping behavior. *Journal of Environmental Psychology, 8,* 287–298.

MOSS, B. W. (1978). Some observations on the activity and aggressive behavior of pigs when penned prior to slaughter. *Applied Animal Ethology, 4,* 323–339.

MOYER, D. B. (1976). Acclimatization and high altitude medical problems in Antarctica. *U.S. Navy Medicine, 67,* 19–21.

MUECHER, H., & UNGEHEUER, H. (1961). Meteorological influence on reaction time, flicker-fusion frequency, job accidents, and medical treatment. *Perceptual and Motor Skills, 12,* 163–168.

MULLEN, B., & FELLEMAN, V. (1990). Tripling in the dorms: A meta-analytic integration. *Basic and Applied Social Psychology, 11,* 33–43.

MUNROE, R., & MUNROE, R. (1971). The effect of environmental experience on spatial ability. *Journal of Social Psychology, 83,* 15–22.

MURPHY, D. L. (1977a). Animal models for mania. In I. Hanin & E. Usdin (Eds.), *Animal models in psychiatry and neurology.* New York: Pergamon.

MURPHY, D. L. (1977b). The behavioral toxicity of monoamine oxidase-inhibiting anti-depressants. In R. J. Schnitzer (Ed.), *Advances in Pharmacology and Chemotherapy, 14,* 71–105.

MURPHY, S. A. (1984). After Mount Saint Helen's: Disaster stress research. *Journal of Psychosocial Nursing and Mental Health Services, 22,* 9–18.

MURPHY-BERMAN, V., & BERMAN, J. (1978). The importance of choice and sex in invasions of interpersonal space. *Personality and Social Psychology Bulletin, 4,* 424–428.

MYERS, K., HALE, C. S., MYKYTOWYCZ, R., & HUGHES, R. L. (1971). Density, space, sociality, and health. In A. H. Esser (Ed.), *Behavior and environment.* New York: Plenum.

NAGAR, D., & PANDEY, J. (1987). Affect and performance on cognitive tasks as a function of crowding and noise. *Journal of Applied Social Psychology, 17,* 147–157.

NAGER, A. R., & WENTWORTH, W. R. (1976). *Bryant Park: A comprehensive evaluation of its image and use with implications for urban open space design.* New York: Center for Human Environments, CUNY.

NAKSHIAN, J. S. (1964). The effects of red and green surroundings on behavior. *Journal of General Psychology, 70,* 143–161.

NAPP, N. (1977, June). Noise drives you crazy—jets and mental hospitals. *Psychology Today,* p. 33.

NASAR, J. L. (1989). Symbolic meanings of house styles. *Environment and Behavior, 21,* 235–257.

NASAR, J. L., & GREENBERG, M. L. (1984). The preparedness and reactions of citizens to warnings and crisis relocation for nuclear attack. *Journal of Applied Social Psychology, 14,* 487–500.

NASAR, J. L., JULIAN, D., BUCHMAN, S., HUMPHREYS, D., & MROHALY, M. (1983). The emotional quality of scenes and observation points: A look at prospect and refuge. *Landscape Planning, 10,* 355–361.

NASH, R. (1967). *Wilderness and the American mind.* New Haven, CT: Yale University Press.

NATIONAL ACADEMY OF SCIENCES (1977). *Medical and biological effects of environmental pollutants.* Washington, DC: National Academy of Sciences.

NEARY, R. S. (1975). *The development and validation of a state measure of the sensation-seeking scale.* Unpublished doctoral dissertation, University of Delaware.

NEARY, R. S., & ZUCKERMAN, M. (1976). Sensation seeking trait and state anxiety and the electrodermal orienting reflex. *Psychopysiology, 13,* 205–211.

NEILL, S. R. ST. J. (1982a). Preschool design and child behavior. *Journal of Child Psychology and Psychiatry, 23,* 309–318.

NEILL, S. R. ST. J. (1982b). Experimental alterations in playroom layout and their effect on staff and child behavior. *Educational Psychology, 2,* 103–119.

NELSON, D. L., REED, V. S., & WALLING, J. R. (1976). Pictorial superiority effect. *Journal of Experimental Psychology: Human Learning and Memory, 2,* 523–528.

NEMECEK, J., & GRANDJEAN, E. (1973). Results of an ergonomic investigation of large-space offices. *Human Factors, 15,* 111–124.

NESBITT, P. D., & STEVEN, G. (1974). Personal space and stimulus intensity at a Southern California amusement park. *Sociometry, 37,* 105–115.

NEWCOMB, M. D., & MCGEE, L. (1991). Influence of sensation seeking on general deviance and specific problem behaviors from adolescence to young adulthood. *Journal of Personality and Social Psychology, 61,* 614–628.

NEWMAN, J., & MCCAULEY, C. (1977). Eye contact with strangers in city, suburb, and small town. *Environment and Behavior, 9,* 547–558.

NEWMAN, O. (1972). *Defensible space: Crime prevention through urban design.* New York: Macmillan.

NEWMAN, O., & FRANCK, K. A. (1982). The effects of building size on personal crime and fear of crime. *Population and Environment, 5,* 203–220.

NG, C. F., & GIFFORD, R. (1984, June). *The office acoustical environment: A survey of office-workers' attitudes.* Paper presented at the annual meeting of the Canadian Psychological Association, Ottawa.

NICKERSON, R. S. (1965). Short term memory for complex meaningful visual configurations: A demonstration of capacity. *Canadian Journal of Psychology, 19,* 155–160.

NICKERSON, R. S. (1968). A note on long term recognition memory for pictorial material. *Psychonomic Science, 11,* 58.

NICOSIA, G. J., HYMAN, D., KARLIN, R. A., EPSTEIN, Y. M., & AIELLO, J. R. (1979). Effects of bodily contact on reactions to crowding. *Journal of Applied Social Psychology, 9,* 508–523.

NIELSEN, J. M., & ELLINGTON, B. L. (1983). Social processes and resource conservation: A case study in low technology recycling. In N. R. Feimer & E. S. Geller (Eds.), *Environmental psychology: Directions and perspectives.* New York: Praeger.

NISBET, R. A. (1962). *Community and power: A study in the ethics of order and freedom.* New York: Oxford University Press.

NOLEN-HOEKSEMA, S., & MORROW, J. (1991). A prospective study of depression and posttraumatic stress symptoms after a natural disaster: The 1989 Lomo Prieta earthquake. *Journal of Personality and Social Psychology, 61,* 115–121.

NORMOYLE, J. B., & FOLEY, J. M. (1988). The defensible space model of fear and elderly public housing residents. *Environment and Behavior, 20,* 50–74.

NORRIS-BAKER, C., & SCHEIDT, R. J. (1990). Place attachment among older residents of a "ghost town": A transactional approach. In R. I. Selby, K. H. Anthony, J. Choi, & B. Orland (Eds.), *Coming of age.* Oklahoma City: Environmental Design Research Association.

NORUM, G., RUSSO, N., & SOMMER, R. (1967). Seating patterns and group task. *Psychology in the Schools, 4,* 276–280.

NOVACO, R. W., STOKOLS, D., CAMPBELL, J., & STOKOLS, J. (1979). Transportation, stress, and community psychology. *American Journal of Community Psychology, 7,* 361–380.

NOVACO, R. W., STOKOLS, D., & MILANESI, L. (1990). Objective and subjective dimensions of travel impedance as determinants of community stress. *American Journal of Community Psychology, 18,* 231–257.

NOWLIS, V. (1965). Research with the Mood Adjective Check List. In S. S. Tomkins & C. E. Izard (Eds.), *Affect, cognition, and personality.* New York: Springer-Verlag.

OBERG, J. E., & OBERG, A. R. (1986). *Living on the next frontier: Pioneering space.* New York: McGraw-Hill.

O'CONNELL, B. J., HARPER, R. S., & MCANDREW, F. T. (1985). Grip strength as a function of exposure to red or green visual stimulation. *Perceptual and Motor Skills, 61,* 1157–1158.

OECHALI, F., & BUECHLEY, R. (1970). Excess mortality associated with three Los Angeles September hot spells. *Environmental Research, 3,* 277–284.

OLDHAM, G. R., & BRASS, D. J. (1979). Employee reactions to an open-plan office: A naturally occurring quasi-experiment. *Administrative Science Quarterly, 28,* 267–284.

OLIVER, D. C. (1991). Psychological effects of isolation and confinement of a winter group at McMurdo Station, Antarctica. In A. A. Harrison, Y. A. Clearwater, & C. P. McKay (Eds.), *From Antarctica to outer space: Life in isolation and confinement.* New York: Springer-Verlag.

OLSEN, M. E. (1981). Consumers' attitudes toward energy conservation. *Journal of Social Issues, 37,* 108–131.

OLSON, D. R., & BIALYSTOK, E. (EDS.). (1983). *Spatial cognition*. Hillsdale, NJ: Erlbaum.

O'NEAL, E. C., BRUNAULT, M. A., CARIFIO, M. S., TROUTWINE, R., & EPSTEIN, J. (1984). Effect of insult upon personal space preferences. *Journal of Nonverbal Behavior, 5,* 56–62.

O'NEAL, E. C., SCHULTZ, J., & CHRISTENSON, T. E. (1987). The menstrual cycle and personal space. *Journal of Nonverbal Behavior, 11,* 26–32.

O'NEILL, G. W., BLANCK, L. S., & JOYNER, M. A. (1980). The use of stimulus control over littering in a natural setting. *Journal of Applied Behavior Analysis, 13,* 379–381.

O'NEILL, M. J. (1986). Effects of computer simulated environmental variables on wayfinding accuracy. In J. Wineman, R. Barnes, & C. Zimring (Eds.), *Proceedings of the 17th Annual Conference of the Environmental Design Research Association,* Atlanta, GA: Environmental Design Research Association.

O'NEILL, M. J. (1991a). Evaluation of a conceptual model of architectural legibility. *Environment and Behavior, 23,* 259–284.

O'NEILL, M. J. (1991b). Effects of signage and floor plan configuration of wayfinding accuracy. *Environment and Behavior, 23,* 553–574.

O'NEILL, S. M., & PALUCK, R. J. (1973). Altering territoriality through reinforcement. *Proceedings of the 81st Annual Convention of the American Psychological Association, 8,* 901–902.

O'RIORDAN, T. (1976). Attitudes, behavior, and environmental policy issues. In I. Altman & J. F. Wohlwill (Eds.), *Human behavior and environment: Advances in theory and research* (Vol. 1). New York: Plenum.

ORLEANS, P. (1973). Differential cognition of urban residents: Effects of social scale on mapping. In R. M. Downs & D. Stea (Eds.), *Image and environment: Cognitive mapping and spatial behavior.* Chicago: Aldine.

ORNE, M. T. (1962). On the social psychology of the psychological experiment: With particular reference to demand characteristics and their implications. *American Psychologist, 17,* 776–783.

OSBORNE, J. G., & POWERS, R. B. (1980). Controlling the litter problem. In G. L. Martin & J. G. Osborne (Eds.), *Helping the community: Behavioral applications.* New York: Plenum.

OSGOOD, C. E., SUCI, G. J., & TANNENBAUM, P. H. (1957). *The measurement of meaning.* Urbana, IL: University of Illinois Press.

OSKAMP, S. (1984). *Applied social psychology.* Englewood Cliffs, NJ: Prentice-Hall.

OSKAMP, S., HARRINGTON, M. J., EDWARDS, T. C., SHERWOOD, D. L., OKUDA, S. M., & SWANSON, D. C. (1991). Factors influencing household recycling behavior. *Environment and Behavior, 23,* 494–519.

OSMOND, H. (1959). The relationship between architect and psychiatrist. In C. Goshen (Ed.), *Psychiatric architecture.* Washington, DC: American Psychiatric Association.

PABLANT, P., & BAXTER, J. C. (1975, July). Environmental correlates of school vandalism. *Journal of the American Institute of Planners,* 270–279.

PACIUK, M. (1990). The role of personal control of the environment in thermal comfort and satisfaction at the workplace. In R. I. Selby, K. H. Anthony, J. Choi, & B. Orland (Eds.), *Coming of age.* Oklahoma City: Environmental Design Research Association.

PAGAN, G., & AIELLO, J. R. (1982). Development of personal space among Puerto Ricans. *Journal of Nonverbal Behavior, 7,* 59–68.

PAGE, R. A. (1977). Noise and helping behavior. *Environment and Behavior, 9,* 559–572.

PAGE, R. A. (1978, May). *Environmental influences on prosocial behavior: The effect of temperature.* Paper presented at the meeting of the Midwestern Psychological Association, Chicago.

PAINTER, M. (1976–1977). Fluorescent lights and hyperactivity in children: An experiment. *Academic Therapy, 12,* 181–184.

PALAMAREK, D. L., & RULE, B. G. (1979). The effects of temperature and insult on the motivation to retaliate or escape. *Motivation and Emotion, 3,* 83–92.

PALINKAS, L. A. (1991a). Group adaptation and individual adjustment in Antarctica: A summary of recent research. In A. A. Harrison, Y. A. Clearwater, & C. P. McKay (Eds.), *From Antarctica to outer space: Life in isolation and confinement.* New York: Springer-Verlag.

PALINKAS, L. A. (1991b). Effects of physical and social environments on the health and well-being of Antarctic winter-over personnel. *Environment and Behavior, 23,* 782–799.

PALLAK, M. S., COOK, D. A., & SULLIVAN, J. J. (1980). Commitment and energy conservation. In L. Bickman (Ed.), *Applied social psychology annual* (Vol. 1). Beverly Hills: Sage.

PALLAK, M. S., & CUMMINGS, W. (1976). Commitment and voluntary energy conservation. *Personality and Social Psychology Bulletin, 2,* 27–30.

PALMER, J. F., & ZUBE, E. H. (1976). Numerical and perceptual landscape classification. In E. H. Zube (Ed.), *Studies in landscape perception.* Amherst, MA: Institute for Man and Environment, University of Massachusetts.

PALMER, M. H., LLOYD, M. E., & LLOYD, K. E. (1978). An experimental analysis of electricity conservation procedures. *Journal of Applied Behavior Analysis, 10,* 665–672.

PARSONS, R. (1991). The potential influence of environmental perception on human health. *Journal of Environmental Psychology, 11,* 1–23.

PARTRIDGE, L. (1974). Habitat selection in titmice. *Nature, 247,* 573–574.

PARTRIDGE, L. (1978). Habitat selection. In J. R. Krebs & N. B. Davies (Eds.), *Behavioral ecology: An evolutionary approach.* Sunderland, MA: Sinnaver Associates.

PASSINI, R. (1984). Spatial representations, a wayfinding perspective. *Journal of Environmental Psychology, 4,* 153–164.

PASSINI, R., & PROULX, G. (1988). Wayfinding without vision: An experiment with congenitally totally blind people. *Environment and Behavior, 20,* 227–252.

PASSINI, R., PROULX, G., & RAINVILLE, C. (1990). The spatio-cognitive abilities of the visually impaired population. *Environment and Behavior, 22,* 91–118.

PATEY, R. C., & EVANS, R. M. (1979). Identification of scenically preferred forest landscapes. In G. H. Elsner & R. C. Smardon (Eds.), *Proceedings of Our National Landscape Conference.* Berkeley, CA: U.S. Department of Agriculture, Forest Service, Pacific Southwest Forest and Range Experiment Station.

PATSFALL, M. R., FEIMER, N. R., BUHYOFF, G. J., & WELLMAN, J. D. (1984). The prediction of scenic beauty from landscape content and composition. *Journal of Environmental Psychology, 4,* 7–26.

PATTERSON, A. H., & CHISWICK, N. R. (1981). The role of the social and physical environment in privacy maintenance among the Iban of Borneo. *Journal of Environmental Psychology, 1,* 131–139.

PATTERSON, M. L. (1975). Personal space: Time to burst the bubble? *Man-Environment Systems, 5,* 67.

PATTERSON, M. L. (1976). An arousal model of interpersonal intimacy. *Psychological Review, 83,* 235–245.

PATTERSON, M. L. (1982). A sequential-functional model of nonverbal exchange, *Psychological Review, 89,* 231–249.

PATTERSON, M. L. (1987). Presentational and affect-management functions of nonverbal involvement. *Journal of Nonverbal Behavior, 11,* 110–122.

PATTERSON, M. L., JORDAN, A., HOGAN, M. B., & FRERKER, D. (1981). Effects of nonverbal intimacy on arousal and behavioral adjustment. *Journal of Nonverbal Behavior, 5,* 184–198.

PATTERSON, M. L., MULLENS, S., & ROMANO, J. (1971). Compensatory reactions to spatial intrusion. *Sociometry, 34,* 114–121.

PAULUS, P. B. (1980). Crowding. In P. B. Paulus (Ed.), *Psychology of group influence.* Hillsdale, NJ: Erlbaum.

PAULUS, P. B. (1988). *Prison crowding: A psychological perspective.* New York: Springer-Verlag.

PAULUS, P. B., ANNIS, A. B., SETA, J. J., SCHKADE, J. K., & MATTHEWS, R. W. (1976). Density does affect task performance. *Journal of Personality and Social Psychology, 34,* 248–253.

PAULUS, P. B., & MATTHEWS, R. (1980). Crowding attribution and task performance. *Basic and Applied Social Psychology, 1,* 3–14.

PAULUS, P. B., MCCAIN, G., & COX, V. C. (1978). Death rates, psychiatric commitments, blood pressure, and perceived crowding as a function of institutional crowding. *Environmental Psychology and Nonverbal Behavior, 3,* 107–116.

PAULUS, P. B., NAGAR, D., & CAMACHO, L. M. (1991). Environmental and psychological factors in reactions to apartments and mobile homes. *Journal of Environmental Psychology, 11,* 143–161.

PEARCE, P. L. (1977). Mental souvenirs: A study of tourists and their city maps. *Australian Journal of Psychology, 29,* 203–210.

PEARSON, J. L., & IALONGO, N. S. (1986). The relationship between spatial ability and environmental knowledge. *Journal of Environmental Psychology, 6,* 299–304.

PEART, B. (1984). Impact of exhibit type on knowledge gain, attitudes, and behavior. *Curator, 27,* 220–237.

PEDERSEN, D. M. (1973). Development of a personal space measure. *Psychological Reports, 32,* 527–535.

PEDERSEN, D. M. (1982). Cross-validation of privacy factors. *Perceptual and Motor Skills, 55,* 57–58.

PELLEGRINI, R. J., & EMPEY, J. (1970). Interpersonal spatial orientation in dyads. *Journal of Psychology, 76,* 67–70.

PELLEGRINI, R. J., & SCHAUSS, A. G. (1980). Muscle strength as a function of exposure to hue differences in visual stimuli: An experimental test of the kinesoid hypothesis. *Journal of Orthomolecular Psychiatry, 9,* 144–147.

PELLEGRINI, R. J., SCHAUSS, A. G., & BIRK, T. J. (1980). Leg strength as a function of exposure to visual stimuli of different hues. *Bulletin of the Psychonomic Society, 16,* 111–112.

PEMPUS, E., SAWAYA, C., & COOPER, R. E. (1975, August). *Don't fence me in: Personal space depends on architectural enclosure.* Paper presented at the meeting of the American Psychological Association, Chicago.

PENNARTZ, P. J. J. (1986). Atmosphere at home: A qualitative approach. *Journal of Environmental Psychology, 6,* 135–153.

PEPONIS, J., ZIMRING, C., & CHOI, Y. K. (1990). Finding the building in wayfinding. *Environment and Behavior, 22,* 555–590.

PEREZ, C., & HART, R. (1980). Beyond playgrounds: Children's accessibility to the landscape. In P. F. Wilkinson (Ed.), *Innovations in play environments.* New York: St. Martin's Press.

PERRET, D. I., & ROLLS, E. T. (1983). Neural mechanisms underlying the visual analysis of faces. In J. P. Ewert, R. R. Capranica, & D. J. Ingle (Eds.), *Advances in vertebrate neuroethology.* New York: Springer-Verlag.

PERSKY, H., ZUCKERMAN, M., BASU, G. K., & THORNTON, D. (1966). Psychoendocrine effects of perceptual and social isolation. *Archives of General Psychiatry, 15,* 499–505.

PETERSON, E. A., AUGENSTEIN, J. S., TANIS, D. C., & AUGENSTEIN, A. G. (1981). Noise raises blood pressure without impairing auditory sensitivity. *Science, 211,* 1450–1452.

PETTERSON, J., SANDBERG, R., & ALERSTAM, T. (1991). Orientation of robins, *Erithacus rubecula,* in a vertical magnetic field. *Animal Behaviour, 41,* 533–536.

PETTY, R. E., & CACIOPPO, J. T. (1985). The elaboration likelihood model of persuasion. In L. Berkowitz (Ed.), *Advances in experimental social psychology* (Vol. 19). New York: Academic Press.

PIAGET, J. (1954). *The child's construction of reality.* New York: Basic Books.

PIAGET, J., & INHELDER, B. (1967). *The child's conception of space.* New York: Norton.

PIAGET, J., INHELDER, B., & SZEMINSKA, A. (1960). *The child's conception of geometry.* New York: Basic Books.

PITT, D. G. (1989). The attractiveness and use of aquatic environments as outdoor recreation places. In I. Altman and E. H. Zube (Eds.), *Public places and spaces.* New York: Plenum.

PITT, D. G., & ZUBE, E. H. (1987). Management of natural environments. In D. Stokols & I. Altman (Eds.), *Handbook of environmental psychology* (Vol. 2). New York: John Wiley and Sons.

PLAISANCE, S. (1984). Learning styles: How people prefer to learn. *American Association of Zoological Parks and Aquariums 1984 Annual Proceedings,* pp. 406–408.

PLATH, K. (1965). *Schools within schools: A study of high school organization.* New York: Teacher's College, Columbia University.

PLATT, J. (1973). Social traps. *American Psychologist, 28,* 641–651.

POGUE, W. R. (1974). Three months in space. *Society of Experimental Test Pilots Technical Review, 12,* 203–217.

POLLEY, C. R., CRAIG, J. V., & BHAGWHAT, A. L. (1974). Crowding and agonistic behavior: A curvilinear relationship. *Poultry Science, 53,* 1621–1623.

PONTING, C. (1990). Historical perspectives on sustainable development. *Environment, 32,* No. 9, 4–9, 31–33.

PORTEOUS, J. D. (1978). The pathology of forced relocation. In S. Kaplan & R. Kaplan (Eds.), *Humanscape: Environments for people.* North Scituate, MA: Duxbury Press.

POTTER, D. R., HENDEE, J. C., & CLARK, R. N. (1973). Hunting satisfaction: Games, guns, or nature? In J. C. Hendee & C. Schoenfeld (Eds.), *Human dimensions in wildlife programs.* Rockville, MD: Mercury.

POULTON, E. C. (1970). *Environment and human efficiency.* Springfield, IL: Charles C Thomas.

POULTON, E. C. (1976). Arousing environmental stress can improve performance, whatever people say. *Aviation, Space, and Environmental Medicine, 47,* 1193–1201.

POULTON, E. C. (1977). Continuous intense noise masks auditory feedback and inner speech. *Psychological Bulletin, 84,* 977–1001.

POULTON, E. C. (1978). A new look at the effects of noise: A rejoinder. *Psychological Bulletin, 85,* 1068–1079.

POULTON, E. C. (1979). Composite model for human performance in continuous noise. *Psychological Review, 86,* 361–375.

POWERS, R. B., OSBORNE, J. G., & ANDERSON, E. G. (1973). Positive reinforcement of litter removal in the natural environment. *Journal of Applied Behavior Analysis, 6,* 579–586.

PRESIDENT'S COMMISSION ON AMERICANS OUTDOORS (1987). *Final report.* Washington, DC: U.S. Government Printing Office.

PRESSON, C. C., & SOMERVILLE, S. C. (1985). Beyond egocentrism: A new look at the beginnings of spatial representation. In H. M. Wellman (Ed.), *Children's searching: The development of search skills and spatial representation.* Hillsdale, NJ: Erlbaum.

PRESTOMON, D. R. (1968). How much does noise bother apartment dwellers? *Architectural Record, 143,* 155–156.

PRINCE-EMBURY, S. (1991). Information seekers in the aftermath of technological disaster at Three Mile Island. *Journal of Applied Social Psychology, 21,* 569–584.

PRINCE-EMBURY, S., & ROONEY, J. F. (1988). Psychological symptoms of residents in the aftermath of the Three Mile Island nuclear accident and restart. *Journal of Social Psychology, 128,* 779–790.

PRINCE-EMBURY, S., & ROONEY, J. F. (1990). Life stage differences in resident coping with restart of the Three Mile Island nuclear generating facility. *Journal of Social Psychology, 130,* 771–779.

PROFESSIONAL BUILDER (1985). What 1986 buyers want in housing. *50,* 68–85.

PROFUSEK, P. J., & RAINEY, D. W. (1987). Effects of Baker-Miller pink and red on state anxiety, grip strength, and motor precision. *Perceptual and Motor Skills, 65,* 941–942.

PROJECT FOR PUBLIC SPACES. (1978). *Exxon minipark: A redesign and management proposal.* New York: Project for Public Spaces.

PROSHANSKY, H. M. (1976). Comment on environmental and social psychology. *Personality and Social Psychology Bulletin, 2,* 359–363.

PROSHANSKY, H. M. (1987). The field of environmental psychology: Securing its future. In D. Stokols & I. Altman (Eds.), *Handbook of environmental psychology* (Vol. 2). New York: John Wiley and Sons.

PROSHANSKY, H. M. (1990). The pursuit of understanding: An intellectual history. In I. Altman & K. Christensen (Eds.), *Environment and behavior studies: Emergence of intellectual traditions.* New York: Plenum.

PROSHANSKY, H. M., FABIAN, A. K., & KAMINOFF, R. (1983). Place identity: Physical world socialization on the self. *Journal of Environmental Psychology, 3,* 57–83.

PROSHANSKY, H. M., ITTELSON, W. H., & RIVLIN, L. G. (EDS.). (1970). *Environmental psychology: Man and his physical setting.* New York: Holt, Rinehart, & Winston.

PROSHANSKY, H. M., ITTELSON, W. H., & RIVLIN, L. G. (1976). Freedom of choice and behavior in a physical setting. In H. M. Proshansky, W. H. Ittelson, & L. G. Rivlin (Eds.), *Environmental psychology.* New York: Holt, Rinehart, & Winston.

PROVINS, K. A. (1958). Environmental conditions and driving efficiency: A review. *Ergonomics, 2,* 63–88.

PURCELL, A. H. (1981, February). The world's trashiest people: Will they clean up their act or throw away their future? *Futurist,* pp. 51–59.

PYLYSHYN, Z. W. (1973). What the mind's eye tells the mind's brain: A critique of mental images. *Psychological Bulletin, 80,* 1–24.

PYLYSHYN, Z. W. (1978). Imagery and artificial intelligence. In C. W. Savage (Ed.), *Perception and cognition issues in the foundations of psychology.* Minneapolis: University of Minnesota Press.

PYLYSHYN, Z. W. (1984). *Computation and cognition.* Cambridge, MA: MIT Press.

RAFFERTY, Y., & SHINN, M. (1991). The impact of homelessness on children. *American Psychologist, 46,* 1170–1179.

RAHE, R. H. (1972). Subjects' recent life changes and their near-future illness reports. *Annals of Clinical Research, 4,* 250–265.

RAJECKI, D. W., NERENZ, D. R., FREEDENBURG, T. G., & MCCARTHY, P. J. (1979). Components of aggression in chickens and conceptualizations of aggression in general. *Journal of Personality and Social Psychology, 37,* 1902–1914.

RAJU, P. S. (1980). Optimum stimulation level: Its relationship to personality, demographics, and exploratory behavior. *Journal of Consumer Research, 7,* 272–282.

RANKIN, R. E. (1969). Air pollution control and public apathy. *Journal of the Air Pollution Control Association, 19,* 565–569.

RAPOPORT, A. (1969). *House form and culture.* Englewood Cliffs, NJ: Prentice-Hall.

RAPOPORT, A. (1980). Environmental preference, habitat selection and urban housing. *Journal of Social Issues, 36,* 118–134.

RAPOPORT, A. (1990). *History and precedent in environmental design.* New York: Plenum.

REDMOND, D. E., & MURPHY, D. L. (1975). Behavioral correlates of platelet monoamine oxidase (MAO) activity in Rhesus monkeys. *Psychosomatic Medicine, 37,* 80.

REED, T., & MINDLIN, A. (1963). Where do visitors come from? *International Zoo Yearbook, 3,* 43–46.

REICH, J. W., & ROBERTSON, J. L. (1979). Reactance and norm appeal in anti-littering messages. *Journal of Applied Social Psychology, 9,* 99–101.

REID, D. H., LUYBEN, P. L., RAWERS, R. J., & BAILEY, J. S. (1976). The effects of prompting and proximity of containers on newspaper recycling behavior. *Environment and Behavior, 8,* 471–482.

REID, E., & NOVAK, P. (1975). Personal space: An unobtrusive measures study. *Bulletin of the Psychonomic Society, 5,* 265–266.

REIFMAN, A. S., LARRICK, R. P., & FEIN, S. (1991). Temper and temperature on the diamond: The heat-aggression relationship in major league baseball. *Personality and Social Psychology Bulletin, 17,* 580–585.

REISER, J. (1979). Spatial orientation in six-month-old infants. *Child Development, 50,* 1078–1087.

REISS, S., & DYDHALO, N. (1975). Persistence, achievement, and open space environments. *Journal of Educational Psychology, 67,* 506–513.

REITER, S. N., & SAMUEL, W. (1980). Littering as a function of prior litter and the presence or absence of prohibitive signs. *Journal of Applied Social Psychology, 10,* 45–55.

RELPH, E. (1976). *Place and placelessness.* London: Pion Ltd.

RENSCH, B. (1957). Aesthetische faktoren bei farb und formbevorzugungen von affen. *Zeitschrift fur Tierpsychologie, 14,* 71–99.

RENSCH, B. (1958). Die wirksamkeit aesthetischer faktoren bei wirbeltieren. *Zeitschrift fur Tierpsychologie, 15,* 447–461.

RIDGEWAY, D., HARE, R. D., WATERS, E., & RUSSELL, J. A. (1984). Affect and sensation seeking. *Motivation and Emotion, 8,* 205–210.

RILAND, D. H., & FALK, J. Z. (1972). *Employee reactions to office landscape environment.* Rochester, NY: Eastman Kodak Co.

RIM, Y. (1975). Psychological test performance during climatic heat stress from desert winds. *International Journal of Biometeorology, 19,* 37–40.

RINGEL, N. B., & FINKELSTEIN, J. C. (1991). Differentiating neighborhood satis faction and neighborhood attachment among urban residents. *Basic and Applied Social Psychology, 12,* 177–193.

RIVLIN, L. G. (1982). Group membership and place meanings in an urban neighborhood. *Journal of Social Issues, 38,* 75–93.

RIVLIN, L. G. (1987). The neighborhood, personal identity, and group affiliations. In I. Altman & H. Wandersman (Eds.), *Neighborhood and community environments.* New York: Plenum.

RIVLIN, L. G., & ROTHENBERG, M. (1976). The use of space in open classrooms. In H. M. Proshansky, W. H. Ittelson, & L. G. Rivlin (Eds.), *Environmental psychology: People and their physical settings.* New York: Holt, Rinehart, & Winston.

RIVOLIER, J., CAZES, G., & MCCORMICK, I. (1991). The International Biomedical Expedition to the Antarctic: Psychological evaluations of the field party. In A. A. Harrison, Y. A. Clearwater, & C. P. McKay (Eds.), *From Antarctica to outer space: Life in isolation and confinement.* New York: Springer-Verlag.

ROBERTS, T. A. (1991). Death in the Gulf: A biologist's view of the Gulf War. *Buzzworm: The Environmental Journal, III,* No. 3, 53–59.

ROBINSON, E. S. (1928). *The behavior of the museum visitor.* Washington, DC: American Association of Museums.

ROBINSON, S. N. (1976). Littering behavior in public places. *Environment and Behavior, 8,* 363–384.

ROBINSON, S. N., & FRISCH, M. H. (1975, April). *Social and environmental influences on littering behavior.* Paper presented at the meeting of the Eastern Psychological Association, New York.

ROCHFORD, E. B. JR., & BLOCKER, T. J. (1991). Coping with "natural" hazards as stressors: The predictors of activism in a flood disaster. *Environment and Behavior, 23,* 171–194.

RODIN, J., SOLOMON, S., & METCALF, J. (1978). Role of control in mediating perceptions of density. *Journal of Personality and Social Psychology, 36,* 988–999.

ROETHLISBERGER, F. J., & DICKSON, W. J. (1939). *Management and the worker.* Cambridge: Harvard University Press.

ROGER, D. B., & SCHALEKAMP, E. E. (1976). Body-buffer zone and violence: A cross-cultural study. *Journal of Social Psychology, 98,* 153–158.

ROHE, W. M. (1982). The response to density in residential settings: The mediating effects of social and personal variables. *Journal of Applied Social Psychology, 12,* 292–303.

ROHE, W. M., & BURBY, R. J. (1988). Fear of crime in public housing. *Environment and Behavior, 20,* 700–720.

ROHE, W. M., & NUFFER, E. L. (1977, August). *The effects of density and partitioning on children's behavior.* Paper presented at the meeting of the American Psychological Association, San Francisco.

ROHE, W. M., & PATTERSON, A. (1974). The effects of varied levels of resources and density on behavior in a day care center. In D. Carson (Ed.), *EDRA V,* 161–171.

ROHNER, R. P. (1974). Proxemics and stress: An empirical study of the relationship between living space and roommate turnover. *Human Relations, 27,* 697–702.

ROSEGRANT, T. J., & MCCROSKEY, J. C. (1975). The effects of race and sex on proxemic behavior in an interview setting. *Southern Speech Communication Journal, 40,* 408–420.

ROSENFIELD, P., LAMBERT, N. M., & BLACK, A. (1985). Desk arrangement effects on pupil classroom behavior. *Journal of Educational Psychology, 77,* 101–108.

ROSENTHAL, N. E., & BLEHAR, M. C. (EDS.). (1989). *Seasonal affective disorders and phototherapy.* New York: Guilford.

ROSENTHAL, N. E., SACK, D. A., CARPENTER, B. S., PARRY, B. L., MENDELSON, W. B., & WEHR, T. A. (1985). Antidepressant effects of light in seasonal affective disorder. *American Journal of Psychiatry, 142,* 163–185.

ROSENTHAL, N. E., SACK, D. A., LEWY, A. M., GOODWIN, F. K., DAVENPORT, Y., MUELLER, P. S., NEWSOME, D. A., & WEHR, T. A. (1984). Seasonal affective disorder: A description of the syndrome and preliminary findings with light therapy. *Archives of General Psychiatry, 41,* 72–80.

ROSENTHAL, N. E., SACK, D. A., SKWERER, R. G., JACOBSEN, F. M., & WEHR, T. A. (1989). Phototherapy for seasonal affective disorder. In N. E. Rosenthal & M. C. Blehar (Eds.), *Seasonal affective disorders and phototherapy.* New York: Guilford.

ROSS, M., LAYTON, B., ERICKSON, B., & SCHOPLER, J. (1973). Affect, eye contact, and reactions to crowding. *Journal of Personality and Social Psychology, 28,* 69–76.

ROSSMAN, B. B., & ULEHLA, Z. J. (1977). Psychological reward values associated with wilderness use: A functional-reinforcement approach. *Environment and Behavior, 9,* 41–66.

ROTHBLUM, E. D. (1990). Psychological factors in the antarctic. *Journal of Psychology, 124,* 253–273.

ROTTON, J. (1987). Hemmed in and hating it: Effects of shape of room on tolerance for crowding. *Perceptual and Motor Skills, 64,* 285–286.

ROTTON, J., & FREY, J. (1985). Psychological costs of air pollution: Atmospheric conditions, seasonal trends, and psychiatric emergencies. *Population and Environment, 7,* 3–16.

ROTTON, J., FREY, J., BARRY, T. MILLIGAN, M., & FITZPATRICK, M. (1979). The air pollution experience and physical aggression. *Journal of Applied Social Psychology, 9,* 397–412.

ROTTON, J., & KELLY, I. W. (1985). Much ado about the full moon: A meta-analysis of lunar-lunacy research. *Psychological Bulletin, 97,* 286–306.

ROTTON, J., SHATS, M., & STANDERS, R. (1990). Temperature and pedestrian tempo: Walking without awareness. *Environment and Behavior, 22,* 650–674.

ROVINE, M., & WEISMAN, G. D. (1989). Sketch-map variables as predictors of way-finding performance. *Journal of Environmental Psychology, 9,* 217–232.

ROWLES, G. D. (1980). Growing old "inside": Aging and attachment to place in an Appalachian community. In N. Datan & N. Lohmann (Eds.), *Transition of aging.* New York: Academic Press.

RUBACK, R. B. (1987). Deserted (and nondeserted) aisles: Territorial intrusion can produce persistence, not flight. *Social Psychology Quarterly, 50,* 270–276.

RUBACK, R. B., CARR, T. S., & HOPPER, C. H. (1986). Perceived control in prison: Its relation to reported crowding, stress, and symptoms. *Journal of Applied Social Psychology, 16,* 375–386.

RUBACK, R. B., & INNES, C. A. (1988). The relevance and irrelevance of psychological research: The example of prison crowding. *American Psychologist, 43,* 683–693.

RUBACK, R. B., & PANDEY, J. (1991). Crowding, perceived control, and relative power: An analysis of households in India. *Journal of Applied Social Psychology, 21,* 315–344.

RUBACK, R. B., PAPE, K. D., & DORIOT, P. (1989). Waiting for a phone: Intrusion on callers leads to territorial defense. *Social Psychology Quarterly, 52,* 232–241.

RUBINSTEIN, R. L. (1989). The home environments of older people: A description of the psychosocial processes linking person to place. *Journal of Gerontology, 34,* 545–553.

RUBONIS, A. V., & BICKMAN, L. (1991). Psychological impairment in the wake of disaster: The disaster-psychopathology relationship. *Psychological Bulletin, 109,* 384–399.

RUDOFSKY, B. (1964). *Architecture without architects.* New York: Doubleday.

RUSSELL, J. A., & LANIUS, U. F. (1984). Adaptation levels and the affective appraisal of environments. *Journal of Environmental Psychology, 4,* 119–135.

RUSSELL, J. A., & MEHRABIAN, A. (1974). Distinguishing anger and anxiety in terms of emotional response factors. *Journal of Consulting and Clinical Psychology, 42,* 79–83.

RUSSELL, J. A., & MEHRABIAN, A. (1977). Evidence for a three-factor theory of emotions. *Journal of Research in Personality, 11,* 273–294.

RUSSELL, J. A., & MEHRABIAN, A. (1978). Environment, task, and temperamental effects on work performance. *Humanitas, 14,* 75–95.

RUSSELL, J. A., & SNODGRASS, J. (1987). Emotion and the environment. In D. Stokols & I. Altman (Eds.), *Handbook of environmental psychology* (Vol. 1). New York: John Wiley and Sons.

RUSSELL, J. A., & WARD, L. M. (1982). Environmental psychology. *Annual Review of Psychology, 33,* 651–688.

RUSSELL, M. B., & BERNAL, M. E. (1977). Temporal and climactic variables in naturalistic observation. *Journal of Applied Behavior Analysis, 10,* 399–405.

RUSTEMLI, A. (1986). Male and female personal space needs and escape reactions under intrusion: A Turkish sample. *International Journal of Psychology, 21,* 503–511.

RUYS, T. (1970). Windowless offices. *Man-Environment Systems, 1,* 49.

SAARINEN, T. F. (1966). *Perception of drought hazard on the Great Plains.* Chicago: University of Chicago Press.

SAARINEN, T. F. (1973). The use of projective techniques in geographic research. In W. H. Ittelson (Ed.), *Environment and cognition.* New York: Seminar Press.

SAARINEN, T. F. (1988). Public perception of the desert in Tuscon, Arizona. *The Journal of Architectural and Planning Research, 5,* 197–207.

SACK, R. D. (1983). Human territoriality: A theory. *Annals of the Association of American Geographers, 73,* 55–74.

SACKETT, G. P. (1972). Exploratory behavior of Rhesus monkeys as a function of rearing experiences and sex. *Developmental Psychology, 6,* 260–270.

SADALLA, E. K., BURROUGHS, W. J., & STAPLIN, L. J. (1980). Reference points in spatial cognition. *Journal of Experimental Psychology: Human Learning and Memory, 6,* 516–528.

SADALLA, E. K., & MAGEL, S. G. (1980). The perception of transversed distance. *Environment and Behavior, 12,* 65–79.

SADALLA, E. K., & MONTELLO, D. R. (1989). Remembering changes in direction. *Environment and Behavior, 21,* 346–363.

SADALLA, E. K., & OXLEY, D. (1984). The perception of room size: The rectangularity illusion. *Environment and Behavior, 16,* 394–405.

SADALLA, E. K., SHEETS, V., & MCCREATH, H. (1990). The cognition of urban tempo. *Environment and Behavior, 22,* 230–254.

SADALLA, E. K., & STAPLIN, L. J. (1980). The perception of transversed distance: Interactions. *Environment and Behavior, 12,* 167–182.

SADALLA, E. K., STAPLIN, L. J., & BURROUGHS, J. E. (1979). Information retrieval and distance cognition. *Memory and Cognition, 4,* 291–296.

SADALLA, E. K., VERSHURE, B., & BURROUGHS, J. (1987). Identity symbolism in housing. *Environment and Behavior, 19,* 569–587.

SAEGERT, S. (1973). Crowding: Cognitive overload and behavioral constraint. *Proceedings of the EDRA IV conference.* Blacksburg, VA: Environmental Design Research Association.

SAEGERT, S. (1978). High density environments: Their personal and social consequences. In A. Baum & Y. M. Epstein (Eds.), *Human response to crowding.* Hillsdale, NJ: Erlbaum.

SAEGERT, S. (1985). The role of housing in the experience of dwelling. In I. Altman & C. Werner (Eds.), *Home environments: Human behavior and environment* (Vol. 8). New York: Plenum.

SAEGERT, S., MACKINTOSH, E., & WEST, S. (1975). Two studies of crowding in urban public spaces. *Environment and Behavior, 7,* 159–184.

SAEGERT, S., & WINKEL, G. H. (1990). Environmental psychology. *Annual Review of Psychology, 41,* 441–477.

SAILE, D. G. (1985) The ritual establishment of home. In I. Altman & C. M. Werner (Eds.), *Home environments.* New York: Plenum.

SAMDAHL, D. M., & CHRISTENSEN, H. H. (1985). Environmental cues and vandalism: An exploratory study of picnic table carving. *Environment and Behavior, 17,* 445–458.

SAMDAHL, D. M., & ROBERTSON, R. (1989). Social determinants of environmental concern: Specification and test of the model. *Environment and Behavior, 21,* 57–81.

SAMUELSON, C. D., & BIEK, M. (1991). Attitudes toward energy conservation: A confirmatory factor analysis. *Journal of Applied Social Psychology, 21,* 549–568.

SAMUELSON, D. J., & LINDAUER, M. S. (1976). Perception, evaluation, and performance in a neat and messy room by high and low sensation seekers. *Environment and Behavior, 8,* 291–306.

SANBORN, D. E., CASEY, T. M., & NISWANDER, G. D. (1970). Suicide: Seasonal patterns and related variables. *Diseases of the Nervous System, 31,* 702–704.

SANDERS, D., WARNER, P., BACKSTROM, T., & BANCROFT, J. (1983). Mood, sexuality, hormones, and the menstrual cycle: I. Changes in mood and physical state: Descriptions of subjects and method. *Psychosomatic Medicine, 45,* 487–501.

SANDERS, J. L. (1978). Relation of personal space to the human menstrual cycle. *Journal of Psychology, 100,* 275–278.

SANDERS, J. L., & BRIZZOLARA, M. S. (1982). Relationships between weather and mood. *Journal of General Psychology, 107,* 155–156.

SANDERS, J. L., HAKKY, V. M., & BRIZZOLARA, M. M. (1985) Personal space amongst Arabs and Americans *International Journal of Psychology, 20,* 13–17.

SANDERS, S. G., & WREN, J. P. (1975). Open space schools are effective. *Phi Delta Kappan, 56,* 366

SAVINAR, J. (1975). The effect of ceiling height on personal space. *Man-Environment Systems, 5,* 321–324.

SCHAEFFER, G. H., & PATTERSON, M J (1980). Intimacy, arousal, and small group crowding. *Journal of Personality and Social Psychology, 38,* 283–290.

SCHAEFFER, M. A., & BAUM, A. (1984). Adrenal cortical response to stress at Three Mile Island. *Psychosomatic Medicine, 46,* 227–237.

SCHAHN, J, & HOLZER, E. (1990). Studies of individual environmental concern: The role of knowledge, gender, and background variables. *Environment and Behavior, 22,* 767–786.

SCHAUSS, A. (1979). Tranquilizing effect of color reduces aggressive behavior and potential violence. *Journal of Orthomolecular Psychiatry, 8,* 218–221.

SCHERER, S. E. (1974). Proxemic behavior of primary school children as a function of their socioeconomic class and subculture. *Journal of Personality and Social Psychology, 29,* 800–805.

SCHETTINO, A. P., & BORDEN, R. J. (1976). Group size vs. group density: Where is the affect? *Personal and Social Psychology Bulletin, 2,* 67–70.

SCHIAVO, R. S. (1987). Home use evaluation by suburban youth: Gender differences. *Children's Environments Quarterly, 4,* 8–12.

SCHIAVO, R. S. (1988). Age differences in assessment and use of a suburban neighborhood among children and adolescents. *Children's Environments Quarterly, 5,* 4–9.

SCHIFF, M. (1977). Hazard adjustment, locus of control, and sensation seeking: Some null findings. *Environment and Behavior, 9,* 233–254.

SCHIFFENBAUER, A. I., BROWN, J. E., PERRY, P. L., SHULACK, L. K., & ZANZOLA, A. M. (1977). The relationship between density and crowding: Some architectural modifiers. *Environment and Behavior, 9,* 3–14.

SCHIFFENBAUER, A. I., & SCHIAVO, R. S. (1976). Physical distance and attraction: An intensification effect. *Journal of Experimental Social Psychology, 12,* 274–282.

SCHMIDT, C. W., & ULRICH, R. E. (1969). Effects of group contingent events upon classroom noise. *Journal of Applied Behavior Analysis. 2,* 171–179.

SCHMIDT, D. E., & KEATING, J. P. (1979). Human crowding and personal control: An integration of the research. *Psychological Bulletin, 86,* 680–700.

SCHMIDT, F. N., & GIFFORD, R. (1989). A dispositional approach to hazard perception: Preliminary development of the Environmental Appraisal Inventory. *Journal of Environmental Psychology, 9,* 57–67.

SCHNEIDER, F. W., & HANSVICK, C. L. (1974). *Gaze direction and distance as a function of variation in the other person's gaze direction.* Unpublished manuscript, University of Windsor, Ontario.

SCHNEIRLA, T. C. (1959). An evolutionary and developmental theory of biphasic processes underlying approach and withdrawal. In M. J. Jones (Ed.), *Nebraska Symposium on Motivation* (Vol. 7). Lincoln, NE: University of Nebraska Press.

SCHOGGEN, P. (1984, August). *Student voluntary participation and high school size.* Address at the meeting of the American Psychological Association, Toronto.

SCHOGGEN, P. (1990). Early days at the Midwest Psychological Field Station. *Environment and Behavior, 22,* 458–467.

SCHOOLER, C., ZAHN, T. P., MURPHY, D. L., & BUCHSBAUM, M. S. (1978). Psychological correlates of monoamine oxidase in normals. *Journal of Nervous and Mental Diseases, 166,* 177–186.

SCHOPLER, J., & STOCKDALE, J. (1977). An interference analysis of crowding. *Environmental Psychology and Nonverbal Behavior, 1,* 81–88.

SCHOUELA, D. A., STEINBERG, L. M., LEVETON, L. B., & WAPNER, S. (1980). Development of the cognitive organization of an environment. *Canadian Journal of Behavioral Science, 12,* 1–16.

SCHROEDER, H. W. (1983). Variations in the perception of urban forest recreation sites. *Leisure Sciences, 5,* 221–230.

SCHROEDER, H. W. (1987). Dimensions of variation in urban park preference: A phychophysical analysis. *Journal of Environmental Psychology, 7,* 123–141.

SCHROEDER, H. W. (1989). Environment, behavior, and design research on urban forests. In E. H. Zube & G. T. Moore (Eds.), *Advances in environment, behavior, and design* (Vol. 2). New York: Plenum.

SCHROEDER, H. W. (1991). Preferences and meaning of arboretum landscapes: Combining quantitative and qualitative data. *Journal of Environmental Psychology, 11,* 231–248.

SCHROEDER, H. W., & ANDERSON, L. M. (1984). Perception of personal safety in urban recreation sites. *Journal of Leisure Research, 16,* 178–194.

SCHUMAN, S. (1972). Patterns of urban heat-wave deaths and implications of prevention: Data from New York and St. Louis during July, 1966. *Environmental Research, 55,* 59–75.

SCHWARTZ, B., & BARSKY, S. F. (1977). The home advantage. *Social Forces, 55,* 641–661.

SCHWEBEL, A. I., & CHERLIN, D. L. (1972). Physical and social distancing in teacher-pupil relationships. *Journal of Education Psychology, 63,* 543–550.

SCIENCE NEWS (1990). Reassessing the costs of keeping baby dry. *138,* 347.

SEARS, D. O., PEPLAU, L. A., & TAYLOR, S. E. (1991). *Social psychology* (7th ed.). Englewood Cliffs, NJ: Prentice-Hall.

SEATON, R. (1968). *Miscellaneous undergraduate research on spatial behavior: A classified and annotated listing.* Berkeley: Department of Architecture, University of California at Berkeley.

SEBBA, R. (1991). The landscapes of childhood: The reflection of childhood's environment in adult memories and in children's attitudes. *Environment and Behavior, 23,* 395–442.

SEBBA, R., & CHURCHMAN, A. (1983). Territories and territoriality in the home. *Environment and Behavior, 15,* 191–210.

SEGAL, B., & SINGER, J. L. (1976). Daydreaming, drug, and alcohol use in college students: A factor analytic study. *Addictive Behaviors, 1,* 227–235.

SELIGMAN, M. E. P. (1975). *Helplessness.* San Francisco: Freeman.

SELYE, H. (1956). *The stress of life.* New York: McGraw-Hill.

SERRELL, B. (1988). The evolution of education graphics in zoos. *Environment and Behavior, 20,* 396–415.

SHAFER, E. L., HAMILTON, J. F., & SCHMIDT, E. A. (1969). Natural landscape preferences: A predictive model. *Journal of Leisure Research, 1,* 1–19.

SHAFER, E. L, JR., & MIETZ, J. (1972). Aesthetic and emotional experiences rate high with Northeast wilderness hikers. In J F Wohlwill & D. H. Carson (Eds.), *Environment and the social sciences: Perspectives and applications.* Washington, DC: American Psychological Association.

SHAFFER, D. R., & SADOWSKI, C. (1975). This table is mine: Respect for marked barroom tables as a function of gender of spatial marker and desirability of locale. *Sociometry, 38,* 408–419.

SHARMA, N. C., KIVLIN, J. E., & FLIEGEL, F. C. (1975). Environmental pollution: Is there enough public concern to lead to action? *Environment and Behavior, 7,* 455–471.

SHARMA, V. M., VASKARAN, A. S., & MANHOTRA, M. S. (1976). Social compatibility under prolonged isolation and high altitude. *Indian Journal of Applied Psychology, 13,* 11–15.

SHARPE, G. W. (1976). *Interpreting the environment.* New York: John Wiley and Sons.

SHAVER, P., & FREEDMAN, J. L. (1976, August). Happiness. *Psychology Today,* pp. 26-32, 75.

SHAW, L. G. (1987). Designing playgrounds for able and disabled children. In C. S. Weinstein & T. G. David (Eds.), *Spaces for children: The built environment and child development.* New York: Plenum.

SHEETS, V. L., & MANZER, C. D. (1991). Affect, cognition, and urban vegetation: Some effects of adding trees along city streets. *Environment and Behavior, 23,* 285–304.

SHEMYAKIN, F. N. (1962). General problems of orientation in space and space representations. In B. G. Ananyev (Ed.), *Psychological science in the USSR*. Arlington, VA: U. S. Office of Technical Reports.

SHEPARD, R. N. (1967). Recognition memory for words, sentences, and pictures. *Journal of Verbal Learning and Verbal Behavior, 6,* 156–163.

SHERMAN, R. C., CROXTON, J., & SMITH, M. (1979). Movement and structure as determinants of spatial representations. *Journal of Nonverbal Behavior, 4,* 27–39.

SHERROD, D. R. (1974). Crowding, perceived control, and behavioral aftereffects. *Journal of Applied Social Psychology, 4,* 171–186.

SHERROD, D. R., & COHEN, S. (1978). Density, personal control, and design. In S. Kaplan & R. Kaplan (Eds.), *Humanscape: Environments for people.* North Scituate, MA: Duxbury Press.

SHERROD, D. R., HAGE, J., HALPERN, P. L., & MOORE, B. S. (1977). Effects of personal causation and perceived control on responses to an aversive environment: The more control the better. *Journal of Experimental Social Psychology, 13,* 14–27.

SHETTEL-NEUBER, J. (1988). Second- and third-generation zoo exhibits: A comparison of visitor, staff, and animal responses. *Environment and Behavior, 20,* 452–473.

SHUMAKER, S. A., & CONTI, G. J. (1985). Understanding mobility in America: Conflicts between stability and change. In I. Altman & C. Werner (Eds.), *Home environments.* New York: Plenum.

SHUMAKER, S. A., & TAYLOR, R. B. (1983). Toward a clarification of people-place relationships: A model of attachment to place. In N. Feimer & E. S. Geller (Eds.), *Environmental psychology: Directions and perspectives.* New York: Praeger.

SIEGEL, A. W., KIRASIC, K. C., & KAIL, R. V., JR. (1978). Stalking the elusive cognitive map: The development of children's representation of geographic space. In I. Altman & J. F. Wohlwill (Eds.), *Children and the environment.* New York: Plenum.

SIEGEL, A. W., & WHITE, S. H. (1975). The development of spatial representations of large-scale environments. In H. W. Reese (Ed.), *Advances in child development and behavior* (Vol. 10). New York: Academic Press.

SILVA, J. M., & ANDREWS, J. A. (1987). An analysis of game location and basketball performance in the Atlantic Coast Conference. *International Journal of Sport Psychology, 18,* 188–204.

SILVER, R. R. (1974, March 17). Arthur, talking aschcan, "eats" C. W. Post trash. *New York Times,* p. 10.

SILVERN, S. B., WILLIAMSON, P. A., & COUNTERMINE, T. A. (1983). *Aggression in young children and video game play.* Paper presented at the biennial meeting of the Society for Research in Child Development, Detroit.

SIMMONS, D. A., TALBOT, J. F., & KAPLAN, R. (1984–1985). Energy in daily activities: Muddling toward conservation. *Journal of Environmental Systems, 14,* 147–155.

SIMS, J. H., & BAUMANN, D. D. (1983). Education programs and human response to natural hazards. *Environment and Behavior, 15,* 165–189.

SINGER, J. E., LUNDBERG, U., & FRANKENHAEUSER, M. (1978). Stress on the train: A study of urban commuting. In A. Baum, J. E. Singer, & S. Valins (Eds.), *Advances in environmental psychology* (Vol. 1). Hillsdale, NJ: Erlbaum.

SIVAK, M., OLSON, P. L., & PASTALAN, L. A. (1981). Effect of driver's age on night-time legibility of highway signs. *Human Factors, 23,* 59–64.

SKINNER, B. F. (1938). *The behavior of organisms.* New York: Appleton-Century-Crofts.

SKINNER, B. F. (1958). *Science and human behavior.* New York: Macmillan.

SKOGAN, W. G., MAXFIELD, M. G., & PODOLEFSKY, D. A. (1981). *Coping with crime: Individual and neighborhood reactions.* Beverly Hills: Sage.

SLOTSKY, R. J. (1973). *Wilderness experience: A therapeutic modality.* San Francisco: California School of Professional Psychology.

SLOVIC, P. (1978). The psychology of protective behavior. *Journal of Safety Research, 10,* 58–68.

SLOVIC, P., KUNREUTHER, H., & WHITE, G. F. (1974). Decision processes, rationality, and adjustment to natural hazards. In G. F. White (Ed.), *Natural hazards: Local, national, global.* New York: Oxford University Press.

SLOVIC, P., LAYMAN, M., & FLYNN, J. H. (1991). Risk perception, trust, and nuclear waste: Lessons from Yucca Mountain. *Environment, 33* (3), 6–11, 28–30.

SMETANA, J., BRIDGEMAN, D. L., & BRIDGEMAN, B. (1978). A field study of interpersonal distance in early childhood. *Personality and Social Psychology Bulletin, 4,* 309–313.

SMITH, A. P. (1991). Noise and aspects of attention. *British Journal of Psychology, 82,* 313–324.

SMITH, C. D. (1984). The relationship between the pleasingness of landmarks and the judgment of distance in cognitive maps. *Journal of Environmental Psychology, 4,* 229–234.

SMITH, D. E. (1982). Privacy and corrections: A reexamination. *American Journal of Community Psychology, 10,* 207–224.

SMITH, G. C. (1991). Grocery shopping patterns of the ambulatory urban elderly. *Environment and Behavior, 23,* 86–114.

SMITH, J. G., & SARGENT, F. P. (1948). Preface to *Midland City* by T. Brennan. London: Dobson.

SMITH, R. J., & KNOWLES, E. S. (1979). Affective and cognitive mediators of reactions to spatial invasions. *Journal of Experimental Social Psychology, 15,* 437–452.

SNYDER, M., & WHITE, P. (1982). Moods and memories: Elation, depression, and the remembering of the events of one's life. *Journal of Personality, 50,* 149–167.

SNYDER, R. L. (1968). Reproduction and population pressures. In E. Stellar & J. M. Sprague (Eds.), *Progress in physiological psychology.* New York: Academic Press.

SOCOLOW, R. H. (1978). *Saving energy in the home.* Cambridge, MA: Ballinger.

SOKOL, R. J. (1976). A psychoanalytic view of vandalism. In *Vandalism and outdoor recreation.* Berkeley, CA: U.S. Department of Agriculture, Pacific Southwest Forest and Range Experiment Station.

SOMMER, R. (1959). Studies in personal space. *Sociometry, 22,* 247–260.

SOMMER, R. (1961). Leadership and group geography. *Sociometry, 24,* 99–110.

SOMMER, R. (1967). Classroom ecology. *Journal of Applied Behavioral Science, 3,* 489–503.

SOMMER, R. (1968). Student reactions to four types of residence halls. *Journal of College Student Personnel, 9,* 232–237.

SOMMER, R. (1969). *Personal space.* Englewood Cliffs, NJ: Prentice-Hall.

SOMMER, R. (1972a). *Design awareness.* New York: Holt, Rinehart, & Winston.

SOMMER, R. (1972b). What do we learn at the zoo? *Natural History, 81,* 26–27, 84–85.

SOMMER, R. (1987). Crime and vandalism in university residence halls: A confirmation of defensible space theory. *Journal of Environmental Psychology, 7,* 1–12.

SOMMER, R., & BECKER, F. D. (1969). Territorial defense and the good neighbor. *Journal of Personality and Social Psychology, 11,* 85–92.

SOMMER, R., & BECKER, F. D. (1971). Room density and user satisfaction. *Environment and Behavior, 3,* 412–417.

SOMMER, R., & OLSEN, H. (1980). The soft classroom. *Environment and Behavior, 12,* 3–16.

SOMMER, R., & STEINER, K. (1988). Office politics in a state legislature. *Environment and Behavior, 20,* 550–575.

SOMMERS, P., & MOOS, R. H. (1976). The weather and human behavior. In R. H. Moos (Ed.), *The human context: Environmental determinants of behavior.* New York: John Wiley and Sons..

SOMMER, R., & ROSS, H. (1958). Social interaction on a geriatrics ward. *International Journal of Social Psychiatry, 4,* 128–133.

SONNENFELD, J. (1969). Personality and behavior in environment. *Proceedings of the Association of American Geographers, 1,* 136–140.

SORENSON, J. H. (1983). Knowing how to behave under the threat of disaster: Can it be explained? *Environment and Behavior, 15,* 438–457.

SORENSON, J. H., SODERSTROM, J., COPENHAVER, E., CARNES, S., & BOLIN, R. (1987). *Impact of hazardous technology: The psycho-social effects of restarting TMI-I.* Albany, NY: SUNY Press.

SOUTHWICK, C. H. (1967). An experimental study of intragroup agonistic behavior in rhesus monkeys, *Macaca mulatta. Behavior, 28,* 182–209.

SOUTHWICK, C. H., & BLAND, V. P. (1959). Effect of population density on adrenal glands and reproductive organs of CFW mice. *American Journal of Psychology, 197,* 111–114.

SPIVAK, M. (1969). The political collapse of a playground. *Landscape Architecture, 59,* 288–291.

SPOEHR, K. T., & LEHMKUHLE, S. W. (1982). *Visual information processing.* New York: W. H. Freeman.

SPOTTS, D. M., & STYNES, D. J. (1984). Public awareness and knowledge of urban parks: A case study. *Journal of Parks and Recreation Administration, 2,* 1–12.

SPREEN, O, TUPPER, D., RISSER, A., TUOKKO, H., & EDGELL, D. (1984). *Human developmental neuropsychology.* New York: Oxford University Press.

SRIVASTAVA, R. K., & PEEL, T. S. (1968). *Human movement as a function of color stimulation.* Topeka, KS: Environmental Research Foundation.

SROLE, L. (1972). Urbanization and mental health: Some reformulations. *American Scientist, 60,* 576–583.

STANDING, L., CONEZIO, J., & HABER, R. N. (1970). Perception and memory for pictures: Single-trial learning of 2560 visual stimuli. *Psychonomic Science, 19,* 73–74.

STANKEY, G. H. (1972). A strategy for the definition and management of wilderness quality. In J. V. Krutilla (Ed.), *Natural environments: Studies in theoretical and applied analysis.* Baltimore: Johns Hopkins University Press.

STANKEY, G. H. (1989). Solitude for the multitudes: Managing recreational use in the wilderness. In I. Altman & E. H. Zube (Eds.), *Public places and spaces.* New York: Plenum.

STANLEY, J. M., & FRANCIS, W. D. (1984, September). *The effects of REST and REST enhanced self-regulation on essential hypertension.* Presented at the 23rd International Congress of Psychology, Acapulco, Mexico.

STANTON, H. E. (1976). Hypnosis and encounter group volunteers: A validational study of the sensation-seeking scale. *Journal of Consulting and Clinical Psychology, 44,* 692.

STEBBINS, R. A. (1973). Physical context influences on behavior: The case of classroom disorderliness. *Environment and Behavior, 5,* 291–314.

STEEL, G. D., & SUEDFELD, P. (1991). Temporal patterns of affect in an isolated group. *Environment and Behavior, 23,* 749–765.

STEINGLASS, P., & GERRITY, E. (1990). Natural disasters and post-traumatic stress disorder: Short-term vs. long-term recovery in two disaster-affected communities. *Journal of Applied Social Psychology, 20,* 1746–1765.

STEINZOR, B. (1950). The spatial factor in face-to-face discussion groups. *Journal of Abnormal and Social Psychology, 45,* 552–555.

STEPHENS, L. S. (1974). *The teacher's guide to open education.* New York: Holt, Rinehart, & Winston.

STERLING, T. D., PHAIR, J. J., POLLACK, S. V., SCHUMSKY, D. A., & DEGROOT, I. (1966). Urban morbidity and air pollution. *Archives of Environmental Health, 13,* 158–170.

STERN, P. C., & OSKAMP, S. (1987). Managing scarce environmental resources. In D. Stokols & I. Altman (Eds.), *Handbook of environmental psychology* (Vol. 2). New York: John Wiley and Sons.

STEVENS, A., & COUPE, P. (1978). Distortions in judged spatial relations. *Cognitive Psychology, 10,* 422–437.

STILGOE, J. R. (1976). Jack O'Lanterns to surveyors: The secularization of landscape boundaries. *Environmental Review, 1,* 14–31.

STIRES, L. (1980). The effect of classroom seating location on student grades and attitudes: Environment or self-selection? *Environment and Behavior, 12,* 241–254.

STOKES, S. J. (1960). *Student reactions to study facilities with implications for architects and college administrators.* Amherst, MA: Committee for the New College. (ERIC Document ED 013 535, EF000078).

STOKOLS, D. (1972). On the distinction between density and crowding: Some implications for future research. *Psychological Review, 79,* 275–277.

STOKOLS, D. (1976). The experience of crowding in primary and secondary environments. *Environment and Behavior, 8,* 49–86.

STOKOLS, D., & NOVACO, R. W. (1981). Transportation and well-being. In I. Altman, J. F. Wohlwill, & P. Everett (Eds.), *Transportation and behavior.* New York: Plenum.

STOKOLS, D., NOVACO, R. W., STOKOLS, J., & CAMPBELL, J. (1978). Traffic congestion, type-A behavior, and stress. *Journal of Applied Psychology, 63,* 467–480.

STOKOLS, D., RALL, M., PINNER, B., & SCHOPLER, J. (1973). Physical, social, and personal determinants of crowding. *Environment and Behavior, 5,* 87–115.

STOKOLS, D., & SHUMAKER, S. A. (1981). People in places: A transactional view of settings. In J. H. Harvey (Ed.), *Cognition, social behavior, and the environment.* Hillsdale, NJ: Erlbaum.

STOKOLS, D., SHUMAKER, S. A., & MARTINEZ, J. (1983). Residential mobility and personal well-being. *Journal of Environmental Psychology, 3,* 5–19.

STOKS, F. (1983). Assessing urban environments for danger of violent crime: Especially rape. In D. Joiner, G. Brinilcombe, J. Daish, J. Gray, & D. Kernohan (Eds.), *Proceedings of the Conference on People and Physical Environment Research.* Wellington, New Zealand: Ministry of Works and Development.

STORMS, M. D., & THOMAS, G. C. (1977). Reactions to physical closeness. *Journal of Personality and Social Psychology, 35,* 412–418

STRODTBECK, F. L., & HOOK, L. H. (1961). The social dimensions of a twelve man jury table. *Sociometry, 24,* 397–415.

STRUBE, M. J., & WERNER, C. M. (1982). Interpersonal distance and personal space: A conceptual and methodological note. *Journal of Nonverbal Behavior, 6,* 163–170.

STRUBE, M. J., & WERNER, C. M. (1984). Personal space claims as a function of interpersonal threat: The mediating role of need for control. *Journal of Nonverbal Behavior, 8,* 195–209.

SUEDFELD, P. (1980). *Restricted environmental stimulation: Research and clinical applications:* New York: John Wiley and Sons.

SUEDFELD, P. (1987). Extreme and unusual environments. In D. Stokols & I. Altman (Eds.), *Handbook of environmental psychology.* New York: John Wiley and Sons.

SUEDFELD, P. (1991a). Groups in isolation and confinement: Environments and experience. In A. A. Harrison, Y. A. Clearwater, & C. P. McKay (Eds.), *From Antarctica to outer space: Life in isolation and confinement.* New York: Springer-Verlag.

SUEDFELD, P. (1991b). Polar psychology: An overview. *Environment and Behavior, 23,* 653–665.

SUEDFELD, P., BALLARD, E. J., & MURPHY, M. (1983). Water immersion and flotation: From stress experiment to stress treatment. *Journal of Environmental Psychology, 3,* 147–155.

SUEDFELD, P., BERNALDEZ, J. P., & STOSSEL, D. (1989). The polar psychology project (PPP): A cross-national investigation of polar adaptation. *Arctic Medical Research, 48,* 91–94.

SUEDFELD, P., METCALFE, J, & BLUCK, S. (1987). Enhancement of scientific creativity by flotation rest (Restricted Environmental Stimulation Technique). *Journal of Environmental Psychology, 7,* 219–231.

SUEDFELD, P., & MOCELLIN, J. S. P. (1987). The "sensed presence" in unusual environments. *Environment and Behavior, 19,* 33–52.

SULMAN, F. G. (1980). *The effect of air ionization, electric fields, atmospherics, and other electric phenomena on man and animal.* Springfield, IL: Charles C Thomas.

SULMAN, F. G., LEVY, D., LEVY, A., PFEIFER, Y., SUPERSTEIN, E., & TAL, E. (1974). Ionometry of hot, dry, desert winds (Sharav) and application of ionizing treatment to weather-sensitive patients. *International Journal of Biometeorology, 18,* 393.

SUNDSTROM, E. (1978). Crowding as a sequential process: Review of research on the effects of population density on humans. In A. Baum & Y. M. Epstein (Eds.), *Human response to crowding.* Hillsdale, NJ: Erlbaum.

SUNDSTROM, E. (1986a). *Work places.* Cambridge, England: Cambridge University Press.

SUNDSTROM, E. (1986b). Privacy in the office. In J. D. Wineman (Ed.), *Behavioral issues in office design.* New York: Van Nostrand Reinhold.

SUNDSTROM, E. (1987). Work environments: Offices and factories. In D. Stokols & I. Altman (Eds.), *Handbook of environmental psychology* (Vol. 1) (pp. 733–782). New York: John Wiley and Sons.

SUNDSTROM, E., & ALTMAN, I. (1974). Field study of territorial behavior and dominance. *Journal of Personality and Social Psychology, 30,* 115–124.

SUNDSTROM, E., & ALTMAN, I. (1976). Interpersonal relationships and personal space: Research review and theoretical model. *Human Ecology, 4,* 47–67.

SUNDSTROM, E., BURT, R. E., & KAMP, D. (1980). Privacy at work: Architectural correlates of job satisfaction and job performance. *Academy of Management Journal, 12,* 101–117.

SUNDSTROM, E., HERBERT, R. K., & BROWN, D. W. (1982). Privacy and communication in an open plan office: A case study. *Environment and Behavior, 14,* 379–392.

SUNDSTROM, E., & SUNDSTROM, M. G. (1977). Personal space invasions: What happens when the invader asks permission? *Environmental Psychology and Nonverbal Behavior, 2,* 76–82.

SUNDSTROM, E., TOWN, J. P., BROWN, D. W., FORMAN, A., & MCGEE, C. (1982). Physical enclosure, type of job, and privacy in the office. *Environment and Behavior, 14,* 543–559.

SUSSMAN, N. M., & ROSENFELD, H. M. (1982). Touch, justification, and sex: Influence on the aversiveness of spatial violations. *Journal of Social Psychology, 106,* 215–225.

SUTTLES, G. D. (1968). *The social order of the slum: Ethnicity and territory in the innter city.* Chicago: University of Chicago Press.

SUTTON, R. W. (1976). Vandalism in the Channel Islands National Monument. In *Vandalism and outdoor recreation.* Berkeley, CA: U.S. Department of Agriculture, Pacific Southwest Forest and Range Experiment Station.

SUTTON, S., & HALLETT, R. (1989). Understanding seat-belt intentions and behavior: A decision-making approach. *Journal of Applied Social Psychology, 19,* 1310–1325.

SWAN, J. (1970). Response to air pollution: A study of attitudes and coping strategies of high school youth. *Environment and Behavior, 2,* 127–152.

SZILAGYI, A., & HOLLAND, W. (1980). Changes in social density: Relationships with functional interaction and perceptions of job characteristics, role stress, and work satisfaction. *Journal of Applied Psychology, 65,* 28–33.

TAGG, S. K. (1973). The rise of multidimensional scaling type techniques in the structuring of the architectural psychology of places. In R. Kuller (Ed.), *Architectural Psychology: Proceedings of the Lund Conference.* Stroudsburg, PA: Dowden, Hutchinson, and Ross.

TALBOT, J. F., & KAPLAN, R. (1986). Judging the sizes of urban open areas: Is bigger always better? *Landscape Journal, 5,* 83–92.

TALBOT, J. F., & KAPLAN, S. (1986). Perspectives on wilderness: Re-examining the value of extended wilderness experiences. *Journal of Environmental Psychology, 6,* 177–188.

TAYLOR, A. J. W. (1991). The research program of the International Biomedical Expedition to the Antarctic (IBEA) and its implications for research in outer space. In A. A. Harrison, Y. A. Clearwater, & C. P. McKay (Eds.), *From Antarctica to outer space: Life in isolation and confinement.* New York: Springer-Verlag.

TAYLOR, D. E. (1989). Blacks and the environment: Toward an explanation of the concern and action gap between blacks and whites. *Environment and Behavior, 21,* 175–205.

TAYLOR, J. G., STEWART, T. R., & DOWNTON, M. (1988). Perceptions of drought in the Oglala Aquifer Region. *Environment and Behavior, 20,* 150–175.

TAYLOR, R. B. (1982). Neighborhood physical environment and stress. In G. W. Evans (Ed.), *Environmental stress.* New York: Cambridge University Press.

TAYLOR, R. B. (1987). Toward an environmental psychology of disorder: Delinquency, crime, and fear of crime. In D. Stokols & I. Altman (Eds.), *Handbook of environmental psychology* (Vol. 2). New York: John Wiley and Sons.

TAYLOR, R. B. (1988). *Human territorial functioning.* Cambridge: Cambridge University Press.

TAYLOR, R. B., & BROOKS, D. K. (1980). Temporary territories? Responses to intrusions in a public setting. *Population and Environment, 3,* 135–145.

TAYLOR, R. B., & FERGUSON, G. (1980). Solitude and intimacy: Linking territoriality and privacy experiences. *Journal of Nonverbal Behavior, 4,* 227–239.

TAYLOR, R. B., & LANNI, J. C. (1981). Territorial dominance: The influence of the resident advantage in triadic decision making. *Journal of Personality and Social Psychology, 41,* 909–915.

TAYLOR, R. B., & STOUGH, R. R. (1978). Territorial cognition: Assessing Altman's typology. *Journal of Personality and Social Psychology, 36,* 418–423.

TAYLOR, T. (1985). The effects of flotation restricted environmental stimulation therapy on learning: Subjective evaluation and EEG measurements. In T. H. Fine & J. W. Turner (Eds.), *Proceedings of the First International Conference on REST and Self-Regulation.* Toledo: Medical College of Ohio.

TEASDALE, J. D., & TAYLOR, R. (1981). Induced mood and accessibility of memories: An effect of mood state or of induction procedure? *British Journal of Clinical Psychology, 20,* 39–48.

TENNEN, H., AFFLECK, G., ALLEN, D. A., MCGRADE, B. J., & RATZAN, S. (1985). Causal attributions and coping with insulin dependent diabetes. *Basic and Applied Social Psychology, 5,* 131–142.

TENNIS, G. H., & DABBS, J. M. (1975). Sex, setting, and personal space: First grade through college. *Sociometry, 38,* 385–394.

TETSURO, W. (1961). *Climate and culture.* Tokyo: The Hokuseido Press.

THALHOFER, N. N. (1980). Violation of a spacing norm in high social density. *Journal of Applied Social Psychology, 10,* 175–183.

THAYER, R. E. (1987). Problem perception, optimism, and related states as a function of time of day (diurnal rhythm) and moderate exercise: Two arousal systems in interaction. *Motivation and Emotion, 11,* 19–36.

THAYER, R. E. (1989). *The biopsychology of mood and arousal.* New York: Oxford University Press.

THAYER, R. E., TAKAHASHI, P. J., & PAULI, J. A. (1988). Multidimensional arousal states, diurnal rhythms, cognitive and social processes, and extraversion. *Personality and Individual Differences, 9,* 15–24.

THEOLOGUS, G. C., WHEATON, G. R., & FLEISHMAN, E. A. (1974). Effects of intermittent, moderate intensity noise on human performance. *Journal of Applied Psychology, 59,* 539–547.

THIESSEN, D. D. (1964). Population density, mouse genotype, and endocrine function in behavior. *Journal of Comparative and Physiological Psychology, 57,* 412–416.

THOMAS, D. R. (1973). Interaction distances in same-sex and mixed-sex groups. *Perceptual and Motor Skills, 36,* 15–18.

THOMPSON, S. C., & STOUTEMEYER, K. (1991). Water use as a commons dilemma: The effects of education that focuses on long-term consequences and individual action. *Environment and Behavior, 23,* 314–333.

THOMSON, G. (1986). *The museum environment* (2nd ed.). Stoneham, MA: Butterworth.

THORNDYKE, P. W. (1981). Distance estimation from cognitive maps. *Cognitive Psychology, 13,* 526–550.

THORNDYKE, P. W., & HAYES-ROTH, B. (1982). Differences in spatial knowledge acquired from maps and navigation. *Cognitive Psychology, 14,* 560–589.

THORNDYKE, P. W., & STASZ, C. (1980). Individual differences in procedures for knowledge acquisition from maps. *Cognitive Psychology, 12,* 137–175.

TIMKO, C., & JANOFF-BULMAN, R. (1985). Attributions, vulnerability, and psychological adjustment: The case of breast cancer. *Health Psychology, 4,* 521–544.

TITCHENER, E. B. (1910). *A textbook of psychology.* New York: Macmillan.

TOGNOLI, J. (1987). Residential environments. In D. Stokols & I. Altman (Eds.), *Handbook of environmental psychology* (Vol. 1). New York: John Wiley and Sons.

TOLMAN, E. C. (1948). Cognitive maps in rats and men. *Psychological Review, 55,* 189–208.

TOLMAN, E. C., RITCHIE, B. F., & KALISH, D. (1946). Studies in spatial learning I. Orientation and the short-cut. *Journal of Experimental Psychology, 36,* 13–24.

TOOBY, J., & COSMIDES, L. (1990). The past explains the present: Emotional adaptations and the structure of ancestral environments. *Ethology and Sociobiology, 11,* 375–424

TOPF, M. (1989). Sensitivity to noise, personality hardiness, and noise-induced stress in critical care nurses *Environment and Behavior, 21,* 717–733.

TRAUB, R. E., & WEISS, J. (1974). Studying openness in education: An Ontario example. *Journal of Research and Development in Education, 8,* 47–59.

TRIGG, L. J., PERLMAN, D., PERRY, R. P., & JANISSE, M. P. (1976). Anti-pollution behavior: A function of perceived outcome and locus of control. *Environment and Behavior, 8,* 307–313.

TRUSCOTT, J., PARMELEE, P., & WERNER, C. (1977). Plate touching in restaurants: Preliminary observations of a food-related marking behavior in humans. *Personality and Social Psychology Bulletin, 3,* 425–428.

TUAN, Y. (1974). *Topophilia: A study of environmental perception, attitude, and values.* Englewood Cliffs, NJ: Prentice-Hall.

TUAN, Y. (1979). *Landscapes of fear.* New York: Pantheon Books.

TURNBULL, C. M. (1961). *The forest people: A study of the Pygmies of the Congo.* New York: Simon and Schuster.

TURNER, J. W., & FINE, T. H. (1983). Effects of relaxation associated with brief restricted environmental stimulation therapy (REST) on plasma cortisol, ACTH, and L. H. *Biofeedback and Self-Regulation, 8,* 115–126.

TURNER, J. W., & FINE, T. H. (1984, September). *Effects of restricted environmental therapy (REST) on self-control of heart rate.* Presented at the 23rd International Congress of Psychology, Acapulco, Mexico.

TURNER, R. K., GRACE, R., & PEARCE, D. W. (1977). The economics of waste paper recycling. In D. W. Pearce & I. Walter (Eds.), *Resource conservation: Social and economic dimensions of recycling.* New York: New York University Press.

TUSO, M. A., & GELLER, E. S. (1976). Behavior analysis applied to environmental/ecological problems: A review. *Journal of Applied Behavior Analysis, 9,* 526.

TVERSKY, B. (1981). Distortions in memory for maps. *Cognitive Psychology, 13,* 407–433.

ULRICH, R. S. (1977). Visual landscape preferences: A model and application. *Man-Environment Systems, 7,* 279–293.

ULRICH, R. S. (1981). Natural vs. urban scenes: Some psychophysiological effects. *Environment and Behavior, 13,* 523–556.

ULRICH, R. S. (1983). Aesthetic and affective response to natural environments. In I. Altman & J. F. Wohlwill (Eds.), *Human behavior and the environment: Vol. 6. Behavior and the natural environment.* New York: Plenum.

ULRICH, R. S. (1984). View through a window influences recovery from surgery. *Science, 224,* 420–421.

ULRICH, R. S., & SIMONS, R. F. (1986). Recovery from stress during exposure to everyday outdoor environments. In *Proceedings of EDRA 17.* Washington, DC: Environmental Design Research Association.

ULRICH, R. S., SIMONS, R. F., LOSITO, B. D., FIORITO, E., MILES, M. A., & ZELSON, M. (1991). Stress recovery during exposure to natural and urban environments. *Journal of Environmental Psychology, 11,* 201–230.

UNGER, D. G., & WANDERSMAN, A. (1983). Neighboring and its role in block organizations: An exploratory report. *American Journal of Community Psychology, 11,* 291–300.

URSANO, R. J., & FULLERTON, C. S. (1990). Cognitive and behavioral responses to trauma. *Journal of Applied Social Psychology, 20,* 1766–1775.

URSANO, R. J., WRIGHT, K., INGRAHAM, L., & BARTON, P. (1988, May). Psychiatric responses to dead bodies. *Proceedings of the American Psychiatric Association Annual Meeting* (p. 132). Washington, DC: American Psychiatric Press.

URSIN, H., BERGAN, T., ENDRESEN, I. M., LUGG, D. J., MAKI, P., MATRE, R., MOLVAER, O., MULLER, H. K., OLFF, M., PETTERSEN, R., SANDAL, G. M., VAERNES, R., & WARNCKE, M. (1991). Psychobiological studies of individuals in small, isolated groups in the Antarctic and in space analogues. *Environment and Behavior, 23,* 766–781.

U.S. DEPARTMENT OF THE INTERIOR: HERITAGE CONSERVATION AND RECREATION SERVICE (1979). *The third nationwide outdoor recreation plan.* Washington, DC: U.S. Government Printing Office.

U.S. NEWS AND WORLD REPORT (April 23, 1990). Living with our legacy. *108,* 60–64.

U.S. NEWS AND WORLD REPORT (December 31, 1990–January 7, 1991). The year that was. *109,* 86–87.

VALINS, S., & BAUM, A. (1973). Residential group size, social interaction, and crowding. *Environment and Behavior, 5,* 421–439.

VAN DER RYN, S., & SILVERSTEIN, M. (1967). *Dorms at Berkeley: An environmental analysis.* Berkeley, CA: Center for Planning and Development Research.

VANDEVEER, D., & PIERCE, C. (EDS.). (1986). *People, penguins, and plastic trees.* Belmont, CA: Wadsworth.

VANETTI, E. J., & ALLEN, G. L. (1988). Communicating environmental knowledge: The impact of verbal and spatial abilities on the production and comprehension of route directions. *Environment and Behavior, 20,* 667–682.

VAN STADEN, F. J. (1984). Urban early adolescents, crowding, and the neighborhood experience: A preliminary investigation. *Journal of Environmental Psychology, 4,* 97–118.

VAUGHAN, E., & NORDENSTAM, B. (1991). The perception of environmental risks among ethnically diverse groups. *Journal of Cross-Cultural Psychology, 22,* 29–60.

VEITCH, J. A., GIFFORD, R., & HINE, D. W. (1991). Demand characteristics and full-spectrum lighting effects on performance and mood. *Journal of Environmental Psychology, 11,* 87–95.

VERDERBER, S., GARDNER, L., ISLAM D., & NAKANISHI, L. (1988). Elderly persons' appraisal of the zoological environment. *Environment and Behavior, 20,* 492–507.

VER ELLEN, P., & VAN KAMMEN, D. P. (1990). The biological findings in posttraumatic stress disorder: A review. *Journal of Applied Social Psychology, 20,* 1789–1821.

VINING, J., & EBREO, A. (1990). What makes a recycler? A comparison of recyclers and nonrecyclers. *Environment and Behavior, 22,* 55–73.

VINSEL, A., BROWN, B. B., ALTMAN, I., & FOSS, C. (1980). Privacy regulation, territorial displays, and effectiveness of individual functioning. *Journal of Personality and Social Psychology, 39,* 1104–1115.

WALBERG, H. J. (1969). Physical and psychological distance in the classroom. *School Review, 77,* 64–70.

WALDEN, T. A., & FORSYTH, D. R. (1981). Close encounters of the stressful kind: Affective, physiological, and behavioral reactions to the experience of crowding. *Journal of Nonverbal Behavior, 6,* 46–64.

WALDEN, T. A., NELSON, P. A., & SMITH, D. E. (1981). Crowding, privacy, and coping. *Environment and Behavior, 13,* 205–224.

WALK, R. D., & GIBSON, E. J. (1961). A comparative and analytical study of visual depth perception. *Psychological Monographs, 75,* No. 15.

WALLER, I., & OKIHIRO, N. (1978). *Burglary: The victim and the public.* Toronto: University of Toronto Press.

WALMSLEY, D. J., & LEWIS, G. J. (1989). The pace of pedestrian flows in cities. *Environment and Behavior, 21,* 123–150.

WALSH, D. P. (1975). Noise levels and annoyance in open-plan educational facilities. *Journal of Architectural Research, 4,* 5–16.

WARD, L. M., & RUSSELL, J. A. (1981). The psychological representation of molar physical environments. *Journal of Experimental Psychology, 110,* 121–151.

WARD, L. M., SNODGRASS, J., CHEW, B., & RUSSELL, J. A. (1988). The role of plans in cognitive and affective responses to places. *Journal of Environmental Psychology, 8,* 1–8.

WARNER, H. D. (1969). Effects of intermittent noise on human target detection. *Human Factors, 11,* 245–250.

WARREN, D. I. (1978). Exploration in neighborhood differentiation. *Sociological Quarterly, 19,* 310–331.

WARZECHA, S., FISHER, J. D., & BARON, R. M. (1988). The equity-control model as a predictor of vandalism among college students. *Journal of Applied Social Psychology, 18,* 80–91.

WATERS, F. (1963). *Book of the Hopi,* New York: Viking Press.

WATSON, O. M., & GRAVES, T. D. (1966). Quantitative research in proxemic behavior. *American Anthropologist, 68,* 971–985.

WAYNE, W., WEHRLE, P., & CARROLL, R. (1967). Oxidant air pollution and athletic performance. *Journal of the American Medical Association, 199,* 901–904.

WEBB, E. J., CAMPBELL, D. T., SCHWARTZ, R. D., & SECHREST, L. (1966). *Unobtrusive measures: Nonreactive research in the social sciences.* Chicago: Rand McNally.

WEBB, E. J., CAMPBELL, D. T., SCHWARTZ, R. D., SECHREST, L., & GROVE, J. B. (1981). *Nonreactive measures in the social sciences* (2nd ed.). Boston: Houghton Mifflin.

WEBLEY, P., & WHALLEY, A. (1987). Sex differences in children's environmental cognition. *Journal of Social Psychology, 127,* 223–225.

WEBSTER, S. K. (1985). Interactive exhibits at the Monterey Bay Aquarium. *American Association of Zoological Parks and Aquariums 1985 Annual Proceedings,* pp. 63–68.

WECKER, S. C. (1964). Habitat selection. *Scientific American, 211,* 109–116.

WEENIG, M. W. H., SCHMIDT, T., & MIDDEN, C. J. H. (1990). Social dimensions of neighborhoods and the effectiveness of information programs. *Environment and Behavior, 22,* 27–54.

WEHR, T. A. (1989). Seasonal affective disorders: A historical review. In N. E. Rosenthal & M. C. Blehar (Eds.), *Seasonal affective disorders and phototherapy.* New York: Guilford.

WEHR, T. A., GEISEN, H., SCHULTZ, P. M., JOSEPH-VANDERPOOL, J. R., KASPER, S., KELLY, K. A., & ROSENTHAL, N. E. (1989). Summer depression: Description of the syndrome and comparison with winter depression. In N. E. Rosenthal & M. C. Blehar (Eds.), *Seasonal affective disorders and phototherapy.* New York: Guilford.

WEIGEL, R. H. (1983). Environmental attitudes and the prediction of behavior. In N. R. Feimer & E. S. Geller (Eds.), *Environmental psychology: Directions and perspectives.* New York: Praeger.

WEIGEL, R. H., TOGNACCI, L. N., & VERNON, D. T. A. (1974). Specificity of the attitude as a determinant of attitude-behavior congruence. *Journal of Personality and Social Psychology, 30,* 724–728.

WEIL, A. T. (1977). The marriage of the sun and the moon. In N. E. Zinberg (Ed.), *Alternate states of consciousness.* New York: Free Press.

WEINSTEIN, C. S. (1979). The physical environment of the school: A review of the research. *Review of Educational Research, 49,* 577–610.

WEINSTEIN, C. S. (1982). Privacy-seeking behavior in an elementary classroom. *Journal of Environmental Psychology, 2,* 23–25.

WEINSTEIN, C. S., & PINCIOTTI, P. (1988). Changing a schoolyard: Intentions, design decisions, and behavioral outcomes. *Environment and Behavior, 20,* 345–371.

WEINSTEIN, C. S., & WOOLFOLK, A. E. (1981). The classroom setting as a source of expectations about teachers and pupils. *Journal of Environmental Psychology, 1,* 117–129.

WEINSTEIN, N. D. (1977). Noise and intellectual performance: A confirmation and extension. *Journal of Applied Psychology, 59,* 548–554.

WEINSTEIN, N. D. (1978). Individual differences in reactions to noise: A longitudinal study in a college dormitory. *Journal of Applied Psychology, 63,* 458–466.

WEINSTEIN, N. D. (1980). Individual differences in critical tendencies and noise annoyance. *Journal of Sound and Vibration, 68,* 241–248.

WEISMAN, G. D. (1981). Evaluating architectural legibility: Wayfinding in the built environment. *Environment and Behavior, 13,* 189–204.

WEISS, L., & BAUM, A. (1989). Physiological aspects of environment-behavior relationships. In E. H. Zube & G. T. Moore (Eds.), *Advances in environment, behavior, and design* (Vol. 1). New York: Plenum.

WELCH, B. L. (1979). *Extra-auditory effects of industrial noise: Surveys of foreign literature.* Dayton, OH: Aerospace Medical Research Laboratory, Wright Patterson Air Force Base.

WELLS, B. W. P. (1965). The psycho-social influence of building environment: Sociometric findings in large and small office spaces. *Building Science, 1,* 153–165.

WENER, R. E. (1989). Advances in evaluation of the built environment. In E. H. Zube & G. T. Moore (Eds.), *Advances in environment, behavior, and design* (Vol. 2). New York: Plenum.

WENER, R. E., & KEYS, C. (1988). The effects of changes in jail population densities on crowding, sick call, and spatial behavior. *Journal of Applied Psychology, 18,* 852–866.

WERNER, C. M., ALTMAN, I., & OXLEY, D. (1985). Temporal aspects of homes: A transactional perspective. In I. Altman & C. M. Werner (Eds.), *Home environments.* New York: Plenum.

WERNER, C. M., ALTMAN, I., OXLEY, D. M., & HAGGARD, L. M. (1985). People, place, and time: A transactional analysis of neighborhoods. In W. H. Jones & D. Perlman (Eds.), *Advances in personal relationships* (Vol. 1). Greenwich, CT: JAI Press.

WERNER, C. M., BROWN, B. B., & DAMRON, G. (1981). Territorial marking in a game arcade, *Journal of Personality and Social Psychology, 41,* 1094–1104.

WERNER, C. M., PETERSON-LEWIS, S., & BROWN, B. B. (1989). Inferences about homeowners' sociability: Impact of Christmas decorations and other cues. *Journal of Environmental Psychology, 9,* 279–296.

WESTIN, A. F. (1967). *Privacy and freedom.* New York: Atheneum.

WESTOVER, T. N. (1989). Perceived crowding in recreational settings: An environment-behavior model. *Environment and Behavior, 21,* 258–276.

WESTOVER, T. N., & COLLINS, J. R., JR. (1987). Perceived crowding in recreation settings: An urban case study. *Leisure Sciences, 9,* 87–99.

WETHINGTON, E., & KESSLER, R. C. (1986). Perceived support, received support, and adjustment to stressful life events. *Journal of Health and Social Behavior, 27,* 78–89.

WEXNER, L. B. (1954). The degree to which colors (hues) are associated with mood-tones. *Journal of Applied Psychology, 38,* 432–435.

WHELDALL, K., MORRIS, M., VAUGHAN, P., & NG, Y. Y. (1981). Rows versus tables: An example of the use of behavioral ecology in two classes of eleven-year-old children. *Educational Psychology, 1,* 171–184.

WHITE, B. L., KABAN, B., & ATTANUCCI, J. (1979). *The origins of human competence.* Lexington, MA: Heath.

WHITE, J. (1986). More than just hands-on! *American Association of Zoological Parks and Aquariums 1986 Annual Proceedings,* pp. 240–245.

WHITE, L. (1967). The historical roots of our ecologic crisis. *Science, 155,* 1203–1207.

WHITE, M. (1975). Interpersonal distance as affected by room size, status, and sex. *Journal of Social Psychology, 95,* 241–249.

WICKER, A. W. (1973). Undermanning theory and research: Implications for the study of psychological and behavioral effects of excess human populations. *Representative Research in Social Psychology, 4,* 185–206.

WICKER, A. W. (1979). *An introduction to ecological psychology.* Pacific Grove, CA: Brooks/Cole.

WIDGERY, R. N. (1982). Satisfaction with the quality of urban life: A predictive model. *American Journal of Community Psychology, 10,* 37–48.

WILLEMS, E. P. (1967). Sense of obligation to high school activities as related to school size and marginality of student. *Child Development, 38,* 1247–1260.

WILLIAMS, M. L. (1976). Vandals aren't all bad. In *Vandalism and outdoor recreation.* Berkeley, CA: U.S. Department of Agriculture, Pacific Southwest Forest and Range Experiment Station.

WILLIAMS, S., RYCKMAN, R. M., GOLD, J. A., & LENNEY, E. (1982). The effects of sensation seeking and misattribution of arousal on attraction toward similar or dissimilar strangers. *Journal of Research in Personality, 16,* 217–226.

WILLIS, C. L. (1975). An empirical study of bathtub and shower accidents. *Proceedings of the Symposium on Environmental Effects on Behavior.* Big Sky, MT: Environmental Design Group of the Human Factors Society.

WILLIS, F. N. (1966). Initial speaking distance as a function of the speakers' relationship. *Psychonomic Science, 5,* 221–222.

WILLIS, F. N., JR., & HAMM, H. K. (1980). The use of interpersonal touch in securing compliance. *Journal of Nonverbal Behavior, 5,* 49–55.

WILSON, C. W., & HOPKINS, B. L. (1973). The effects of contigent music on the intensity of noise in junior high home economics classes. *Journal of Applied Behavior Analysis, 6,* 269–275.

WILSON, E. O. (1975). *Sociobiology: The new synthesis.* Cambridge: Harvard University Press.

WILSON, G. D. (1966). Arousal properties of red versus green. *Perceptual and Motor Skills, 23,* 947–949.

WINEMAN, J. D. (1982). Office design and evaluation: An overview. *Environment and Behavior, 14,* 271–298.

WINEMAN, J. D. (1986). *Behavioral issues in office design.* New York: Van Nostrand Reinhold.

WINETT, R. A. (1976). Efforts to disseminate a behavioral approach to energy conservation. *Professional Psychology, 7,* 222–228.

WINETT, R. A., HATCHER, J. W., FORT, T. R., LECKLITER, E. N., LOVE, S. Q., RILEY, A. W., & FISHBACK, J. F. (1982). The effects of videotape modeling and daily feedback on residential energy conservation, home temperature and humidity, perceived comfort, and clothing worn: Winter and summer. *Journal of Applied Behavior Analysis, 15,* 381–402.

WINGFIELD, A., & BYRNES, D. L. (1981). *The psychology of human memory.* New York: Academic Press.

WINKEL, G., OLSEN, R., WHEELER, F., & COHEN, M. (1976). *The museum visitor and orientational media: An experimental comparison of different ap-*

proaches in the Smithsonian Institution and National Museum of History and Technology. New York: City University of New York Center for Environment and Behavior.

WINKELHAKE, C. (1975). Personal space and interpersonal space. *Man-Environment Systems, 5,* 351–352.

WINKLER, R. C., & WINETT, R. A. (1982). Behavioral interventions in resource management: A systems approach based on behavioral economics. *American Psychologist, 37,* 421–435.

WITMER, J. F., & GELLER, E. S. (1976). Facilitating paper recycling: Effects of prompts, raffles, and contests. *Journal of Applied Behavior Analysis, 9,* 315–322.

WITTIG, M. A., & SKOLNICK, P. (1978). Status versus warmth as determinants of sex differences in personal space. *Sex Roles, 4,* 493–503.

WOHLWILL, J. F. (1974). Human response to levels of environmental stimulation. *Human Ecology, 2,* 127–147.

WOHLWILL, J. F. (1976). Environmental aesthetics: The environment as a source of affect. In I. Altman & J. F. Wohlwill (Eds.), *Human behavior and the environment* (Vol. 1). New York: Plenum.

WOHLWILL, J. F. (1983). The concept of nature: A psychologist's view. In I. Altman & J. F. Wohlwill (Eds.), *Human behavior and environment: Behavior and the natural environment* (Vol. 6). New York: Plenum.

WOLFE, M. (1975). Room size, group size, and density: Behavior patterns in a children's psychiatric facility. *Environment and Behavior, 7,* 199–224.

WORCHEL, S., & BROWN, E. H. (1984). The role of plausibility in influencing environmental attributions. *Journal of Experimental Social Psychology, 20,* 86–96.

WORCHEL, S., & SHACKELFORD, S. L. (1991). Groups under stress: The influence of group structure and environment on process and performance. *Personality and Social Psychology Bulletin, 17,* 640–647.

WORCHEL, S., & TEDDLIE, C. (1976). The experience of crowding: A two-factor theory. *Journal of Personality and Social Psychology, 34,* 36–40.

WORCHEL, S., & YOHAI, S. (1979). The role of attribution in the experience of crowding. *Journal of Experimental Social Psychology, 15,* 91–104.

WOTTON, E., & BARKOW, B. (1983). An investigation of the effects of windows and lighting in offices. *Proceedings of the 1983 Daylighting Conference,* Phoenix. Washington, DC: AIA Service Corporations.

WRIGHT, G. (1981). *Building the dream: A social history of housing in America.* New York: Pantheon.

WRIGHT, R. J. (1975). The affective and cognitive consequences of an open education elementary school. *American Educational Research Journal, 12,* 449–468.

WULF, K. M. (1977). Relationship of assigned classroom seating area to achievement variables. *Educational Research Quarterly, 21,* 56–62.

WYNNE-EDWARDS, V. C. (1962). *Animal dispersion in relation to social behavior.* Edinburgh-London: Oliver and Boyd.

WYON, D. P. (1974). The effects of moderate heat stress on typewriting performance. *Ergonomics, 17,* 309–318.

YANCEY, W. L. (1971). Architecture, interaction, and social control: The case of a large-scale public housing project. *Environment and Behavior, 3,* 3–21.

YERKES, R. M., & DODSON, J. D. (1908). The relation of strength of stimulus to rapidity of habit-formation. *Journal of Comparative and Neurological Psychology, 18,* 459–482.

YOORS, J. (1967). *The Gypsies.* New York: Simon and Schuster.

ZEHNER, R. B. (1972). Neighborhood and community satisfaction: A report on new towns and less planned suburbs. In J. F. Wohlwill & D. H. Carson (Eds.), *Environment and the social sciences: Perspectives and applications.* Washington, DC: American Psychological Association.

ZEIDBERG, L. D., PRINDLE, R. A., & LANDAU, E. (1964). The Nashville air pollution study: III. Morbidity in relation to air pollution. *American Journal of Public Health, 54,* 85–97.

ZEISEL, J. (1981). *Inquiry by design.* Pacific Grove, CA: Brooks/Cole.

ŽENTALL, S. S. (1983). Learning environments: A review of physical and temporal factors. *EEO: Exceptional Education Quarterly, 4,* 90–115.

ZIFFERBLATT, S. M. (1972). Architecture and human behavior: Toward increased understanding of a functional relationship. *Educational Technology, 12,* 54–57.

ZILLMANN, D., BARON, R. A., & TAMBORINI, R. (1981). Social costs of smoking: Effects of tobacco smoke on hostile behavior. *Journal of Applied Social Psychology, 11,* 548–561.

ZIMBARDO, P. G. (1969). The human choice: Individuation, reason, and order versus deindividuation, impulse, and chaos. In W. J. Arnold & D. Levine (Eds.), *Nebraska symposium on motivation.* Lincoln, NE: University of Nebraska Press.

ZIMMER, H. R. (1951). *Philosophies of India.* New York: Pantheon Books.

ZLUTNICK, S., & ALTMAN, I. (1972). Crowding and human behavior. In J. F. Wohlwill & D. H. Carson (Eds.), *Environment and the social sciences: Perspectives and applications.* Washington, DC: American Psychological Association.

ZUBE, E. H. (1976). Perception of landscape and land use. In I. Altman & J. F. Wohlwill (Eds.), *Human behavior and environment* (Vol. 1). New York: Plenum.

ZUBE, E. H. (1978). The natural history of urban trees. In S. Kaplan & R. Kaplan (Eds.), *Humanscape: Einvironments for people.* North Scituate, MA: Duxbury Press.

ZUBE, E. H. (1980). *Environmental evaluation: Perception and public policy.* New York: Cambridge University Press.

ZUBE, E. H. (1990). Landscape research: Planned and serendipitous. *Human Behavior and Environment: Advances in Theory and Research, 11,* 291–313.

ZUBE, E. H., PITT, D. G., & ANDERSON, T. W. (1975). Perception and prediction of scenic resource values of the Northeast. In E. H. Zube, R. O. Brush, & J. G. Fabos (Eds.), *Landscape assessment: Values, perceptions, and resources.* Stroudsburg, PA: Dowden, Hutchinson, and Ross.

ZUBE, E. H., PITT, D. G., & EVANS, G. W. (1983). A lifespan developmental study of landscape assessment. *Journal of Environmental Psychology, 3,* 115–128.

ZUBEK, J. P. (ED.). (1969). *Sensory deprivation: Fifteen years of research.* New York: Appleton-Century-Crofts.

ZUCKERMAN, M. (1971). Dimensions of sensation seeking. *Journal of Consulting and Clinical Psychology, 36,* 45–52.

ZUCKERMAN, M. (1974). The sensation seeking motive. In B. A. Maher (Ed.), *Progress in experimental personality research* (Vol. 7). New York: Academic Press.

ZUCKERMAN, M. (1979). *Sensation seeking: Beyond the optimal level of arousal.* Hillsdale, NJ: Erlbaum.

ZUCKERMAN, M. (1980). To risk or not to risk. In K. R. Blankstein, P. Pliner, & J. Polivy (Eds.), *Assessment and modification of emotional behavior.* New York: Plenum.

ZUCKERMAN, M. (1983). A biological theory of sensation seeking. In M. Zuckerman (Ed.), *Biological basis of sensation seeking, impulsivity, and anxiety.* Hillsdale, NJ: Erlbaum.

ZUCKERMAN, M. (1990). The psychophysiology of sensation seeking. *Journal of Personality, 58,* 313–345.

ZUCKERMAN, M., BONE, R. N., NEARY, R., MANGELSDORFF, D., & BRUSTMAN, B. (1972). What is the sensation seeker? Personality trait and experience correlates of the Sensation Seeking Scales. *Journal of Consulting and Clinical Psychology, 39,* 308–321.

ZUCKERMAN, M., BUCHSBAUM, M. S., & MURPHY, D. L. (1980). Sensation seeking and its biological correlates. *Psychological Bulletin, 88,* 187–214.

ZUCKERMAN, M., EYSENCK, S., & EYSENCK, H. J. (1978). Sensation seeking in England and America: Cross-cultural, age, and sex comparison. *Journal of Consulting and Clinical Psychology, 46,* 139–149.

ZUCKERMAN, M., KOLIN, E. A., PRICE, L., & ZOOB, I. (1964). Development of a sensation-seeking scale. *Journal of Consulting Psychology, 28,* 477–482.

ZUCKERMAN, M., & LUBIN, B. (1985). *Manual for the MAACL-R: The Multiple Affect Adjective Check List.* San Diego: Education and Industrial Testing Service.

ZUCKERMAN, M., NEARY, R. S., & BRUSTMAN, B. A. (1970). Sensation Seeking Scale correlates in experience (smoking, drugs, alcohol, "hallucinations," and sex) and preferences for complexity (designs). *Proceedings of the 78th Annual Convention of the American Psychological Association.* Washington, DC: APA.

ZUCKERMAN, M., SCHULTZ, D. P., & HOPKINS, T. R. (1967). Sensation seeking and volunteering for sensory deprivation and hypnosis experiments. *Journal of Consulting Psychology, 31,* 358–363.

ZUCKERMAN, M., TUSHUP, R., & FINNER, S. (1976). Sexual attitudes and experience. Attitude and personality correlates and changes produced by a course in sexuality. *Journal of Consulting and Clinical Psychology, 44,* 7–19.

ZURAVIN, S. J. (1986). Residential density and urban child maltreatment: An aggregate analysis. *Journal of Family Violence, 1,* 307–322.

ZWEIGENHAFT, R. (1976). Personal space in the faculty office — desk placement and the student-faculty interaction. *Journal of Applied Psychology, 61,* 529–532.

Name Index

Subject Index

Credits

These pages constitute an extension of the copyright page.

Chapter 2: 30, Figure 2.1 from *Environmental Psychology,* by C. J. Holahan. Copyright © 1982 by McGraw-Hill, Inc. Reprinted by permission. **33,** Figure 2.2 from "The Stellar-Orientation System of Migratory Birds" by S. T. Emlen, 1975. Copyright © by the Scientific American. All rights reserved. **34,** Figure 2.3 courtesy of Alex Paul. **38,** Box from *Maps in Minds,* by R. M. Downs and D. Stea. Copyright © 1977 by Harper & Row. Reprinted by permission of the authors. **Chapter 3: 56,** Figure 3.2 from "Adaptation Level and the Affective Appraisal of Environments" by J. A. Russell and U. F. Lanius, 1984, *Journal of Environmental Psychology, 4,* pp. 119–135. Copyright © 1984 Academic Press Inc. (London) Ltd. Reprinted by permission of Rights and Permissions, Academic Press Inc. (London) Ltd., London, England. **Chapter 4: 79,** Figure 4.1 from "Defining Trauma: Terminology and Generic Stressor Dimensions" by B. L. Green, 1990, *Journal of Applied Social Psychology, 20,* pp. 1632–1634. Copyright © by V. H. Winston & Son, Inc. Reprinted by permission. **80,** Table 4.1 reprinted with permission from *Journal of Psychosomatic Research,* vol. 11, by T. H. Holmes and R. H. Rahe, "Social Readjustment Scale," Copyright © 1967, Pergamon Press. **91,** Quote from "Life in Antarctica" in A. A. Harrison, Y. A. Clearwater, and C. P. McKay (Eds.), *From Antarctica to Outer Space.* Copyright © 1991 by Springer-Verlag. Reprinted by permission. **Chapter 5: 110,** Figure 5.1 from "An Arousal Model of Interpersonal Intimacy" by M. L. Patterson, 1976, *Psychological Review, 83,* pp. 235–245. Copyright © 1976 by The American Psychological Association. **112,** Figure 5.2 from "A New Measure and Social-Learning Model for Interpersonal Distance" by M. P. Duke and S. Nowicki, 1972, *Journal of Experimental Research in Personality, 6,* pp. 119–132. Copyright © 1972 by Academic Press. Reprinted by permission. **Chapter 6: 124,** Figure 6.1 from "The Role of the Social and Physical Environment in Privacy Maintenance Among the Iban of Borneo" by A. H. Patterson and N. R. Chiswick, 1981, *Journal of Environmental Psychology, 1,* pp. 131–139. Copyright © 1981 by Academic Press Inc. (London) Ltd. Reprinted by permission of Rights and Permissions, Academic Press Inc. (London) Ltd., London, England. **139, 140,** Figures 6.2a and 6.2b reprinted by permission of Barbara Brown. **Chapter 7: 147,** Figure 7.1 from "Population Density and Social Pathology" by J. B. Calhoun. Copyright © 1962 by Scientific American, Inc. All rights reserved. **Chapter 8: 168, 169,** Figures 8.1 and 8.2 from *Personal Space: The Behavioral Basis of Design* by R. Sommer. Copyright © 1969 by Prentice-Hall. Reprinted by permission of the author. **170,** Cartoon reprinted with special permission of King

Features Syndicate, Inc. **173,** Figure 8.4 from Daniel Kahneman, *Attention and Effort,* © 1973, p. 10. Reprinted by permission of Prentice-Hall, Englewood Cliffs, New Jersey. **175,** Figure 8.5 from *Manual for the Questionnaire Measure of Stimulus Screening and Arousability* by A. Mehrabian, 1976. Reprinted by permission of the author. **Chapter 9: 190,** Figure 9.1 from *The Teacher's Guide to Open Education* by L. S. Stephens. Copyright © 1974 by Holt, Rinehart and Winston, Inc. Reprinted by permission of the publisher. **193,** Figures 9.3a and 9.3b from *Environmental Psychology: People and Their Physical Setting,* Second Edition, by Harold M. Proshansky, William H. Ittelson and Leanne G. Rivlin. Copyright © 1976 by Holt, Rinehart and Winston, Inc. Reprinted by permission of the publisher. **196,** Table 9-1 from "Children's Play and Urban Playground Environments: A Comparison of Traditional, Contemporary, and Adventure Playground Types" by D. G. Hayward, M. Rothenberg, and R. B. Beasley, 1974, *Environment and Behavior, 6,* pp. 131–167. Copyright © 1974 by Sage Publications, Inc. Reprinted by permission. **202,** Quote from "Exhibit Design and Visitor Behavior: Empirical Relationships" by S. Bitgood, D. Patterson, and A. Denefield, 1988, *Environment and Behavior, 20,* pp. 474–491. Copyright © 1988 by Sage Publications, Inc. Reprinted by permission. **Chapter 10: 225,** Box from *Topophilia* by Y. F. Tuan, 1974. Reprinted by permission of the author. **Chapter 11: 243,** Quote from *Prairyerth: A Deep Map* by William Least Heat-Moon. Copyright © 1991 by William Least Heat-Moon. Reprinted by permission of Houghton Mifflin Company. All rights reserved. **Chapter 12: 276–277,** Figure 12.1 and quotes from "Instructions as a Determinant of Paper-Disposal Behaviors" by E. S. Geller, J. F. Witmer and A. L. Orebaugh, 1976, *Environment and Behavior, 8,* pp. 417–439. Copyright © by Sage Publications. Reprinted by permission. **290,** *Frank & Ernest* cartoon reprinted by permission of NEA, Inc.

Photo Credits

Chapter 1: 5, Courtesy, Archives of the History of American Psychology, University of Akron. **6, 7, 8,** Courtesy, Paul Gump and the University of Kansas. **22,** Photos by Peter Bailley. **Chapter 2: 40,** National Park Service/Jefferson National Expansion Memorial Archives. **Chapter 3: 73,** Photo by Michael D. Peterson. **Chapter 4: 86,** AP/Wide World Photos. **95,** Courtesy, NASA. **102,** Photo by Peter Bailley. **Chapter 5: 102, 103,** Photos by Peter Bailley. **108,** (left) Photo by Peter Bailley. **108,** (right) UPI. **Chapter 6: 128,** Photos from Leuthold, W. (1977). *African Undulates.* Berlin: Springer-Verlag. Used by permission. **129, 132, 133, 137, 138,** Photos by Peter Bailley. **Chap-**